ISBN 978-1-333-81581-3
PIBN 10618181

This book is a reproduction of an important historical work. Forgotten Books uses
state-of-the-art technology to digitally reconstruct the work, preserving the original format
whilst repairing imperfections present in the aged copy. In rare cases, an imperfection in
the original, such as a blemish or missing page, may be replicated in our edition. We do,
however, repair the vast majority of imperfections successfully; any imperfections that
remain are intentionally left to preserve the state of such historical works.

N. POPOV

OUTLINE HISTORY *of the* COMMUNIST PARTY *of the* SOVIET UNION

Part II

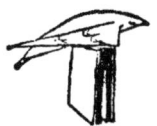

LONDON
MARTIN LAWRENCE LIMITED

Edited by H. G. Scott

TABLE OF CONTENTS

Page

The struggle of the Party for a Bolshevik solution of the grain problem. The Shakhty case and the problem of cadres. The Party in
the struggle against the Right deviation as the main danger. The
Comintern in the struggle against the Right deviation as the main
danger. The Sixth Congress of the Comintern. The C.P.S.U. and the
Comintern expose the anti-Leninist platform of the Rights and conciliators and suppress their factional struggle. The mobilisation of the
masses for a Bolshevik overcoming of difficulties. The struggle
against the revision of Leninism, the anti-Party slander and the kulak
platform of the Rights. The Sixteenth Party Conference. The struggle
of the Party against bureaucracy. The general purging of the Party
ranks and the enrolment of workers. The Party in the struggle on
two fronts in the period of the extended socialist offensive. The
struggle against Right opportunism and against the conciliators in
the Comintern. The Plenum of the Central Committee in November
1929. From restricting and sqeezing out the kulak to the liquidation
of kulakdom. The Party in the struggle against anti-middle peasant
excesses. The Sixteenth Party Congress. The socialist offensive along
the whole front. The national question at the Sixteenth Congress.
After the Sixteenth Congress.

CHAPTER XI

THE PARTY IN THE PERIOD OF THE BREST-LITOVSK PEACE TREATY AND AFTER

Consolidation of the Soviet power after October—Dissolution of the Constituent Assembly—The task of creating the state apparatus of the proletarian dictatorship—Lenin's fight against Trotsky and the "Lefts" for the conclusion of peace—The German offensive and the conclusion of peace—The Seventh Party Congress—The resolution of the Seventh Congress on peace— The Party changes its name—Lenin on the tactics of the Party after the conclusion of peace—The "Left" Communists and the petty-bourgeois environment—The first stage of the Civil War—Red terror—The policy of War Communism—The annulment of the Brest peace—The military and political alliance of the working class and peasantry—The Party after the October Revolution.

Consolidation of the Soviet Power after October

Having come to power and having commenced to create its own state apparatus, the working class was compelled to overcome the furious resistance of its class enemies. In the very first months of the October Revolution the Soviet government had to withstand violent civil war. The Mensheviks and Socialist-Revolutionaries moved the Cossack regiments of General Krasnov against revolutionary Petrograd, and organised an uprising of the *Junkers** within the city itself. Under the leadership of the Party, the working class heroically repulsed these first attacks of the counter-revolution on the Soviet government.

After this failure, the Mensheviks and Socialist-Revolutionaries, who acted as the initiators of counter-revolution, attempted to organise sabotage by the officials in all government institutions. In the Ukraine, the Central Rada,** which was headed by the

---

* *Junkers:* cadets at tsarist military academies.—*Ed.*

** The Rada was composed of representatives of bourgeois Ukrainian organisations, most of which bore socialist names, and included also representatives of bourgeois organisations of the national minorities in the Ukraine (Russian, Jewish and Polish).

Ukrainian Mensheviks and Socialist-Revolutionaries, proclaimed itself the supreme power; in Rostov the Cossack General Kaledin set up the headquarters of all-Russian counter-revolution; the supreme command at army headquarters refused to carry out the orders of the Soviet government; the Cossack ataman Dutov stirred up an uprising among the Orenburg and Ural Cossacks; in Finland, close to Petrograd, civil war broke out between the workers and the bourgeoisie, between the Red and White Guards; in Siberia, the Right Socialist-Revolutionaries attempted to offer resistance to the Soviets. In the ensuing struggle, however, the decisive superiority of the Soviet government quickly became apparent. The Decree on Peace, issued by the Second All-Russian Congress of Soviets on October 26, 1917, had at once secured for it tremendous sympathy in the army both at the front and in the rear. The army perceived that the Soviet government had resolutely and irrevocably thrown overboard the policy of sabotaging peace and protracting the war, that the cause of peace was in the firm hands of the working class. In the very first days of its existence the Soviet government had succeeded in winning over the broadest masses of the peasantry by means of the Land Decree. This decree, as is well known, was adopted in the form drafted by the Socialist-Revolutionaries and did not exactly conform to our Party programme on the agrarian question. As early as 1906, at the Fourth Congress, Lenin and the Bolshevik Party strongly opposed the Menshevik programme for the municipalisation of the land and advocated our agrarian programme for the nationalisation of the land, but did not preclude the possibility of the landlords' estates being divided up among the peasantry if it was not found possible to carry out the nationalisation programme. The land decree as formulated in October reflected the desires and moods of the broad peasant masses as expressed in 242 instructions.* For this reason the Party, without the slightest hesitation, adopted this decree, which strengthened the Soviet government, consolidating as it did the bond between this government and the broad peasant masses.

The most essential and basic aspect of the decree was that it

* Instructions given by the peasants to their deputies to the First All-Russian Congress of Peasant Deputies, held in Petrograd, May 4-28, 1917.—*Ed.*

signified the abolition of private ownership of land and the transfer of the landlords' estates, without any compensation, to the
peasantry. The main thing, according to Lenin, was "that the
peasantry received complete assurance that there were to be no
more landlords in the countryside—let the peasants themselves
settle all questions, let the peasants themselves arrange their own
lives."*

Its essential aim was to secure for the Soviet government the
sympathy and support of the broadest peasant masses. This aim
was fully attained by the decree.

Only the Soviet government, the government of the triumphant
proletariat, could have given and did give the land to the peasantry, thus settling the age-old conflict between the toiling peasantry and the feudal landlords.

To be sure, the broad peasant masses saw in the equal labour
land tenure** salvation not only from exploitation by the landlords but from capitalist exploitation as well. Equal labour land
tenure, as the Bolsheviks had shown on many occasions when
they criticised the programme of the Socialist-Revolutionaries,
could not have given them such salvation if it had been put into
effect by the Socialist-Revolutionaries who regarded it as their
ultimate ideal. Actually, being put into effect by the Soviet government, which abolished landlordism in the villages, it served only
as the first step towards the socialist reconstruction of agriculture
and the final obliteration of the age-old savagery and "idiocy" of
village life. •

At the Peasant Congress which was held in November 1917,
though convened by the Executive Committee which was controlled by the Right Socialist-Revolutionaries, the majority sided
with the Soviet government. Under pressure from this Congress,
the Left Socialist-Revolutionaries dropped their demand for the
formation of a coalition government with the Mensheviks and
Right Socialist-Revolutionaries, and were given representation
in the Soviet government.

The Left Socialist-Revolutionaries were at that time supported

---

* Lenin, "Report at the Second All-Russian Congress of Soviets,' *Collected
Works*, Vol. XXII.
** Equal in the sense that each family receives as much land as it can
cultivate by its own efforts, without employing wage labour.

by certain sections of the poorest peasantry. This is precisely what Comrade Stalin had in mind when he wrote:

"We marched towards October under the slogan of the dictatorship of the proletariat and the poorest peasantry, and in October achieved it formally, inasmuch as we had a *bloc* with the Left Socialist-Revolutionaries and shared the leadership with them, although actually the dictatorship of the proletariat already existed, since we Bolsheviks constituted the majority."

Reporting to the All-Russian Central Executive Committee of the Soviets on the conditions of the agreement with the Left Socialist-Revolutionaries, Lenin quite clearly emphasised that this agreement in no way signified a retreat from the socialist principles of the October Revolution.

"In Russia the proletarian socialist revolution has begun. The popular masses want to be the masters of their fate. Our agreement is only possible on a socialist platform, otherwise it is not an agreement." *

And the October Revolution, by a whole series of decrees—on workers' control, nationalisation of the banks, etc.—from the very first, set about fundamentally changing the capitalist relationships of production, overcoming the sabotage of the manufacturers, merchants and officials by means of confiscations, requisitions, arrests.

This was, as Lenin afterwards expressed it, a Red Guard attack on capital, which was attempting to prevent the establishment of the proletarian dictatorship and the realisation of its historic task, the expropriation of the expropriators.

In the very first days of its existence, the Soviet government issued a Declaration of the Rights of the Peoples of Russia, proclaiming the right of nations to self-determination, including the right of secession.

After coming into power, the working class had to demolish the old state apparatus of the imperialist bourgeoisie and to replace it with a new state apparatus based on the Soviets.

As Comrade Stalin has observed:

" . . . the Soviets are the most all-embracing mass organisations of the proletariat, for they and they alone embrace all workers without exception.

" . . . the Soviets are the only mass organisations that take in all the oppressed and exploited workers, soldiers and sailors; and for this

* Lenin, *Collected Works,* Vol. XXII. . . .

reason, the political leadership of the mass struggle by the vanguard, by the proletariat, can be most easily and most completely exercised through them. ... The Soviets are the direct organisation of the masses themselves, *i.e.,* they are *the most democratic,* and therefore the most authoritative organisations of the masses, that provide them with the maximum facilities for participating in the building up of the new state and its administration; they develop to their fullest extent the revolutionary energy, the initiative and the creative faculties of the masses in the struggle for the destruction of the old system, in the struggle for the new proletarian system.

"The Soviet power is the unification and the crystallisation of the local soviets into one general state organisation, into a state organisation of the proletariat which is both the vanguard of the oppressed and the exploited masses and 'the ruling class—it is their unification into the republic of soviets." *

By the end of the year, the Soviet government was established throughout the whole territory of the country and at the front, except in the Ukraine, in the Don region, in Transcaucasia and part of Finland. An armistice was concluded with the Austro-German coalition. Peace negotiations were begun. This was the period of the "triumphant march" of the Soviet power.

Dissolution of the Constituent Assembly

But in order to consolidate itself further, it still had to overcome one serious political obstacle. Two weeks after the October Revolution the elections to the Constituent Assembly were held, and despite the fact that the overwhelming bulk of the proletariat voted for the Bolsheviks and in spite of the tremendous electoral successes of the Bolsheviks at the front and in a number of peasant districts (in the Central and Western provinces), they resulted as a whole in a majority for the Right Socialist-Revolutionaries, who—together with the Mensheviks and Cadets (Constitutional Democrats)—had carried through the whole preparatory work for the elections.

The reasons for this result were fully and clearly explained in the *Theses on the Constituent Assembly* by Lenin.

"The calling of the Constituent Assembly in our revolution on the basis of candidate lists which had been presented in the middle of

* Stalin, "Foundations of Leninism," *Leninism,* Vol. I.

October 1917, took place under conditions which precluded the possibility that the will of the people in general and of the toiling masses in particular would be correctly reflected by the elections to this Constituent Assembly.

"... The party which, between May and October, had the largest following among the people and particularly among the peasantry, the party of Socialist-Revolutionaries, nominated integral lists of candidates to the Constituent Assembly in the middle of October 1917, but split after the elections to the Constituent Assembly and before its convocation.

"Owing to this, the composition of the deputies to the Constituent Assembly does not and cannot even formally correspond to the will of the electors in their mass.

"... Secondly, an even more important, not formal or legal, but social-economic class source of the discrepancy between the will of the people, on the one hand, and the composition of the Constituent Assembly, on the other, is the fact that the elections to the Constituent Assembly occurred at a time when the overwhelming majority of the people could not yet know the whole scope and significance of the October, Soviet, proletarian-peasant revolution, which began on November 7 [October 25], 1917, i.e., after the lists of candidates for the Constituent Assembly had been entered." *

The Constituent Assembly, dominated as it was by the Right Socialist-Revolutionaries who had fought the Bolsheviks in October, inevitably had to place itself in opposition to the October Revolution. This concrete example was to serve as a means of contrasting formal bourgeois democracy to the Soviet government. The Party had previously put forward the demand for the calling of the Constituent Assembly, since this was the highest form of democracy under the conditions of a bourgeois republic. But the Party had emphasised from the very beginning of the revolution in 1917 that a Soviet republic is a higher form of democracy than an ordinary bourgeois republic with a Constituent Assembly.

Even in April 1917, Lenin had declared that the Soviet form of state power, and not formal bourgeois democracy, corresponds to the interests of the proletarian revolution. At the April Conference, the Party definitely adopted the slogan of Soviet power. But the Party did not as yet abandon the demand for the calling of the Constituent Assembly. This demand played a revolutionary role against the coalition government of Kerensky. After the October Revolution when the Soviet government dissolved the So-

* Lenin, *Collected Works*, Vol. XXII.

cialist-Revolutionary and Menshevik city councils in Moscow and Petrograd, new elections were held in Petrograd on the basis of universal suffrage which resulted in a majority for our Party.

But the organisation of the Soviet government and its work very soon rendered the existence of any kind of democratic governing institutions side by side with the Soviets clearly and obviously superfluous. After the results of the elections had been ascertained, the slogan "all power to the Constituent Assembly" became the slogan of the entire bourgeois counter-revolution against the Soviet government. Under such conditions, certain democratic illusions, a certain fetishism of the Constituent Assembly and of universal suffrage, which the Party could not but take into account until now, began very rapidly to disappear among the working masses and in the Party. In the theses which were written by Lenin and published in *Pravda* on December 26, 1917, the question of the Soviet government versus the Constituent Assembly was presented quite clearly and unequivocally.

"Any attempt, direct or indirect, to consider the question of the Constituent Assembly from a formal, legal aspect, within the framework of customary bourgeois democracy, without taking into account the class struggle and the civil war, is a betrayal of the cause of the prole- tariat and desertion to the viewpoint of the bourgeoisie. To forewarn each and all against this error, into which some of the leaders of Bolshevism, who were incapable of appraising the October uprising and the tasks of the proletarian dictatorship, are falling, is the absolute duty of revolutionary Social-Democracy." *

Vacillations within the Party on the question of the Consti- tuent Assembly were quite insignificant and affected only indi- vidual members. The Party showed exceptional unanimity on this question. The Constituent Assembly was opened on January 5, 1918, and, after refusing to endorse the Soviet government and its peace and land decrees, it was dissolved. Not a ripple was caused by its dissolution, save for small anti-Soviet demonstra- tions of scattered groups of intellectuals and petty bourgeoisie in Moscow and Petrograd. **

* Lenin, *Collected Works*, Vol. XXII.
** The Central Committee of the Socialist-Revolutionary Party was prepar- ing a *coup d'état* for January 5, and relied on the participation of certain military units. This plot ended in complete failure.

By the beginning of 1918, on all fronts of the civil war which sprang up immediately after the October Revolution—in the Ukraine, in the Don region, in Siberia—everywhere the decisive victory of the Soviet government had become apparent.

The Task of Creating the State Apparatus of the Proletarian Dictatorship

Colossal work was required to create a state apparatus in place of the old apparatus which had been demolished, to create a new proletarian army, to get rid of all elements of anarchy which were fostered by the conditions prevailing in the transition period, when the apparatus of the bourgeois state was being destroyed while the state apparatus of the proletarian dictatorship was only in its inception.

"In bourgeois revolutions," Lenin afterwards wrote, "the principal task of the toiling masses was to carry out negative or destructive work, to destroy feudalism, the monarchy, mediaevalism. The positive or constructive work of organising the new society was carried out by the property-owning bourgeois minority of the population. And the latter carried out this task with comparative ease, despite the resistance of the workers and poorest peasants, not only because the masses, exploited by capital, could at that time offer but feeble resistance owing to their unorganised and ignorant state, but also because the basic organising force of the anarchically built capitalist society is the national and international market, anarchically growing in breadth and depth.

"On the other hand, the principal task of the proletariat, and of the poorest peasantry led by the proletariat, in every socialist revolution—hence also in the socialist revolution in Russia, begun on October 25, 1917*—is the positive or constructive work of creating an extremely complex and subtle network of new organisational relationships comprising the planned production and distribution of goods which are essential for the existence of scores of millions of people. Such a revolution can be successfully realised only through the independent historical creative work of the majority of the population, above all of the majority of the toilers."**

"The state, which for centuries has been the organ for the oppression and plunder of the people, has left us as its legacy the greatest hatred and mistrust on the part of the masses towards everything connected with the state. To overcome this is a very difficult task, a task

* New style—November 7.
** Lenin, "The Immediate Tasks of the Soviet Government," *Collected Works*, Vol. XXII.

which the Soviet government alone can cope with but for which it, too, requires a long space of time and tremendous persistence. This 'legacy' makes itself felt with particular keenness on the question of accounting and control, this root question for the socialist revolution on the morrow of the overthrow of the bourgeoisie. A certain period of time will inevitably elapse before the masses, who have for the first time felt themselves free after the overthrow of the landlords and bourgeoisie, will comprehend—not from books, but from their own *Soviet* experience—will grasp and will *feel* that, without comprehensive state accounting and control of the production and distribution of goods, the power of the toilers, the freedom of the toilers, cannot be maintained, that a return to the yoke of capitalism is *inevitable*. Besides this, all the habits and traditions of the bourgeoisie and petty bourgeoisie are particularly opposed to *state* control, and for the inviolability of 'sacred private property,' of 'sacred' private enterprise. We can now see especially clearly to what extent the Marxist proposition is correct, that anarchism and anarcho-syndicalism are *bourgeois* tendencies, in what irreconcilable conflict they stand to socialism, proletarian dictatorship, communism." *

` The problem of creating the new state apparatus of the proletarian dictatorship, the problem of organising accounting and control, of carrying out measures for the creation of a new socialist social system, arose in all its urgency. Immense labour and struggle were called for in this direction. The struggle to destroy the old and to create the new state apparatus commenced from the very first day of the Soviet government's existence.

But at the time of Brest-Litovsk, when the first country of the proletarian dictatorship, almost defenceless (in a military sense), stood face to face with German and world imperialism, the most pressing question was the task of organising the workers' and peasants' Red Army as a component part of the new state apparatus of the dictatorship of the proletariat.

Lenin's Fight Against Trotsky and the "Lefts" for the Conclusion of Peace

To carry on the war any longer was impossible. The army at the front was deserting its positions, leaving behind all military supplies which it could not carry along.

At Brest-Litovsk, the Soviet government had done everything in its power to expose German imperialism as well as the imper-

* *Ibid.*

ialism of the Entente, whose governments had refused to join in the peace negotiations. The situation now demanded the *speediest possible conclusion of a separate peace, the neutralising of German imperialism,* which constituted a deadly menace to the Revolution, and the concentration of all the internal forces of the Party on the *task of strengthening the dictatorship of the proletariat* for the suppression of the resistance of the exploiters, for winning over the broadest masses of the toilers to the side of the working class, for the building of socialism.

Lenin, from the very first, resolutely upheld this view. On January 7, he presented his theses to the Central Committee of the Party, showing the necessity of *immediately concluding a separate peace with Germany,* even on the severe terms which Germany offered.

According to these terms, we had to renounce all claim to Poland, Lithuania, Courland, part of Livonia and White Russia, and the Moon Sound Archipelago (the islands Esel, Dago, etc.). The army was to be demobilised. The Soviet government had to undertake to pay Germany a definite sum for the maintenance of the Russian war prisoners who were kept in Germany during the imperialist war. In his theses of January 7, Lenin expressed himself categorically in favour of *concluding peace* on these terms.

"It would be a mistake to base the tactics of the socialist government in Russia," Lenin wrote, "on attempts to determine whether or not the European and particularly the German socialist revolution will occur within the next half year (or a similar brief term). Since it is quite impossible to determine this, all such attempts would objectively be tantamount to sheer gambling." *

Trotsky and Bukharin opposed the conclusion of peace believing that by delaying to conclude peace we would inevitably cause a revolution in Germany.

In his theses Lenin also decidedly challenged the argument that by concluding peace we were playing into the hands of German imperialism, an argument which was especially popular in Defencist circles, but which also exercised some influence over certain sections of the Party.

---

* Lenin, "Thesis on the Question of the Immediate Conclusion of a Separate and Annexationist Peace," *Collected Works,* Vol. XXII.

"Our tactics must now be based, not on the principle of which of the two imperialisms it would now be more advantageous to aid, but on the principle of how it is possible more surely and safely to guarantee the socialist revolution a chance to consolidate itself or at least to maintain itself in one country until the other countries join in." *

One of the strongest arguments of those who opposed the conclusion of peace was to cite previous declarations of the Party regarding the need for it to wage revolutionary war after the conquest of power by the proletariat. This argument, too, was rejected by Lenin.

"It is said that we have plainly 'promised' a revolutionary war in a number of Party declarations, and that the conclusion of a separate peace would be a betrayal of our pledge.

"This is incorrect. We have said that for a socialist government in the epoch of imperialism it is *necessary* to '*prepare for and to wage*' revolutionary war. We said this in order to combat abstract pacifism, to combat the theory which altogether rejects 'defence of the fatherland' in the epoch of imperialism, finally to combat the purely selfish instincts of some of the soldiers. But we have not pledged ourselves to start a revolutionary war without taking into account how far it is possible to wage such war at any particular moment." **

Lenin's view did not find sufficient support at the conference of the members of the Central Committee, which was attended by some delegates to the Third All-Russian Congress of Soviets, although a number of Central Committee members headed by Comrade Stalin resolutely supported this viewpoint.

The Third Congress of Soviets, meeting after the conference, adopted a resolution which, on the one hand, recommended to drag out the peace negotiations and refused to accept the terms proposed by German imperialism, but at the same time authorised the government, in case of extreme necessity, to conclude a separate peace.

When the German imperialists definitely refused to modify their demands, the answer was the famous formula proposed by Trotsky, which the Central Committee adopted in spite of Lenin: *Neither peace nor war.* The German delegation was informed that the Soviet government did not accept the peace terms but at the same time discontinued the war. This formula was put

* *Ibid.*
** *Ibid.*

forth in the belief that the German army commanders would not succeed in forcing the masses of soldiers into an offensive. Lenin emphatically objected to this formula, describing it as the scrapping of the revolution. He once more proposed to conclude peace, in the very last moment after the armistice, before the German army commenced the inevitable offensive.

Somewhat earlier, at the meeting of the Central Committee on January 24 (11), Lenin gave the following argument for his proposal in favour of the immediate signing of peace:

"The Bolsheviks never rejected defence, but this defence and protection of the fatherland had to have a definite, concrete situation, such as we have at the present time, namely: the defence of the socialist republic against an unusually strong international imperialism. The only question we must consider is, how are we to defend the fatherland, the socialist republic. The army is excessively war-weary; the condition of the horses in such that we will not be able to get the artillery away in case of an offensive; the position of the Germans on the Baltic islands is so good that, in case of an offensive, they will be able to take Reval and Petrograd with their bare hands. Should we continue the war under such conditions, we will strengthen German imperialism to an unusual degree; peace we will have to conclude anyhow, only the peace will then be worse.... Unquestionably, the peace which we are compelled to conclude at the present time is a dirty peace. But should war be renewed, our government will be swept aside and peace will be concluded by another government.

"At present we have the support not only of the proletariat but of the poorest peasantry as well, and the latter will desert us if the war is continued. The prolongation of the war is in the interests of French, British and American imperialism.... Those who favour a revolutionary war, point out that we will thereby be in a state of civil war with German imperialism and will thus arouse the revolution in Germany. But Germany is as yet only pregnant with revolution, while we have already given birth to a quite healthy baby, the socialist republic, which we may kill if we resume the war.

"We need a delay to effect social reforms (take only the transport). We need to grow strong, and for this, time is necessary. We must utterly throttle the bourgeoisie, and for this we must have both our hands free. By having done this, we shall set free both our hands, and then we shall be in a position to wage a revolutionary war against international imperialism. The *échelons* of the volunteer revolutionary army which have now been formed—these are the officers of our future army.

"What Comrade Trotsky proposes—discontinuance of the war, refusal to sign peace and the demobilisation of the army—means an international political demonstration. All we will achieve by withdrawing our troops is to surrender the Esthonian socialist republic to the Germans. By signing peace. . . we enable our gains to gather strength. If the Germans begin to advance, we will be forced to sign any kind of peace, and then the peace will of course be worse." *

In this speech of his, Lenin depicted with extraordinary clarity the prime necessity of a breathing space for the Soviet republic and outlined, with the foresight of genius, the entire future course which events would take if his proposal were rejected.

The rejection of Lenin's proposal and the acceptance of Trotsky's proposal, which was supported by the "Left" Communists, was paid for very dearly by our country and Party.

The German Offensive and the Conclusion of Peace

On February 17, 1918, the German and Austrian armies started a determined offensive. Thereby imperialist Germany placed the Soviet power in an exceptionally difficult position.

The movement of the German and Austrian troops encountered almost no resistance. The immense military supplies which were at the front, consisting of thousands of guns, colossal stores of ammunition, etc., fell into the hands of German imperialism. The Germans were advancing on a wide front, extending from the Baltic Sea to the Rumanian border, meeting with virtually no resistance. Lenin raised the question of resuming negotiations point-blank. The Central Committee decided that the German government be informed by wire of the readiness of the Soviet government to accept the terms which had been offered before by German imperialism. But the German general staff of course understood that Germany was now in a position to propose much more onerous terms than in January, before the negotiations were broken off and the German troops started their offensive.

In the event of German imperialism forcing us into war, Lenin, contrary to the "Left" Communists who were sunk in the bog of petty-bourgeois revolutionary phrasemongering, deemed it possible to utilise the contradictions in the camp of international imperialism in the interests of the Soviet government and to accept military assistance from the "brigands of Anglo-French imperialism."

* Lenin, "Speech on War and Peace at the Session of the R.S.D.L.P., Jan. 1918," *Collected Works*, Vol. XXII.

When after three days, during which no reply had been received from Germany and her troops continued uninterruptedly to advance, the German terms were finally received, they proved radically different from the old terms. This was the direct outcome of the tactics of the "Left" Communists and of Trotsky, who had prevented the conclusion of peace. In the course of their advance, the German troops occupied the whole of Latvia and Esthonia, came close to Petrograd, seized Pskov, Dvinsk and Mogilev, i.e., almost entire White Russia, and invaded a good part of the Ukraine. This immense territory and all the supplies accumulated there during the years of the imperialist war fell into the hands of German imperialism. Germany demanded that all of this territory remain for the present in her hands, promising to evacuate a part of it upon the conclusion of the war on the Western front. Germany also demanded that the Soviet troops immediately evacuate the whole of Finland and the Ukraine, and that peace be concluded with the White Guard governments of these territories; that the whole army be demobilised, including the units which had been organised by the Soviet government; and that a number of politically and strategically important points in Transcaucasia—Batum, Kars, Ardagan, Artvin—be surrendered to Turkey.

But the Soviet government now had no choice. The situation was extremely grave both at the front and within the country. The very fact of the German offensive, the very fact of the defencelessness of the Soviet power in the face of the German advance caused a certain confusion in the state of feeling among the masses and encouraged all the enemies of the Soviet government.

When the Central Committee of the Party took up the question of whether or not to accept the new German terms, Lenin, in view of the tremendous responsibility which rested at this moment with the Party for the fate of the proletarian dictatorship, declared that if there were continued hesitation in face of the mortal danger he would resign from the Central Committee and from the government. *The new German terms were accepted,* but this decision of the Central Committee evoked emphatic protest from a certain section of the Party leaders, producing a real danger of a split.

The Moscow Regional Bureau which had the leadership over the organisations of the Central Industrial region, the Moscow and Petrograd committees of the Party and a number of members of the Central Committee and of the People's Commissariats issued an emphatic protest against the Brest terms. The resolution of the Moscow Regional Bureau declared outright that a split in the Party was inevitable and that, should the German terms be accepted, the Soviet government would become a mere formality, having no value whatever from the standpoint of international revolution.

In his article, *Strange and Monstrous,* Lenin with the greatest indignation branded the political irresponsibility of this declaration as an act of shameful political despair. But the opponents of peace persisted in their policy of disorganising the Party. A number of comrades announced their immediate resignation from leading positions (Lomov, Uritsky, V. M. Smirnov, Bukharin, Bubnov, Yakovleva, Pyatakov and others).

It was these very comrades who opposed the acceptance of the Brest terms who formed the core of the "Left" Communist faction which existed within the Party for several months and which on all basic questions proposed its own line in opposition to the Party line.*

This faction launched a determined struggle against the Brest peace, endangering the existence of the Party as an integral whole. It took great efforts and tremendous energy on the part of the whole Party, above all on the part of Lenin, before this group, under the determined pressure of the entire Party, abandoned its attempts at a virtual split in the Party, which is what they were heading for originally.

We have already noted that during the imperialist war as well as at the Sixth Congress of the Party, Bukharin, who now appeared as the leader of the "Left" Communists, had held views bordering on Trotsky's theory of "permanent revolution." According to this view, the working class of our country, after winning power, could not count on winning over the peasant masses,

---

* How far the "Left" Communist faction went in its attacks on the Party and on Lenin can be seen from the fact that Comrade Bukharin in his articles set Lenin on a par with Kautsky, calling him a phrasemonger of opportunism.

but had to build socialism while fighting the peasants. According to the Trotskyists, the working class could count on receiving aid only from the workers of the more advanced capitalist countries. Trotsky during the years of the war emphatically opposed the Leninist theory of the possibility of building socialism in one country. It followed from this that, if the Soviet government in our country should not succeed in immediately calling forth a socialist revolution in other countries, it must inevitably perish. Here lay the root of the adventurist tactics of the "Left" Communists, whose real inspirer was Trotsky.

The Seventh Party Congress

The Seventh Congress of the Party was convened to make a final decision on the question of the Brest peace. It was held on March 6-8, 1918. It was a very small congress, each delegate representing five thousand Party members. The Central Committee had neither the time nor the possibility to call the congress with full representation.

The German troops halted on the territory of White Russia and at the approaches to Petrograd. But in the Ukraine they continued to advance rapidly and there was no assurance whatever that they would not advance further. All the forces of counter-revolution began to raise their head. It was under such conditions that the Seventh Party Congress had to decide the question whether to approve or disapprove the acceptance of the Brest terms by the government. At the end of stormy debates on Lenin's report in favour of peace and Bukharin's against peace, the Congress, by a majority of thirty votes against twelve, decided, in spite of the violent opposition of the "Left" Communists, *to ratify the Brest peace*. The breathing space, which was as vitally necessary to the country as light and air, was now assured. Lenin's viewpoint was completely victorious, but the Party's procrastination, the time that was lost before the Brest terms were accepted, cost the Soviet government very dear. There can be no doubt that any further delay would have been absolutely fatal. We are still feeling the effects of that delay and procrastination.*

* The 'Left' Communists declared that the acceptance of worse peace terms by the Soviet government at the point of the revolver deprived its enemies

The Soviet government ceased to exist in Finland, Esthonia, Latvia, White Russia and the Ukraine. The Soviet government was later restored on half of the territory of White Russia and on the greater part of the Ukraine, but in western White Russia, Finland, Latvia and Esthonia, in a whole number of districts where the proletariat had marched in the forefront of the revolution in 1905 and 1917, bourgeois power continues to exist to this day. To this day the frontiers of the capitalist powers surrounding the Soviet republics are within gunshot of Leningrad; we still feel the consequences of the disastrous tactics of Trotsky and his followers, the "Left" Communists, who were intoxicated with revolutionary phrases.* As Lenin declared at the Seventh Congress, arguing against Bukharin: "By manoeuvring *à la* Bukharin a good revolution may be killed."

The Resolution of the Seventh Congress on Peace

The resolution on the ratification of the Brest peace, proposed by Lenin and adopted by the Seventh Congress, was not made public at the time (only the fact of the ratification was reported, since we could not show our hand before German imperialism). It did not become known to broad circles of Party members until after the *Minutes of the Seventh Congress* were published, in 1923. The resolution ascribed the acceptance of the "most onerous, most humiliating" peace treaty with Germany to the absence of an army, the unsound state of the demoralised forces at the front,

of the right to speak of an alliance between the Soviet government and German imperialism. We know, however, that the enemy nevertheless continued to speak of such an alliance. As to exposing German imperialism, the Soviet government had already done enough in this respect before the question of accepting the German terms became an urgent one.

* "Revolutionary phrasemongering," Lenin wrote on the eve of the decision on the conclusion of peace, "is a disease which most frequently affects revolutionary parties under conditions when these parties, directly or indirectly, effect a connection, coalescence, or intertwining of the proletarian and petty-bourgeois elements and when the course of revolutionary events produces great and rapid changes. Revolutionary phrasemongering is the repetition of revolutionary slogans without regard to the objective conditions at the given turn of events, in the particular situation. Superb, fascinating, intoxicating slogans—without any basis under them—is the essence of revolutionary phrasemongering." (Lenin, "On Revolutionary Phrasemongering," *Collected Works*. Vol. XXII.

and the necessity óf utilising even the slightest breathing space before imperialism launched an attack on the socialist Soviet republic.

"In the present period, when the era of socialist revolution has commenced," the resolution further declared, "repeated military attacks by the imperialist states (both in the West and in the East) against Soviet Russia are historically inevitable. The historical inevitability of such attacks, in view of the present extremely exacerbated state of all internal state relations, class relations, and international relations alike, may result at any moment, in the most immediate future, even within a few days, in new imperialist wars of aggression against the socialist movement in general and against the socialist republic in particular.

"The Congress therefore declares that it recognises it to be the foremost and basic task alike of our Party, of the entire vanguard of the conscious proletariat and of the Soviet government to adopt the *most energetic, mercilessly resolute and draconian measures to raise the self-discipline and discipline of the workers and peasants of Russia,* to explain the inevitability of Russia historically approaching a national and socialist war of liberation, to create everywhere and at all places the most strictly bound mass organisations cemented by a single-minded iron will, organisations capable of united self-sacrificing action both in ordinary times and in particularly critical moments in the life of the people, finally, for comprehensive, systematic and universal training of the adult population, irrespective of sex, in military science and military operations."

The resolution spoke of the need for the Party, despite all difficulties of the internal situation in the country, "to support the fraternal revolutionary movement of the proletariat of all countries" in every way.

Ryazanov, upon the adoption of this resolution, announced to the Congress his resignation from the Party.

This gesture of Ryazanov was a vivid example of Menshevik posing and political instability.

Ryazanov, who had taken up a glaringly liquidationist, capitulatory position in the October days, demanding as he did the surrender of power to the Mensheviks and Socialist-Revolutionaries, now acted together with the "Lefts."

By his actions at the Congress, Ryazanov clearly exposed the Menshevik-capitulatory character of his position, of the position of Trotsky and the "Left" Communists, against signing the peace treaty.

"I knew," Ryazanov stated, "that the proletarian Party to which we belong ... would be faced with a dilemma at the moment when it seized power, that it would have to decide the question of whether to rely on the peasant masses or on the proletariat of Europe, would have to ponder before taking the decisive step."

What the whole Ryazanov philosophy amounted to was that it was necessary to ponder before October (hence his capitulatory tactics after October).

It is impossible to rely on the peasantry. Refusal to sign peace is a desperate gesture designed to call forth a revolution in Europe. If no revolution results, the Soviet government will perish. Nothing else is possible, since socialism cannot be built in our backward country. Such was Ryazanov's reasoning.

Lenin's efforts, by means of signing peace, to save the existence of Soviet Russia as the focus of world revolution, Ryazanov had the insolence to describe as a desire to "build in Russia a peaceful haven under the protection of German bayonets."

Trotsky, who, like Ryazanov, deemed it impossible to build socialism in our country, continued to uphold the viewpoint of a revolutionary war at the Congress, but abstained from voting against the signing of peace, stating that with the Party in a split condition it would be impossible to wage a revolutionary war. This was nothing but a jesuitical evasion. Trotsky tried to shift the responsibility of the acceptance of the German peace terms on to the shoulders of Lenin and the majority of the Party.

Shortly before the Congress, at the Central Committee meeting on February 23, Comrades Krestinsky and Yoffe, who then shared Trotsky's opinion, defended their viewpoint in the following fashion:

"If the split which was declared by Lenin through his ultimatum should occur, and if we had to wage a revolutionary war against German imperialism, the Russian bourgeoisie and part of the proletariat headed by Lenin, the resulting situation would be more dangerous for the Russian revolution than if peace were signed."

Lenin was thus virtually placed on a par with German imperialism and the Russian bourgeoisie.

During the Brest period, Trotsky held essentially the same position as the "Left" Communists. He was in fact their inspirer.

Trotsky, however, resorted to somewhat peculiar manoeuvring and this manoeuvring of his had the concealed aim of discrediting Lenin personally as the leader of the Party.

It is no accident that part of the leaders of the "Left" Communists during the Brest period subsequently joined the Trotskyist opposition. This was emphasised by Comrade Stalin in his speeches against Trotskyism in 1923.

The Party Changes Its Name

A question of tremendous importance which the Seventh Congress had to settle after ratifying the Brest peace, was the question of the Party programme and the name of the Party. This question had already been on the order of the day for a year. The April Conference had already expressed itself in favour of a radical re-drafting of the Party programme. The old programme had been adopted in 1903, and after the Revolution of 1905-07, after the World War, after the February Revolution, and finally, after the October Revolution it was quite out of date. It was necessary to change it, while retaining that part of it which contained an analysis of the pre-imperialist phase of the capitalist system from the standpoint of revolutionary Marxism.

Lenin had already raised the question of changing the name of the Party in April 1917, stating that it was necessary to cast off the old soiled shirt, to drop the name of social-democracy which had been defiled by the opportunists and social-patriots of all countries, including the Russian Mensheviks, and to adopt the name Communist. Lenin proposed that the Party resume the name which Marx and Engels adopted in 1847.*

* In one of the prefaces to *The Communist Manifesto*, Engels answers the question why he and Marx had already then, in 1847, chosen the word "Communist" and not "Socialist" for the name of the party: "In 1847 two kinds of people were considered socialist. On the one hand were the adherents of the various Utopian systems, notably the Owenites in England and Fourierists in France, both of whom at that date had already dwindled to mere sects slowly dying out. On the other hand, manifold types of social quacks who wanted to eliminate the social ills by means of their universal panaceas and all kinds of tinkering, without in the least hurting capital and profits.... However, the section of the working class which, convinced that mere political revolution was not enough, demanded radical reconstruction of society—that section then called itself *Communist*.... Socialism in 1847 stood for a bourgeois movement, communism for a working class movement."

Lenin's proposal to change the Party name was adopted by the Seventh Congress. Instead of the Russian Social-Democratic Labour Party (Bolsheviks), as the Party called itself in 1917-18, it adopted the name of Russian Communist Party (Bolsheviks). Steklov proposed the name Russian Social-Democratic Party (Communists). Larin favoured leaving the word "Labour" in the name of the Party.

The word "Labour" was quite superfluous, since communism meant the consistent revolutionary point of view of the proletariat, the only thorough-going revolutionary class.

It was clearly necessary to drop the old, theoretically incorrect name of social-democracy which had been defiled by the opportunists. On the other hand, in spite of Steklov's proposal, the Congress by an overwhelming majority decided to keep the word "Bolsheviks" in the name of the Party. It thereby emphasised the fact that the Bolsheviks had not changed their tactics, had not discarded Bolshevism, had not repudiated their past, as Trotsky contended, that they remained true to the old Bolshevik traditions of irreconcilable struggle against opportunism.

The Congress adopted a short resolution on changing the Party programme.

In this resolution the Congress recognised the necessity of changing the political section of the programme which

". . . should consist of as precise and circumstantial a characterisation as possible of the Soviet republic as a new type of state, as a form of the dictatorship of the proletariat and as the continuation of those gains of the international workers' revolution which began with the Paris Commune."

"The programme should point out that our Party would not reject the utilisation of bourgeois parliamentarism if the outcome of the struggle should throw us back for a certain time from this historical stage which our revolution has now passed. In any case and under all circumstances, the Party will fight for a Soviet republic as a type of state higher in point of democracy and as a form of the dictatorship of the proletariat, for the overthrow of the yoke of the exploiters and the suppression of their resistance.

". . . The economic, including the agrarian, sections of our programme, together with the pedagogical and other sections, should also be re-drafted in the same sense and with the same tendency. The centre of gravity should be made the precise definition of the economic and other changes introduced by our Soviet government, coupled with a concrete analysis of the immediate concrete tasks which confront the Soviet government and which follow from the practical steps already taken by us for the expropriation of the expropriators."

The Seventh Congress elected a commission which was instructed to proceed immediately with the final drawing up of a new Party programme for presentation to the next (the Eighth) Congress. The Seventh Congress was of tremendous significance in the history of our Party. Under the most difficult conditions of a turn from the triumphant march of the revolution to heavy defeats and trials the Party succeeded at this Congress in enforcing and consolidating the correct Leninist line, succeeded in saving the proletarian dictatorship in our country from the catastrophe into which it was being propelled by Trotsky and the "Left" Communists.

Lenin on the Tactics of the Party After the Conclusion of Peace

Immediately after the Seventh Party Congress, the Fourth Congress of Soviets was held, the Communist fraction of which already had *an overwhelming majority in favour of signing the peace treaty*. Peace was finally ratified by the Congress of Soviets. The "Left" Communists abstained from voting, and made public their declaration. The ratification of peace was fought at the Congress by the Left Socialist-Revolutionaries as well as by the Right Socialist-Revolutionaries and Mensheviks (headed by Martov), who were well aware that a war with Germany would jeopardise the existence of the Soviet government. In spite of their efforts, the Party obtained the breathing space of which Lenin spoke and most energetically set about the work of government on the territory which remained under Soviet control. This territory was very much reduced: it had been stripped of immense regions in the west and south, including the Ukraine and the Don region, where counter-revolutionary governments had been formed under the protection of the German Army of Occupation. The Soviet government was cut off from oil (Baku and Grozny), from the principal coal supply and metallurgical base (the Donbas), from the chief districts which supplied it with grain (the Ukraine and the Northern Caucasus) and sugar (the Ukraine); it was completely cut off from the Black Sea and had lost almost all contact with the Baltic. But the Party and the Soviet government, albeit at a heavy price, had nevertheless obtained a breathing space. The question arose of the further tactics to be pursued by the state of proletarian dictatorship, which had to suppress the resistance of the exploiters, to win over the broadest toiling masses to the side of the working class and to build socialism under the most difficult historical conditions. The question arose of what methods were to be employed, what economic policy was to be pursued in building the new state. During the consideration and solution of these questions, a struggle developed between Lenin together with the majority of the Party on the one hand, and the "Left" Communists—the opposition within the Party which was formed during the Brest negotiations and the conclusion of the Brest peace—on the other hand.

Arguing against the "Left" Communists and Left Socialist-Revolutionaries, Lenin declared that our country would have to go through a most difficult transition period on its way to communism, that during this period the Party would have to permit state capitalism, utilising it to accelerate the transition from scattered petty peasant farming towards socialism. Lenin perceived that this was to be achieved, on the one hand, by means of a policy of concessions, by attracting foreign capital to the development of the natural resources of the country, allowing it a certain profit. On the other hand, it meant that part of the enterprises which belonged to the Russian capitalists would be left in the hands of their owners, that they would be organised into trusts, operating under the control of the proletarian state. This was a peculiar anticipation of the N.E.P. (New Economic Policy), one of the characteristic features of which was the toleration of capitalism within certain limits and under the control of the proletarian state.

Lenin saw five forms of economy in our economic system after the establishment of the power of the proletariat: patriarchal, natural (self-sufficing) economy; petty commodity production; private capitalism; state capitalism; and socialism. The elements of socialism Lenin saw in the already nationalised enterprises. State capitalism he defined as capitalism controlled and regulated by the state, in this case by the proletarian state. Concretely, Lenin regarded the trading and industrial enterprises, concession enterprises and bourgeois co-operatives as belonging to the category of state capitalism.

In 1918, as also in 1921 (see his pamphlet *The Food Tax*),

"Lenin conceived of state capitalism as the possibly basic form of our economic activity, while considering the co-operatives in combination with state capitalism."*

Lenin's premise was that economically speaking, from the standpoint of developing the productive forces, state capitalism was a tremendous step towards socialism compared with patriarchal, natural, self-sufficing economy as well as compared with private capitalism and scattered peasant farming. The Soviet government carried on negotiations with foreign and even with Russian capitalists (as, for instance, Mestchersky) regarding the formation of privately owned trusts under state control.

International capital, however, refused to take up concessions in the Soviet country. It preferred to invest its money in organising counter-revolution against the Soviet government.

Similarly the Russian capitalists with whom negotiations were carried on for the organisation of trusts under the control of the Soviet government preferred the path of counter-revolutionary civil war.

From the first moment of the October Revolution, Lenin raised the question of the need for the Party, during the transition period, to create a strong centralised state apparatus as an absolutely essential instrument for the working class, as a weapon of its class dictatorship.

The Party had immediately to tackle the long and serious job of building this apparatus; it had first of all to undertake the creation of a reliable regular army to defend the proletarian country.

The Party had put forth the slogans of the destruction of the bourgeois state apparatus and of the imperialist army, which are weapons of the class rule of the bourgeoisie.

* Stalin, *On the Opposition.*

This was understood even by the undeveloped masses who were imbued with a burning hatred for the old slavery and oppression. Even anarchistically inclined elements had been close to the Party during this period. Various anarchist groups also considered themselves to a certain degree as "travelling companions" of the Bolsheviks in the struggle against the power of the bourgeoisie.

The Party, in building the proletarian state apparatus, now had to strike hard against the petty-bourgeois anarchic tendencies which existed even among Party members, particularly among the young members who had not gone through the hard Leninist-Bolshevik school of centralism and discipline. It was necessary to smash these petty-bourgeois anarchic tendencies, to strengthen the Party as a monolithic organism, to consolidate the state apparatus, weld it into one whole and at the same time to carry through tremendous educational work among the masses, to establish socialist labour discipline and on the basis of the latter to raise the productivity of labour.

In connection with these tasks, the Soviet government took a number of decisive steps against the anarchists, disarming their militia, etc. Anarchism was played out as a revolutionary force and under the conditions of the proletarian dictatorship, it was becoming one of the forms of bourgeois counter-revolution. A new type of counter-revolutionary appeared, the underground anarchist, who hated the Soviet government no less than did the Mensheviks and Right Socialist-Revolutionaries.

"We, the Party of the Bolsheviks, have *convinced* Russia. We have *wrested* Russia away—from the rich for the poor, from the exploiters for the toilers. We must now govern Russia. And the whole peculiarity of the present moment, the whole difficulty consists in grasping the special character of the transition from the main task of convincing the people and of the military suppression of the exploiters to the main task of *governing*." *

"We have frequently been reproached by the lackeys of the bourgeoisie with having carried out a 'Red Guard' attack on capital. An absurd reproach, worthy indeed of these lackeys of the cash bag. For the 'Red Guard' attack on capital, *at the time when it took place*, was ab-

* Lenin, "The Immediate Tasks of the Soviet Government," *Collected Works.* Vol. XXII.

solutely dictated by circumstances.... Military resistance cannot be crushed in any other way than by military means.

". . . We have won by using methods of suppression, and we will be able to win by using methods of government.

"... The epoch which is now knocking at the door is one in which the proletarian state power must utilise bourgeois specialists for such a re-ploughing of the soil as may render quite impossible the growth of any bourgeoisie."*

Whereas formerly the Party headed the struggle of the working class in the enterprises against the engineering and technical staffs who acted as agents of the owners of the enterprises, the Party had now to create its own apparatus to direct the economy of the country and to place a trained staff of old specialists at its disposal. To attract specialists and to induce them to work conscientiously, it was necessary to pay them more than the wages of the average worker.

"Without guidance by specialists in various branches of knowledge, technique and experience, the transition to socialism is impossible, for socialism demands a conscious and mass movement forward to higher productivity of labour as compared with capitalism.... Socialism must realise this forward movement *in its own way,* by its own methods, to put it more specifically—by *Soviet* methods. And the specialists, in their mass, are inevitably bourgeois, by virtue of the whole environment of that social life under which they became specialists. If our proletariat, having won power, had quickly solved the problem of accounting, control and organisation on a nation-wide scale—which was impossible owing to the war and the backwardness of Russia—then, after crushing sabotage, we would have completely subordinated the bourgeois specialists to ourselves by means of universal accounting and control.

"Owing to considerable 'lateness' in effecting accounting and control in general, although we have succeeded in overcoming sabotage, we have *not yet* created conditions calculated to place the bourgeois specialists at our disposal. Numerous saboteurs 'accept jobs,' but the best organisers and biggest specialists could be utilised by the state either in the old, bourgeois fashion (*i.e.,* for high pay) or in the new, proletarian fashion (*i.e.,* by creating those conditions of nation-wide accounting and control from below which would inevitably, and of its own force, subject and attract the specialists).

"At present we would have to resort to the old bourgeois method and to agree to very high remuneration for the 'services' of the biggest bourgeois specialists." **

* *Ibid.*
** *Ibid.*

Lenin's views met with great objections and fundamental opposition from the "Left" Communists. They regarded Lenin's position as a retreat from fundamental revolutionary principles, almost as a betrayal of the international revolution. The theses published by the "Left" Communists stated that the Party had virtually abandoned the position of international revolution in concluding a separate peace with German imperialism, that it was necessary to wage a revolutionary war against German imperialism. Only such a war, the "Left" Communists contended, could unleash the revolution in the West. By choosing the path of peace, the Party, according to the "Left" Communists, had beaten a retreat before the peasant environment, had surrendered to the petty bourgeoisie. The notorious theory of the degeneration of the Party, which was later trotted out by every opposition and which had been used against the Bolsheviks by the Mensheviks, starting with the notorious articles of Axelrod in 1904, was now applied by the "Left" Communists to the Leninist Party leadership. In passing this judgment on the position adopted by the majority of the Party at the Seventh Congress, the "Left" Communists emphasised that all the measures which the Party was now advocating—to raise labour discipline, not hesitating to employ measures of compulsion, to restore the prestige of the technical staff, in place of the disorderly seizure of individual factories by groups of workers, to establish strong state management over industry, to increase the productivity of labour, etc., all of this, they alleged, signified a return to the bourgeois system, the renunciation of the principal gains of the October Revolution. The "Left" Communism of 1918 rejected the Leninist teachings on the building of socialism in our country which formed the basis for the strategy and tactics of the Party both before and since the winning of power in October.

Actually it denied the Leninist doctrine of the dictatorship of the proletariat, the state of proletarian dictatorship in the period of transition from capitalism to socialism, the leadership which the working class, having come to power, gives to the broadest peasant masses and the winning over of these masses to the cause of socialist construction.

The "Left" Communists were in fact opposing the organisation of a new state machinery—in place of the old state machinery which had been demolished—as a weapon for the suppression of the exploiters and as an instrument for the leadership of the non-proletarian toiling masses. Thereby they became abettors of the Mensheviks* and Socialist-Revolutionaries, who in their turn exerted every effort to prevent the creation of a strong apparatus of working class state power.

The "Left" Communists and the Petty-Bourgeois Environment

Consequently the "Left" Communists, while charging the Party with every deadly petty-bourgeois sin, found themselves in company with the typically petty-bourgeois party of the Left Socialist-Revolutionaries. After the Brest peace, when the leading "Left" Communists announced their resignation from their posts, the Left Socialist-Revolutionaries resigned from the Council of People's Commissars.

This similarity in tactics alone was in itself a clear indication that it was not the Party which occupied a petty-bourgeois position, but those who attempted to criticise the Party from the

---

* In his article on *"Left" Childishness and Petty-Bourgeois-ism*, which brilliantly exposes the intrinsic petty-bourgeois character of "Left" Communism, Lenin compares the thesis of the well-known Menshevik Isuv with the thesis of the "Left" Communists.

Isuv wrote: "Devoid, from the very beginning, of a true proletarian character, the policy of the Soviet government has of late been ever more openly coming to terms with the bourgeoisie and is assuming an open anti-labour character. Under the pretext of nationalising industry, it is pursuing a policy of developing industrial trusts; under the pretext of restoring the productive forces of the country, attempts are being made to abolish the eight-hour working day, to introduce piece rates, the Taylor system and blacklists. This policy threatens to deprive the proletariat of its principal gains in the economic field and to make it the victim of unlimited exploitation by the bourgeoisie." (Cited from Lenin, *Collected Works*, Vol. XXII.)

The "Left" Communists wrote:

"The introduction of labour discipline in connection with the restoration of the leadership of the capitalists in industry cannot substantially increase labour productivity, but it will lower the class initiative, activity and organisation of the proletariat. It threatens the enslavement of the working class, and will arouse discontent both in the backward sections and in the vanguard of the proletariat. In view of the prevailing hatred among the proletariat against the 'sabotaging capitalists,' the Communist Party would have to rely on the petty bourgeoisie against the workers in order to put this system into effect, and would thereby kill itself as the party of the proletariat." (Cited from Lenin, *Collected Works*, Vol. XXII.)

"Left." It was no accident that the criticism of the "Left" Communists should immediately have been seized upon and utilised by the Mensheviks against the Party and the Soviet government in general.

The Party was striving to apply the principle of proletarian dictatorship to the whole field of economic life, to establish firm order, such as must prevail in a country in which proletarian power has been set up, to destroy the elements of anarchy, of laxity and lack of discipline, which were rooted in the petty-bourgeois environment represented by the Left Socialist-Revolutionaries.* But in this the "Left" Communists, in opposition to their own Party, aided and abetted the Left Socialist-Revolutionaries. How close the Left Socialist-Revolutionaries were at this time to the "Left" Communists can be seen from the fact, reported by Comrade Bukharin during a discussion in 1923, that the Left Socialist-Revolutionaries proposed to the "Left" Communists that they should together organise a *coup d'état* and arrest the Council of People's Commissars, including Lenin; and that, although this proposal was rejected by the "Left" Communists, they did not even inform the Central Committee about it at that time. The Party did not learn of this until 1923.

Such was the situation in the spring of 1918· An *opposition within the Party* was formed against the Party line at a time when violent agitation was being carried on outside the Party by anti-

---

* "Dictatorship is a great word," Lenin wrote, "and great words should not be used in vain. Dictatorship is iron power, revolutionarily bold and swift, merciless in the suppression of both exploiters and hooligans. And our power is unduly soft; it often resembles not so much iron as jelly. It must not be forgotten for a minute that the bourgeois and petty-bourgeois elemental forces fight against the Soviet government in two ways: on the one hand, acting from the outside, by the methods of Savinkov, Gotz, Gegechkori, Kornilov, by conspiracies and insurrections, by their foul 'ideological' backwash, by floods of falsehood and slander in the press of the Cadets, Right Socialist-Revolutionaries and Mensheviks; on the other hand, these elemental forces act from within, utilising every element of decay and every weakness for the purpose of bribery, for increasing the lack of discipline, corruption and chaos. The closer we approach the complete military suppression of the bourgeoisie, the more dangerous does the elemental force of petty-bourgeois anarchy become for us. This elemental force cannot be combated just by propaganda and agitation, just by organising competition, just by selecting organisers. It must be combated also by means of coercion." (Lenin, "The Immediate Tasks of the Soviet Government," *Collected Works,* Vol. XXII.)

Soviet elements and everything within the country was in a turmoil. Under these conditions, the Party, under the leadership of Lenin, carried out its policy with a firm hand in spite of all obstacles. The opposition of the "Left" Communists was gradually reduced to nought, thanks to the energetic struggle which the Party waged against them. The "Left" Communists lost their following in Moscow, Petrograd and the Urals, and were removed by these basic Party organisations from the elective Party posts which they had held. The unity of the Party was being strengthened, and this meant the creation of the main factor necessary for economic and state construction on a planned basis. But within the country, in which a radical transformation of social relations was taking place, a new wave of counter-revolution was rising on the basis of the desperate resistance of the bourgeoisie.

The First Stage of the Civil War

The petty-bourgeois anarchic forces which had risen against the establishment of a firm state order capable of really securing the proletarian dictatorship in the country, the petty-bourgeois anarchic forces headed by the kulaks, broke through to the surface in the July rebellion of the Left Socialist-Revolutionaries.

"The criminal terroristic act and rebellion," Lenin said, with regard to the action of the Left Socialist-Revolutionaries, "completely opened the eyes of the broad masses of the people to the abyss towards which the criminal tactics of the Left Socialist-Revolutionary adventurers were propelling the people's Soviet Russia.

"...And if anyone rejoiced at the action of the Left Socialist-Revolutionaries and maliciously rubbed their hands, it was only the White Guards and the henchmen of the imperialist bourgeoisie. The worker and peasant masses allied themselves yet more closely, yet more strongly, during these days, to the Communist-Bolshevik Party, which truly expresses the will of the masses of the people." *

Until the October Revolution, the Left Socialist-Revolutionaries were in one party side by side with Chernov and Kerensky. When the October Revolution took place, when the Decree on Land caused a' tremendous wave of sympathy and support towards the

* Lenin, "Interview with the Representative of the *Izvestia* on the Rebellion of the Left Socialist-Revolutionaries," *Collected Works*, Vol. XXIII.

Soviet government among the broadest masses of the peasants, the Left Socialist-Revolutionaries, under the pressure of these masses, entered the Soviet government, calling themselves the representatives of the poorest peasantry. However, those elements among the poorest peasantry who followed the Left Socialist-Revolutionaries after the October Revolution lost all their illusions with regard to the Left Socialist-Revolutionaries and broke away from them. The Left Socialist-Revolutionaries came to reflect the interests and aspirations of the well-to-do part of the peasantry which met the October Revolution with sympathy, inasmuch as it signified the abolition of the landlords' estates, but who were averse to any thought of socialism. On the other hand, they expressed the aspirations of the wavering middle peasantry, of the wavering petty bourgeoisie, who were helplessly vacillating between the camp of revolution and that of counter-revolution.

"The social source of such types is the small property owner, who has become enraged at the horrors of war, of sudden collapse, of the unheard-of torments of starvation and ruin, who hysterically rushes about, seeking salvation and a way out, wavering between confidence in and support of the proletariat, on the one hand, and fits of despair on the other.

"We must clearly understand and firmly grasp the fact that on such a social base no socialism can be built. The toiling and exploited masses can be led only by the class which keeps to its path without any wavering, which does not lose courage and does not fall into despair at the most difficult, hard and dangerous marches. Hysterical impulses are of no use to us. What we need is the measured tread of the iron battalions of the proletariat." *

The proletarian revolution inherited a completely ruined economy from tsarism and from the Provisional Government. At first, before the proletarian power succeeded in suppressing the capitalists, the violent resistance of the latter to the carrying out of the workers' control still further increased the disorder. The rich and well-to-do peasantry seized part of the landlords' estates, accumulated large stores of grain and refused to surrender them to the state organs. The destruction of the old state apparatus and the fact that the new state apparatus had not yet been sufficiently organised enabled this section of the peasantry complete-

---

* Lenin, "The Immediate Tasks of the Soviet Government," *Collected Works*, Vol. XXII.

ly to evade all obligations to the state. By selling grain at exorbitant prices they accumulated in their hands large quantities of valuable goods from the towns. The strengthening of the Soviet government which began to reach into the villages in an organised fashion, and the organisation of the poor peasants on whom the Soviet government naturally had to rely, impelled the kulak and well-to-do part of the peasantry, who did not at all wish to part with their accumulated possessions, to the path of active counterrevolutionary actions against socialism and the dictatorship of the proletariat. These kulak elements found leadership first of all in the Left Socialist-Revolutionaries. The Left Socialist-Revolutionaries made an attempt to seize power in Moscow on July 5-7, 1918. The attempt was accompanied by the murder of Count Mirbach, the German Ambassador, as a result of which the country was once more confronted with the danger of war. The Soviet government proved strong enough to suppress the rebellion of the Left Socialist-Revolutionaries by quick and decisive measures, and at the same time succeeded in steering clear of a conflict with German imperialism and in avoiding a war, which would have been fatal at that time. The adventurist attempt of the Left Socialist-Revolutionaries met with almost no response in the country.

But the flames of civil war had extended to new parts of the country. They were drawing closer to Moscow itself. At the end of May 1918 an insurrection of Czecho-Slovaks broke out along the entire Siberian railway line from Penza to Vladivostok, an insurrection which was prepared for and financed by the French mission. In alliance with the internal forces of counter-revolution, with the kulaks, counter-revolutionary officials and officers, with the landlords who had been driven from their estates, the expropriated capitalists and merchants and part of the urban lower middle classes and petty bourgeoisie, the Czecho-Slovaks crushed the Soviet government in Siberia and entrenched themselves in the Middle Volga region.* The Soviet government, which had been cut off from the Ukraine and the Don region, now faced an even more difficult situation. It was now cut off from the

* On the territory occupied by the Czecho-Slovaks, a Socialist-Revolutionary committee of the Constituent Assembly was formed, which had the support of the bourgeoisie and the Mensheviks.

grain regions of Siberia and the Volga as well. During the same summer of 1918, Entente troops landed in the North, occupying Archangel and Murmansk, and in alliance with the local White Guards began to advance southward, aiming to effect a junction with the Czecho-Slovaks. The internal forces of counter-revolution received organised support not only from allied imperialism but from German imperialism as well. In the Ukraine, German imperialism, which had occupied the entire country, replaced the "socialist" Central Rada with the openly bourgeois and landlord government of the hetman Skoropadsky. With the aid of the Germans, the Cossack ataman Krasnov seized the entire Don region, and his troops advanced as far as Voronezh and Tsaritsyn. Only here, especially under the walls of Red Tsaritsyn, which was later called the Soviet Verdun, they met with a crushing repulse. In the Kuban, in the rear of Krasnov and the German bayonets which in fact protected him, new counter-revolutionary forces were organised with funds supplied by Anglo-French imperialism—the army of General Denikin.

This situation showed most clearly the great harm inflicted on the Soviet government by the policy pursued by Trotsky on the question of the Brest peace, as a result of which the favourable moment for concluding peace with German imperialism was let slip. It was just because of this policy that the forces of counter-revolution received such extensive aid and support from the bourgeoisie abroad and such an immense base for the organisation of their forces, for the organisation of a military struggle against the Soviet power on such large territories as the Ukraine, the Crimea, the Don region and the Kuban.

It was on this very territory that the most formidable and menacing forces of the counter-revolution were collected and grew; it was here that Denikin prepared for his march on Moscow, which was carried out in the autumn of 1919, when the counter-revolutionary White bands occupied Orel and almost reached Tula.

By the summer of 1918 the only territory remaining in the hands of the Soviet government was the northern part of former European Russia, the eastern borders of which were marked by the Urals and the Middle Volga. In Moscow itself, the Right Socialist-Revolutionaries made an attempt on the life of Lenin, who was wounded by several bullets and thus prevented for a considerable period from taking part in the government of the country. In Leningrad, too, the Right Socialist-Revolutionaries assassinated Uritsky and Volodarsky. In various localities within the country, insurrections took place in the village, headed by kulaks.

The insurrections extended also to the cities. The petty-bourgeois counter-revolution headed by the kulaks assumed the most variegated outward colours and forms, appearing under the banner of anarchism, Left and Right Socialist-Revolutionarism, Menshevism, counter-revolutionary monarchist priesthood and anti-Semitism.

Red Terror

At this moment, in a situation so critical for the Soviet government, the system of mass Red terror proved a weapon of tremendous importance in its hands. This system came down with all its severity upon the heads of the landlord and bourgeois counter-revolution, on its leading forces: on the White officers, big tsarist officials, and the most prominent figures among the nobility, the clergy and the capitalists. In destroying the organisers, inspirers, and active participators in counter-revolution, the Soviet government could make no exception for those of them who called themselves socialists, could allow no impunity to those parties which engaged during this very time in organising terrorist acts against Soviet leaders. The Socialist-Revolutionaries and Mensheviks knew what they were doing when they undertook an armed struggle against the Soviet government.*

The overwhelming majority of the victims of the Red terror consisted of generals and higher officers of the tsarist army, of

---

* The Socialist-Revolutionaries were at the head of the Samara government which, in August 1918, together with other White governments (in particular, the Siberian), formed the Ufa Directorate with the Socialist-Revolutionary Avksentyev as chairman, which was two months later suppressed by Admiral Kolchak. The Mensheviks in the Volga and Ural regions supported the Samara Committee of the Constituent Assembly and participated in the formation of the Ufa Directorate, although no Menshevik was included in the Directorate. As to the Central Committee of the Mensheviks (headed by Martov), which was in Moscow, it pursued a policy of "neutrality." Martov explained that this neutrality was to be understood as hostile towards the Bolsheviks and friendly to the Czecho-Slovak hirelings of the Entente.

police, gendarmerie and judicial officials, of rural prefects,* marshals of the nobility and reactionary priests—in short, of the sort of people by whose aid Russian tsarism had terrorised the country for centuries.

In terrorising its enemies, the proletarian revolution was acting in accordance with Marx's instructions. It took all measures necessary to curb the bourgeoisie, in order to secure for itself "the first essential—time for prolonged action."

But the rich classes who had been overthrown still had considerable wealth at their disposal. It was necessary not only to crush them politically but also to complete their economic expropriation. This was attained by the policy of merciless confiscation of the enterprises, money deposits, houses, apartments and all possessions of the bourgeoisie, including articles of consumption which could be expropriated in one form or another. Meanwhile the hidden paper currency quickly depreciated as a result of the policy pursued by the Soviet government with regard to the issue of money.

The Policy of War Communism

At the end of June 1918, the Soviet government issued a decree for the nationalisation of the large industrial enterprises, à certain number of which were still in the hands of private capital.**

This measure was caused by the determined resistance of the bourgeoisie to the enforcement of workers' control in industry, by the attempts of the owners to disrupt and sabotage every kind of production at all costs and by their refusal to submit to the regulations introduced by the proletarian state.

The bourgeoisie, confident in its strength, confident of the support of international imperialism and encouraged by the fact that an immense amount of Soviet territory was occupied by the

* In Russian, *Zemski Nachalnik*. Officials whose function was to keep the peasants in subjection to the landlords. The *Zemski Nachalnik* was a member of the nobility in his province and exercised both administrative and judicial authority over the local peasant population.

** Decrees had already been issued for the nationalisation of the land (on October 26, 1917), of the banks (December 1917), and of water transport (January 26, 1918).

troops of German and allied imperialism, preferred open war against the Soviet government.

To this war the Soviet government retaliated with decisive measures for the suppression of the resistance of the bourgeoisie.

The most difficult task was, to cope with the village kulak.

After all the roads for shipping grain from the East and South had been cut off, it became necessary at all costs to obtain grain within the country. But the government' did not have a sufficient quantity of commodities at its disposal with which to pay for the grain. This forced the government to take the course of simply expropriating grain, of vigorously enforcing the grain requisitions, of sending armed detachments into the villages. The best workers, mobilised by the Party and the trade unions, marched into the villages *en masse* to obtain grain, to aid the poor peasants. This was the time when Lenin proclaimed his historic slogan: "The struggle for bread is the struggle for socialism."

The kulaks, by placing themselves at the head of petty-bourgeois elemental forces, attempted to get a stranglehold on the proletarian dictatorship, to deprive the proletarian cities of bread. However, this move of theirs did not succeed.

The Soviet government united the broad masses of the poor peasants around the slogan of the expropriation of grain from the kulaks. The Committees of the Poor became the organ of the poor peasants which were to provide active support for the Soviet government in its seizure of grain from the kulaks and for the consolidation of the Soviet power in the countryside. Not only the stocks of grain, but also the excess land, farm implements, etc., which were in the hands of kulaks, were expropriated. The kulaks, who had been so lovingly cherished by tsarism, particularly in the last years of its existence, were thus dealt a severe blow.

The expropriation of the kulaks which was carried out by the broad masses of the poor peasantry under the leadership of the proletariat and the Party in the summer of 1918 was a real socialist revolution in the countryside, as Lenin often called it, although it did not lead, and under the existing conditions could not lead, to the organisation of socialist production in agriculture. But after the expropriation of the landlords and capitalists, it inflicted a crushing blow on the kulaks.

The blow inflicted on the kulaks was not a' mortal or a final one, since petty peasant farming still remained. On the basis of this petty peasant-economy, kulak-capitalist elements in. the country-side were given a chance.to grow under the conditions of the N.E.P.

In 1918, the Committees of the Poor, under the leadership of the working class, having expropriated the land, implements and cattle of the kulaks, distributed them among the poor and middle peasants. .

In 1929-30, the Party initiated the policy of the liquidation of the kulaks as a class on the basis of all-round collectivisation.

The implements of production which were expropriated from the kulaks were and are being used to strengthen the collective farms, which unite the broadest masses of the poor and middle peasantry, which put an end to petty individual peasant farming and which close every loophole for the growth of the kulak-capitalist in the countryside.

In 1918 Lenin wrote of the kulaks:

"The kulaks are the most brutal, most ruthless and most savage of exploiters, who more than once in the history of other countries have restored the power of the landlords, tsars, priests and capitalists. . . . During the war these bloodsuckers grew rich out of the poverty of the people; they accumulated thousands and hundreds of thousands of rubles by forcing up the price of bread and other products. These spiders grew fat at the expense of the peasants ruined by the war, at the expense of the starving workers. These leeches sucked the blood of the toilers, becoming richer the more the workers in the towns and in the factories starved. These vampires grabbed, and are continuing to grab, the estates of the landlords; they are again and again enslaving the poor peasants."*

The expropriation of the kulaks was a most vital factor in consolidating the proletarian dictatorship throughout the whole country.

"A year after the proletarian revolution in the capitals, under its influence and with its aid, came the proletarian revolution in the remote villages which finally consolidated the Soviet power and Bolshevism, which finally proved that there were no forces within the country which could oppose it."**

The mass expropriation of the urban bourgeoisie and of the kulaks and the economic policy of War Communism were the

* Lenin, "Comrades-Workers! We Are Going to the Last, Decisive Fight," *Collected Works*, Vol. XXIII.

** Lenin, "The Proletarian Revolution and the Renegade Kautsky," *Collected Works*, Vol. XXIII.

results of the blockade and intervention, the results of the extreme sharpening of the class struggle within the country.

At first, it was primarily a system of more or less planned distribution of the small resources which the country had at its disposal at the time. These small resources had to be used with extreme economy.

On the other hand, political necessity dictated the expropriation of the enterprises which were owned by capitalists, the concentration in the hands of the centralised state apparatus not only of distribution but of production as well. The concentration of production in the hands of the proletarian state power and the strict regulation of distribution by the same power bore a certain external resemblance to the immediate realisation of socialism.

In April 1918, Lenin outlined a plan for permitting not only foreign but also Russian capital to participate in the work of restoring the country's economy. But the altogether exceptional situation which arose in the country forced the Soviet government to drop the economic policy outlined by Lenin in his speeches and articles of April 1918 and to enter upon the path of so-called War Communism.

The measures which had been outlined by Lenin for strengthening the state apparatus of the proletarian dictatorship, and which had been met with protests from the "Left" Communists, were steadfastly being put into effect.

The Soviet apparatus was being built up as a single centralised unit. Correct relations were being established between the central and the local organs of the Soviet government and an apparatus was being formed for all the various institutions, both the central and the local ones—those of the *gubernia, uyezd,* and *volost* executive committees and their departments.

All this immense work was being carried on under the leadership of the Party on the basis of the broadest initiative on the part of the working class and peasant masses themselves. And this work was bearing fruit.

The state apparatus of the proletarian dictatorship was being developed and strengthened.

The most sober elements among the "Left" Communists and those sections of the Party who sympathised with them very soon came to see the complete failure of the theory and tactics of

"Left" Communism. This failure became apparent even before the rebellion of the Left Socialist-Revolutionaries—shortly before the closest allies of the "Left" Communists—had demonstrated who, in the final analysis, benefited by the propaganda of the "Left" Communists. The Communist fraction of the Fifth Congress of Soviets, which was in session at the time of the rebellion of the Left Socialist-Revolutionaries, almost unanimously (only a few members abstaining) approved the policy pursued by the Soviet government since the Brest peace. And in the autumn, the leaders of the "Left" Communists, Comrades Bukharin and Radek, declared that they were entirely wrong in their policy of opposition to the Brest peace and recognised the correctness of Lenin's position.

Thanks to the measures taken by the Party in line with the decisions of the Seventh Congress, thanks to the fact that now at last a state apparatus and an army had been created, thanks to the mobilisation, the rallying, the intensive effort of all the forces of the workers and poor peasantry, the Soviet government was already able to repulse its main enemies on the civil war fronts in the second half of the summer of 1918, even before a radical change for the better had occurred in the international situation as a result of the November revolution in Germany. On February 23 a decree was issued on the organisation of the Red Army. On the basis of this decree strong Red Army units were created, and masses of toilers were drawn into the Red Army on the principle of obligatory military service. A clean-up was carried out in all the principal parts of the state apparatus, and the lack of co-ordination which had existed between the central and local authorities was considerably reduced. Owing to these measures, which were effected as a result of the greatest heroism and enthusiasm on the part of the working class and poor peasantry, the chief foe of the Soviet power—the Czecho-Slovaks and the army of the Constituent Assembly Committee which was organised under the protection of Czech bayonets—who had pushed forward almost to the walls of Moscow and had already seized Kazan, were, by the end of October, thrown back far beyond the Volga.

The Annulment of the Brest Peace

The German revolution, which broke out in the beginning of November, *most radically altered the whole external situation.* The Brest Peace Treaty, of course, now became a 'dead letter. The frontier line which cut through the living body of the Soviet country ceased to exist. The Soviet government was established on half the territory of Esthonia, most of Latvia, almost all of the Ukraine, White Russia and part of Lithuania. This occurred at the very time when the wave of the revolutionary movement was rising in Germany, when the Spartakus Bund, led by Karl Liebknecht and Rosa Luxemburg, was extending its activities ever wider and wider.

The collapse of German imperialism under the blows inflicted on it from within and from without radically changed the international situation in favour of the Soviet republic.

But we must emphasise that even before this the proletarian state created by the October Revolution, drawing its strength from its internal forces, the working class and poor peasantry, had demonstrated its power in the struggle against counter-revolution, had inflicted a series of crushing blows on the latter, and had succeeded in creating a strong state apparatus and army.

This created the basis for a change of front on the part of the petty-bourgeois masses in favour of the October Revolution —the middle peasantry, certain sections of the intelligentsia and specialists. It was of this that Lenin wrote in his article *The Valuable Admission of Pitirim Sorokin* and in a number of other articles. This change of front, which took place as a result of the actually proven strength of the Soviet government, had become clearly apparent by the end of 1918.

The German revolution acted only as a new and powerful impulse to the consolidation of the Soviet government.

But the country and Party were confronted with a further hard struggle. Describing the road along which the Soviet government had travelled during the first year of its existence, Lenin, speaking at the Sixth Congress of Soviets, said:

"From workers' control, these first steps of the working class, from managing all the resources of the country, we have advanced right up to the creation of workers' administration in industry. From the struggle for land by, the peasantry as a whole, from the struggle of the peasants against the landlords—a struggle which was of an all-national, bourgeois-democratic character—we have advanced to the stage when the proletarian and semi-proletarian elements have become prominent in the countryside, when those who toil especially hard, those who are exploited, have come to the fore, have risen to build a new life. The most oppressed section of the rural population has entered upon a fight to the finish with the bourgeoisie including their own village kulak bourgeoisie.

"Furthermore, from the first steps of Soviet organisation, we have advanced to the point where, as was correctly remarked by Comrade Sverdlov who opened the Congress, there is not a remote corner in Russia where Soviet organisation has not been firmly implanted, where it does not form an integral part of the Soviet Constitution which was formulated on the basis of a prolonged experience of struggle on the part of all toilers and oppressed people." *

Military and Political Alliance of the Working Class and Peasantry

The situation of the country, encircled as it was within narrow boundaries, cut off from the sources of raw materials and fuel and having but limited stores of grain and commodities, imperatively dictated the *enforcement of the system of War Communism,* one of the chief characteristics of which was the food quotas, *i.e.,* taking the surplus of grain from the villages without adequate compensation, since the impoverished and exhausted state did not have the necessary means at its disposal. The Soviet government had to take as much as possible of the surplus, and the peasantry was thus deprived of almost all possibility of disposing of any surplus from the crop. The state was not in a position to supply an adequate quantity of such goods as the peasants formerly obtained from private traders.

This had its effect upon the state of feeling among the peasantry and hence also upon the state of feeling in the army.

A certain factor in the military defeats which we suffered at times in 1918-19 was the vacillating temper of the middle peasant masses. The White armies, wherever they were victorious, restored landlordism and the police regime. The Soviet government waged a merciless struggle against the landlords but

* Lenin, *Collected Works,* Vol. XXIII.

was at the same time compelled to deprive the middle peasants of their grain surplus and to prohibit free trade.

The peasantry formed a very large part of the population of the country, and this caused great difficulties, which were utilised by the kulaks to organise anti-Soviet actions.

The Party could not have finally crushed the Whites as it did in 1919, had it not, under the leadership of Lenin, taken steps to confirm the change of front on the part of the middle peasant masses—a change which occurred as a result of the crushing of the kulaks in the summer of 1918 and of a number of victories won by the Soviet government over the forces of internal counter-revolution, as a result of the obvious stability of the Soviet government and dictatorship of the proletariat.

This policy of the Party was clearly expressed in the decisions of the Eighth Congress in March 1919.

They involved, first of all, the question of strengthening the war alliance between the working class and the poor peasants on the one hand and the masses of middle peasants on the other. Without strengthening this alliance, the working class could not achieve decisive victory over the forces of counter-revolution. The middle peasant masses had received the land from the working class. And only the victory of the working class over the armies which stood for bourgeois-landlord and kulak restoration could definitely secure the land for the peasantry. Thus, the war alliance against the bourgeois-landlord restoration was dictated by the interests of both sides.

But in order to cement this alliance, it was necessary to take a number of economic and political measures, so that, despite the vacillations of the middle peasantry between the two belligerent forces, we might nevertheless turn the scale in our favour and *definitely win over the middle peasant to the side of the Soviet government.* As a result of these measures, which were put into effect after the Eighth Congress of the Party, the middle peasantry, at the end of 1919, acted as the decisive factor on all fronts of the Civil War in favour of the Soviet government.

In the period under consideration, which was one of the most critical and most dangerous in the life of the Soviet government, Lenin upheld the policy of paying the most serious consideration (in our peasant country) to the interests and the state of feeling of the broad masses of the middle peasantry, the policy of winning over these masses to our side, while at the same time mercilessly suppressing the kulaks. When the country was in the throes of civil war, Lenin clearly perceived and grasped that our Party would not be able definitely to defeat the enemy in this civil war, would not be able to consolidate the proletarian dictatorship in the country and to secure the necessary conditions for the building of socialism, unless it was able to find common ground with the middle peasantry.

Even at the end of 1918 Lenin wrote:

"In the countryside, our task is to destroy the landlord, to break down the resistance of that exploiter and speculator, the kulak. In this we can rely with certainty *only* upon the semi-proletarians, the poor peasants. But the middle peasant is no enemy of ours. He has wavered, he is wavering, and will waver. The task of influencing the wavering elements is *not identical* with the task of overthrowing the exploiter and of winning victory over the active enemy. To know how to arrive at an understanding with the middle peasantry, without for a moment relinquishing the struggle against the kulak and relying firmly only on the poor peasant—this is the task of the moment, for just at this time the turn of the middle peasantry towards our side is inevitable."

At the Eighth Congress, Lenin resolutely and explicitly raised the question of an alliance with the middle peasant as the question by which the victory of the Soviet power in the Civil War would be secured.

At that time middle peasant farming could have developed along either of two ways: along the capitalist path, by becoming a kulak form of economy; or along the socialist path, the path of large-scale socialised farming on the basis of collectivisation.

It was this dual character of middle peasant farming which determined the neutral position adopted by the middle peasantry at the time when the working class was fighting for its dictatorship as against the dictatorship of the bourgeoisie.

But the October Revolution in Russia gave the peasants the landlords' estates, saved them from further ruin and extermination and put an end to the war. This explains the attitude of sympathy towards the dictatorship of the proletariat taken by

---

* Lenin, "The Valuable Admission of Pitirim Sorokin," *Collected Works*, Vol. XXIII.

the middle peasants after the October Revolution; for the latter, in passing, fulfilled the tasks of the bourgeois-democratic revolution and gave them a way out of the war from which the middle peasants were suffering.

The proletarian dictatorship consolidated itself in spite of the desperate resistance of the bourgeoisie, demonstrated its power and vitality and showed that the most practicable path of development for the middle peasantry was the socialist path of development under the leadership of the working class.

The October socialist revolution was carried out by the forces of the working class and the poorest peasantry, while neutralising the middle peasantry. But the measures taken by the October Revolution to obliterate the remnants of serfdom and to abolish landlordism met with the sympathy of the entire peasantry.

However, it was not only the fact that the Party continued to fight against the restoration of landlordism which ensured the turn of the middle peasantry in favour of the Soviet government; it was also the strengthening of the dictatorship of the proletariat which ensured this.

"The middle peasant whined and vacillated between revolution and counter-revolution as long as the bourgeoisie was being overthrown, and as long as the Soviet power was not consolidated; therefore, it was necessary to neutralise him. The middle peasant began to turn towards us when he began to convince himself that the bourgeoisie had been overthrown 'for good'; that the Soviet power was being consolidated, that the kulak was being overcome, and that the Red Army was beginning to triumph on the fronts of the civil war." *

The Soviet government won decisive and conclusive victories against the forces of White counter-revolution on the basis of the alliance with the middle peasantry. But even before this, the proletarian dictatorship under the leadership of the Party had already demonstrated its tremendous stability and strength, and this was a decisive factor in turning the middle peasant in favour of the Soviet government.

The international position of the Soviet government in the first year of its existence was very largely determined by the fact that the imperialist war was still proceeding. Both imperialist coalitions endeavoured to reap all the benefit of the temporary

* Stalin, "Reply to Comrade Yan—sky," *Leninism*, Vol. I.

weakness of the Soviet republic. They occupied and despoiled its territory. German imperialism seized the Ukraine and dominated the Don region and Transcaucasia. Allied imperialism seized the Far East, Siberia, Murmansk, Archangel and the territory beyond the Caspian. The Baku oil fields first fell into the hands of the British imperialists, who were invited there by the Mensheviks; later the British were forced out of Baku by the Turks who had the backing of German imperialism. Both Allied and German imperialism extended all possible aid to the anti-Soviet counter-revolutionary forces. But they were too absorbed in their mutual struggle, and consequently their aid proved insufficient for the overthrow of the Soviet government, although imperialism as a whole was incomparably stronger than we. In the Far East, the imperialist contradictions between Japan and the United States appeared in their most accentuated form.

The imperialist slaughter in the West, and the sharpening of the struggle between Japan and the United States in the East, hindered any co-ordinated action on the part of the imperialists against the Soviet government.

On the other hand, the October Revolution gave a powerful impulse to the development of the revolutionary movement in capitalist countries. In the beginning of 1918, a wave of political strikes swept over Germany and Austria. The German-Austrian army of occupation in the Ukraine was clearly going to pieces in the struggle with the growing guerrilla movement among the peasants.

Discontent was increasing among the workers even in the armies of the Allied countries.

An increasing process of disintegration was to be observed within the Social-Democratic Parties. Even in 1917, the Centrists deemed it necessary to dissociate themselves in words from the open social-chauvinists, though the "Independents" were, of course, incapable of pursuing any sort of revolutionary tactics.

The revolutionary political strikes which took place in Germany in the beginning of 1918, and which at one time assumed quite large dimensions, were suppressed by the Independents, together with the Scheidemann or government socialists.

Even after the October Revolution, the German Lefts were unable to break the organisational fetters which bound them to the Centrists. They could not grasp and accept the Leninist tactics, particularly on the question of the Brest peace. At the meeting of the Central Committee, on January 11, 1918, Lenin said:

> "We have in our hands a circular letter of the German Social-Democrats; we have information concerning the attitude towards us of two tendencies of the Centre, one of which believes that we have been bribed and that at Brest-Litovsk a comedy is now being enacted with previously assigned roles. This group attacks us for the armistice. The other group of the Kautskyists declares that the personal honesty of the Bolshevik leaders is beyond all question but that the behaviour of the Bolsheviks is a psychological riddle." *

It is characteristic that on this question the German Lefts were not far removed from the Kautskyists. This was due in part to the influence of the Polish Social-Democrats, followers of Rosa Luxemburg, who in Russia took the same stand as the "Left" Communists on the question of the Brest peace.

Liebknecht and Rosa Luxemburg were in prison. In her pamphlet which she wrote in prison, Rosa Luxemburg severely criticised the policy of the Bolsheviks, although she acknowledged their great revolutionary services.

Franz Mehring, at the time one of the leaders of the Spartakus Bund, gave a more or less correct appraisal of the policy of the Bolsheviks on the questions of the Brest peace and' Red terror against the counter-revolution.

But among the masses of the workers in imperialist countries the influence of Bolshevism was increasing, and this made it extremely difficult for the imperialist governments to carry out their interventionist policy against the Soviet government, which had not yet grown sufficiently strong.

The revolution in Germany and Austria, the formation of Soviets of Workers' and Soldiers' Deputies, and the collapse of the Brest peace furnished convincing evidence of the correctness of the Bolshevik policy which secured the establishment and consolidation of the dictatorship of the proletariat on one-sixth of the globe.

* Lenin, *Collected Works*, Vol. XXII.

The Party After the October Revolution

The Party won a great victory in October owing to a correct policy and to the superb organisation which it had succeeded in creating on the basis of the experience gained in decades of struggle against tsarism. As Lenin afterwards wrote, the absolute centralisation and strict discipline of the proletariat constituted one of the fundamental conditions for the victory over the bourgeoisie.

The Party succeeded in maintaining firm organisation and iron discipline in its ranks after emerging from underground and after the winning of power, when scores of thousands of new members—workers, soldiers and intellectuals—joined its ranks. This testifies to the strength and vitality of the old Bolshevik traditions. The old generation of Party members which came to the forefront in the Revolution of 1905-06 (and also in the period preceding this revolution), in the period of reaction, in that of advance and, finally, in the period of the imperialist war, was reinforced after 1917 by a new generation of Bolsheviks which gave the Party large forces of very valuable workers, both in political and practical spheres.

The Party organisation, which had a membership of about 70,000 at the time of the April Conference in 1917, had increased its membership to 230,000 by the time of the October Revolution and continued to grow after that. Alongside with the Party organisations and under their leadership there were the organisations of the Young Communist League, which rapidly developed their work and formed a powerful transmission belt between the Party and the masses of proletarian and peasant youth. Having exposed the bourgeois nature of the policy pursued by the Mensheviks and Socialist-Revolutionaries, the Party definitely secured the support of the broadest proletarian masses by the time of the October Revolution. Immediately before and after the October Revolution, the Party won the overwhelming majority of the Soviets of Workers' Deputies and became the dominant force in the trade union movement, although here and there Menshevik trade union bureaucrats, supported by individual groups of skilled workers and particularly office employees, held on for some time.

At the First All-Russian Congress of Trade Unions, held in the beginning of 1918, the Bolsheviks gained control of the leading organ of the trade unions in Russia, the All-Russian Central Council of Trade Unions. During the first months of 1917, during the period when the struggle for Soviet power was developing, and up to the very moment of the victorious consummation of this struggle, the Party had to overcome the influence of a patriotic Defencist, petty-bourgeois, Menshevik ideology over individual strata among its ranks. The Party was able successfully to ward off this danger; it firmly and resolutely enforced the line of consistent proletarian internationalism.

The Party successfully overcame the attempts of the Right opportunists to pull it over to the side of the Mensheviks. In the first half of 1918, the Party had to pass through a period of extremely bitter struggle against "Left" tendencies. This period bears considerable resemblence to the period of reaction when the Party waged a struggle against the "Vperyod-ists." Just as in the latter case, "Leftist" feelings affected a considerable number of Party leaders. But this time the Party overcame these feelings much more quickly and escaped a split. The "Vperyod" crisis and split reflected the desertion of Bolshevism by a section of the Party intellectuals who succumbed to the influence of bourgeois and petty-bourgeois ideology. In 1917 a tremendous number of new elements came to the Party, flowing into its ranks on the crest of the revolutionary wave. Together with the Party, they stormed the positions of bourgeois rule and went into battle against the forces of counter-revolution. But when, having taken into account the real correlation of forces, the Party had to relinquish the idea of an offensive against German and international imperialism, had to retreat before the imperialist-forces and to set about doing prolonged and painstaking work within the country, it was very difficult for many members of the Party who had not been politically trained and hardened, for the raw elements of the proletariat, to grasp these new tactics which were forced upon the Party. We must especially note that our Party, which had put forward radical demands on the question of peace and on the agrarian and national minority questions, had now been joined by non-proletarian elements who were imbued with petty-bourgeois laxity and who found it extremely difficult to assimilate proletarian discipline and organisation. Clearly, these latter elements could not immediately take a positive attitude towards the organic work of socialist construction, towards the Party line of establishing rigorous state order, of enforcing labour discipline without hesitating to resort to measures of compulsion. The petty-bourgeois feelings within the Party found their ideological expression among the so-called "Left" Communists, who almost brought the Party to a split. As is known, the "Left" Communists included some old Party workers, but they, too, yielded to the influence of the petty-bourgeois environment. During the early part of the war, Bukharin, as is well known, had already manifested certain anarchist tendencies—a failure to grasp Lenin's teachings on the dictatorship of the proletariat and on the function of the proletarian state in the period of transition from capitalism to communism. We know also of the dispute which Lenin had with Bukharin (Nota-Bene) during the war on the question of the state.* An exhaustive analysis of this dispute and of the position taken by Bukharin in it was given by Comrade Stalin in his speech at the Plenum of the Central Committee in April 1929. Bukharin's position of that period was characterised by Comrade Stalin as a repudiation of "the state in the period of transition from capitalism to socialism. Comrade Bukharin here overlooked a 'trifle,' namely, the whole transition period, during which the working class cannot get along without its own state, if it really wants to crush the bourgeoisie and build socialism."**

To the anarchist theory of "blowing up" the state—the theory which was defended by Bukharin—Lenin opposed the "theory of the *creation* of a new state after the overthrow of the bourgeoisie, namely, the state of the proletarian dictatorship." The attempts to line up the Party for a struggle against any kind of state, including the proletarian state, were further developed in the theory and practice of "Left" Communism, which threatened to defeat the measures taken by the Party for the building of a state apparatus of proletarian dictatorship. It was the irony of history

* See Lenin's article "The Youth International," *Collected Works*, Vol. XIX, in which he criticises Bukharin's semi-anarchist views on the state, expressed by him when writing under the pen name of Nota-Bene.
** Stalin, "The Right Deviation in the C.P.S.U." *Leninism*, Vol. II.

that the "Left" Communists, wallowing as they were in the petty-bourgeois swamp, should have charged the Party and its leader, Lenin, with petty-bourgeois tendencies. However, the "Left" Communists were not the original authors of this charge. Many years before them similar charges had been put forward by the Mensheviks.

"The 'Left' Communists," as Stalin afterwards observed, "criticised the Party from the 'Left,' opposing the Brest peace and characterising the policy of the Party as opportunist, non-proletarian and conciliatory towards the imperialists. But in actual fact it has been shown that the 'Left' Communists, by opposing the Brest peace, hindered the Party from gaining a breathing space for the organisation and consolidation of the Soviet power, aided the Socialist-Revolutionaries and Mensheviks, who at the time also opposed the Brest peace, and made things easy for imperialism, which was striving to nip the Soviet power in the bud."*

The comparative rapidity with which the opposition of the "Left" Communists was overcome, testified to the strength and political maturity of the Party.

While overcoming this crisis, the Party was able simultaneously to carry out a number of political tasks: to rally around the working class the broad masses of the poor peasantry; to crush the kulaks; to crush the urban bourgeoisie; to build up, albeit only in outline, a Soviet state and economic apparatus; to organise the Red Army, which became a formidable force to its enemies, and to raise in good earnest the question of establishing a firm alliance with the broad masses of the middle peasantry.

* Stalin, *On the Opposition.*

CHAPTER XII

THE PARTY IN THE PERIOD OF CIVIL WAR AND OF WAR COMMUNISM

The achievements of the Soviet government in 1918—The break-up of the compromising parties—Towards alliance with the German revolution—The vacillations of the middle peasantry—International imperialism in the struggle against the Soviet government—The founding of the Communist International—The Eighth Party Congress—The discussion on the programme—Our attitude to the middle peasantry—The national question at the Eighth Congress—The military question at the Eighth Congress—The Eighth Congress on the social composition of the Party—Victories on the fronts—The struggle with Trotskyism in the Civil War period—The Eighth Party Conference in December 1919—The Ninth Party Congress—Shock methods and one-man management—The faction of "Democratic Centralism"—The significance of the Ninth Congress—The Second Congress of the Communist International—The war with Poland—The political state of the peasantry—The Ninth Party Conference, September 1920—The end of the Civil War—The Party on the eve of the N.E.P.

The Achievements of the Soviet Government in 1918

By the autumn of 1918, the Soviet regime, its economic and provisioning apparatus, and the whole system of government had been greatly strengthened. The Party had been vigorously sweeping away that petty-bourgeois laxity and semi-anarchist slackness which had been so much in evidence in the work of the Soviet apparatus during the first few months of its existence. This slackness was the result of the influence of the petty-bourgeois environment on the work of the Soviet apparatus. And this to a great extent accounts for the weakness of the Soviet state when faced with the offensive of German imperialism. Immediately after the Brest peace, Lenin raised the question of a struggle against the elemental forces of petty-bourgeois anarchy as the immediate task of the Party.

By successfully getting rid of the petty-bourgeois laxity and slackness in the state apparatus, in economic life, etc., by overcoming the influence of the petty-bourgeois environment in its own ranks, the Party itself became stronger. The setting to rights of the state and Party apparatus was carried on under the direct guidance of so exceptionally gifted an organiser as Y. M. Sverdlov, one of Lenin's closest aides during this critical period, and who was at that time Chairman of the All-Russian Central Executive Committee and virtually secretary of the Central Committee of the R.C.P.

The Break-Up of the Compromising Parties

The fact that by the end of 1918 the Soviet government had grown strong, and that not only the middle peasantry but also considerable masses of the intellectuals and urban petty-bourgeoisie had changed their attitude in its favour, gave a new impulse to the breaking up of the compromising Socialist parties, which had attempted to unite around the Ufa Directorate. After the Directorate had been abolished by Admiral Kolchak, the leaders of these parties were compelled to change their tactics. Instead of waging an armed struggle against the Soviet government in alliance with the forces of open counter-revolution—a policy which antagonised their own rank and file—the Socialist-Revolutionaries and Mensheviks adopted the policy of formal hypocritical support of the Soviet government. By these tactics they determined to camouflage their real struggle against the Soviet government: they were speculating on the difficulties. Some of the members of the Committee of the Constituent Assembly, who had escaped from Kolchak, took refuge on Soviet territory and proclaimed a cessation of the civil war against the Soviet government. A similar declaration was shortly after made by the Central Committee of the Right Socialist-Revolutionaries. Still earlier, in November 1918, the Central Committee of the Mensheviks had declared their opinion that the German revolution and the transfer of power in Germany into the hands of Social-Democracy had made it possible to effect certain measures of a socialist character in Russia as well. At the same time the Central Committee of the Mensheviks adopted a resolution, recognising the necessity of supporting the Soviet government against the Anglo-French intervention. In the Ukraine, certain leaders of the Bund and of the Ukrainian Social-Democrats, striving to hold back their rank and file from joining the Bolsheviks under the influence of what the Civil War had taught them, adopted the platform of the Soviet government. But the manoeuvre of the Mensheviks and Socialist-Revolutionaries was very poorly camouflaged. In their newspapers, which were published for a short time in Moscow in the beginning of 1919, they exposed themselves by carrying on demagogic agitation against the measures of the Soviet government, demanding the dissolution of the extraordinary commissions, the abolition of the death penalty for spies and counter-revolutionaries, and freedom of speculation. Many rank and file members of the Menshevik and Socialist-Revolutionary parties, perceiving the hypocrisy and duplicity of their leaders who, despite their professed recognition, of the Soviet government, continued to play into the hands of the counter-revolution by their demagogic agitation against that government and to cause demoralisation in the rear of the Soviet forces in face of the White Guard armies, broke with the compromisers and joined the ranks of the Communist Party By the end of 1919, the ranks of the Mensheviks and Socialist-Revolutionaries were greatly reduced.

Towards Alliance with the German Revolution

The German revolution contributed in the highest degree to the further strengthening of the Soviet power. It would have seemed that there was nothing to prevent the *closest alliance* between our country and the German proletariat which had overthrown the Wilhelm monarchy. But this alliance was not effected, above all through the fault of German Social-Democracy, which was in power for several months, and owing to the fact that the Entente, aided by the bourgeoisie of the national minorities who had formerly been oppressed by tsarism and by the help of German counter-revolutionary forces, succeeded in erecting a partition between Soviet Russia and Germany in the form of a number of bourgeois states (Esthonia, Latvia, Lithuania, Poland).

In all this, the German Social-Democratic government acted as the loyal servant of the Entente, ready to undertake any form of police action against the Soviet government. Its anti-Soviet ardour was restrained only by the profound sympathy of the German toiling masses towards the Soviet government and their refusal to fight against it.

The extension of Soviet territory into districts which had formerly been occupied by German troops did not reach the frontiers of Germany, although it occurred at a time when the Spartacists were fighting on the streets of Berlin. Besides the difficulties which the revolutionary movement encountered in these districts, this was due to the fact that the work done within the Soviet country to strengthen the state apparatus and the army was still insufficient, to the great difficulties, to the fact that the country had suffered too great ravages, and that the main forces of the Red Army, which had been organised but a short time before, had to be concentrated in the East, since it was there that they had to withstand the most violent onslaught of the counter-revolution.

The Soviet advance westward came to a halt. The Soviet government reached the frontiers of Poland, Galicia and Bessarabia when the wave of revolution in Western Europe had mounted especially high, when Soviet republics were proclaimed in Hungary and then in Bavaria, when Germany became the arena of the most violent civil war. But with the aid of the parties of the Second International, the Entente succeeded in confronting the Soviet troops in the West with a front of the newly-formed bourgeois states and in the South and East with a front of internal counter-revolutionary forces. On the latter front were the armies of Kolchak, who had overthrown the Socialist-Revolutionary Ufa Directorate in the East, and the Denikin army in the South. The struggle against these armies was exceptionally difficult, since the middle peasantry, despite a definite change of attitude in favour of the Soviet government, had not yet by any means got rid of its vacillating tendencies. To be sure, the character of these vacillations had undergone a considerable change. Ever more frequently it became a question not of vacillating between the Soviet government and the forces of counter-revolution, but of vacillating between active support of the Soviet government and neutrality.

There were of course considerable contradictions between the counter-revolutionary forces of Denikin and Kolchak, which were trying to resurrect old monarchist Russia, one and indivisible, and the buffer states of the White republics which had been formed in the West.

The bourgeoisie of these republics were not inclined to take their troops far beyond the borders of their territory, and were not at all disposed to restore the tsarist Russia of former days.

The Esthonian, Latvian and Finnish bourgeoisie, after taking vengeance on the revolutionary working class in their territories, could even conclude peace with Soviet Russia in spite of Entente pressure, as actually happened later, on the initiative of the Soviet government, which adroitly utilised the contradictions in the camp of its enemies.

With Kolchak, Denikin, and later Wrangel, there could be no other course than that of a merciless struggle to the death.

The Vacillations of the Middle Peasantry

Even in the summer of 1918, there had been a considerable number of uprisings, in which the leading role was played by the kulaks and a certain section of the middle peasantry. These uprisings played an important part in the formation of the Urals-Volga, Krasnov and Denikin fronts and in the fall of the Soviet government in Siberia and the Northern Caucasus.

The vacillations of the middle peasants were due to the intermediate character of their social position, and were intensified at this stage by certain distortions of our policy in the countryside—distortions which not infrequently found their expression in the organisation of communes and state farms by administrative methods from above, without having the necessary base of technical equipment and without sufficiently taking into account the interests of the middle peasantry—this despite the fact that the Party had recommended that the organisation of the peasants into collectives should take place on a voluntary basis, and looked upon state farms, under the conditions of that period, only as model farms. The Committees of Poor Peasants, which originally formed a weapon in the hands of the Soviet government for the expropriation of the kulaks, after fulfilling this basic task of theirs, began in some cases to manifest anti-middle peasant tendencies. These distortions were utilised by counter-revolutionary elements to persuade the peasants that the Soviet government was aiming at forcibly compelling all the peasants to join communes.

If such widespread excesses against the middle peasants were possible in the spring of 1930, and if kulak provocation very often played a big part in these excesses, it must not be overlooked that, in the spring of 1919, there were much more favourable conditions for such kulak provocation, since our apparatus in the countryside was much less well organised and was much more infested with alien elements.

Experienced and militant workers, devoted to the cause of the proletarian revolution, had been mobilised for the fronts of the Civil War, while the young and untried forces of our Party in the countryside were not always able to expose and determinedly to repulse the cases of kulak provocation and anti-middle peasant excesses in the building of state farms and communes.

The White republics which were formed in Esthonia, Latvia, Poland and Lithuania did not only rely on the bourgeoisie and kulaks in the struggle against the Soviet government, but were also able partly to win over certain individual sections of the toilers, who for centuries had been brought up in a spirit of mistrust towards tsarist Russia, and who feared that the Soviet government would continue the same policy towards the national minorities.

The lack of stability in the state of mind of the middle peasantry, which was fostered in the former border regions, among other reasons, by national motives, was one of the causes of the fact that the Civil War during the second half of 1918 and up to the fall of 1919 was always waged with variable success, rapid advances of the Soviet troops giving way to rapid retreats.

The forces of internal counter-revolution which were fighting against the Soviet government made extensive use of these vacillations on the part of the peasantry. It must not be forgotten, however, that these vacillations now occurred at a time when the middle peasantry were already turning in favour of the Soviet government—a fact which Lenin had already noted in the end of 1918.

"In the final analysis," Lenin wrote in his article *The Elections to the Constitutent Assembly and the Dictatorship of the Proletariat* at the end of 1919, "it was just these vacillations of the peasantry as the chief representative of the mass of petty-bourgeois toilers which were deciding the fate of the Soviet government and of the Kolchak-Denikin government. But before this 'final analysis,' there was a sufficiently lengthy period of hard struggle and agonising ordeals, which have not yet ended in Russia after two years, have not ended, that is to say, in Siberia and in the Ukraine."*

The whole policy of the White governments in the regions occupied by them, the unconcealed policy of the restoration of landlordism, and the acts of violence and brutality against the peasants, were a very strong factor in helping to change the vacillations of the middle peasantry into support of the Soviet government.

International Imperialism in the Struggle Against the Soviet Government

International imperialism was the directing force of the internal counter-revolution. As we have seen, the Soviet government after the October Revolution was established almost throughout the entire territory of former tsarist Russia.

Only the invasion of German troops caused the triumph of the counter-revolution in the Ukraine, the Don region, in Finland, Esthonia and Latvia. Only under the protection of the Czecho-Slovak hirelings of French imperialism was it possible to form the Urals-Volga front of the Constituent Assembly, which was headed by the Mensheviks and Socialist-Revolutionaries; and the same is true of the Northern front.

Japanese, American and British troops, and the Czecho-Slovak legions, which were under the direction of the French General Staff, occupied the Far East, Siberia, the Urals, the Volga region and the North.

The Denikin Volunteer Army, protected on the North by Krasnov who received arms and munitions from German imperialism, and supported by counter-revolutionary elements among the Kuban and Terek Cossacks, gradually began to consolidate its position in the Northern Caucasus.

Even during the first period of its existence, the Soviet government proved sufficiently strong to administer a determined rebuff

* Lenin, *Collected Works*, Vol. XXIV.

to the forces of internal counter-revolution, despite the support extended to them by both of the two hostile imperialist coalitions. The Soviet government took full advantage of the fact that the main forces of both coalitions were engaged in mutual struggle.

At the end of 1918, however, German imperialism collapsed. Its troops evacuated the occupied territories. But no sooner was the armistice signed, in November 1918, than a French fleet entered the Black Sea, transports arrived at Novorossisk with military supplies for Denikin's army and several divisions of French troops were landed in the Crimea and at Odessa.

The first campaign of the Entente had commenced. The Allies sent money and arms to support the troops of Finland, Esthonia, Latvia, Poland, Lithuania and the Petlura bands in the Ukraine, which fought against the Soviet government in the West. They took over the work of supplying the Denikin and Kolchak armies. British troops occupied Transcaucasia, forming the main support of the Georgian Mensheviks, of the Armenian Dashnyaks* and Azerbaidjan Mussavatists* against the revolutionary workers and peasants.

However, the Soviet government had powerful allies, even beyond the boundaries of its country. The revolutionary movement in Europe did not diminish, but on the contrary grew stronger after the conclusion of the armistice, not only in the defeated countries, but in the victorious countries as well. The masses of soldiers were in no mood to let themselves be forced into a fight against the Soviet government. The efforts of the Allied governments to force the German troops in the Ukraine to fight against the Bolsheviks proved of no avail. And they had no better luck with their own troops.

The mutiny of the French Black Sea Fleet, connected as it is with the name of Comrade Marty, and the extremely effective Bolshevik propaganda among the French troops which were landed in Odessa, were the most outstanding but by no means the only facts which showed how difficult it was for the Allied governments to crush the Soviet power by armed force. And it was precisely owing to this difficulty that in 1919 vacillation was already to be observed among the ruling circles of the Allied pow-

* Bourgeois nationalist parties.

ers between the policy of armed intervention and a policy of abandoning intervention. This vacillation found its expression in the project to call a conference on the Prinkipo Islands, near Constantinople, of the Soviet government and the White Guard governments, with Allied representatives participating. However, the ruling circles of the Allied powers, hoping that the Whites would be victorious, abandoned this project and continued the policy of intervention.

The Founding of the Communist International

The revolutionary movement in 1918-19, wherever it assumed more or less extensive proportions and took on the form of a direct struggle with the imperialist governments, utilised, although quite inadequately, the experience of the victorious struggle of the Russian Bolsheviks, creating Soviets of Workers' and Soldiers' Deputies as the embryos of revolutionary power.

This was the case in Germany, Austria, Hungary and Poland. However, it was only in Hungary and Bavaria that the Soviets succeeded, even temporarily, in taking power. In Germany and Austria, the Social-Democrats—the Scheidemann group and the Independents—were able to reduce the Soviets into impotent and meaningless appendages of the capitalist state power, so that they imperceptibly put an end to their existence. This was also the case in Poland, where the members of the Polish Socialist Party prevented the Soviets from becoming the organs of proletarian dictatorship. But the fact that the revolutionary masses had created these Soviets was a further striking proof of the international significance of the experience of the Russian revolutions, testifying to the correctness of the strategy and tactics of Bolshevism not only for Russia but on an international scale as well.

The October Revolution and the subsequent revolutionary events in Central Europe in 1918 and 1919 made it an urgent necessity to set about the immediate creation of a Communist International as a revolutionary organisation to lead the international proletariat on the basis of the principles of Marxism-Leninism regarding programme, tactics and organisation.

During the World War, Lenin had made a tremendous contribution to the treasury of Marxism. He gave a profound and complete analysis of the imperialist phase in the development of capitalism, investigated the effect of 'the law of the uneven development of capitalism under the conditions of imperialism and proved the possibility of socialism being victorious, of socialism being built up, in individual countries.

In 1917 Lenin put forward a programme for the creation of a Soviet type of state as a higher type compared with a bourgeois parliamentary republic. Comrade Stalin wrote on this question:

"In 1915 Lenin did not yet know of the Soviet power as the state form of the proletarian dictatorship. Lenin was already aware in 1905 that individual Soviets are the embryo of revolutionary power in the period of the overthrow of tsarism. But at that time he had not yet conceived of the Soviet power united on a national scale as the state form of the proletarian dictatorship. The republic of Soviets as the state form of the proletarian dictatorship Lenin discovered only in 1917."*

In the autumn of 1917, Lenin published his famous book *State and Revolution,* expounding in a systematic form and developing the teachings of Marx and Engels and completely exposing the opportunists and Centrists.

The state is a product of the irreconcilable class contradictions in a society which is divided into classes. It grew up as an organisation for the domination of one part of society over the other, as the organisation of the dominant class. The weapon of this domination is the state apparatus, armed forces, prisons, etc.

The destruction of the class rule of the bourgeoisie demands that the victorious proletariat destroy the bourgeois state, smash its machinery. For this task, formulated on many occasions by Marx and Engels, the opportunists wanted to substitute the task of getting control of the bourgeois state apparatus, of winning a majority in the bourgeois parliament.

Communism will bring with it the elimination of the division of society into classes, and consequently also the abolition of the state. But the working class, in carrying out the violent overthrow of the bourgeoisie, cannot confine itself to the destruction of the bourgeois state machinery.

In place of the bourgeois state machinery which has been destroyed, the working class must create its own state of the type of

* Stalin, *On the Opposition.*

the Commune, of the type of the Soviets, which will be the last historical form of the state, the state of the proletarian dictatorship and of the building of socialism.

This proletarian state will wither away with the coming of communism.

The opportunists of the Social-Democratic camp have rejected the overthrow of capitalism, the destruction of the bourgeois state, rejected the proletarian dictatorship and the creation of a state of the Soviet type as the organ of this dictatorship. The highest, ideal type of state power was, in their opinion, bourgeois democracy, bourgeois parliamentarism.

The anarchists, while advocating the destruction, the blowing up of the bourgeois state, do not recognise the proletarian state, the state of the proletarian dictatorship, as the organ for suppressing the resistance of the exploiters, for re-moulding the non-proletarian classes of the working population and for building socialism.

This is connected with their rejection of the role of a political party as the main weapon in the struggle for the proletarian dictatorship and as the main instrument of this dictatorship, and also with their refusal to utilise various forms and institutions of the bourgeois state in the interests of the working class struggle against the bourgeoisie and for the proletarian dictatorship.

In the anarchist view, the blowing up of the bourgeois state as a result of sporadic revolutionary actions by individual groups and persons (without systematic struggle by an organised working class) is bound up with the destruction of every kind of state, with the destruction of state power in general, with the passing of mankind to existence without a state, to an existence which the anarchists conceived in the form of disconnected anarchist communes.

In a number of basic questions regarding the proletarian and bourgeois state, the "Left" Communists in Russia (Bukharin) approached the anarchist point of view. Similar attitudes were to be met with among individual groups adhering to the Zimmerwald Left wing in Germany, Great Britain and Holland.

The First, Constituent, Congress of the Communist International was held at the beginning of March 1919. It was attended by delegates from Russia, the Ukraine, Poland, Latvia, Germany, the United States, Norway, Hungary, Switzerland, Finland, Britain and other countries. The central question at the Congress was that of bourgeois democracy and proletarian dictatorship, the report on this question being made by Lenin. In his introductory speech at the opening of the Congress, Lenin said:

"It is only necessary to find that practical form which will enable the proletariat to realise its domination. Such a form is the Soviet system with the proletarian dictatorship. Heretofore the words 'proletarian dictatorship' sounded Latin to us. Thanks to the spread of the Soviet system, this Latin has been translated throughout the world into all modern languages; the working class masses have found a practical form of proletarian dictatorship. It has become comprehensible to the broadest masses of the workers, thanks to the Soviet power in Russia, thanks to the Spartacists in Germany and similar organisations in other countries, as for instance, the 'Shop Stewards' Committees' in England."

It should be noted that at first some of the delegates to the Congress, including Eberlein, who represented the German Spartacists, opposed the organisation of the Communist International, hesitating to make a final break with the Centrists. This was in line with the semi-Centrist tendencies and vacillations of the German Lefts both before .nd during the war, and which we have already had occasion to note. Rosa Luxemburg was particularly affected by these tendencies and vacillations; even in 1918, while in prison, she wrote the pamphlet *The Russian Revolution,* in which she emphatically condemned not only the agrarian and national policy of the Soviet government, but even the dissolution of the Constituent Assembly, the disfranchisement of the propertied classes, the denial of freedom of the press to the bourgeoisie and its "socialist" henchmen, not to mention the Red terror. Fortunately, this pamphlet was not Rosa Luxemburg's last word. Upon her release from prison she recognised and corrected in deeds a good part of her errors, became a leader of the German Communist Party and was brutally murdered at her post by White Guards acting on the instructions of the Social-Democrats then in power.

However, the basic political theses of the pamphlet *The Russian Revolution* remain characteristic of the inconsistency and vacillation of Luxemburgism, of its opportunist Menshevik tendencies.

The Eighth Party Congress

The Eighth Congress of the Party* met between March 18 and March 23, almost immediately after the First Congress of the Communist International. This Congress was of great importance in the history of the Party. The previous Congress had adopted a new name for the Party. The Eighth Congress adopted a new Party programme, which, to the analysis of pre-imperialist capitalism contained in the old programme, added an analysis of imperialism. The analysis was made by Lenin in his book *Imperialism as the Highest Stage of Capitalism*, written in 1916, and it represents one of Lenin's most valuable contributions to the theory of Marxism. The Party programme adopted by the Eighth Congress contains a concise formulation of the doctrine of Marx and Engels on the state—the dictatorship of the proletariat, which constitutes the main point in Marxism. This doctrine was developed by Lenin, especially in his book *State and Revolution*. On the basis of the experience of the three Russian revolutions, the state form of proletarian dictatorship proposed by the programme was Soviet power.

"This victory of the world proletarian revolution calls for the greatest confidence, the closest fraternal union and the greatest possible unity of revolutionary action on the part of the working class in progressive countries.

"These conditions cannot be achieved unless a determined rupture is made on matters of principle, and a ruthless struggle is waged against the bourgeois distortion of socialism which has gained the upper hand among the leaders of the official Social-Democratic and Socialist parties.

"Such a distortion is, on the one hand, the opportunist and social-chauvinist trend which professes to be socialist in words, yet is chauvinist in practice, and covers up the defence of the rapacious interests of their own bourgeoisie under the false slogan of defending the fatherland, both in general and especially during the imperialist war of 1914-18. This trend was created by the fact that in the progressive capitalist countries the bourgeoisie, by robbing the colonial and weak nations, were able, out of the surplus profits obtained by this robbery, to place the upper stratum of the proletariat in their countries in a

* The Congress was attended by 286 delegates with a decisive vote and 100 delegates with a consultative vote, representing a total membership of 313,000. The delegates included representatives of the regions which had been recently delivered from the hands of the Whites and which had become Soviet republics, *viz.*, the Ukraine, White Russia, Lithuania and Latvia.

privileged position, to bribe them, to secure for them in peace time tolerable, petty-bourgeois conditions of life, and to take into their service the leaders of that stratum. Opportunists aand social-chauvinists, being the servants of the bourgeoisie, are actually the direct class enemies of the proletariat, especially now, when, in alliance with the capitalists, they are suppressing by force of arms the revolutionary movement of the proletariat both in their own countries and in foreign countries.

"On the other hand, the 'centrist' movement is also a bourgeois distortion of socialism. That movement is also found in all capitalist countries. It vacillates between the social-chauvinists and the Communists, advocates union with the former, and strives to revive the bankrupt Second International. The only leader in the proletarian struggle for emancipation is the new, Third, Communist International, of which the Communist Party of the Soviet Union is a detachment. This International was created by the formation in a number of countries, particularly in Germany, of Communist Parties which were made up of the genuinely proletarian elements of former Socialist Parties. It was formally established in March 1919, at its First Congress, held in Moscow. The Communist International, which is winning increasing sympathy among the masses of the proletariat of all countries, reverts to Marxism, not only in name, but also in its entire ideological and political content, and in all its activities applies the revolutionary teachings of Marx, purged of bourgeois opportunist distortions."*

The Soviet power was envisaged by the programme as the socialist dictatorship of the proletariat.

"The October Revolution ... in Russia," states the first paragraph of the Party programme adopted by the Eighth Congress, "brought about the dictatorship of the proletariat, which with the support of the poorest peasantry, or semi-proletariat, began to lay down the foundation of · communist society. The course of the revolution in Germany and Austria-Hungary, the growth of the revolutionary movement of the proletariat in all the progressive countries, the spread of the Soviet form of this movement, i.e., a form which directly aims at the establishment of the dictatorship of the proletariat—all this showed that the era of world proletarian communist revolution had begun." **

The programme of the Communist International which was adopted later also emphasises that

"As has been shown by the experience of the October Revolution of 1917 and by the Hungarian Revolution, which immeasurably enlarged the experience of the Paris Commune of 1871, the most suitable form

* *Programme and Constitution of the C.P.S.U.(B)*, Preamble.
** *Ibid.*

of proletarian state is the Soviet state—a new type of state, which differs in principle from the bourgeois state, not only in its class content, but also in its internal structure. This is precisely the type of state which, emerging as it does directly out of the broadest possible mass movement of the toilers, secures the maximum of mass activity and is, consequently, the surest guarantee of final victory.

"The Soviet form of state, being the highest form of democracy, namely, proletarian democracy, is the very opposite of bourgeois democracy, which is bourgeois dictatorship in a masked form. The Soviet state is the dictatorship of the proletariat, the rule of a single class—the proletariat. Unlike the bourgeois democracy, proletarian democracy openly admits its class character, and aims avowedly at the suppression of the exploiters in the interests of the overwhelming majority of the population."*

After the October Revolution the Soviet government, under the leadership of the Party, carried out a tremendous work in bringing the bourgeois-democratic revolution to completion.** But the main problems which had confronted it then and continued to confront it now were the problems of socialist construction. In solving these problems, emancipating itself in the process of their solution, and heading for the abolition of classes, the proletariat was at the same time emancipating all toilers and oppressed people, and above all the peasantry. The theoretical and concretely practical part of the programme adopted by the Eighth Congress was based on the consideration that the proletarian dictatorship existed in our country as an actual historical fact.

---

* *Programme of the Communist International,* Section IV, par. 2.

** "One of the greatest merits of the dictatorship of the proletariat lies in the fact that it completed the bourgeois revolution and entirely swept away the debris of mediævalism. This was of supreme and indeed decisive importance for the rural districts; without it that association of peasant wars with the proletarian revolution of which Marx spoke in the second half of the last century could not have been achieved. Without it the proletarian revolution itself could not have been consolidated. Moreover, the following important circumstance should be borne in mind. The completion of the bourgeois revolution was not a single act. In fact it was spread over a whole period embracing not only parts of 1918, as you assert in your letter, but also parts of 1919 (the Volga provinces and the Urals) and of 1919 and 1920 (the Ukraine), I am referring to the advance of Kolchak and Denikin, when the peasantry *as a whole* was faced with the danger of the restoration of the power of the landlords and when the peasantry precisely *as a whole* was obliged to rally around the Soviet power in order to ensure the completion of the bourgeois revolution and to preserve the fruits of that revolution." (Stalin, "Reply to Comrade Yan—sky," *Leninism,* Vol. I.)

At the Seventh Congress, the Party had launched a resolute struggle against the "Left" Communists, who were under the influence of the petty-bourgeois environment and who did not understand that at that specific moment it was necessary for the Party to conclude the Brest peace, to beat a retreat, in order to avoid a disadvantageous struggle with German imperialism. At the Eighth Congress Lenin said:

"From the standpoint of a revolutionary, those who condemned this retreat were occupying in reality a basically incorrect and non-Marxist position. They had forgotten under what conditions, after how long and difficult a development during the Kerensky epoch, at what a price of vast preparatory work in the Soviets, we reached the point where, after the severe July defeats, after the Kornilov affair, the determination and readiness among the vast masses of the toilers to overthrow the bourgeoisie and the material organised force which was necessary for this task finally matured in October. Clearly, anything of this kind on an international scale was at that time quite out of the question."*

The "Left" Communists by their tactics were objectively propelling the Soviet government to the path of disaster. The opposition which the "Left" Communists together with the Left Socialist-Revolutionaries offered after the Seventh Congress to the practical measures of the Soviet government for the creation and strengthening of a state apparatus, for raising labour productivity, for establishing discipline in the mills and factories, continued to act as grist to the mill of the petty-bourgeois forces of counter-revolution.

The Discussion on the Programme

The Eighth Party Congress in its turn had to fight the so-called "Left" but actually petty-bourgeois deviations in the discussion of the programme and of the tactical resolutions on the three main questions before the Congress—the peasant question, the national question and the military question. Bukharin and his associates had recognised the correctness of Lenin's position at the time of the conclusion of the Brest peace, but they had not yet by any means repudiated their entire ideology of "Left" Communism, which was closely interwoven with "Left" Social-Democratic Centrism and which, in Bukharin's case for instance, had already developed in its essential features during the early part of

* Lenin, *Collected Works*, Vol. XXIV.

the war. Bukharin, on the basis of his anti-Leninist theory of pure imperialism, thought it superfluous to include an analysis of the capitalist system in the programme. Lenin, in his report on the Party programme, was compelled to take a decided stand against this distortion and underestimation of the significance of the elements of capitalism which existed in our country, against this tendency to skip over difficulties.

"We are now experiencing in Russia the consequences of the imperialist war and the beginning of the proletarian dictatorship," Lenin said. "At the same time, in a large number of regions in Russia which had been cut off from each other, we are experiencing in many places, to a greater extent than formerly, a revival of capitalism and the development of its first stage. This cannot be evaded. If we were to write the programme as Comrade Bukharin wanted, the programme would be incorrect. It would, at best, reproduce the best that has been said of finance capitalism and imperialism but would not reproduce reality, since there is no such completeness in this reality."

"What does the collapse of transport in the imperialist system signify?" Lenin continued. "It means the return to the most primitive forms of commodity production. We are quite familiar with the bag carriers.* These cannot be placed under any category that fits in with the proletarian dictatorship, they belong to the lowest stages of capitalist society and commodity production." **

Lenin demonstrated the necessity of including in the new programme the theoretical part of the old programme which contained an analysis of pre-imperialist capitalism, saying:

"That capitalism which was depicted in 1903 continues to exist also in 1919 in the Soviet proletarian republic, precisely because of the decomposition of imperialism, because of its collapse.

"... In a period when the Civil War is rending the country asunder,

* Private food speculators who used to go to the country, buy up bagfuls of food and sell it at exorbitant prices in the cities.
**Lenin, Collected Works, Vol. XXIV. As can be seen from the above quotations, Bukharin's main error in 1919 during the discussion of the programme was to underestimate, or even to ignore, the elements of capitalism existing under Soviet conditions. In contradistinction to Lenin, who pointed out that capitalism is spontaneously generated by petty commodity production, Bukharin offered his original theory. "Although we now see the peasant 'commodity producer,' " said Bukharin, "or the artisan who revives on the basis of the disintegration of large-scale capitalism, 'the formation of the old simple commodity form cannot yet serve by any means as a basis for the generation of a new capitalism." Underestimation of the elements of capitalism in Soviet economy was a "Left" slip on the part of Bukharin in 1919

we will not soon emerge from this situation, from this bag carrying. . . . We must grasp all this, for only by reckoning with reality will we be able to solve such questions as, for instance, our attitude to the middle peasantry. Indeed, whence could the middle peasant arise in an epoch of pure imperialist capitalism? He was not to be found even in coun: tries of ordinary capitalism? If we attempt to solve the question of our attitude to this almost mediæval phenomenon (to the middle peasantry) exclusively from the standpoint of imperialism and the dictatorship of the proletariat. . . we come out all over bruises. . . . This is the A B C of capitalism, which should be indicated since we have not yet got out of this A B C stage. To evade this, and to say: 'Why should we bother about the A B C if we have already learned finance capitalism,' would be very frivolous procedure."*

Our Attitude to the Middle Peasantry

Up to the time of the Eighth Congress, certain individual elements within the Party took a too simplified view of the problem of the transition of petty peasant farming to socialism. Local organisations sometimes went so far as to merge peasant farms into communes by forcible means. However, there were hundreds of thousands and millions of such small peasant farms, and it was on the leadership of these millions by the proletariat -that the fate of the Civil War ultimately depended. The final text of the Party programme adopted by the Eighth Congress contains a number of items which speak of the necessity of state aid for individual farms, of the fact that the Soviet government would still have to reckon with individual peasant farms for a long time to. come, helping them to unite into collectives, not by issuing orders, not by means of compulsory expropriation, but by means of model social cultivation of the soil, by means of voluntary union.

Besides elucidating this question in the course of the discussion on the programme, the Congress also adopted a special reso· lution on the attitude to the middle peasantry.** The entire Con-

---

* Lenin, *Collected Works*, Vol. XXIV.
** "At the present time the state of utter ruin, caused in all countries of the world by the four years of the imperialist war waged in the interests of capitalist plunder—ruin which is particularly severe in Russia—has placed the middle peasantry in a difficult situation.

"Taking this into account the law of the Soviet government on the special tax, in contradistinction to all the laws of all the bourgeois governments in the world, insists on placing the entire burden of the tax on the

gress was marked by a change to the new slogan of an alliance
with the middle peasantry. The resolution adopted by the Congress spoke of aid from the then scanty state resources to individual peasant farming, and repeatedly emphasised that the Soviet government, under the leadership of the Communist Party,
does not aim at the forcible transformation of individual peasant
farming into collective farming. The resolution further charged
the Soviet apparatus with the task of waging a relentless struggle against all abuses in regard to the middle peasantry. This was
all the Party could offer the middle peasantry at the time, but
it proved sufficient to determine once and for all the position of
the middle peasantry in the struggle between the Soviet power and
the forces of landlord-monarchist counter-revolution, to turn the
balance of peasant feeling definitely in favour of the Red Army
and thereby to decide the issue of the Civil War. This would not
have been possible had not the "Left" deviations on the peasant
question been overcome.*

kulaks, on the comparatively few representatives of the exploiting peasantry
who have grown especially rich during the war. While the middle peasantry
should be taxed quite moderately, only to an extent which they are fully able
to bear and which is not a burden to them.

"The Party demands that the collection of the special tax be mitigated
under all circumstances in the case of the middle peasantry, even if this
should involve a reduction in the total amount of the tax."

The same resolution continues:

"While encouraging co-operative societies of all kinds, including agricultural communes of middle peasants, the representatives of the Soviet government should not tolerate the least degree of compulsion in their organisation. Only those associations are valuable which are developed by the
peasants themselves, on their own initiative, the advantages of which have
been tested by them in practice. Excessive haste in this work is harmful,
for it is calculated only to strengthen the prejudice of the middle peasantry
against new methods."

* "We have no benefits," Lenin said, in the report of the Central Committee at the Eighth Congress, "which we can give to the middle peasant,
and he is a materialist, a practical man and demands concrete material benefits. These we cannot furnish at present and the country will have to get
along without them perhaps for months of difficult struggle, which now
promises us complete victory. But we can do a great deal in our administrative practice. We can improve our apparatus, we can correct a great many
abuses. We can correct the line of our Party, which has not been sufficiently
directed towards a *bloc*, an alliance, an agreement with the middle peasantry
—we can and must rectify and correct this line." (Lenin, *Collected Works*,
Vol. XXIV.)

At the proper time, in 1905 and 1917, the Party carried through the agrarian revolution against tsarism and against the landlords with the forces of the entire peasantry.

"We carried through the October Revolution so easily," Lenin said at the Eighth Congress, "because the peasantry as a whole supported us, because it opposed the landlords, because it saw that we were going to see this thing through."

Lenin of course had in mind the incidental solution of the tasks of the bourgeois-democratic revolution by the October Revolution. As a socialist revolution, the working class, under the leadership of the Party, carried through the October Revolution in alliance with the poorest peasantry against the kulak, while neutralising the middle peasantry. This was the main slogan with regard to the peasantry at that stage. After the October Revolution, too, the Party fought against the bourgeoisie in the towns and the kulaks in the countryside with the aid of the poorest peasantry, while neutralising the middle peasants. By the joint efforts of the working class and poor peasants, against the kulaks, the socialist revolution was accomplished in the countryside in the summer of 1918. This revolution expropriated the capitalist elements, but could not yet, under the conditions of that time, create a system of large-scale socialist production in agriculture. Later, after the kulaks had been routed and after the link with the poor peasantry, as representing the support of the Party, had been strengthened, the Party undertook the task of establishing a firm alliance between the working class and the middle peasantry, of turning the middle peasant into an active helper of the Soviet power.

"The best representatives of socialism of the old days—when they still believed in revolution and served it in theory and ideology—spoke of the neutralisation of the peasantry, i.e., of transforming this middle peasantry into a social stratum, which, if it did not actively aid the revolution of the proletariat, at least would not hinder our work, would remain neutral and would not take the side of our enemies. This abstract, theoretical statement of the task is perfectly clear to us. But it is not enough. We have entered a phase of socialist construction in which we must draw up concrete and detailed basic rules and instructions which have been tested by the experience of our work in the rural districts, by which we must guide ourselves in order to achieve a *stable alliance* with the middle peasantry." *

This is what Lenin said at the Eighth Congress.

The National Question at the Eighth Congress

We have already seen how the Allies exploited the nationalist feelings to be met with among the toiling masses of those peoples who had formerly been oppressed by tsarism, and how this played a tremendous important part in the organisation of opposition to the Soviet government in the West. In spite of this, however, there were to be found comrades who loudly proclaimed their views at the Eighth Party Congress to the effect that the Soviet government should not treat the national question as an urgent one, that it was a question of the past, that in the imperialist epoch the national question could not play a revolutionary role and that there was no need to include in the Party programme anything about the right of nations to self-determination.

These ideas were expressed at the Congress by the former "Left" Communists, who shared the Luxemburgist viewpoint on the national question and who went so far as to state that the demand in our programme for the right of nations to self-determination, including the right of secession, would play into the hands of counter-revolution. Proposals were made by Bukharin, Pyatakov and others to replace Lenin's formula of the right of nations to self-determination, including the right of secession, by the formula demanding the right of self-determination for the toilers. Lenin determinedly fought against such Luxemburgist "nihilism" on the national question.

The programme of the Party, in accordance with Lenin's view, retained the demand for *the right of nations to self-determination, including the right of secession.* In his closing speech on the programme, Lenin gave a merciless rebuff to all the liquidatory arguments of the "Lefts" on the national question, all of which were based on an erroneous, Luxemburgist treatment of the national question, while in reality their "Leftism" served to conceal the most ordinary Great-Russian chauvinism.

* Lenin, "The Eighth Congress of the R.C.P.(B)," *Collected Works,* Vol XXIV.

"Scratch certain Communists," declared Lenin outright, "and you will find a Great-Russian chauvinist. . . . For instance, there are some Communists among us who say: We have a unified school system, therefore you must not dare to teach in any language other than Russian. In my opinion such a Communist is a Great-Russian chauvinist. There is a trace of this chauvinist in many of us, and we must fight him.".*

Such an attitude towards the national question, veiled by "Left" phrases, did tremendous harm to the Party and was of no less tremendous benefit to the forces of counter-revolution, which took every opportunity of playing upon the nationalist feeling to be met with among the formerly oppressed peoples. Lenin had on frequent past occasions pointed out that Luxemburgism on the national question was nothing more or less than grist to the mill of Great-Russian chauvinism.

The Party Programme adopted by the Eighth Congress contained a special point recognising the necessity of a federative union of those governments which were organised on a Soviet basis. In practice the Party had already put this into effect, immediately after the October Revolution. But the pre-October resolutions of the Party spoke of national territorial autonomy. The broad scope of the national movement, the profound mistrust among the toiling masses of the oppressed nationalities towards any manifestations of centralism which were not directly dictated by their own interests (military alliance, etc.), demanded greater elasticity in establishing forms of contact and union between the Soviet republics. Among these forms was the federative union approved by the Party programme.

Recognising the right of nations to self-determination, including the right of secession, and applying this principle to the actual circumstances of Soviet life, our Party formed autonomous and independent Soviet republics. The creation of these republics was a factor in the successful termination of our civil war, helping to free a considerable section of the peasantry, petty bourgeoisie and even certain sections of the proletariat from the influence of petty-bourgeois nationalist parties and to win their support for the Soviet government.

We have already noted that petty-bourgeois Luxemburgist views and feelings on the national question were to be met with

* *Ibid.*

during the period of the war and at the April Conference. Lenin and Stalin had to carry on a severe struggle at this conference against the united forces of the Russian and Polish Luxemburgists.

The correct national policy of the Bolshevik Party was a tremendous factor in creating the necessary conditions for the victory of the October Revolution.

But whereas prior to October the national question in our country was a part of the question of the bourgeois-democratic revolution which was evolving into the socialist revolution, it now became part of the question of the dictatorship of the proletariat.

In connection with the national question, there were a number of most important measures put into effect by the Party after the victory of the October Revolution, and which became a powerful weapon for the consolidation of the proletarian dictatorship in our country.

Among these measures was, first of all, the Declaration of the Rights of the Peoples of Russia, signed by Lenin and Stalin, which proclaimed:

1. The equality and sovereignty of the peoples of Russia.

2. The right of free self-determination, including that of secession.

3. The abolition of all national and national-religious privileges and restrictions of every kind.

4. The free development of the national minorities and ethnical groups inhabiting the territory of Russia.

Another very important document which constituted part of the programme of the Soviet government was the address to the working Mohammedan population of Russia and the East, signed by Lenin and Stalin, which was published in December 1917. The carrying out of the Leninist national policy became a powerful weapon for the consolidation of the proletarian dictatorship in our country. The Luxemburgist practice of ignoring and underestimating the national question, ignoring the national demands of the broad toiling masses of those nationalities which had formerly been oppressed by tsarism, was only playing into the hands of the nationalist forces of counter-revolution.

This fact was especially apparent in the Ukraine, where Luxemburgist tendencies on the national question (the most outstanding spokesman for which in the Party was Bukharin) had very grave consequences. Individual comrades went so far as to deny the existence of an Ukrainian nation and Ukrainian culture, or to describe the latter as a backward, village culture doomed to be inevitably supplanted by the advanced culture of Russia. The practical consequences of this was an attitude of disapprobation towards the Ukrainisation of the state apparatus and of the schools, towards the carrying on of Party work and political work in general in the Ukrainian language, etc.

"The revolution would not have triumphed in Russia, and Kolchak and Denikin would not have been crushed, if the Russian proletariat did not have on its side the sympathies and the support of the oppressed peoples in the former Russian empire. But to win the sympathies and the support of these peoples, it had first of all to break the chain forged by Russian imperialism and free these peoples from the yoke of national oppression. Without this it would have been impossible firmly to establish the Soviet power, to implant true internationalism and to create that remarkable organisation for the collaboration of nations which is called the Union of Soviet Socialist Republics and which is the living prototype of the future union of nations in a single world economic system." *

The Military Question at the Eighth Congress

The leader of the opposition on the military question was V. M. Smirnov, but yesterday a "Left" Communist, and later on a protagonist of "democratic centralism." He was supported by Safarov, Pyatakov and others. The Central Committee's point of view was defended by Lenin and Stalin. The differences of opinion on this question at the Congress were extremely sharp. They were a continuation of those differences which had already made their appearance in our Party after the Brest peace, when the question arose of how an army was to be formed. On this basis there was a dispute between those who favoured the formation of a regular, disciplined and centralised army and those who favoured so-called guerrilla warfare. The Left Socialist-Revolutionaries consistently advocated guerrilla warfare, and as a result of the state of feeling engendered by them, the struggle against specialists, which they, in conjunction with the "Left" Communists, had carried on in industry, was now continued in the army as well. Guer-

---

* Stalin, "Foundations of Leninism," *Leninism.* Vol. I.

rilla methods, however, remained in vogue even after the Party of the Left Socialist-Revolutionaries had disappeared from the scene. These methods, which were supported by some of our Party workers, though not, it is true, in such direct and consistent form as by the Left Socialist-Revolutionaries, constituted one of the reasons why the army did not attain a sufficient degree of organisation. The Eighth Party Congress also had to give a resolute rebuff to certain "Left" deviations on the military question, which had their source in the views of "Left" Communism and of its theoretical leader, Comrade Bukharin, with regard to the state, the state apparatus and the proletarian dictatorship in the period of transition from capitalism to communism. It was no accident that the leading nucleus of the opposition on the war question should have been composed in the main of former "Left" Communists. The Congress decided that to advocate the idea of guerrilla detachments in place of a planfully organised and centralised army (as preached by the Left Socialist-Revolutionaries and their like) was nothing but a travesty of political thought and an expression of the frivolity of the petty-bourgeois intelligentsia.

"Guerrilla methods of struggle were forced on the proletariat in the first period by its oppressed position in the state, just as it was forced to use primitive underground printshops and secret meetings of small groups. The winning of political power has enabled the proletariat to utilise the state apparatus for the planful building of a centralised army, whose unity of organisation and unity of leadership alone can secure the achievement of the greatest results with the minimum of sacrifice. To preach guerrilla methods as a military programme is the same as recommending a reversion from large-scale industry to handicraft production. Such preaching is fully in accord with the character of intellectual groups who are incapable of holding state power, who are even incapable of seriously undertaking the task of winning such power and who expend their energy in guerrilla attacks (polemical or terrorist) on the working class government."

So reads the resolution on the military question which was adopted by the Eighth Congress.

The Eighth Congress on the Social Composition of the Party

By the time of the Eighth Congress, a year and a half after the October Revolution, a considerable change was to be observed in the composition of the Party. Whereas at the time of the October

Revolution the overwhelming majority of Party members were workers, a large number of peasant elements had now come into the Party, both through the Red Army, and also through the village nuclei and the Young Communist League. It would have been inconceivable that a proletarian party, governing a peasant country, should not have peasants in its ranks. But besides peasants, not a few intermediate petty-bourgeois elements had also joined the Party. As a result of the position of our Party as the ruling Party in the country, there were to be found among the new recruits certain elements who had entered under false colours. The presence in the Party of these elements led to considerable abuses. The Party was joined by politically alien elements who pursued a policy which had nothing in common with the policy of the Soviet government and the Communist Party. It was on this problem that the Eighth Congress centred its attention. The Congress adopted a decision calling, on the one hand, for a general re-registration of Party members and, on the other hand, emphasising that the Party should henceforth pay all possible attention to the question of its social composition. The subsequent Party congresses had to return to this question on more than one occasion and it is one which still continues to confront our Party to some extent even now, though, to be sure, in nothing like such an acute form as at the Eighth Congress. A report on the formation of the Third International was delivered at the Congress, which fully approved the platform of the International. The Congress instructed the Central Committee to extend all possible aid to the organisation and activity of the Third International.

The decisions of the Eighth Congress, starting with the extended programme of the Party which it adopted, contain the main tenets of the strategy and tactics of our revolution in its third phase. According to Comrade Stalin's definition, the third phase of our strategy (assuming that the first phase terminated in February 1917 and the second in October 1917),

"... commenced after the October Revolution. Aim: consolidation of the dictatorship of the proletariat in one country, using it as a stronghold for the overthrow of imperialism in all countries. The revolution goes beyond the confines of one country and the period of world revolution commences. The main forces of the revolution: the dictatorship of the proletariat in one country and the revolutionary movement of the proletariat in all countries. Main reserves: the semi-proletarian and small peasant masses in the advanced countries and the liberation movement in the colonies and dependent countries. Direction of the main blow: the isolation of the petty-bourgeois democrats and the isolation of the parties of the Second International which constitute the main support of the policy of *compromise* with imperialism. Plan for the disposition of forces: alliance of the proletarian revolution with the liberation movement of the colonies and the dependent countries." *

Victories on the Fronts

The Eighth Congress was followed by decisive events in our Civil War: the spring offensive of Kolchak, and later the summer and autumn offensive of Denikin. In both of these offensives the heroism of the working class and the support of the poorest and middle peasantry, who formed the mass of the Red Army, decided the question of the outcome of the Civil War. If this question was decided in our favour, it was due to a large extent to the decisions of the Eighth Party Congress, and to the inability of the White Guard counter-revolutionary forces, which were organically connected with landlordism, with the bourgeoisie and international imperialism, to win over the peasantry to their side.

"Is it not a fact," Lenin wrote, "that the peasants in the Urals and Siberia, who in the elections to the Constituent Assembly gave the lowest percentage of Bolsheviks, generally supported the front of the Constituent Assembly which was at that time the front of the Mensheviks and Socialist-Revolutionaries? Is it not a fact that these peasants were the best human material against the Communists? Is it not a fact that Siberia was a country in which there was no landlordism and in which we could not immediately help the peasant masses as we helped all the Russian peasants?"**

At the beginning of May, Kolchak, who had almost reached the Volga, was dealt a decisive blow near Buguruslan by a section of our army led by M. V. Frunze, after which commenced the uninterrupted retreat of the Kolchak armies towards the East. In the autumn of 1919, Yudenich's attempt to get possession of Leningrad was defeated once and for all. The struggle against Deni-

* Stalin, "Foundations of Leninism," *Leninism*, Vol. I.
** Lenin, "Seventh All-Russian Congress of the Soviets," *Collected Works*, Vol. XXIV.

kin was more protracted, the principal reason for this being that here the main front of struggle was in the Ukraine and it was precisely in the Ukraine that the largest number of errors had been committed both on the peasant and on the national questions—a fact which found its reflection in the attitude of the peasantry there.

At the end of 1919, Lenin was compelled once more to return to the national question in the Ukraine. In his article, *The Elections to the Constituent Assembly and the Dictatorship of the Proletariat,* he wrote as follows:.

"The author of these lines has been charged by some comrades with unduly emphasising the national question in the Ukraine. The figures on the elections to the Constituent Assembly show that even in November 1917, the *Ukrainian* Socialist-Revolutionaries and Socialists obtained a majority in the Ukraine.... In the face of this situation, to ignore the importance of the national question in the Ukraine—an error which is often committed by Great-Russians (and which is also committed, though perhaps less frequently, by the Jews)—means committing a profound and dangerous error.... And as internationalists, we are bound... to combat with particular energy the remnants (sometimes unconscious) of Great-Russian imperialism and chauvinism among the 'Russian' Communists."*

By its national policy, the Soviet government won the support of the broad masses of the oppressed nationalities. What the Kolchak-Denikin counter-revolutionary forces had to offer these nationalities, on the other hand, was the restoration of the old Russian empire, one and indivisible, a prison of the nations comprised within its borders. And thus it was that Denikin and Kolchak did not succeed in creating any sort of stable united front with White Poland, Finland and the Baltic republics. At the time when the most violent struggle was raging between the Red Army and Denikin on the southern front, the Polish army remained inactive.

The Struggle with Trotskyism in the Civil War Period

The decisive victories gained in the Civil War over the chief enemies of the Soviet power, Kolchak and Denikin, were won by the Party under Lenin's leadership, and by rejecting Trotsky's plans.

* Lenin, *Collected Works,* Vol. XXIV.

We are not going to deny that Trotsky played a certain role in the Civil War as an agitator and as an executor of the decisions of the Central Committee, when he did carry them out. But Trotsky's whole policy and strategy suffered from a number of organic defects, which would have had disastrous consequences had not the Central Committee, under the leadership of Lenin, corrected Trotsky at every step.

The most characteristic feature of Trotsky's policy and strategy was a profound mistrust in the power of the proletariat to lead the peasantry and in the power and ability of the Party to lead the Red Army. Hence his policy based exclusively on formal discipline, on methods of compulsion similar to the bourgeois armies. Hence his efforts to keep the Party away from the army. Hence his excessive confidence in bourgeois specialists, his underestimation of the strength of the Red Army as against the White Guard armies—tendencies which reflected the psychology of the former tsarist generals who were serving on our staff. This underestimation greatly affected Trotsky's strategy. At the end of 1918, Trotsky together with the specialists on the general staff, emphatically opposed the offensive in the Ukraine. The arguments against it were quite simple: Why an additional front? It was of no importance that a mighty wave of revolution was rising in the Ukraine, that vast material resources and inexhaustible human reserves were concentrated there, that it was the road to the Donbas and the Black Sea!

The offensive commenced in the end of December 1918, in spite of Trotsky's advice, and resulted in brilliant successes for the Soviet government and Red Army.

In the summer of 1919, the Red Army won a number of victories over Kolchak. The whole of Siberia was swept with uprisings. The Central Committee insisted on pressing on with the offensive. Ahead was the Ural region with its factories which constituted the industrial base of Kolchak's army. In Siberia, there were scores of thousands of guerrilla fighters who were ready to join the Red Army. But Trotsky opposed the offensive. Together with the specialists of the general staff, he believed that it was impossible to carry on offensive warfare simultaneously both against Denikin and against Kolchak.

In spite of Trotsky's opposition, the offensive was continued and culminated in the complete smashing of Kolchak.

Finally, the decisive campaign against Denikin on the southern front was launched after Trotsky had been removed from the command on the southern front.   . ,   .

Echoing the views of the military specialists who surrounded him, unable to give a Bolshevik estimate of the political circumstances in which the Civil War was being waged, Trotsky attempted to put into effect a plan for the destruction of Denikin by means of an offensive through the Don region, where the Whites had behind them their strongest support and where the Red Army would come up against a population among whom revolutionary tendencies were weakest.

According to the plan for the destruction of Denikin, which was proposed by Comrade Stalin and approved by the Central Committee, the decisive stroke was to be delivered through the Ukraine and the Donbas, avoiding the Cossack regions. This plan counted on the assistance of the proletariat in the Donets Basin and of the Ukrainian peasantry, who were hostile to Denikin.

This plan was carried out with brilliant success.

As chairman of the Revolutionary War Council, Trotsky had to carry out the line of the Party, which called for the creation of a strong regular army as against the guerrilla method. But he systematically distorted this line, and that not only by his attempts to weaken the guiding influence of the Party over the army and to replace conscious revolutionary discipline by the spiritless discipline of bourgeois armies. Even the struggle against the guerrilla tendencies was systematically distorted into a struggle against the utilisation of revolutionary initiative of the worker and peasant masses, into supercilious disregard of the guerrilla movement, which played a very important part in the Civil War, particularly in the Ukraine, Siberia and the Far East. Trotsky looked at the guerrilla movement through the eyes of the bourgeois specialists who surrounded him.

The credit for the organisation of the victories of the Red Army belongs above all to the Party and its leader, Lenin. The closest and truest assistant of Lenin in military affairs was Comrade Stalin.

He played a leading role in the brilliant defence of Tsaritsyn in the autumn of 1918, against the then most serious foe of the Soviet power, Krasnov. Tsaritsyn, in the hands of the Soviet troops, was at that time of vital importance as a wedge driven between the two main groups of White Guard troops, in the South and in the East. With the active participation of Comrade Stalin as leader, the advance of Kolchak's forces in the northern sector of the eastern front was brought to a standstill in the beginning of 1919. In the first half of 1919, Comrade Stalin did great work on the western and north-western fronts. And finally, he was the author of the plan which resulted in the crushing of Denikin on the southern front in the autumn of 1919.

The Eighth Party Conference in December, 1919

The Eighth Conference of the Party, in December 1919, took place at the very moment when a victorious struggle was being waged against Denikin in the South. Very few written documents are now available regarding this Conference. Even a complete record of the work of the Conference is not available. The Conference adopted the Party Constitution which had been drafted on the instructions of the Eighth Congress of the Party and which remained in force until the autumn of 1922. Besides this, the December Conference considered the question of inner-Party education. The Conference met immediately after the Party recruiting week, in November 1919, when an appeal was issued to all workers and toilers, urging them to join the Party. This took place at the most critical moment in the existence of the Soviet government, at the time of the Denikin offensive. Several scores of thousands of workers and peasants joined the Party, and in consequence the question arose of giving political education to these comrades as well as to the other scores of thousands of Party members who had joined the ranks of the Party during the Civil War.

Thus, in the same year, 1919, while the Party Congress raised the question of the social composition of the Party in its full scope, the Conference also raised a question of first-rate importance, the question of inner-Party education. The two questions were intimately connected, and both of them had to be raised because of the rapid growth of the Party since the October Revolution and the urgent need of re-moulding and educating the vast mass of human material that had entered the Party.

The Conference met at the time when the Red Army was engaged in victorious operations on all fronts, when the working class was displaying the greatest heroism and when the crisis in the economy of the country was at its most acute stage. Having hurled back its White Guard enemies—a task involving the utmost exertion of its strength—the country was starving, freezing to death, ravaged by epidemics. "To give bread, to give fuel, to kill the louse"—these were the main points emphasised by Lenin in the introductory speech with which he opened the Conference. Lenin delivered another brilliant speech at the Conference, *On the Organisation of the Soviet Power in the Ukraine,* though here again no stenographic notes were taken. In this speech, Lenin mercilessly analysed the errors on the peasant and national questions which had been committed in the Ukraine in the beginning of 1919 and which contributed to the fall of the Soviet government there.* In his closing speech on this question, Lenin, arguing against the Trotskyist Rakovsky, said:

"We must recognise that only a very small number of the well-managed farms ought to be turned into Soviet farms, otherwise we will

* The resolution of the Central Committee of the Russian Communist Party "On the Soviet Government in the Ukraine" (which was approved by the Conference) reads as follows (we quote the passage relating to the national question):

"1· Unswervingly enforcing the principle of the self-determination of nations, the Central Committee of the Russian Communist Party deems it necessary once more to emphasise the fact that the R.C.P. favours recognition of the independence of the Ukrainian Socialist Soviet Republic.

"2. Holding as it does that no Communist or class conscious worker can question the necessity of the closest union of all Soviet republics in their struggle against the menacing forces of world imperialism, the R.C.P. maintains that the form of this union will be definitely determined by the Ukrainian workers and toiling peasants themselves.

". . . 4. In view of the fact that Ukrainian culture (language, schools, etc.) has for centuries been suppressed by tsarism and the exploiting classes of Russia, the C.C. of the R.C.P. makes it obligatory for all members of the Party to help in every way to get rid of all obstacles to the free development of the Ukrainian language and culture. Owing to centuries of oppression, nationalist tendencies are to be found among the backward sections of the Ukrainian masses, and in view of this fact it is the duty of members of the

not get a *bloc* with the peasantry, and this *bloc* is essential to us . . . .
Do we need a *bloc* with the Ukrainian peasantry, do we need a policy
similar to that which we were in need of at the end of 1917 and during
many months of 1918? I maintain that we do need such a policy, and
we must therefore assign a large number of Soviet farms for virtual
distribution of the land."*

The Conference approved the resolution of the Central Committee of the R.C.P. on the tasks of the Soviet government in the
Ukraine, in which the main emphasis was laid on a determined
struggle against "Left" excesses on the peasant question and
against national "nihilism" which was particularly dangerous
under the conditions then obtaining in the Ukraine.

The Party Conference held in December 1919 also had to deal
with "Left" deviations in the discussion on the question of Soviet
construction. Sapronov, a former "Left" Communist and future
leader of the "Democratic Centralism" faction, again spoke as an
ardent apologist of decentralised government.

· Essentially, this was a continuation of the struggle of the
"Left" Communists against the creation of a centralised state apparatus; it reflected Bukharin's view on the blowing up of the
state, which implied that there was no difference between bourgeois and proletarian states. Sapronov's new interpretation of
this view, like the interpretation of the "Left" Communists, was
a curious intermingling of elements of anarchism' and of Menshevism. Its distinguishing feature was its vociferous demagogy,
which later caused Lenin to characterise the "democratic centralism" faction headed by Sapronov as the faction "which out-
shouted all shouters."

R.C.P. to treat them with the utmost forbearance and discretion, putting before them a comradely explanation of the identity of the interests of the toiling masses of the Ukraine and of Russia. Members of the R.C.P. on the
territory of the Ukraine must really enforce the right of the toiling masses to
study in the Ukrainian language and to use it in all Soviet institutions, resisting in every way all attempts to place the Ukrainian language artificially in a
secondary position, striving, on the contrary, to render the Ukrainian language a weapon for the Communist education of the toiling masses. Steps
must immediately be taken to assure a sufficient number of employees in all
Soviet institutions who know the Ukrainian language, and to see that in the
future all employees should be able to speak Ukrainian."

* Lenin, "The All-Russian Conference of the R.C.P. (B)" *Collected Works*,
Vol. XXIV.

The Conference decisively rejected the anarcho-Menshevik, essentially petty-bourgeois criticism of the Party policy by Sapronov and his associates. At the same time the Conference called upon the forthcoming Seventh Congress of Soviets to define more precisely the inter-relationship between the Soviet government organs in the sense of subordination, both "vertically" (commissariat and department) and "horizontally" (department and provincial executive committee). This was a new step towards strengthening the Soviet government apparatus and towards overcoming "Left" distortions about "local government" and excessive bureaucratic centralism; this last phenomenon was developing, on the one hand, as a result of the backwardness of the country and the unpreparedness of the masses to take active part in the government of the state, and, on the other hand, as a result of the government apparatus becoming clogged with alien bourgeois and bureaucratic elements.

The Ninth Party Congress

The Ninth Congress of our Party met in the beginning of April 1920.* In the interval between the Eighth and Ninth Congresses the Party membership had almost doubled. The basis for this increase was the heroic upsurge of the working class, which had borne upon its shoulders all the privations and burdens of the Civil War and had displayed extraordinary force and energy in coping with these burdens.

It was just at this time that socialist competition and Communist *subbotniks*,** to which Lenin devoted his famous article, *The Great Initiative*,*** began to acquire widespread popularity.

---

* The Congress was attended by 554 delegates with a decisive vote and 162 delegates with a consultative vote, representing a total membership of over 600,000.

** *Subbotnik*—organised public work performed voluntarily and gratuitously outside of working hours—*Ed.*

*** Of socialist competition Lenin had already written in January 1918 in his article *How to Organise Competition*.

"Socialism," he wrote, "not only does not extinguish competition but on the contrary creates for the first time the possibility of applying it on a really *wide*, on a really *mass* scale, of really drawing the vast majority of toilers into work in which they can develop their abilities, which can reveal talent among the people that has never been tapped and that capitalism trampled on, crushed and strangled in thousands and millions." (Lenin, *Collected Works*, Vol. XXII).

"The Communist *subbotniks,* arranged by workers on their own initiative," Lenin wrote in this article, "are of truly colossal significance. Obviously, this is only a beginning, but it is a beginning of extraordinarily great importance. It is the beginning of a revolution which is more difficult, more essential, more radical, more decisive, than the overthrow of the bourgeoisie, since it means a victory over their own sluggishness, laxity, petty-bourgeois egoism, over those habits which accursed capitalism has left as a heritage to the worker and peasant. When this victory has been secured, then and only then will a new social discipline, socialist discipline, have been created, then and only then will a return to capitalism have become impossible and communism have been rendered really invincible." *

The rapid growth of the Party was to a considerable extent due to the enormous increase in the territory of the Soviet republics. At the time when the Ninth Party Congress was held, the Soviet government had become firmly consolidated in Siberia and the North. Contact had been established with Turkestan. The remnants of the Denikin bands were being driven out of the Caucasus. The Ukraine was also represented at the Congress. But there were no representatives from Latvia, Lithuania and the greater part of White Russia, which the Soviet troops evacuated in 1919** and which had been seized by the interventionists. In April 1920 the Soviet government extended over almost the same territory as at present.

The main enemies on almost all external fronts had been defeated, but the Red Army still had three and a half million men under arms and they could not possibly be demobilised, since the struggle with Poland had not yet terminated and there were still remnants of Wrangel's and Denikin's forces in the Crimea and Caucasus.

Great victories had been won by the proletariat, under the leadership of the Party, over international imperialism and the counter-revolutionary forces at home.

* Lenin, *Collected Works,* Vol. XXIV.
** The defeat of the Soviet government in Latvia and Lithuania was to a considerable extent due to the Trotskyist-Luxemburgist errors with regard to the peasantry, which were analogous to the errors committed in the Ukraine but in an even cruder form. A typical mistake was the complete ignoring of the middle peasantry and the fact that the former landlord estates were generally turned into Soviet farms. Such errors were also characteristic of the Hungarian Soviet Republic and later, in 1920, of the Polish Revolutionary Committee.

"Russian soil," Lenin said, summing up the results of these victories at the Ninth Congress, "has proved to be a soil on which soldiers of another country cannot wage war. The soil on which the Soviet revolution has been accomplished has proved very perilous for all countries. It has been shown that the Russian Bolsheviks, who under tsarism succeeded in creating unity among the workers, were right; and the work- ers succeeded in creating small nuclei which met all those who trusted them, French workers and British soldiers, with agitation in their native language.

"We have achieved a situation where they dare not send us either British or French soldiers, because they know from experience that such an experiment turns against them.'

"In the spring of last year, our military situation was extremely diffi- cult; we still had ahead of us, as you remember, quite a few defeats, and new tremendous unexpected offensives by the representatives of counter- revolution and the representatives of the Entente, which we had not anticipated. It is therefore quite natural that a large part of this period should have been taken up with activities for the carrying out of the military task, the task of the Civil War, which had seemed insoluble to all the faint-hearted, let alone the Menshevik and Socialist-Revolu- tionary parties and other representatives of petty-bourgeois democracy and the mass of intermediate elements, and which caused them quite sincerely to contend that this task was insoluble, that Russia was backward and weakened and could not defeat the capitalist system of the entire world, since the revolution in the West has been delayed. And therefore we had to stand our ground and declare with complete firmness, preserving absolute confidence, that we would win; we had to carry through the slogan 'Everything for Victory' and 'Everything for the War.' For the sake of this, we were compelled to reconcile our- selves, quite consciously and openly, to neglecting a number of the most vital needs, frequently leaving very many people without any aid, in the conviction that we had to concentrate all our resources on the war and to win this war which the Entente had forced upon us. And only because the Party was on guard, because the Party was most strictly disciplined and because the authority of the Party united all the departments and institutions, and scores, hundreds, thousands and, in the final analysis, millions of people marched as one man to the slogan issued by the Central Committee, only because unheard-of sac- rifices were made—only this has rendered possible the miracle which has occurred. Only because of this did we prove able to win, in spite of the double, triple and quadruple campaign of the imperialists of the Entente and of the imperialists of the entire world. Of course, we do not stress this aspect of the matter alone, but we must bear in mind that this aspect of the matter carries a lesson that without discipline and without centralisation, we could never have realised this task." *

* Lenin, "Ninth Congress of the (R.C.P.(B)," *Collected Works,* Vol. XXV.

The general line of the Ninth Congress was a continuation of the line of the Seventh and Eighth Congresses. It kept to the path of creating a centralised Party, state and economic apparatus. At the Ninth Party Congress, this line had to be particularly firmly enforced, since the Soviet government was spreading over vast new territories for the first time. In these territories, everything had to be created anew. It was necessary to carry out the work there which had already been carried out in the central regions in 1918. In the provinces there were still to be met with many of the shortcomings, manifestations of slackness, petty-bourgeois laxity and pseudo-democratism against which Lenin had fought so persistently since 1918. The Party, which had grown to a membership of 600,000, contained many quite raw, politically untrained and undeveloped elements who succumbed to petty-bourgeois demagogy.

Such, for example, was the situation in the Ukraine, where at the beginning of 1920 the Party had to deal, under the guise of "Democratic Centralism," with manifestations of the most unrestrained *ataman** tendencies and demagogy.

The Fourth All-Ukrainian Party Conference, which met in March 1920, elected a Central Committee which was immediately dissolved by the Central Committee of the R.C.P. ·

At the Fourth All-Ukrainian Conference a group of supporters of "Democratic Centralism," led by Sapronov, came forward as the political exponents of the ideas of certain groups within the Party which had succumbed to the direct influence of petty-bourgeois and kulak elements. They emphatically opposed the independent organisation of the poor peasants, the formation of Committees of Poor Peasants in the Ukraine. Yet without such organisation, it would have been impossible to expropriate the land of the powerful class of Ukrainian kulaks, it would have been impossible to carry out in the Ukrainian villages the socialist revolution which had been effected in the Russian villages in the summer and autumn of 1918.

By fighting against the socialist revolution in the Ukrainian countryside, the Sapronov group acted, in effect, as the agents of the Ukrainian kulaks.

---

* *Ataman:* a headman of Cossack detachments or of local irregular forces In the Ukraine.

On the other hand, this group was also backed by petty-bourgeois elements for whom *ataman* rule, local government and
"Soviet democracy" served as a cover for favouritism to the local
bourgeoisie or petty bourgeoisie under the pretext of reckoning
with peculiar local conditions. Under the influence of Sapronov
and his supporters, the Fourth All-Ukrainian Conference adopted
a decision against the introduction of one-man management in
industry.

The military situation in the Ukraine and the struggle against
the kulak bandit groups made it imperative for the Party to take
the most resolute measures to overcome the disorganising activities of the "Democratic Centralism" faction, and these measures
were taken by the Central Committee of the R.C.P. under Lenin's
leadership. These measures included the dissolution of the Central Committee elected by the Fourth Conference, and the withdrawal from the Ukraine of a number of functionaries, headed
by Sapronov.

The Party was confronted with a particularly big task in the
economic field, since the victory which the Soviet government
had achieved in the Civil War was won at an extremely high
price.

At the time of the Ninth Congress, our transport was in a catastrophic state. A railway trip between Moscow and Kharkov
lasted ten days! And a trip between Moscow and Tashkent lasted
a month or thereabouts.

Shock Methods and One-Man Management

In the field of supplying industry and of providing the urban
working class population and the army with food products, prolonged hitches were constantly occurring. The Ninth Party Congress therefore raised as an urgent problem that of tackling a
number of vital tasks of an economic character by shock methods and of assuring preferential treatment in regard to food
supplies to certain industrial enterprises and certain groups of
workers. .The situation demanded heroic measures in order to set
things going properly. The deepening economic chaos constituted
a direct menace to the proletarian dictatorship. Less debating,
less talk, more action, more responsibility and discipline—this
was the elementary, simple form which the problem then took.

In accordance with this, the principle of one-man management was put forward in the economic field. At the Ninth Party Congress it was decided that an enterprise should be managed not by five persons but by one. At present, this seems quite natural to us, and we cannot even imagine how it was possible to tolerate five directors managing a mill, especially when industry was in a state of collapse. But when the Ninth Party Congress did away with this state of things and introduced one-man management, many comrades regarded this as a violation of the principles of democracy and socialism. Among those who protested were not only representatives of the "Democratic Centralism" faction, which formed the main opposition at the Congress, but important economic and trade union leaders (Comrades Rykòv, Tomsky and others). Lenin had to come out strongly in defence of the principle of one-man management and also of the practice of employing bourgeois specialists—a question which he had already dealt with on a number of other occasions.

"Too often," Lenin said, "the arguments in favour of collegiate management are imbued with a spirit of ignorance, with an attitude of opposition to specialists. With such an attitude, it is impossible to win. In order to win, it is necessary to understand the whole profound history of the old bourgeois world and in order to build communism it is necessary to take hold of technique and science and to set them going for wider circles of the population. But we cannot take them anywhere except from the bourgeoisie. This basic question must be set in sharp relief, must be placed among the main tasks of economic construction. We must manage the industries with the help of individuals from the class which we have overthrown, individuals who are imbued with the prejudices of their class and whom we must re-educate. At the same time we must recruit our own managers from the ranks of our own class, we must utilise the whole state apparatus to see that the schools, out-of-school education and practical training, that all of these, under Communist guidance, be placed at the service of the proletarians, of workers and toiling peasants." *

Thus, Lenin treats the problem of utilising the old specialists in close connection with the problem of training new forces.

"The Brest peace," Lenin continued, "was imposed upon us because we were powerless in all fields . . . . This was a period of impotence,

* Lenin, "Ninth Congress of the R.C.P.(B)," *Collected Works*, Vol. XXV.

from which we emerged as victors. This was a period when collegiate management was the general rule. You cannot escape from this historical fact by saying that the collegiate system is a school of management.... We cannot stay forever in the beginners' class at school! That won't do at all. We are grown up now, but we will get thrashed and thrashed again in every field if we go on acting like schoolboys. We must go forward. By dint of energy and united will, we must rise higher. The trade unions have tremendous difficulties to cope with. We must see to it that they master this task in a spirit of struggle against the remnants of notorious democratism. All this clamour about appointments from above, all this old and noxious trash which finds its way into various resolutions and discussions must be swept out. Otherwise we cannot win. If we have not mastered this lesson in the course of two years, then we are backward, and the backward will be beaten." *

The Ninth Party Congress had to decide the question of the utilisation of the army in the interests of the national economy. The war was over, but the Red Army had three million men under arms. To demobilise these men at a time when it took weeks for a train to cover the distance from Moscow to Kharkov would have meant wasting two years in mobilising them again in case of need; it would have meant completely disarming the country and leaving it exposed to an attack by its enemies abroad.

The only way out of the situation was to utilise the demobilised armies on the industrial front, and the Ninth Party Congress approved this experiment.

This was a grave necessity, although some were inclined to make a virtue of this necessity. Trotsky, for instance, went so far as to argue as though methods of military compulsion applied to industrial armies were almost the best of all possible methods of building socialism. This was wholly consistent with Trotsky's standpoint regarding the peasantry. The Party as a whole and Lenin in particular emphatically rejected Trotsky's bureaucratic leanings. The enforcement of the principle of one-man management, the organisation of industrial armies, the militarisation of certain branches of industry, notably the transport, the policy of attracting the trade unions to participate more closely in the organisation of economy—such was the gist of the resolutions adopted by the Ninth Party Congress. The Ninth Congress decided to apply the preferential principle in our industrial life. The country was in an extremely difficult situation,

* *Ibid.*

and the national economy was sinking ever deeper into the quagmire of collapse. With the slender resources which were at the disposal of the central authorities, it was absolutely impossible to guarantee systematic and regular improvement in all branches of production. The single economic plan which was adopted by the Ninth Party Congress called for a gradual expansion of production, the first enterprises and branches of industry to be developed being those most vital to the life of the country (transport, fuel, metallurgy). The restoration of these branches was achieved at a high price to the country. The workers in them were given a small food ration, but it was necessary to deny such rations to the workers in all other enterprises. This, however, was the only solution in the desperate situation in which the country was placed at the time.

The Faction of "Democratic Centralism"

In carrying into effect those measures which were rendered imperative by the difficult situation of the country, the Ninth Congress of the Party again had to fight the ideology of "Left" Communism against which the Party had fought at the Seventh and Eighth Congresses. To be sure, the representatives of the "Left" deviation appeared at the Ninth Congress under new colours, under the colours of the so-called faction of "Democratic Centralism." This faction was headed exclusively by the "Left" Communists of 1918—Ossinsky, Sapronov, Maximovsky, V. Smirnov and others. They used the same arguments against one-man management, against industrial armies, against the militarisation of individual branches of industry as were used by the "Left" Communists two years earlier against the establishment of strict discipline in mills and factories, against the abolition of "the full power of the local authorities," against the creation of a strong centralised state apparatus, in fact against the proletarian dictatorship.

In the discussion on the political report of the Central Committee which was submitted by Lenin, Sapronov declared that the Congress could not be satisfied with this report. "He has told us of matters about which we have heard at five Congresses and at ten Conferences (!!). There has been no report from the Central Committee, but only an attempt to distract attention from the activity of the Central Committee." Sapronov attacked Lenin further, saying that in the past he had not objected to "Democratic Centralism," that "when a definite opinion was demanded of him, he began to manoeuvre (?!) and to retreat before the opinion of the masses in order not to carry it into effect later on."

. Sapronov continued to fulminate against Lenin, saying:

"It is quite superfluous to read us a lecture about the bourgeoisie having at one time enlisted feudal officials in, the government, since we ourselves have enlisted the services of bourgeois specialists, and there is no need to obscure the question and to distract attention from the real issue by referring to the feudalism of ancient times.

"We know ourselves that we have invited bourgeois specialists to the Soviet farms, who developed there such counter-revolutionary activity that the local Party workers requested that they be withdrawn. . .

"No matter how much you may talk of suffrage, of the proletarian dictatorship. . . in reality this leads to the dictatorship of Party officialdom."

Such was the tone in which the leaders of "Democratic Centralism" spoke against Lenin. However, this did not prevent them a few years later, when they had completely sunk to an anarcho-Menshevik position and were attacking the Leninist Party from this position, from hiding behind the name of the very same Lenin whom they had attacked in such demagogic fashion when he was still alive.

The Significance of the Ninth Congress

In his concluding speech at the close of the Ninth Congress, Lenin spoke of the complicated position in which the Party had been placed by its tremendous growth.

"There is a very real danger, due to the fact that the rapid growth of our Party did not always proceed hand in hand with the training of this mass for its actual tasks. We must always bear in mind that this army of 600,000 must be the vanguard of the working class, that without iron discipline it would scarcely have been possible to carry out its tasks in the course of two years. The basic condition for the enforcement and maintenance of our strict discipline is loyalty. All old means and sources for the enforcement of discipline have been destroyed. We have based our activity solely on the foundation of a high degree of understanding and consciousness. This has enabled us to realise a discipline which is superior to the discipline of any other state and which rests on a different foundation from the discipline that somehow continues to be maintained, if it can still be maintained, in capitalist society. We must therefore remember that our task for the next year, after the brilliant successes in the war, consists not so much in enlarging the Party, as in internal work in the sense of developing the membership of our Party."*

The Ninth Congress met in the period of War Communism in our economic policy and in our Party practice which took the form of a peculiar militarisation of the Party. The decisions of this Congress and their realisation are a clear illustration of how necessary this policy was in the actual historical conditions in which the country and the Party were situated at the time.

At present, looking back, we must recognise that if the Party had not resorted to these military methods in its policy and practice, it would have been extremely difficult for it to survive in the struggle. The path of "collegiate management," of "broad democracy," so called, of an equalitarian policy, the path of the faction which "outshouted all shouters" and which represented the petty-bourgeois anarchic forces, would have been disastrous for the Soviet government, and the Party emphatically rejected this path.

We can now recognise that, if it proved possible to cope with the profound economic collapse, if the country proved able to withstand civil war for the space of almost a whole year more, this was of course due to the fact that the Ninth Party Congress, on the basis of the whole line of the Party, adopted perfectly correct decisions, the realisation of which, although at the price of the greatest sacrifices, enabled the Soviet government to carry the Civil War to a victorious conclusion.

The Second Congress of the Communist International

The Second Congress of the Comintern was held shortly after the Ninth Party Congress. It coincided with the new campaign of the Entente against the Soviet power, the Soviet-Polish war, and with a marked rise in the labour and revolutionary movement in the capitalist countries.

* Ibid.

In contrast to the First, Constituent Congress of the Comintern, which was attended by a few delegates from small groups, the Second Congress was attended by representatives from numerous organisations with a membership of tens and hundreds of thousands. A great number of the future leaders of the Second and Two-and-a Half Internationals, future bitter opponents of communism, applied for admission to the Communist International. German, French and Italian Independent Socialists (Crispien, Diettmann, Longuet, Modigliani) pleased for admission in person or by letter. Their insistent efforts to sneak into the Comintern were a reflection of the tremendous mass movement in favour of the Soviet government which had at that time taken hold of the proletariat of Western Europe. Despite the defeats suffered in Germany in 1919, the wave of revolution was still running very high. The attempt at a monarchist coup in Germany in 1920 was crushed by a general strike of the German proletariat. In a number of districts in Germany, particularly in the Ruhr, a Red Army had been formed. The widespread movement of the working masses which had developed was only suppressed as a consequence of the treachery of the Social-Democratic leaders.

The wave of revolution had mounted very high in Italy, where somewhat later, in the autumn of 1920, the metal workers began to seize the mills and factories.

The revolutionary movement was also very strong in the countries of the Balkan peninsula.

The Second Congress of the Comintern set up a Bolshevik barrier to guard the ranks of the international revolutionary Communist organisation from the intrusion of all kinds of opportunist elements who during a period of a revolutionary upswing camouflage themselves with revolutionary colours. The Congress adopted the famous "twenty-one conditions" for all parties who joined the Comintern. The most important of these conditions were the recognition in actual fact of the proletarian dictatorship and of Soviet government as a form of this dictatorship, recognition of revolutionary means for the winning of power, recognition of illegal work, etc. These conditions were directed in the main against opportunist, semi-Centrist and Centrist elements. But along with this, a serious struggle was also waged at this Congress against the "Left" opportunist elements who rejected work in the trade unions and the utilisation of bourgeois parliamentarism, as a weapon of agitation. It was to this struggle against the "Left" opportunist elements in particular that Lenin devoted his famous pamphlet *"Left-Wing" Communism, An Infantile Disorder* which was published on the eve of the Congress. In its decisions the Congress stressed the role of the Party as the vanguard in the class struggle of the proletariat and as the chief weapon of this struggle both before and after the winning of power by the proletariat, the necessity of Party leadership in the work of the trade unions, of all mass organisations of the working class, and also for parliamentary fractions, etc.

Essentially, the decisions transmitted the experience of the victorious proletariat of our country—who succeeded, on the basis of the experience of the international struggle, in creating the most powerful and united party and winning power under its leadership—to other countries, where the Communist Parties were only in the process of formation in the political and organisational sense.

The opportunist elements, both at the Congress and after it, opposed the Bolshevik principles regarding programme, tactics and organisation, on the pretext of the alleged inapplicability of these principles to the conditions of the advanced capitalist countries. Following in the footsteps of the Social-Democrats, they attempted to represent Bolshevism-Leninism as a product of Russian national peculiarities, in particular of the economic backwardness of Russia. Thus, these gentlemen, on the one hand, made political capital by praising the Bolshevik Party before their own masses and saying that the line it was carrying out was a perfectly correct one for Russia; while on the other hand, under cover of their reputation as friends of Bolshevism and Soviet Russia, they continued to carry on Social-Democratic tactics in their own countries, on the pretext that Bolshevism could not be applied under the conditions of the "cultured" democratic West.

Lenin took a very active part in the whole work of the Congress and in all the preparations for it.

He delivered the general report on the international situation and on the tasks of the Communist International. In his speech on the role of the Communist Party and on the use to be made of parliamentarism, he emphatically opposed all semi-anarchist, Leftist tendencies.

Lenin reported at the plenary session of the Congress on behalf of the commission on the national and colonial questions.

Lenin energetically defended the twenty-one conditions of af-filiation with the Communist International, in opposition to "Left" Social-Democrats of the type of Crispien who were present at the Congress and against Communists of the type of Serrati who took a conciliatory attitude towards the "Left" Social-Democrats. In a short article on the results of the Congress, published in the magazine *Kommunistka*, Lenin wrote:

"The Congress, which concluded its sessions on August 7, already united not only the advanced forerunners of the proletarian revolution but delegates from strong and powerful organisations which are con-nected with masses of proletarians. A world army of the revolutionary proletariat now supports communism, an army which achieved its organisation and a clear, precise, detailed programme of action at this Congress." *

Of tremendous significance were the decisions of the Second Congress on the national-colonial and the peasant questions.

In these decisions the Congress stressed the division of the capitalist world into a small number of oppressing nations, above all, the "great" imperialist powers, and a vast majority of op-pressed nations (colonial, semi-colonial and subject countries). The Congress pointed out the role of the national liberation move-ment as a mighty factor in the struggle against imperialism, and the possibility of backward agricultural colonial countries developing towards socialism, and escaping the capitalist stage, relying on the help of more advanced countries where the work-ing class is in power, as for instance, the U.S.S.R.

As is well known, Marx and Engels admitted the possibility of the Russian peasantry developing from the primitive commune directly towards socialism, in the event of a revolution taking place in Russia and of its being aided by the socialist proletariat of the West.

* Lenin, "The Second Congress of the Communist International," *Col-lected Works*, Vol. XXV.

Marx and Engels considered it possible that other backward countries, too, might take a similar path of development, skipping over the capitalist stage.

The theses of the Second Congress and Lenin's speeches were in full accord with the views of Marx and Engels on this point.

As regards the question of the peasantry, the Congress, on the basis of the whole experience of the international labour movement and on the basis of the experience gained in Russia, resolved that the task of the parties in the more developed capitalist countries where the working class had not yet come to power, was to win over the poor peasants, while neutralising the middle peasants.

The War with Poland

Almost immediately after the Ninth Congress was over, war broke out with Poland, which had the backing of the Entente and above all of France. Poland, as Lenin wrote, had been closely connected from the very first days of its existence with the whole system of international imperialism.* The war was forced upon the Soviet government by Entente and Polish imperialism, in spite of the policy of peace which the Soviet government pursued. This was, as Comrade Stalin wrote at the time, the third campaign of the Entente against the Soviet power.

"The first campaign," Stalin wrote, "was launched in the spring of 1919. This was a combined campaign, for it involved a joint attack of Kolchak, Denikin, Yudenich and mixed Anglo-Russian forces in Turkestan and Archangel (the centre of gravity of the campaign being in Kolchak's zone). . . . The second Entente campaign was launched in the autumn of 1919. This, too, was a combined campaign, for it involved a joint attack by Denikin, Poland and Yudenich (Kolchak had already been eliminated). The centre of gravity of the campaign was this time in the South, in Denikin's zone.

. "There can be no doubt that the campaign of landlord Poland against worker-and-peasant Russia was essentially an Entente campaign. The main thing is that Poland could not have undertaken its attack on Russia without aid from the Entente, that France above all, and later also Britain and the United States, gave all possible support to the Polish attack with arms, equipment, money and instructors. The differences among the Allies on the Polish question do not alter matters,

* Lenin, "Speech at the Congress of Workers and Employees of the Leather Industry," Oct. 2, 1920, *Collected Works*, Vol. XXV.

since they involve only the question of how to support Poland, and not the question of whether or not it should be supported." *

From the very beginning of the formation of the Polish bourgeois republic, which became an indissoluble component part of the Versailles system, the Polish bourgeoisie pursued an aggressive imperialist policy towards the Soviet government, aspiring to the so-called 1772 frontier, striving to annex White Russia and the western part, if not the whole, of the Ukraine.

In the beginning of 1919 the Polish legions seized Vilna and advanced far into White Russian territory. In the autumn of the same year they occupied Minsk and a considerable part of the provinces of Podolsk and Volhynia.

True, the Polish army remained more or less inactive at the very height of the struggle of the Red Army against Denikin, in the end of 1919. This was undoubtedly due to the antagonism between the imperialist aspirations of the Polish bourgeoisie with regard to the Ukraine and White Russia, and Denikin's policy which aimed at a united and indissoluble Russia and which was a direct continuation of the national policy of tsarism.

But as soon as the Denikin army had suffered decisive defeats, the activity of the White Polish troops immediately revived. In January 1920, together with the White Latvian troops, they occupied Dvinsk and forced the Soviet troops to evacuate Latgalia; in March 1920, the White Polish troops occupied Mozir; and finally in April, under the personal direction of Pilsudski, the Polish armies launched a determined offensive against the Ukraine under the slogan of the restoration of the Petlura government, which had been driven out by an uprising of the Ukrainian workers and peasants in 1919, and with which Pilsudski now concluded a military alliance.

The war with Poland, which was forced upon the Soviet government, was of great significance for the issues of the international revolution.

"The approach of the Red Army to Warsaw," said Lenin, "constituted an international crisis. This is why it caused such excitement in the entire bourgeois press. The situation was such that had the victorious advance of the Red Army continued for another few days,

* Stalin, "The New Entente Campaign Against Russia," *Pravda*, No. 111 for 1920.

not only would Warsaw have been taken (which would have been of no great importance), but the Versailles peace treaty would have been destroyed." *

But the offensive which the Soviet government launched in the West in 1920, in resistance to its enem.es, and which brought the Red troops to the walls of Warsaw, did not succeed, although the principal aim of the war, the defence of the Soviet frontiers from a new external attack, was achieved. In the autumn of 1920 White Poland was forced to conclude peace and to recognise the Soviet government—a recognition which for two years we had striven in vain to obtain from her.

The Warsaw defeat coincided with the beginning of the most severe crisis, which the Soviet government was only able to overcome by d.nt of tremendous exertions and which ended with the transition to the New Economy Policy.

The Warsaw defeat was, of course, no accident. At the time of this defeat we had 5,500,000 men under arms in the Red Army. Out of these 5,500,000 men we could only send into battle near Warsaw about 50,000 to 60,000 men at the decisive moment. It required tremendous efforts to get together the army of 100,000 men which smashed the Poles at the rivers Dvina and Berezina, and which reached Warsaw with only half its strength.

Our advancing army could get practically no reinforcements, owing to the grave situation in regard to transport. Budenny had to march with all h.s cavalry from the Kuban to the western part of the Ukraine. But while the cavalry could be adapted to making forced marches of hundreds of kilometres, it was much more difficult to move the artillery, infantry and military supplies in the same way. Reaching Warsaw almost without field-guns and without cartridges, unclothed, unshod and without military supplies, our army had to fight against the numerically superior Polish forces which had been equipped by France. An important factor in our defeat near Warsaw was the weakness of the revolutionary movement in Poland, the weakness of the Polish Communist Party and the errors committed by the Polish revolutionary government (Revolutionary Committee) in regard to the peasant and national questions—errors of a Luxemburgist char-

* Lenin, "Speech at the Congress of Workers and Employees of the Leather Industry," Oct. 2, 1920. *Collected Works*, Vol. XXV.

acter. These errors alienated the broad masses of the peasantry and of the oppressed nationalities from the Party. A large part of the Polish proletariat was under the influence of the Polish Socialist Party and believed its lying demagogic propaganda to the effect that the Soviet government aimed at depriving Poland of its independence, that it was continuing the policy of tsarist Russia.*

* We must point out here, however, that there is nothing more lying and despicable than the yarns concocted by the Mensheviks of all hues about the "Red imperialism" of the Soviet government, which, so they would have it, was manifested in the advance on Warsaw. Not Soviet Russia, but land-lord Poland, headed by the "socialist" Pilsudski, was the initiator of the war. Poland ignored our repeated peace proposals and even refused an armistice, in spite of the fact that in the spring of 1920 the Soviet government was ready to recognise *de facto* the frontier line as it existed at the time, *i.e.*, to leave in the hands of Poland huge territories inhabited by Ukrainians and White Russians (larger than Poland occupies at present). In April 1920, after all our peace proposals, Poland started an offensive on the Ukraine.

What did Soviet Russia demand of the Polish government, after the Red Army had repulsed the Polish offensive and had thrown back the White Polish troops into the territory of ethnographic Poland? As far as territory is concerned, Soviet Russia offered Poland more than the Allied Coun-cil, which in 1919 had fixed the Polish frontiers along the rivers Bug and San. But Soviet Russia demanded guarantees against new attacks, guarantees consisting of the disarmament of the White Polish army and *the arming of the Polish working class*. Whether the Red Army should have or should not have crossed the Bug and moved on Warsaw, is a different question. This was a purely strategic problem. The War Depart-ment was of the opinion that our forces were sufficient to take Warsaw, *i.e.*, for a quick termination of the war. This opinion was based on a gross over-estimation of our forces and underestimation of the forces and technique of the enemy. This was the great mistake of the War Department, which was at that time headed by Trotsky. Stalin speaks of this with exhaustive clarity in his article, "Reply to Comrades on Collective Farms."

"When can an advance be successful, in the military sphere, let us say? When the advancing force does not confine itself simply to moving forward headlong, but tries at the same time to *consolidate* the positions captured, to *regroup* its forces in accordance with the changed circumstances, to *strengthen* the rear and to *bring up* reserves. Why is all that necessary? As a protection against surprises, in order to close up possible breaches in the line of attack, which may happen in every advance, and thus to prepare for the complete liquidation of the enemy. The mistake that the Polish armies made in 1920, if we take only the military side of the matter, was that they ignored this rule. . . . The mistake the Soviet forces made in 1920, again if we take only the military side of the question, was that, in their advance on Warsaw, they repeated the error committed by the Poles." (Stalin, "Reply to Comrades on the Collective Farms," *Leninism,* Vol. II.)

Trotsky now tries to make capital by claiming that he was opposed to the Warsaw offensive alleging that he had foreseen its disastrous results. Trotsky even dares to draw an analogy between Brest-Litovsk and Warsaw: in 1918

The Political State of the Peasantry

The Warsaw defeat was also due to the grave economic situation in our country and the change for the worse in the state of feeling among the masses of middle peasants, which in its turn, affected the state of feeling in the army. During the retreat from Warsaw whole divisions surrendered. The new detachments that were brought up to reinforce the retreating army proved very unreliable, and this forced the army into further retreat.

The continuation of the war demanded large resources and large grain supplies, above all for the army. As a result of this, our food requisitions became more and more burdensome for the peasantry with every year. Owing to the collapse of the old state apparatus and to the fact that our state apparatus was not immediately created and strengthened, the grain monopoly could not be developed with complete success during the first period of the Soviet government's existence. During the fiscal year of 1916-17 Kerensky's Provisional Government, and the tsarist government before it, took 5,241,758 tons of grain from the peasants and partly from the landlords, to supply the army and for other state requirements. In 1917-18 the Soviet government collected only one-tenth of the amount of grain taken by the Provisional and tsarist governments. It was helped by the previously accumulated stocks of grain, by the stores of textile goods which were exchanged for grain, etc. The Soviet government itself during the first year of its existence collected only 491,803 tons of grain; the rest remained with the peasants. But by 1918-19, when the Soviet state apparatus had sufficiently improved, the grain collections had already increased to three and a half times as much as in the preceding

Lenin warned the Party of the danger, while in 1920 it was he, Trotsky, who sounded the warning.

Actually Trotsky was opposed to the advance on Warsaw, not because he considered our forces insufficient (on the contrary, the War Department which was under his charge, gave its assurance that Warsaw would be taken on August 16), but due to a Social-Democratic prejudice to the effect that it was wrong to carry revolution into a country from the outside.

For these same reasons Trotsky was opposed to the Red Army aiding the rebels in Georgia in February 1921.

Trotsky's anti-Bolshevik, Kautskyist reasoning was emphatically rejected by the Central Committee, both in July 1920 in the case of Poland and in February 1921 in the case of the Menshevik government in Georgia.

year, totalling 1,801,854 tons, while in 1919-20 they reached a total of 4,258,928 tons. At our congresses of that period these figures were looked upon as evidence of the great achievements of the Soviet government. Of course, the achievements were indubitable, but owing to the civil war which was forced upon the Soviet government, the countryside was in a state of ruin, the area under cultivation had greatly diminished (by 1920 the cultivated area in the Central Black Soil Region, at that time the principal granary of the Soviet government, had been reduced by half) and the state of political feeling among the peasantry was growing steadily worse. A basis was developing for all kinds of anti-Soviet actions. Another means of drawing in the resources from the countryside was the issue of currency, which caused the depreciation of the supplies of money which had been accumulated in the countryside during the war. The issues of currency gave the Soviet government 523,000,000 pre-war rubles in 1918-19, 300,000,000 rubles in 1919-20 and 186,000,000 rubles in 1920-21. As can be seen from these figures, the scope of the currency issues declined in proportion as that of the food requisitions increased.

Owing to the lack of trained forces, the development of the centralised state apparatus led to a strengthening of its bureaucratic features. The bureaucracy of the state apparatus was carried over into certain sections of the Party apparatus. This happened the more easily because of the alien elements who had insinuated themselves into the Party and because of a change for the worse which had taken place in the social composition of the Party.

The Ninth Party Conference, September 1920

For this reason the Party most determinedly tackled the question of overcoming bureaucracy, of overcoming the tendency of individual links of the Party organisation to isolate themselves from the masses, etc. The Party Conference in September 1920, at which the Central Committee raised the question of our future course of international policy and of the conclusion of peace with Poland, adopted a very important resolution on the immediate tasks of Party construction.

The resolution called for the strengthening of the contact of Party organisations with the masses, for a wider application of the principle of electing Party functionaries. It called for certain measures against inequality in the position of Party members and for transferring a number of the Party members, who had lost contact with the masses, to the mills and factories. The whole resolution was imbued with the spirit of bringing the upper circles of the Party into closer contact with the rank and file and of strengthening the connection between the Party and the mass of workers. To combat manifestations of decay within the ranks of the Party and violation of Party ethics, the Conference passed a decision creating control commissions, whose functions were later considerably enlarged.

But the Conference and the Central Committee quite clearly perceived that the shortcomings of the Party apparatus were connected with the militarisation of the Party, which in its turn, was a result of the war.

The protracted war was having serious effects upon the Party, the government apparatus and the whole economy of the country. The war was becoming unbearable for the country, which was in a state of utter collapse.

It was necessary to resort to all available measures to end the war. It was clear that the country could not go on with this war any longer. The Conference approved the proposal of the Central Committee, in particular of Lenin, to conclude an immediate peace with Poland even on hard and unfavourable terms. It further decided that, without awaiting the conclusion of peace with Poland, the best forces should be immediately transferred from the Polish front to the Wrangel front, in order to finish as quickly as possible with Wrangel, who had united under his command the remnants of Denikin's troops, and to set about the restoration of economy, not under war conditions, but in an environment of peace.

Lenin showed a perfect grasp of the whole political situation. With Poland it was possible to conclude a peace of compromise, just as it was with Esthonia, Latvia and Finland. The Polish bourgeoisie was not interested, as was the Russian bourgeoisie, in fighting the Soviet government to a finish. The Polish bourgeoisie had no reason to count on friendly relations with a White Guard Russian government. With Poland it was possible to conclude peace. Wrangel, however, had to be crushed.

The End of the Civil War

This daring manoeuvre, which involved colossal sacrifices, was successful. Having gained the annexation of Western White Russia and Western Volhynia (in the Ukraine) and the renunciation of our claim to Eastern Galicia, and having forced us to accept frontier lines which were extremely disadvantageous from a strategic point of view, Poland agreed to conclude an armistice, since it was itself completely spent.

In the beginning of November 1920, the Wrangel army, which in September had reached Ekaterinoslav and the Donbas, was hurled back into the sea by the large forces which were brought up from all parts of the country and which were numerically far superior to the enemy. Under the skilful leadership of Frunze on the Southern front and thanks to the heroism of the Workers' and Peasants' Red Army which covered itself with glory, the Perekop and Sivash positions, which blocked the way to the Crimea, were conquered. The crushing of Wrangel and the victorious termination of the Civil War on all fronts* created a firm base for overcoming manifestations of crisis in the national economy. The Eighth Congress of Soviets, which met immediately after the crushing defeat of the Wrangel army, was characterised by a transition to peaceful economic construction.

In view of the termination of the war, the Congress considered a plan for the electrification of the country on a grand scale, for the fundamental reconstruction of all industry and agriculture on a new technical foundation. But things were still very far from what they should be. The September Party Conference took note of the dangerous manifestations of bureaucratisation in individual links of the Party. The Conference laid great stress on the question of strengthening the connection between the upper circles of the Party and the rank and file. No less urgent was the necessity of strengthening the connection between the Party and the working masses. The latter was largely identical with the question of the trade unions in which the broad masses of the

---

* The war still continued in the Far East. Remnants of the Kolchak army, supported by Japan, were strongly entrenched in that part of the country. The Japanese troops did not evacuate Vladivostok until the autumn of 1922 and did not leave Northern Sakhalin until 1924.

workers were organised, the question of reviving the work of the trade unions. The attention of the Party was riveted upon the trade unions. But the fundamental solution of the question and the beginning of recovery depended, not only on the correction of shortcomings in the apparatus of the Party and of the trade unions, but on correcting that relationship between the working class and the peasantry which had been created under the conditions of War Communism and Civil War.

The Party on the Eve of the N.E.P.

The period between the end of 1918 and the end of 1920 was a period of the most dogged and difficult civil war for the Soviet government. The war was waged on two fronts: against the Russian counter-revolutionary forces (Kolchak, Denikin, Yudenich, Miller and Wrangel), who aimed at the restoration of the former Russian empire, one and indivisible, and against the bourgeois nationalist counter-revolutionary forces of the formerly oppressed peoples (Poland, Finland, the Ukraine, the Baltic and Transcaucasian bourgeois republics, etc.). Both these forces were backed by allied imperialism, which gave them vast material support. This support, however, did not decide the outcome of the struggle, since the Allies were not in a position to utilise their huge armies after the defeat of Germany, inasmuch as the military forces which the Allies moved into the sphere of operations refused to fight against the Soviet government. The White Guard governments therefore had to organise their own armies by forcibly mobilising the peasant masses. Only in those regions where the kulaks were strong and owned much land and where the peasants were well-to-do (above all in the Cossack regions) did this mass of peasants furnish the counter-revolutionary forces with more or less suitable human material. But even these were not sufficiently staunch and could not withstand any serious trials. As to the mass of poor and middle peasants, including the former soldiers of the imperialist army, who had gone through two revolutions, it proved absolutely impossible to win over this mass to support the cause of restoring the monarchy and landlordism, although the feeling of discontent which penetrated into the broad peasant masses as a result of the enforcement of the policy of War

Communism was utilised by the White Guard counter-revolutionary forces and undoubtedly prolonged the resistance of the latter
in certain sectors.

At any rate, the Soviet government was already able to win
decisive victories over the forces of internal Russian counter-revolution by the end of 1919, and it was only the attack by Poland,
which diverted almost all the Soviet forces, that helped Wrangel
to hold out until the end of 1920. But in the struggle with the
bourgeois nationalist counter-revolutionary forces in the former
border provinces of tsarist Russia, the Soviet government succeeded in winning only partial success. Soviet rule was established in
the Ukraine, in Transcaucasia and in the Tyurkic regions in the
East of former Russia. In Poland, Lithuania, Finland and the
Baltic coastlands the Soviet government did not succeed in maintaining itself. The government of Soviet Russia found it necessary to reconcile itself to the temporary triumph of the counter-
revolution in all of these countries and to conclude peace treaties
with their bourgeois governments.

On their part, the bourgeois governments of Poland and the
Baltic countries, according to the peace terms, formally undertook
not to support the forces of counter-revolution on Soviet territory.

To be sure, they did not live up to their obligations. This is
particularly true of Poland. In spite of the terms of the peace
treaty, the territory of Western Ukraine and Western White Russia which was annexed to Poland became a real base and place
of refuge for White Guard bands who crossed over on to Soviet
territory.

However, peace with Poland and the Baltic republics was
nevertheless concluded.

This took place during 1920 and the beginning of 1921. By
the end of 1920, the Soviet government had been set up on the
overwhelming bulk of the former territory of tsarist Russia. This
success was achieved by the Party thanks to its correct policy and
powerful organisation.

"The dictatorship of the proletariat," wrote Lenin in the spring of
1920, "is a persistent struggle—sanguinary and bloodless, violent and
peaceful, military and economic, educational and administrative—against
the forces and traditions of the old society. The force of habit of millions
and tens of millions is a terrible force. Without an iron party steeled

in the struggle, without a party enjoying the confidence of all that is honest in the given class, without a party capable of keeping track of and influencing the mood of the masses, it is impossible to conduct such a struggle successfully."

Fortunately for the working class of former Russia, it had such a party. Thanks to its unity and ideological consolidation, thanks to the fact that petty-bourgeois and anarchist tendencies in the Party ranks were overcome and destroyed, a strong and united state apparatus of the proletarian dictatorship was created in the country, even though it suffered from bureaucratic distortions and some of its individual links were too cumbersome and un-wieldy. This apparatus formed a colossal organisation of economy and of food distribution, extending its feelers to all corners of the country and serving tens of millions of people. Never before in history has there been an example of a state organisation embracing such vast human masses as the Soviet apparatus in the epoch of War Communism. The creation of such an organisation required incredible efforts, energy and enthusiasm on the part of the million-strong masses who had risen to revolutionary struggle, above all of the working class. But the fact that these masses lacked political experience, the force of traditions and habits which were inherited from the past and which clung to the masses, the necessity of attracting scores of thousands of former tsarist officials to the task of building up the state apparatus, organising industry and creating a machinery for distribution—all this meant that in the Soviet state and economic apparatus, which had been created with such tremendous efforts and had developed such vast activities there very quickly sprang up elements of bureaucracy, tendencies to isolation from the masses and the influence of alien and hostile classes. Even at the Eighth Congress of the Party, and later on at the Eighth Congress of Soviets, the question of bureaucracy in the Soviet apparatus had to be raised very seriously. However, bureaucracy continued to grow and by the end of 1920 it had assumed large dimensions, manifesting a tendency in individual links of the Soviet apparatus to eliminate altogether all contact with the masses and to replace it entirely with measures of external compulsion towards these masses. This tendency undoubtedly led to degeneration and decay in these links of the Soviet apparatus.

In 1918-19, and in the first half of 1920, the Party was fighting first and foremost against those elements in its individual sections who did not understand the significance of a centralised state and economic, military and Party apparatus, who had not out-lived their petty-bourgeois anarchist state of mind, or who unconsciously succumbed to its influence.*

These included above all the "Left" Communists and their direct successor, the group of Democratic Centralism. Their principal weapon of struggle against the Party was that of "Left" revolutionary phrasemongering. It was not for nothing that Lenin had characterised the group of Democratic Centralism as the faction which out-shouted all shouters, although this very same group at times came out with open Right opportunist propaganda for Right opportunism. In the second half of 1920, the situation changed to a certain extent. The struggle continued against the influences of the anarchist and petty-bourgeois environment, against the "Left," pseudo-revolutionary phrase-mongering, which had become particularly dangerous in view of the accentuated economic crisis. On the other hand, a struggle was also developing against a certain section among the leaders of the Party, who had yielded to some extent to the influence of the bourgeois and specialist elements in the Soviet apparatus, who had not sufficiently grasped the danger of the bureaucratisation of the Soviet apparatus and who saw no other means for improving the execrable work of the state and economic apparatus save their further bureaucratisation, i.e., their further alienation from the worker and peasant masses. This constituted a very serious Right

---

* Engels wrote in the 'seventies with regard to the anarchists: "Have these gentlemen ever seen a revolution? A revolution is undoubtedly the most authoritarian thing that could possibly be. A revolution is an act in which part of the population imposes its will on the other part by means of rifles, bayonets, cannon—all these, very authoritarian means. And the victorious party must maintain its rule by means of that fear which its weapons inspire in the reactionaries. Had not the Paris Commune made use of the authority of an armed people against the bourgeoisie, could it have lasted more than a day? On the contrary, have we not a right to blame the Commune for the fact that it did not make sufficient use of this authority? And so, either one way or the other. Either those who are 'against all authority' don't know themselves what they are talking about, and in that case they only saw confusion. Or they do know, and in that case they betray the cause of the proletariat. In either case, they only serve the cause of reaction."

danger for the Party and a danger of bureaucratic degeneration and class degeneration for the Soviet government, led by the Party.

The Party thus approached the period of the New Economic Policy, carrying on a firm and determined policy of a struggle on two fronts.

The Party itself had tremendously increased its membership in the first years of the Soviet government. By the time of the Ninth Congress, the Party had a membership of about 600,000. A powerful and well-knit Party apparatus had been created, which in spite of all its shortcomings and imperfections, established firm connection between the Party leadership and the rank and file of the Party.

During these years (1918-20), the underground Party organisations in the districts which were occupied by the imperialists and White Guards—the Ukraine, the Crimea, the Northern Caucasus, the Urals, Siberia and the Far East—had greatly enlarged their ranks. This underground work cost the working class enormous efforts and sacrifices, but it played a tremendous role in the victorious outcome of the Civil War, and forged new cadres of Bolshevik fighters.

In old tsarist Russia and later in bourgeois imperialist Russia, the Party developed, under Leninist leadership, into the fighting vanguard of the working class, into the weapon for the winning of proletarian dictatorship by revolutionary means.

Now the Party has become the weapon of the already established proletarian dictatorship, the guiding force of the state apparatus and mass labour organisations, the guiding force in the construction of socialism in this country.

"Marx and Engels gave the main outlines of the idea of the Party as being the vanguard of the proletariat, without which (the Party) the proletariat could not achieve its emancipation, could not capture power or reconstruct capitalist society. Lenin's new contribution to this theory was that he developed these outlines further and applied them to the new conditions of the proletarian struggle in the period of imperialism and showed: a) that the Party is a higher form of the class organisation of the proletariat as compared with the other forms of proletarian organisation (labour unions, co-operative societies, state organisation) and, moreover, its function was to generalise and direct the work of these organisations: b) that the dictatorship of the proletariat may be realised only through the Party as its directing force; c) that the dictatorship of the proletariat can be complete only if it is led by a single party, the Communist Party, which does not and must not share leadership with any other party; and d) that without iron discipline in the Party, the tasks of the dictatorship of the proletariat to crush the exploiters and to transform class society into socialist society cannot be fulfilled." *

The Communist Party, having won power, proved able under the most difficult conditions to extricate the country from the imperialist war, proved able to build, for the first time in history, a state apparatus of proletarian dictatorship, proved able to carry the Civil War to a victorious conclusion. It was now confronted in its full scope with the task of building a socialist economy. A substantial part of this work was carried out during the period of the Civil War. The entire industry was concentrated in the hands of the state, but industry was in a state of collapse, there was an acute shortage of raw materials and fuel, the equipment was worn out, and there was a food crisis in the cities which undermined the efficiency of the workers. Moreover, the best of the workers were still away fighting in the Civil War. The demobilisation of the army was only just beginning.

In the impoverished country, with its predominance of petty-peasant economy, with industry half destroyed and the proletariat semi-declassed as a result of the Civil War, the Party was now confronted with the urgent tasks of the construction of socialism. The Central Committee of the Party, headed by Lenin, submitted to the Eighth Congress of Soviets, which met at the end of 1920, a grand project for the electrification of the entire country, for the construction of large district electric power stations in various parts of the country as a base for the socialist reconstruction of the whole national economy.

"Communism is Soviet power plus electrification of the whole country," Lenin declared at the Eighth Congress of Soviets, explaining the electrification plan of the Goelro.** "Otherwise the country will remain a small peasant one, and we have got to realise that clearly. We are weaker than capitalism, not only world capitalism, but even our own domestic capitalism. That we all know. We realised this, and we shall

---

* Stalin, "Interview with the First American Labour Delegation in Russia," *Leninism*, Vol. I.
** Goelro: State Commission for the Electrification of Russia.

see to it that the basis of small peasant economy is replaced by the basis of large-scale industry. Only when the country is electrified, when industry, agriculture and transport are placed on the technical basis of modern large-scale production—only then will our victory be complete."

In a letter to Lenin, Comrade Stalin expressed his opinion as follows on the electrification plan, which was published in book form after its approval by the Eighth Congress of Soviets:

"An excellent well-composed book. A masterly outline of a really unified and really national economic plan. The only Marxist attempt in our time to place a truly real, the only possible technical production base under the Soviet superstructure of economically backward Russia. Do you remember Trotsky's plan of last year (his theses) for the 'economic revival' of Russia on the basis of the mass application of the unskilled peasant-worker mass (the labour army) to the fragments of pre-war industry? What puerility, what backwardness compared to the plan of the Goelro."

The Eighth Congress of Soviets adopted the magnificent plan for the electrification of the country. But it was extremely difficult to set about realising it in practice. The Civil War was over. The grounds for military-political alliance of the working class with the broad masses of the peasantry against the bourgeois-landlord forces of counter-revolution had already largely disappeared. It was only the Civil War, the direct and imminent threat of counter-revolution, which had reconciled the peasant masses to the system of War Communism. But with the transition to peace, it became absolutely impossible to continue to develop the relations of the working class with the peasantry on the basis of this system.

The question of abandoning War Communism, the question of finding a new form for the relations between the working class and the peasant masses, of a new economic policy, arose as a question involving the very existence of the Soviet government.

CHAPTER XIII

THE PARTY DURING THE TRANSITION TO THE N.E.P.

The Eighth Congress of Soviets and the beginning of the discussion on the trade unions—The anti-Leninist platforms of Trotsky, of the "Workers' Opposition" and of Bukharin—The platform of the Leninist core of the Central Committee in the discussion on the trade unions—The crisis of 1921—The Tenth Party Congress—The food quotas replaced by a tax in kind—Securing the unity of the Party—The tax in kind and commodity exchange—The Tenth Party Conference—The slogan "Learn How to Trade"—The international situation and the Third Congress of the Comintern—The Eleventh Party Conference and the all-Russian verification of Party membership—The Eleventh Party Congress—The struggle against the remnants of the "Workers' Opposition"—The first results of the New Economic Policy—The Party after the transition to the N.E.P.

The Eighth Congress of Soviets and the Beginning of the Discussion on the Trade Unions

The Party had won a brilliant victory in the Civil War. Over a tremendous part of the territory of former Russia the White Guard forces of counter-revolution had been smashed. The imperialist armies, which had occupied large districts of this territory, were compelled to evacuate them (except the Far East). But the transition from civil war to peaceful construction involved very great difficulties for the Land of Soviets. At the moment of the transition to a "peaceful breathing space" the peasantry was not faced with an immediate threat of the restoration of landlordism. A new basis was necessary for a political alliance between the working class and the peasantry; an economic base was needed for this alliance. Actually, however, no such economic base was as yet in existence. Industry, which was in a state of collapse, could give only very little aid to peasant farming.

The broad masses of the middle peasantry were reconciled to the policy of War Communism only so long as there was war. But the war was over, and the discontent of the peasant masses

112

with the policy of War Communism became ever more pronounced.

Thus, a serious threat arose to the alliance between the working class and the peasantry.

The weakening of this alliance was the main factor in the political crisis through which the Soviet government passed in the beginning of 1921. As Lenin later stated at the Fourth Congress of the Comintern:

> "We were up against a great—I believe, the very greatest—internal political crisis of Soviet Russia, which led to discontent not only among a considerable part of the peasantry but among the workers as well...
>
> "The reason was that in our economic offensive we had advanced too far, that we had not secured a sufficient base, that the masses had sensed that which we ourselves could not as yet consciously formulate, but which we, too, admitted shortly after, in a few weeks' time—namely, that the direct transition to purely socialist forms, to purely socialist distribution, was beyond our strength, and that, unless we proved able to execute a retreat in order to confine ourselves to easier tasks, we would be threatened with disaster." *

At the Eighth Congress of Soviets, in December 1920, the question of the policy to be pursued in the countryside was among the most important questions discussed. A report was submitted to the Congress on the grave state of agriculture, on the uninterrupted reduction of the cultivated area, which continued from year to year. This reduction was particularly rapid in the case of crops furnishing raw materials for industry. The production of hemp in 1920 was only 10 per cent compared with 1913, the production of flax 25 per cent, of beets 15 per cent, of cotton 11 per cent and of tobacco 10 per cent. There was an equally sharp decline in the number of cattle. In view of this, the Congress adopted a decision which pointed out the urgent need of increasing the cultivated area by means of agitation and state compulsion, and of creating special "sowing committees" in each *volost* ** as administrative and social organs whose task was to see that the area under cultivation in their *volost* was enlarged. The Congress at the same time considered the question of awarding premiums to efficient farmers. The Party fraction of the Con-

---

* Lenin, "Five Years of the Russian Revolution and the Prospects of World Revolution," *Collected Works*, Vol. XXVII.

** *Volost*: a former administrative unit in rural areas, now abolished.

gress of Soviets at first rejected the proposal that premiums should be given not only to collective enterprises but to individual farmers as well. Only when the Central Committee, at the instance of Lenin, insisted on this point, did the fraction reconsider its decision and agree to the award of premiums to individual farmers.

But while the Congress of Soviets was considering questions connected with the crisis in agriculture, the Party organisations had their attention concentrated on the discussion of trade union questions—a discussion which was begun in real earnest immediately after the Eighth Congress of Soviets was over. The discontent among the peasantry was also reflected among the working class, above all, among those of its sections which were connected with the peasantry. The acute character of the trade union question was undoubtedly connected with the obvious necessity of strengthening the Party's connection with the non-Party working masses. It was just this necessity that compelled the Party to seek various ways and means to improve the whole system of trade union work. On this question two groups were formed within the Party in opposition to the main kernel of the Party which supported Lenin. One group, which virtually constituted a faction, was represented by the Trotskyists, the other was the "Workers' Opposition."

The Anti-Leninist Platforms of Trotsky, of the "Workers' Opposition" and of Bukharin

In a number of statements Trotsky defined his position—a position opposed to that of Lenin—as the viewpoint of industrial democracy. In substance, however, it amounted to transforming the trade unions into state organs, into bureaucratic administrative organs, and to selecting the leading apparatus of the trade unions accordingly, *i.e.*, by rigorous selection from above, or, as Trotsky expressed it, by "sandpapering the trade unions." The Ninth Party Congress had adopted a policy of one-man management, of a firm administrative system, coupled with measures of compulsion in those cases where nothing could be done without such measures. After the Ninth Congress, however, Lenin emphasised, when speaking at the Eighth Congress of Soviets, that our Party should use measures of compulsion only as supplementary to measures of persuasion. This was said with especial reference to the working class. Comrade Stalin, who supported Lenin against Trotsky and against the latter's attempts to carry over military methods into the trade unions, to reduce everything to compulsion, wrote as follows:

"Democracy in the trade unions, *i.e.*, the thing that is usually called 'the normal methods of proletarian democracy within the trade unions,' is the conscious democracy which is characteristic of the mass labour organisations and which presupposes an understanding of the necessity and usefulness of systematically applying methods of persuasion to the millions of the working masses who are being organised into trade unions." *

Trotsky, however, attached exceptional importance to measures of compulsion, to measures of pressure from above, to administrative measures from above. He refused, as Lenin said, to see "the degeneration of centralism and militarised forms of work into bureaucracy, arbitrary action, red tape," etc. Objectively considered, Trotsky's viewpoint expressed the tendencies of the bureaucratised elements in the upper circles of the Soviet apparatus, who not only failed to see the correct and real means for the solution of the crisis through which the country and Party were passing, but even urged the Party to intensify still further those negative features of bureaucracy which had already made their influence strongly felt in the Party and Soviet apparatus. These tendencies exercised an influence over some of our Party leaders. The transformation of the trade unions into state organs could not, of course, have saved them from bureaucratisation but would only have made this bureaucratisation more acute. Here Trotsky again and again showed his lack of confidence in the power of the Party and the working class. Moreover, by transforming the trade unions into state organs, and entrusting them with the direct guidance of industry, by converting them into administrative organs, the main functions of the trade unions, the functions of educating the working masses and of defending their interests, would actually have been reduced to nothing. And Trotsky's proposal to take the guidance of the economic activities out of the hands of the Soviet organs, in which the peasantry

* Stalin. "Our Differences," *On the Opposition.*

8*

were represented, was additional evidence of his complete ignoring of the peasantry as an ally of the proletariat. This tendency to ignore the peasantry was the distinctive characteristic of the political ideology of Trotsky, even after he had joined the Party.

"Trotsky's error," Lenin wrote, "if not recognised and corrected, will lead to the collapse of the dictatorship of the proletariat."

It is highly characteristic of Trotsky that he coupled his proposals for the transformation of the trade unions into state organs with propaganda in favour of petty-bourgeois equalitarianism.

"In the field of consumption," Trotsky wrote, "*i.e.*, in the conditions of private existence, it is essential to pursue a policy of equalitarianism. in the domain of production, shock methods will still remain decisive for us for a long time." *

Lenin described these arguments of Trotsky's as an example of theoretical confusion.

"Shock methods imply preference, and preference without consumption is nothing. . . . Preference in shock work means preference in consumption. Without this, shock work is a dream, a cloud, and we, after all, are materialists."**

The equalitarian demagogy of Trotsky is the best evidence of the fact that in the struggle against the Central Committee and Lenin he strove to get the support of the most backward strata among the workers, of those strata that were most infected with petty-bourgeois prejudices.

With no less energy and determination Lenin opposed the platform of the so-called "Workers' Opposition." This anti-Leninist platform, in certain features, had an outward resemblance to the plaform of Trotsky, particularly to Bukharin's version of this platform. The resemblance of the platform of the "Workers' Opposition" to Trotsky's platform was that, while Trotsky spoke of turning the trade unions into organs of the state, the "Workers Opposition" spoke of the trade-unionising of the state.

Trotsky said that the trade unions should become state organs. The "Workers' Opposition" said that the state should transfer its functions to the trade unions. Both Trotsky and the "Workers'

* Quoted in Lenin, "On the Trade Unions," *Collected Works*, Vol. XXVI
** *Ibid.*

Opposition" agreed that the functions of the trade unions should
be of an administrative and industrial character. The function
of the trade unions should be, not to organise and serve the
working class, the way in which the Party, headed by Lenin,
put the question—not to defend the workers' interests, not to
struggle against the bureaucratic distortion of the state machine,
but to organise production. The "Workers' Opposition" and the
Trotskyists were in agreement upon this point. But the "Workers'
Opposition" even went so far as to demand that the trade unions,
as the organisers of production, should take the place not only
of the Soviet apparatus but of the Party as well. One of the theses
in the platform of the "Workers' Opposition" stated outright that
all our industry should be managed by the trade unions, the
highest organ of which, according to the opinion of Shlyapnikov
and his supporters, should be an all-Russian congress of the
producers. On account of this thesis Lenin charged the "Workers' Opposition" with an anarcho-syndicalist deviation, since the
distinctive characteristic of syndicalism in France, Britain and
America consisted precisely in the fact that it advocated the idea
of putting industry under the control of the trade union con-
federations, rejecting the idea of the state and of the political
party as the leading organ of the proletarian struggle both before
and after the winning of proletarian dictatorship.

Comrade Bukharin and a number of other comrades at first
took a so-called "buffer" standpoint. They agreed with Trotsky's
proposals to hand over the functions of organisation and production to the trade unions, going even further than Trotsky on this
point and taking an outright syndicalist position, but they did
not share Trotsky's predilection for administrative and militar-
ising measures which found its classical expression in the formula
about "sandpapering the trade unions."

Finally, however, the Trotskyists and adherents of the "buffer" group presented one platform in which the Trotskyist tendencies towards administrative orders and "sandpapering" were
somewhat modified and toned down. The function of the "buffer"
faction, objectively considered, was to act as a screen for Trotskyism. This caused Lenin to declare that this faction, more than
any other, had inflicted harm and introduced confusion, that it

had proved itself an abettor of the worst and most harmful factionalism.

The Bukharin faction was essentially a buffer between the Trotskyists and the "Workers' Opposition." Hence its unrestrained propaganda of "industrial democracy," regarding which Lenin wrote:

"Industrial democracy engenders certain ideas which are radically false. It is not so long ago that we were advocating one-man management. It is wrong to sow confusion by creating the danger that people may get mixed up and not know when they have to do with democracy, when with one-man management and when with dictatorship." *

It was for this reason that Lenin dealt with extreme severity with the position of Bukharin, in particular with his demand, that the nominations of the trade unions for the various economic posts should be taken as binding; Lenin described this as "a complete break with communism and desertion to the position of syndicalism," as "a complete failure to grasp that formal democracy should be subordinated to revolutionary expediency," as the substitution of eclectics for dialectics.

Trotsky, who was trying to confuse the ranks of the Party cadres among the leaders of the trade union movement, was not averse to making use of Bukharin's anarcho-syndicalist tendencies for this purpose, tendencies which had their roots in the latter's failure to understand the nature of the state of proletarian dictatorship. This lack of understanding was clearly manifested by Bukharin both during the period of the imperialist war and during that of the Brest peace.

Both Trotsky and Bukharin were very far from seeking a way out of the difficulties, with which the Soviet government was confronted, along the path of adjusting the mutual relations between the working class and the peasantry.

Lenin had already pointed out this path at the very beginning of the discussion on the trade union question.

The anarcho-syndicalist tendencies of the "Workers' Opposition," were akin to the views of Bukharin during the first years of the imperialist war (it was no accident that Bukharin was now in favour of making trade union nominations to economic posts

---

*Lenin, "On the Trade Unions," *Collected Works*, Vol. XXVI.

binding); they were also akin to the criticism which the "Left" Communists levelled at Lenin after the Brest peace; and they were supplemented with charges, at one time borrowed from the Mensheviks by the "Left" Communists, that the Soviet govern- ment had abandoned the class standpoint of the proletariat in favour of the standpoint of the peasantry, etc.

Such clearly Menshevik, anti-Soviet arguments in the mouths of the "Workers' Opposition" were particularly dangerous, since the working masses were in a hard situation; they were having to go without the most vital necessaries of life, and some of them might have believed this demagogic slander.

What were the practical proposals of the "Workers' Opposi- tion"? On the one hand, they proposed "to trade-unionise the state," to transfer the industries to the trade unions; they further wanted to free the trade unions from "petty Party tutelage": and finally, the "Workers' Opposition" proposed to pass to a regime of unlimited democracy within the Party and trade union organisations.

"Democratisation" of the Party in the spirit of the "Workers' Opposition" meant the complete repudiation of the Bolshevik organisational principles of democratic centralism; it meant the collapse and ruin of the Party as the weapon of proletarian dictatorship. The restrictions of broad democracy, against which the "Workers' Opposition" demagogically protested, were abso- lutely necessary under the conditions of civil war.

It was just the iron discipline in our Bolshevik Party (ap- proaching military discipline in the years of the Civil War) and which was based on the Bolshevik principle of democratic cen- tralism which had been tested in the course of decades, it was just the persistent struggle of Lenin (and the Bolsheviks) in the course of almost a score of years for a new type of proletarian party, it was just the irreconcilable and relentless struggle of the Bolsheviks on two fronts against opportunism and against a conciliatory attitude towards opportunism, for a split in the Rus- sian Social-Democratic Labour Party and in the Second Inter- national—it was just this that secured for the proletarian dic- tatorship in our country a victory of world historical significance against the forces of international and internal counter-revolu- tion.

During the years of the Civil War too, in spite of the extraordinary difficulties and dangers unprecedented in the history of the revolution, our Bolshevik Party—by means of periodical mass re-registrations of its organisations and its members, by means of Party weeks for the mass recruitment of workers and peasants into its ranks, and through a number of other tried Bolshevik methods—fought to secure the fighting proletarian character of its organisations, its iron discipline, its monolithic character, and the purity of Marxist-Leninist principles. The Party carried on a determined struggle to purge its ranks of individual elements who might chance to enter it under false colours, which was bound to happen even in the land of proletarian dictatorship, where our Party has fought and continues to fight as the ruling party, as the sole and single party in the system of the proletarian dictatorship.

But our Party also included petty-bourgeois elements in its ranks (peasants, intellectuals, office employees), while the majority of the proletarian members of the Party were in the army or in the state apparatus and were thus taken away from production work. The educational activities of the Party were insufficiently developed. The hard situation of the workers who remained in the industries, and the privations of the Civil War, affected the state of feeling among the workers, and this was also reflected in the Party.

When under *such* conditions, the "Workers' Opposition" put forward their practical proposals for unrestricted democracy, proposals which met with a response among individual sections of the masses, they were, objectively speaking, carrying out the social orders of the enemy. Had the plans of the "Workers' Opposition" been carried into effect, this would have given the Mensheviks and Socialist-Revolutionaries a free hand to carry on anti-Soviet activities. It was no accident that all anti-Soviet parties applauded with especial zeal the criticism offered by the opposition.* The phrase in Kollontai's pamphlet to the effect

---

* The Mensheviks, in particular, lavished their Judas kisses upon the "Workers' Opposition," which is not surprising: first, the Mensheviks readily supported anything that tended to disrupt the Party; secondly, in demanding democracy at all costs, in fighting for the emancipation of the trade unions from "petty Party tutelage," etc., the "Workers' Opposition" was voicing purely Menshevik sentiments.

that the proletariat in our country was in a *pitiful condition* and other similar statements were cited by all Social-Democrats abroad against our Party and the Soviet government. That is why Lenin was obliged to launch a most determined struggle against the "Workers' Opposition." That is why the Party administered such a decided rebuff to the "Workers' Opposition."

Later, at the Tenth Congress, Lenin stated outright that "the 'Workers' Opposition,' which screens itself behind the proletariat, actually represents the petty-bourgeois, anarchic elemental forces."*

The Platform of the Leninist Core of the Central Committee in the Discussion on the Trade Unions

The Leninist platform stressed the role of the trade unions in the task of defending the interests of the working class and in the struggle against bureaucratic distortions; and it likewise emphasised their role as a school of socialist construction, as a school of communism.**

"The trade unions," said Lenin, "are a school, a school of unity, of solidarity, a school of the defence of their own interests, a school of economic management, a school of administration.

"The state is the sphere of compulsion. It would be insanity to renounce compulsion, particularly during the epoch of the dictatorship of the proletariat. In this sphere, 'administrative' measures and an administrative attitude to things are obligatory. The Party is the direct ruling vanguard of the proletariat, the Party is the leader. The specific Party method of exerting pressure, its method of purifying and hardening the vanguard is not compulsion, but expulsion from the Party. The trade unions are a reservoir of the state power, a school of communism, a school of economic management. The specific and principal feature in this sphere is *not* administration, but 'contact between the central' (and, of course, also local) 'government administration, the

* The "Workers' Opposition" was led by Shlyapnikov and supported by a number of trade union leaders and business managers (S. Medvedev, M. Vladimirov, a metal worker, Tolokontsev, Brudno, P. Orlov, Kiselev, Kutuzov, Chelyshev, Perepechko, etc.). Kollontai, who also belonged to this group, published a pamphlet, *The Workers' Opposition*, the only literary production which contains a more or less comprehensive and complete statement of the views of the "Workers' Opposition."

** The Leninist platform was signed by "a dozen" member of the Central Committee, including Lenin, Stalin, Kalinin, Rudzutak, Artem (Sergeyev) and others.

national economy and the *broad masses* of the toilers' (as the programme of our Party states in paragraph 5 of the economic section,
dealing with the trade unions).

"An incorrect approach to this question, a failure to understand this
inter-relation runs like a red thread through Trotsky's whole pamphlet
containing his platform." *

Besides this, Lenin and his associates stressed the fact that,
essentially, our crisis was not due to any particular shortcoming
in the trade union apparatus; such a defect should, of course,
be corrected, but it was not necessary to resort to giving the
Party a shake-up for this purpose. Lenin believed that the discussion on the trade unions was an unnecessary luxury.** But
inasmuch as, on the initiative of Trotsky supported by Shlyapnikov, the discussion had flared up, the Leninist core of the
Central Committee, while pointing out the positive functions
which the trade unions had to exercise, at the same time criticised
the proposals which were put forward by Trotsky and by the
"Workers' Opposition" and which would have been disastrous for
the Soviet government and the Party.

On one hand, there was the danger of excessive state compulsion, of coercion, of putting on the screw too hard. This would
have led to the bureaucratisation of the government and trade
union apparatus.

On the other hand, there was the danger that, under the
slogans of unrestrained democracy, of "emancipating" the working masses from "government" and "Party tutelage," the petty-
bourgeois anti-Soviet anarchic forces would triumph. The so-
called "Workers' Opposition" was the weapon of these anarchic
forces.

The Crisis of 1921

The Eighth Congress of Soviets met at a time when the economic crisis in the country had not yet become particularly

* Lenin, "Once More About the Trade Unions," *Collected Works*, Vol.
XXVII.
** This was literally what Lenin said at the opening of the Tenth Congress: "We have permitted ourselves the luxury of discussions and disputes
within our Party. For a party which is surrounded by enemies, by the most
powerful and mighty enemies uniting the entire capitalist world, for a party
which has an unheard-of burden to bear—such luxury was truly amazing."
Lenin, *Collected Works*, Vol. XXVI.

acute. Within a few weeks this crisis was sharply accentuated, owing to the shortage of fuel and food supplies. Almost all of the operating plants had to close down,* while the situation on the railways became much worse and the supply of food in the large industrial centres also deteriorated.

This gave the kulak elements, who were resisting the Soviet government, an opportunity to make extensive use, for their own ends, of the increased discontent among the middle peasantry.

Railway connections with the most important grain supplying districts, as for instance with Siberia, were interrupted for weeks. ✓ The situation with regard to the peasantry was more complex now than in 1918. Since then the middle peasantry had become a considerably greater force in the countryside. This was because the peasantry, above all the poor peasants, had appropriated the landlord and kulak land, and from this standpoint the growth of the middle peasants represented a great achievement of the Soviet power. But, in view of the discontent prevailing among the broad peasant masses with the policy of War Communism, there was a growing danger of the countryside, with its increased proportion of middle peasantry, coming into opposition to the work- ✓ ing class and the Soviet government. The discontent of the peasantry, owing to the aggravated food situation, spread to those sections of the workers who were connected with the peasantry. The state of feeling among the peasantry likewise affected the Red Army. There were cases of individual groups deserting to the side of the bandits against whom they were sent to fight. Finally, at the moment of the greatest accentuation of the crisis, on the eve of the Tenth Party Congress, an uprising occurred in Kronstadt under the slogan: "Soviet power without the Communists." This slogan was put forward by the White Guard leaders of the uprising and was later seized upon by the White Guard press abroad. (Milyukov's *Posledniye Novosti*.)

The White Guards were compelled, by using the slogan of

---

* In 1920 our industry reached its maximum decline. Although 43 per cent of the pre-war number of workers were engaged in the industries, their output was only 18 per cent of the pre-war level. Particularly catastrophic was the situation in heavy industry. In 1920 we produced but 2.8 per cent of the pre-war output of pig iron. The acute crisis in the beginning of 1921 paralysed even the pitiful remnants of the heavy industry which were still operating in 1920.

Soviet power as a screen, to admit the popularity of this slogan among the masses. What they were striving for, however, was to separate the Soviet government from the Party and thus to unite around themselves the petty-bourgeois elements, who would not have supported openly counter-revolutionary slogans.

The Kronstadt uprising might have caused very great complications, had not the Soviet government and the Party taken the most determined measures to suppress it.

The rebels had in their hands a strong fortress, located right on the frontier, with enormous stores of military supplies and all the warships of the Baltic fleet. This would have enabled the forces of counter-revolution, particularly in case of external assistance, to resume the civil war against the Soviet government, which the latter, at the price of tremendous exertion, had but a short time ago succeeded in bringing to a victorious conclusion. The White Guard émigrés, from the monarchists to the Left Socialist-Revolutionaries, developed tremendous agitation in favour of supporting Kronstadt. The forces of monarchist counter-revolution, represented by the remnants of the Cadet Party (Milyukov), eagerly defended the slogan "Soviet power without the Communists." They understood very well that the abolition of the proletarian dictatorship, no matter under what pretext it might be carried out, would open the way for the restoration of the power of the capitalists and landlords.

But the bourgeoisie within the country had been crushed. They were unable to extend any aid to the Kronstadt rebellion.

The Party found the solution for the crisis by changing the economic policy, by abandoning the system of War Communism, while relentlessly suppressing all counter-revolutionary attempts and strengthening its unity.

As we have seen above, the system of War Communism had been forced upon the Party and the Soviet government by the iron logic of civil war. The war necessitated the merciless expropriation of the bourgeoisie, the nationalisation of the entire industry, the concentration in the hands of the state and the planned distribution of all supplies, the firm enforcement of the grain monopoly by which the peasants were obliged to surrender all their grain surplus to the government, and in connection with this, 'the suppression of free trade.*

The programme of the Communist International later defined the policy of War Communism as

"the organisation of rational consumption for the purpose of military defence accompanied by a system of intensified pressure upon the capitalist groups (confiscation, requisitions, etc.), with the more or less complete liquidation of freedom of trade and market relations, and a sharp disturbance of the individualist economic stimuli of the small producers, which results in a diminution of the productive forces of the country. This policy of War Communism, while it undermines the material basis of the strata of the population in the country that are hostile to the working class, secures a rational distribution of the available supplies and facilitates the military struggle of the proletarian dictatorship—which is the historical justification of this policy—nevertheless, cannot be regarded as the 'normal' economic policy of the proletarian dictatorship."**

As Lenin later wrote:

"We committed the error of deciding to carry out a direct transition to communist production and distribution. We decided that the peasants through the grain quotas would give us the necessary amount of bread, which we would distribute to the mills and factories, and the result would be communist production and distribution."

The workers were to have satisfied their essential needs from the state supplies. The peasants who surrendered their grain sur-

* An attempt to provide a theoretical basis for the whole practice of War Communism was made by Comrade Bukharin in his book *The Economics of the Transition Period.* In this book Bukharin considered the economic policy of War Communism as the only possible policy under the conditions of the proletarian dictatorship during the transition from capitalism to socialism, completely failing to see the specific conditions which called this policy into being. Attempting to prove that state capitalism was impossible under the dictatorship of the proletariat, Bukharin opposed the economic plan of Lenin, who in 1918 had already expressed himself in favour of allowing capitalism on condition that it be controlled and regulated by the proletarian state. Bukharin also expressed himself in advance against the New Economic Policy, which was described by Comrade Stalin as a policy planned to allow capitalism on condition that the commanding positions remained in the hands of the proletarian state. The book contains a number of other crass theoretical errors, characteristic of Bukharin, which Lenin at the time pointed out in his notes on *The Economics of the Transition Period.* Particularly notable is the tendency to overestimate the elements of organisation and to gloss over the elements of anarchy and competition in the system of capitalist imperialism, as well as the attempt to consider this system as "pure imperialism."

** *Programme of the Communist International,* p. 33.

plus to the state also had the right to be supplied with the products of the state industries. Money, which, to be sure, had almost completely lost its value, could, it would seem, be entirely discarded, the country passing to accounting without money.β

The organic defects of the policy of War Communism were now completely revealed.

The shortage of bread was felt most acutely. Even the villages experienced a shortage of bread and gave almost nothing to the cities. The workers in the cities got very little from the state. Under such conditions the Party had only one solution: to abandon the system of War Communism, *i.e.,* to abandon the policy of the direct realisation of socialism and to take the path which had already been outlined in the spring of 1918 in the articles and speeches of Lenin. The first step in this direction was the substitution of a tax in kind for the food quotas, and this was inevitably followed by further measures.

It was absolutely necessary to make concessions to the peasantry. The more so since, while previously the peasants were ready to make sacrifices for fear of the restoration of landlordism, they were not now confronted with such a direct menace, since the country, after the crushing of the White Guard armies, had entered upon a period of a "peaceful breathing space."

On the other hand the cities and the industries could not exist without bread. It was impossible to reckon on their restoration unless agriculture were lifted out of the rut, unless an increase in agricultural production were obtained at all costs. Under the existing conditions, when industry produced only 20 per cent of the pre-war output and heavy industry even less, this could be attained only on the basis of individual peasant farming, by giving the peasant a personal interest in increasing his production, by allowing him the right to dispose of his grain surplus himself.

The Tenth Party Congress

Such was the atmosphere in which the Tenth Party Congress opened its sessions, under the thunder of the guns from Kronstadt.* The Congress adopted a resolution calling for the replacement of the food quotas by a tax in kind.

* There were 990 delegates at the Congress, 694 with a decisive vote and 296 with a consultative vote, representing a membership of 730,000. In the in-

"We have passed through a year," Lenin said in opening the Congress, "which was very rich in developments both in international and in our internal history. Starting with the international situation, I must state that we meet here for the first time in circumstances when the Communist International has ceased to be merely a slogan and has really become a powerful organisational structure which has its foundation, a real foundation, in the largest advanced capitalist countries. What had only been outlined in resolutions at the Second Congress of the Communist International, has been realised during the past year, has found its expression and confirmation in such countries as Germany, France and Italy. It is sufficient to name these three countries to see that in all the largest advanced European countries the Communist International, since the Second Congress which was held last summer in Moscow, has become the cause of the labour movement in each of these countries—more than this, it has become a basic factor in international politics. This, comrades, is such an immense conquest, that no matter

---

terval between the Ninth and the Tenth Congresses, the Soviet government was established in Transcaucasia. The Azerbaijan Soviet Republic was formed as early as April 1920. The Baku oil fields were wrested from the grasp of the imperialists. At the end of 1920 Armenia became Sovietised. Finally, on the very eve of the Tenth Congress, the Soviet government was established in Georgia, which had been ruled in the two preceding years by a government of Georgian Mensheviks, at first in alliance with German imperialism and, after the collapse of the latter, in alliance with the Entente.

During the Tenth Congress the Bund joined forces with the R.C.P. For several decades the Bund had maintained an ideological, and later also an organisational connection with the Mensheviks. Together with the Mensheviks, the Bund carried on a bitter struggle against the October Revolution and the Soviet government. However, the hardships of the Civil War period destroyed the Menshevik faith in bourgeois democracy among the working class membership of the Bund. In the Ukraine some members of the Bund, under pressure from the workers, adopted a Soviet platform as early as 1918-19, later joining our Party. In Soviet Russia and White Russia the Bund organisation was more slow in getting rid of its ingrained Menshevik and nationalist prejudices. Not until the spring of 1920 did the Bund definitely break with the Mensheviks, changing its name to the Communist Bund and offering to join the R.C.P. with the rights of an autonomous exterritorial organisation. But for the R.C.P. this principle was absolutely unacceptable. The question was carried to the Comintern, which proposed to the Bund that it should join the R.C.P. This proposal was accepted by the Central Committee of the Bund.

Thus, whereas in the period after the October Revolution the Bund, together with the Mensheviks, found itself on the other side of the barricade, now the best elements of the Bund consciously accepted "self-liquidation," instead of continuing, together with their former comrades in arms, the Mensheviks, to serve the cause of bourgeois restoration.

The elements who were faithful to the opportunist and nationalist traditions of the Bund, such as Abramovich, Lieber, etc., remained in the camp of the Mensheviks, sharing their disgraceful fate.

how difficult and severe the various trials which may yet await us—and we can never and ought never to lose sight of them—no one can take it away from us.

"Further, comrades, we meet for the first time in Congress in circumstances where there are no longer any enemy troops, supported by the capitalists and imperialists of the whole world, on the territory of the Soviet Republic. For the first time thanks to the victories of the Red Army during the past year, we open the Party Congress under such circumstances. Three and a half years of unheard-of severe struggle, but no enemy armies left on our territory—that is what we have won! Of course, we are still far from having won everything thereby, and we have not by any means won thereby what we ought to win—real security from invasions and interference on the part of the imperialists . . . . The transition from war to peace—that transition which we welcomed at the last Congress of the Party and were already attempting to realise, attempting to adjust the work in this direction —this transition is not yet completed even now. Our Party is still confronted with incredibly difficult tasks, not only involving the economic plan—in which we have made not a few errors—not only involving the foundations of our economic construction, but involving the foundations of the very relations between classes in our society, in our Soviet Republic."*

In his report on behalf of the Central Committee, Lenin drew a vivid picture of the tremendous difficulties which confronted the Party at the moment of demobilisation, of a crisis in the mutual relations between the working class and the peasantry, on the one hand, and between the working class and the Party, on the other.

"Now that the problems of war have been solved, a large part of the army is coming up against immeasurably worsened conditions, is coming up against incredible difficulties in the countryside and is unable, owing to this and to the general crisis, to find employment for its labour. The result is something midway between peace and war. The demobilisation has engendered continuation of the war, only in a new form. When scores and hundreds of thousands of the demobilised men cannot find employment for their labour, return to their homes impoverished and ruined, men who are used to engage in warfare and regard it almost as their only trade—we find ourselves drawn into a new form of war, into a new kind of warfare, which can be summarised by the word banditry."**

* Lenin, "Speech at the Opening of the Party Congress on March 8," *Collected Works*, Vol. XXVI.
  ** *Ibid.*

The petty-bourgeois environment was also making itself felt in the mills and factories.

"This state of feeling has very extensively affected the proletariat. It has affected the enterprises in Moscow, it has affected the enterprises in a number of places in the provinces. This petty-bourgeois counterrevolutionary attitude is undoubtedly more dangerous than Denikin, Yudenich and Kolchak taken together, since we are dealing with a country where the proletariat constitutes a minority, with a country in which a state of ruin has been revealed in peasant property. . . .

"If the discontent of the peasantry with the proletarian dictatorship is increasing, if the crisis in farming has reached its limit, if the demobilisation of the peasant army is throwing out hundreds of thousands of ruined people who can find no occupation, people who have become used to engage in war as their only trade and who engender banditry, then this is no time to engage in disputes about theoretical deviations. And we must plainly state at the Congress: We will not permit disputes about deviations. [Lenin had in mind a continuation of the pre-congress discussion—N.P.] We must put an end to this. The situation is becoming extremely perilous, is becoming an outright menace to the dictatorship of the proletariat." *

Lenin, in the very first report, squarely raised the question of changing the economic inter-relations between the working class and the peasantry, of replacing the food quotas by a tax in kind. In the discussion on Lenin's report the Trotskyists and spokesmen of the "Workers' Opposition" quite clearly manifested a defeatist and capitulatory attitude, characteristic of both these factions which fought against Lenin and, objectively speaking, played the role of agents of the bourgeoisie. Particularly characteristic from this standpoint was the speech of the Trotskyist, Sosnovsky. He declared:

"It has been quite correctly established [by whom?—N.P.], though, in my opinion, the point was not fully developed, that we are now entering upon a phase of capitulation to the petty bourgeoisie, that this capitulation will result at the next congress in capitulation to the same petty-bourgeois environment, depending upon how the revolution will develop in Europe. This should have been said quite plainly to the Party, in order that it might be able to understand the meaning of the change, of the alteration in policy—today in the food policy, tomorrow in the agrarian and some other policy. I don't know what the comrades who work in the provinces think, but it seems to me that for many districts in Russia this concession which we are now about to discuss will prove in some places to be belated or insufficient."

* *Ibid.*

9 Popov II E

This was a characteristic Trotskyist approach. If there is no revolution in Europe, then capitulate to the petty-bourgeois environment, abolish the proletarian dictatorship.

The event, however, did not justify the prediction of this former aide-de-camp of Trotsky's, but quite the reverse. The next (Eleventh) congress of the Party did not bring the capitulation of the Party to the petty-bourgeois forces over which the kulak attempted to gain the leadership (what the Trotskyists had reckoned on). It brought a halt in the retreat (what the Party had reckoned on).

After hearing the report of the Central Committee, the Tenth Congress, by an overwhelming majority, adopted a resolution which approved "the home and foreign policy of the Central Committee as generally correct."

The Congress at the same time noted

"the lack of unity in the Central Committee, manifested of late in the discussion of a number of burning questions, particularly on the role and tasks of the trade unions,' which resulted in an extreme exacerbation of the discussion in the ranks of the Party and undue dissipation of the Party forces to the detriment of other Party tasks, particularly that of extending and consolidating the influence of the Party among the broad non-Party masses."

This was aimed at those members of the Central Committee who supported the factional policy of Trotsky and helped him to precipitate a discussion at a very critical moment for the proletarian dictatorship, thus undermining the work which the Party was doing to strengthen its influence among the non-Party masses.

The Congress adopted a decision on Party democracy. This decision did no more than to supplement, systematise and develop the resolution of the Party Conference of the previous September. In a separate resolution which was adopted on Party unity and on the anarcho-syndicalist deviation, the Congress set definite limits to inner-Party democracy, categorically prohibiting factions and groupings.

The Party Congress put an end to the discussion on the trade unions. The overwhelming majority of the delegates—several hundred as against fifty Trotskyists and approximately the same number of the "Workers' Opposition"—voted for Lenin's theses.

On the basis of Comrade Stalin's report, the Congress adopted theses on the national question. These theses were adopted as a further development of the corresponding points of our Party programme which had been approved by the Eighth Congress. They contained an analysis of two deviations in the Party on the national question: the deviation towards Great-Russian chauvinism and the deviation towards local national chauvinism. Besides this, they contained a number of practical proposals, aimed at solving the national question (providing for the use of native languages of the population in the government apparatus, schools, press and Party apparatus, etc.). The theses particularly stressed the policy of raising the productive forces in the backward border republics inhabited by national minorities.

The congress adopted a decision regarding the policy of the Soviet Republics in the surrounding ring of capitalist states. This resolution outlined the fundamental principles of the foreign policy of the Soviet government towards the surrounding capitalist countries.

"For three years the capitalist powers attempted to overthrow the Soviet government by means of armed attacks, to reduce Russia to the role of a colony and thereby to convert Russian raw materials and Russian workers and peasants into a source of profit for foreign capital. Through the heroic efforts of the toilers, the Soviet Republic repulsed these attempts, thereby gaining for itself the possibility of entering into communication with the capitalist state as an independent state on the basis of reciprocal obligations of a political and commercial character.

"On the other hand, the failure of intervention and the avidity of the various capitalist groups, which are competing on the world arena to increase their profits by utilising the natural resources of Russia, forces a number of capitalist states to establish treaty relations with the Soviet Republic.

"The possibility of new relations based on treaties and conventions between the Soviet Republic and the capitalist countries should be utilised first of all in order to raise the productive forces of the Republic, to improve the situation of the principal productive force, the working class.

"This, the main problem confronting the Soviet Republic, cannot be solved on a wide scale and within a previously fixed period without the utilisation of foreign technique, of foreign equipment, of means of production manufactured abroad."

9*

To pursue a policy of peace, to utilise the technique of the advanced capitalist countries, to accumulate strength for new battles on the internal and international arena—such was the problem presented.

The concessions represented one of the practical measures designed to increase the productive forces of the Soviet country and to utilise foreign technique. A decree regarding concessions had already been published at the end of November 1920, a few months before the launching of the New Economic Policy. This decree authorised the Soviet government to lease sections of land and industrial establishments to foreign capitalists. The question of concessions was dealt with at length in Lenin's report to the Eighth Congress of Soviets. The Tenth Congress of the Party decided that the Soviet government, upon certain conditions, should lease out the natural resources of the country in concessions to be developed by foreign capital. The economic situation of the country was so critical that the Tenth Party Congress even authorised the Central Committee to conduct negotiations on the leasing out of the Baku and Grozny oil fields. However, it proved unnecessary to carry this decision into effect. The New Economic Policy strengthened the economic position of the Soviet Republic and enabled it by its own efforts to improve conditions not only in the Baku and Grozny districts but in all our large industries as well. At present the Baku and Grozny districts are in the van of Soviet industry, having fulfilled the first Five-Year Plan in two and a half years.

The Tenth Congress at a closed session heard Trotsky's report on the condition of the army. On Lenin's categorical proposal, which was adopted by the Congress in spite of Trotsky's opposition, no stenographic record was taken of this report. The most essential supplies of the army had been gravely affected by the economic crisis. Demobilisation had only just begun. The discontent among the peasants affected the temper of the Red Army men and even that of the commanding staff. All these facts were presented by Trotsky in his report with an overemphasis and exaggeration amounting to panic, the result being an entirely distorted picture of the actual state of affairs in the Red Army. From what Trotsky said, only one conclusion was possible—that the Soviet government would collapse within a very short time.

This appraisal of the Red Army by Trotsky manifested his characteristic lack of faith in the strength of the Party and the working class, his lack of faith in the ability of the Soviet government to maintain and consolidate its position in our country. This appraisal was in line with the specific methods which Trotsky used in his military work, attempting to destroy the Party influence, showing boundless trust in the bourgeois specialists and failing to take into account the peculiar features which distinguished our Red Army as the army of the proletarian dictatorship. The defeatist and liquidationist view taken by Trotsky of the situation in the Red Army logically led him to a position which was hostile to the Soviet government and the proletarian dictatorship. As Trotsky put it after the Congress: "The cuckoo has cuckooed the end of the Soviet government." Lenin emphatically repudiated this appraisal of the situation in the Red Army. The Congress outlined a number of measures to strengthen the Red Army in connection with the demobilisation and the reduction of its numerical strength.

The Food Quotas Replaced by a Tax in Kind

The most important decision of the Tenth Party Congress was the resolution which called for the replacement of the food quotas by a tax in kind. As Lenin stated in his report at the Congress on this question:

"The question of replacing the quotas by a tax is above all and pre-eminently a political question, since it is essentially a question of the relation of the working class to the peasantry. The placing of this question on the order of the day means that the relation between these two principal classes, a struggle or an agreement between which determines the fate of our revolution, must be subjected by us to a new, or, I should perhaps say, more circumspect and correct supplementary consideration and a certain revision. I do not need to deal in detail with the causes for such a revision. All of you are, of course, well aware of what sum total of events, particularly on the basis of the extreme exacerbation of the hardships caused by the war, ruin, demobilisation and the extremely serious failure of crops—of what sum total of circumstances has rendered the conditions of the peasants particularly difficult and acute, inevitably increasing their tendency to waver from the proletariat towards the bourgeoisie. . . .

"The problem of satisfying the middle peasantry must be solved. The peasantry has become much more middle-peasant than in the past, contradictions have been smoothed out, the land has been much more equally divided for use, the kulak has been undermined and to a considerable extent expropriated—in Russia more than in the Ukraine, in Siberia' less so. But on the whole, the statistical data show beyond dispute that the village population has been levelled, equalised, *i.e.,* that the sharp extremes—the kulaks and the landless peasants— have been smoothed out."*

Lenin was fully alive to the difficulties of transforming the economics of petty peasant farming.

"Only the material base, technique, the application of tractors and machines to agriculture on a mass scale, electrification on a mass scale, can settle this question in relation to the small husbandman, and, so to speak, sanitise his whole psychology." **

However, for this purpose tremendous industrial development was necessary, whereas our industry at this time was producing less than 20 per cent of its pre-war output.

The restoration of industry was directly dependent on an increase in the agricultural resources of the country, and for this purpose it was necessary to satisfy the demands of the middle peasantry, to give them an incentive for work, for the present on the basis of their small individual farming.

The first and most important point of the resolution which was adopted by the Congress reads as follows:

"In order to ensure that farming be carried on in a more proper and regular manner on the basis of the agricultural producer being more free to dispose of his economic resources; in order to strengthen peasant farming and raise its productivity; and also for the purpose of fixing exactly the obligations of the agricultural producer to the state, the quotas as a method of state collections of food products, raw materials and fodder are to be replaced by a tax in kind."

This resolution did no more than outline the transition to the New Economic Policy, which did not yet exist in its more highly developed form. It was merely a question of allowing the peasants the opportunity to dispose of their surplus within the limits of so-called local trade. There was no talk as yet of removing the numerous special detachments which were stationed at all points on the railways to prevent the carrying of grain even in

* Lenin, "Report on the Food Tax," *Collected Works,* Vol. XXVI.
** *Ibid.*

small quantities from one district to another. There was no talk of a radical reconstruction of industry, of a stable currency.*
But the main lines of the N.E.P. had already been laid down in Lenin's report on the food tax at the Tenth Congress of the Party. The working class could build socialism only in the closest alliance with the peasant masses. The majority of the peasants were discontented with the form of relations between them and the working class which existed under the system of War Communism. The psychology of scores of millions of petty producers could not be transformed in the course of three years so that they would work exclusively for the public weal. It was necessary to give them an incentive, stimulating them thereby to produce more products. This incentive was the freedom to dispose of their grain surplus. By giving the middle peasant this incentive to improve his individual farming, the proletarian state power was not weakening but strengthening itself, as it was securing not only an improved condition in peasant farming but was also strengthening the political alliance of the working class with the peasantry.

By adopting the decision to substitute a tax in kind for the food quotas, the Congress took a big step forward towards establishing a form of inter-relations between the working class and the peasantry which, unlike War Communism, provided a real basis for socialist construction over a prolonged period in the country which had endured the ravages of the Civil War.

"The shortest possible period," said Lenin, "in which it would be possible so to organise large-scale industry that it might create a fund for the harnessing of agriculture is estimated at ten years. This is the shortest possible period, assuming unusually favourable technical conditions. But we know that we are situated in unusually unfavourable conditions.

"We have a plan for developing Russia on a basis of modern large-scale industry. This is the electrification plan which was drawn up by scientists. This plan establishes the minimum period at ten years."**

Despite the most unfavourable conditions, the working class, under the leadership of its Leninist Central Committee, has, within

* Preobrazhensky delivered a brief report at the Congress on the issue of silver money, but it was assumed that this would play an extremely insignificant part in exchange.
** Lenin, "Report on Party Unity and the Anarcho-Syndicalist Deviation," *Collected Works,* Vol. XXVI.

ten years after the launching of the New Economic Policy, succeeded not only in carrying out the electrification plan in the main
but also in securing a decisive and definite turn of the peasant
masses towards socialism, in building a foundation of socialist
economy, and in placing on the order of the day as an immediate
practical task the elimination of the capitalist elements and of
classes in general, the building of a classless socialist society.

Securing the Unity of the Party

The resolutions adopted by the Tenth Party Congress regarding Party unity and the anarcho-syndicalist deviation were of
tremendous importance. The appearance of this deviation in the
Party, as the Congress resolution stated, "was partly due to the
fact that elements who have not yet fully assimilated the Communist viewpoint have joined the ranks of the Party. But principally, this deviation was caused by the influence on the proletariat and on the R.C.P. of the petty-bourgeois environment,
which is exceptionally strong in our country and which inevitably
engenders vacillation towards anarchism, particularly at moments
when the condition of the masses has sharply deteriorated in
consequence of the crop failure and the disastrous effects of the
war and when the demobilisation of the huge army is releasing
hundreds and hundreds of thousands of workers and peasants
who cannot at once find employment and means of subsistence."

The resolution characterised the views of the "Workers' Opposition" and its theses and statements as a complete break with
Marxism and communism.

"Marxism teaches—and this teaching has not only been formally
endorsed by the whole Communist International in the decision of the
Second Congress of the Comintern on the role of the political party
of the proletariat, but has been practically tested by the whole experience of our revolution—that only the political party of the working
class, i.e., the Communist Party, can unite, train and organise such a
vanguard of the proletariat and of all the toiling masses as may be
able to resist the inevitable petty-bourgeois vacillations of these masses,
the traditions and inevitable recrudescence of craft narrow-mindedness
or craft prejudices among the proletariat and to guide all sides of the
proletarian movement, which means to guide all the toiling masses.
Without this, the dictatorship of the proletariat is inconceivable. The
incorrect understanding of the role of the Communist Party in its rela-

tion to the non-Party working masses, on the one hand, and the equally incorrect understanding of the role of the working class in its relation to the whole mass of toilers, on the other hand, represent a fundamental theoretical retreat from communism and a deviation towards syndicalism and anarchism, which deviation pervades all the views of the "Workers' Opposition."

The Congress declared the views of the "Workers' Opposition" to be an anarcho-syndicalist deviation, the defence of which was incompatible with membership in the R.C.P.*

Proceeding from the basic organisational principles of Bolshevism, and fully taking into account the grave situation in which the country and the Party then were, the Congress adopted a decision to secure firm unity within the Party, dissolving all factional groupings and prohibiting such groups in the future under the threat of expulsion from the Party. Moreover, the resolution of the Tenth Party Congress, in one point which was not made public, gave the Central Committee the right during the intervening periods between Congresses to reduce members of the Central Committee to the status of candidates and even to expel them from the Party, if they carried on factional politics, provided that two-thirds of the membership of the Central Committee voted for such action.** "We are going to put an end to opposition now, to put the lid on it; we have had enough of oppositions!" Lenin said at the opening of the Congress. In circumstances when the entire national economy was in a grave condition, when a considerable part of the proletariat had become declassed, when the discontent among the peasantry was breaking out in the form of counter-revolutionary banditry, what was

---

* How far the "Workers' Opposition" went in its criticism of the Party line at the Tenth Congress, to what extent the views of Shlyapnikov and his associates really were incompatible with membership in the R.C.P., is shown by the statements of the spokesmen of the "Workers' Opposition" at the Congress.

Shlyapnikov, discussing the report which was made by Lenin, stated that the causes of the discontent of the workers were to be sought for in the Kremlin. Milonov explained why the "Workers' Opposition" was accused of syndicalism as follows: "Comrade Lenin is the chairman, he directs our Soviet policy. It is evident that any movement, no matter where it comes from, which hinders this work of governing, is looked upon as a petty-bourgeois movement, as an extremely harmful movement."

** This point was subsequently made public in accordance with a decision adopted by the Thirteenth Party Conference.

demanded of the Party was the maximum degree of coherence, the maximum degree of unity, and this was what the Tenth Party Congress secured under the firm leadership of Lenin.

The Tax in Kind and Commodity Exchange

The Tenth Congress had begun the transition to the New Economic Policy. At first the peasants were only given the right to exchange their grain surplus, to utilise this surplus within the limits of local trade. Lenin was of the opinion that the state should receive part of the grain from the peasants in the form of a tax and that this part should be considerably smaller than what had been procured through the food quotas. Formerly the peasant had to surrender all the grain to the state at so-called fixed prices, except the part which he himself consumed. This was now changed. Part of the grain the peasants were to give to the state in the form of a tax, and another part the state was to procure from them in exchange for goods by means of so-called commodity exchange.

Lenin dealt with the question of the tax in kind and commodity exchange precisely in this fashion in the pamphlet *On the Tax in Kind* which was written after the Tenth Congress. But in the same pamphlet he wrote of the necessity of extending free trade beyond the limits of local exchange. On the basis of free trade, Lenin considered that, in view of the prevalence of petty peasant economy in the country, there would inevitably be a development of capitalist elements, which the Soviet government was interested in directing into the channels of state capitalism. The elements of state capitalism in our economy whose progressive character Lenin continued to emphasise, as compared with petty commodity production which lends itself with great difficulty to regulation, could be strengthened by attracting foreign capital into concessions. In his pamphlet *On the Tax in Kind* Lenin enumerated the following forms of state capitalism: Concessions, leased enterprises, private commission trade acting as intermediary between state and petty producers, petty-bourgeois co-operatives regulated by the state (Lenin specifically excepted the workers' co-operatives, stating that they cannot be included in the category of state capitalism). The development of capitalist elements in the countryside was a natural result of the development of commodity production, of commodity circulation on the basis of petty peasant farming.

The development of commodity production and of commodity circulation resulted in a real increase in the output of agriculture. This was also a primary condition for the restoration of large-scale industry, the main foundation of the proletarian dictatorship. Only through the restoration of large-scale industry and through its further development was it possible to turn the petty commodity production of small peasant farming onto the path of socialism.

Lenin warned the Party that the development of capitalist elements in our country might result in increased activity by the Mensheviks and Socialist-Revolutionaries, who pinned their hopes on the "political N.E.P." as they expressed it, *i.e.*, who were striving not only for a certain freedom of trade but also for freedom of the press and freedom of political activity for the bourgeoisie and the petty-bourgeoisie parties. Lenin said that the Socialist-Revolutionaries and Mensheviks had to be kept fast in prison. The transition to the N.E.P., coupled with the resultant economic concessions to the peasantry and the introduction of a limited freedom of trade was envisaged by Lenin as a means for strengthening the proletarian dictatorship, and for bringing increased pressure to bear on the part of the state apparatus of this dictatorship on the politically hostile elements.

The question of commodity exchange became the central question discussed at the next Party Conference, held in the end of May 1921.

The Tenth Party Conference

The Tenth Party Conference had to be called almost immediately after the Congress because it was necessary, on the basis of the general propositions contained in the decisions of the Tenth Congress, to outline concretely the course to be taken by the New Economic Policy, to ensure that all sections of the Party fully understood and appreciated the necessity of the turn effected by the Tenth Congress and definitely to implant in the minds of the Party forces the idea which Lenin had expressed in his closing speech at the Tenth Conference—that the New Economic

Policy was to be enforced *in earnest and for a long time, although not forever*. The Tenth Party Conference, at which Lenin reported in behalf of the Central Committee of the Party on the new tasks of the Soviet government in the economic field, adopted a decision to the effect that six and a half million tons of grain which the Soviet government had to have to satisfy the needs of the army, the government apparatus and industry, was to be raised in part by means of the tax in kind (about four million tons) while the rest was to be procured by means of commodity exchange. The role of intermediary between the state and the peasantry in commodity exchange was to be played by the co-operatives, which had been turned into a state organisation during the period of War Communism, but which by a decision of the Tenth Congress again became, not a state, but only a public organisation.

In his report at the Tenth Party Conference, Lenin strongly emphasised that the measures of the New Economic Policy adopted by the Party were in the interests of socialist industry, and of the working class, in the interests of strengthening the proletarian dictatorship.

"An error, a delusion has been produced among the comrades, who fail to understand why the chief attention must now be paid to the peasantry. Some workers complain: They are allowing the peasants certain favours, but giving us nothing. Such talk has been heard, and it should be said that such talk is, I believe, not so very widespread; for it must be said that such talk is dangerous, as it reflects the Social-ist-Revolutionaries' approach to the question. There is clear evidence here of political provocation and, besides this, of the remains of the workers' craft prejudices—not class prejudices but trade-unionist ones —when the working class regards itself as one part of capitalist socie-ty with equal rights, unconscious of the fact that it continues to take its stand on the same capitalist basis as before: 'They've granted the peasant favours, released him from the quotas, given him the right to exchange the free part of his surplus; and we, the workers, stick at our jobs and we want to have the same . . . .'

"What is the basis of this viewpoint? The same essentially petty-bourgeois ideology. Inasmuch as the peasants form a component part of capitalist society, the working class also remains a component part of this society. Hence, if the peasant engages in trade, we should also engage in trade. In this the old prejudices which rivet the worker to the old world are undoubtedly reviving." *

* Lenin, "Report on the Tax in Kind," *Collected Works*, Vol. XXVI.

It was one of the most important tasks of the Party to fight these prejudices, to fight the petty-bourgeois state of mind among the working class. But in order to effect this task, in order to protect the working class from becoming diffused and declassed, it was necessary to concentrate the food supplies in the hands of the state, to promote agricultural production.

"Without concentrating large stores of food in the hands of the state, the restoration of industry is out of the question," said Lenin.*

"At present," said Lenin in closing the Conference, "we are exercising our main influence on the international revolution by our economic policy. All eyes are turned on the Soviet Russian Republic, all the toilers in all countries of the world, without exception and without any exaggeration. That has been achieved. The capitalists cannot hush up or screen anything; that is why they are all the more ready to seize upon our economic mistakes and our weakness. The struggle on this field is now being waged on a world scale. If we solve this problem, then we shall have won on an international scale for certain and finally." **

The Slogan "Learn How to Trade"

In the task of organising commodity exchange, the Soviet government did not achieve the expected results. This was due partly to the organisational weakness of the co-operatives, partly to the famine of 1921, partly to the shortage of commodities in the hands of the organisations which were carrying on commodity exchange. The chief reason was the organisational weakness of the co-operatives, which were not capable of any flexibility in manoeuvring with the commodities at their disposal. Besides this, the very serious crop failure in 1921 dealt a severe blow at a number of grain producing districts (the Volga region and part of the Ukraine). The amount of grain obtained by means of commodity exchange was very small and proved quite insufficient for the needs of the state.

But the same crop failure also caused a considerable decrease in the total raised through the tax in kind. What recourse was left to the mills and factories which the state could not supply with a sufficient quantity of bread? The bread which could not be obtained by means of organised exchange, through the medium

* *Ibid*
** Lenin, "Concluding Speech at the All-Russian Conference of the R.C.P.," *Collected Works*, Vol. XXVI.

of the state, had to be procured either through direct exchange of the products of the particular enterprise or through purchasing with money. This still further enhanced the importance of money and of the monetary system—a point which had already been noted by Lenin at the Tenth Congress. With the aid of money, by means of purchase and sale, even with the unstable and depreciated Soviet ruble, the state industry managed to procure an amount of bread which somehow just sufficed to supply the workers employed in state enterprises.

But the state procured this bread with money. Individual enterprises could also procure bread with money. The workers at these enterprises could get it on the market for money. The enterprises had to get this money by selling their products. The workers, who were at first paid with a ration or with part of the products of their enterprise, had to take these products to the market and sell them, and to buy bread with money. Later, the workers began to get their pay directly in the form of money.

This produced a number of practical problems for the further development of the New Economic Policy. First of all, the question of creating a stable monetary unit, which had already been considered at the Tenth Congress, now became even more acute. To be sure, the legalisation of the market immediately raised the demand for currency and this resulted in a certain stabilisation of the ruble. But its real value was gradually approaching the value of the paper which was marked with the words "million," or "billion." This depreciation of the ruble made it difficult to establish anything like normal commodity exchange. In the villages the ruble was accepted with great reluctance. The Soviet government was thus compelled to undertake the task of creating a stable ruble.

But the stable ruble could be established only as a result of putting an end to the currency emissions, on the basis of a balanced budget and of the radical reorganisation of the entire industry, which would have to adopt a strict system of business accounting or of paying its own way.

Hence the efforts of the Soviet government to establish a stable monetary unit in the country, together with a correct budget in which the revenues and expenditures were exactly fixed. Hence the fact that the enterprises were transferred to the system of business accounting, and hence the new slogan which Lenin addressed to the Communists, to the members of the Party, in the autumn of 1921—"Learn how to trade." The correlation between the main elements of the economy of the country under the conditions of the N.E.P. was already taking shape: On the one hand, state industry which was beginning to produce for the market, and the petty commodity production of peasant farming; and on the other hand, the capitalist elements which took their rise from the latter, private trade which attempted to establish itself as an intermediary between state industry and the peasantry. The elements of socialism and the elements of capitalism were thus struggling with each other on the arena of the market. And the question of which would down the other could no longer be settled merely by physical force. This made it necessary for the Party to adapt itself as far as possible to the new situation, to master methods of controlling the market, to learn how to trade.

"The whole question is, who will come in first? If the capitalists succeed in organising first, they will drive out the Communists, and that's all there is to it. We must confront these facts soberly—Who will defeat whom? Or the proletarian state power, relying on the peasantry, will prove capable of holding Messieurs the Capitalists properly in check in order to direct capitalism into state channels and to create a capitalism subordinated to the state and serving it." *

"We should not count on a direct transition to communism. We should build on the basis of the personal interests of the peasantry. We are told, 'the personal interest of the peasant means the restoration of private property.' No, private ownership of objects of consumption and of implements, this we have never infringed upon with regard to the peasantry. We have abolished the private ownership of land. The peasant has carried on farming without private ownership of the land, as for instance on rented land. This system has existed in very many countries. There is nothing economically impossible in this. The difficulty is in developing personal interest. We must also provide an incentive for every specialist in order to get him interested in developing production.

"Have we been able to do this? No, we have not! We believed that merely by virtue of the Communists giving orders, production and distribution would be carried on in a country with a declassed prole-

* Lenin, "The New Economic Policy and Tasks of Political Instructors," *Collected Works*, Vol. XXVII.

tariat .... Never before in history have such tasks had to be tackled. If we attempted to carry out this task directly, by a frontal attack as it were, then we suffered a defeat. Such errors occur in every war and they are not considered as errors. Since the frontal attack has failed, we will turn the flank, we will use the methods of siege and sapping." *

"Transition to the New Economic Policy which was started in the spring—this retreat of ours to the ways, means and methods of action of state capitalism—has it proved sufficient for us to stop the retreat and already begin preparing for an offensive? No, it has not yet proved sufficient .... We now find ourselves in circumstances where we must execute a further slight retreat, not only to state capitalism, but also to state regulation of trade and of money circulation. Only by this path, which is even longer than we had supposed, can we restore our economic life. The restoration of a correct system of economic relations, the restoration of petty peasant farming, the restoration of large-scale industry, and the task of raising it up on our own shoulders. Without this we will not get out of the crisis." **

"After the retreat which we had to execute in the spring of 1921 from socialist construction [Lenin has in mind War Communism— N.P.] to state capitalism, we see that an immediate question is that of the regulation of trade and money circulation. No matter how far removed from communism the field of trade may seem to us, it is nevertheless precisely in this field that we are confronted with a peculiar problem. Only after solving this problem will we be able to set about meeting the economic needs which are absolutely pressing, and only in this way can we secure the possibility of restoring large-scale industry by a longer but more certain path, which is at present the only path open to us." ***

Thus Lenin spoke in the autumn of 1921 in his reports delivered at the All-Russian Congress of Political Instructors and at the Party Conference of the Moscow province.

"We shall endeavour to determine our tasks on this new, higher stage of the struggle with supreme, with threefold circumspection. We shall fix these tasks as modestly as possible. We shall make more concessions, of course within the bounds of what the proletarian *can* concede while remaining the dominant class. The quickest possible collection of a moderate tax in kind and the utmost possible freedom for the development, strengthening and restoration of peasant farming. We shall lease out those enterprises, which are not absolutely essential, to contractors, including private capitalists and foreign concessionaires. We must have a *bloc* or an alliance of the proletarian state with state

* *Ibid.*
** Lenin, "The New Economic Policy," *Collected Works*, Vol. XXVII.
*** *Ibid.*

capitalism against the petty-bourgeois anarchic forces. This alliance must be effected skilfully, according to the rule: 'Measure your cloth seven times before you cut it.' We shall leave the smallest possible field of work directly for ourselves, only what is absolutely essential. We shall concentrate the weakened forces of the working class on a *smaller* field, but we shall consolidate our position the more firmly, check up the results of our work on the basis of practical experience not once or twice but many times. Step by step, inch by inch—in any other way such an 'army' as ours *cannot* at present move forward over so difficult a road, in such a difficult situation, in the face of such dangers. Whoever considers such work as 'tedious,' 'uninteresting,' 'incomprehensible,' whoever turns up his nose or becomes panicky, or finds himself ranting about the lack of 'the former *elan*,' of 'the former enthusiasm,' etc., such persons had better be 'relieved of their duties' and shelved, so that they may not be able to do any damage, for they either do not desire or are unable to give thought to the peculiarity of the present stage, of the present phase of the struggle." *

The International Situation and the Third Congress of the Comintern

Our retreat within the country coincided with a serious change in the situation in the surrounding capitalist countries. A certain lull had set in after the tremendous upsurge of the revolutionary wave in those countries. The bourgeoisie had coped with the difficulties of demobilising the army and of restoring industry to peace-time production, and had suppressed the revolutionary action of the workers in individual countries. In March 1921, the German bourgeoisie, supported by Social-Democracy and the reformist trade unions, suppressed the uprising of the Communist vanguard of the proletariat. In a number of countries the bourgeoisie developed an offensive against the working class.

A certain equilibrium was established between the forces of revolution and of counter-revolution on an international scale, between the forces of the bourgeoisie and the proletariat, of the Soviet power and the capitalist countries. In this equilibrium as Lenin declared at the Third Congress of the Communist International which was held in July 1921,

"the chief support of capitalism in the industrially developed capitalist countries is precisely that part of the working class which is organ-

* Lenin, "New Times, the Old Mistakes in a New Form," *Collected Works*, Vol. XXVII.

ised in the Second and the Two-and-a-Half Internationals. If it [the bourgeoisie—N.P.] did not have the support of this part of the working class, of the counter-revolutionary elements within the working class, the international bourgeoisie would be absolutely unable to maintain its power." *

In view of this, the Third Congress of the Comintern declared it to be the militant task of all Communist Parties to win over the majority of the proletariat by methods of persistent everyday work. In its decisions, the Third Congress repudiated the centrist vacillations in individual parties, which became more pronounced as a result of the suppression of the revolutionary movement, as a result of the strengthening of the power of the bourgeoisie and of a certain improvement in the economic situation following the crisis in the post-war period. The Congress approved the expulsion from the Communist Party of Germany of the Levi group, which, in renegade fashion, accused the Party leaders of "putschism" because they had placed themselves at the head of the revolutionary uprising of the German workers in March. The Congress approved the firm enforcement of the twenty-one conditions, a policy which was directed against centrist and semi-centrist elements; this applied particularly to Italy, where a group of leaders of the former Socialist Party headed by Serrati refused to expel the reformists, thus obliging the revolutionary elements to split off and form a separate party. The Congress at the same time dealt a resolute blow at the "Left" sectarian attitude which found its expression in the inability or refusal to draw the necessary conclusions from the new changed situation, in a tendency to underestimate the work in trade unions, in elevating into a principle the tactic of an offensive under all conditions, in denying the necessity of winning over the broad masses of the Social-Democratic workers to the side of the Communist Parties. This attitude was reflected at the Congress in the speeches of some of the delegates from Germany, Poland, Italy and other countries.

Following a special report by Lenin, the Congress unreservedly approved the tactics of the R.C.P. as expressed in the transition to the New Economic Policy, recognising that this transi-

* Lenin, "Report on the Tactics of the R.C.P.," *Collected Works*, Vol. XXVI.

tion was calculated to preserve and strengthen the Soviet power in Russia, whose interests were closely linked up with those of the revolution on an international scale.

The adoption of this resolution was of great significance for the workers of capitalist countries, among whom the Social-Democrats were busily spreading the demagogic yarn that the transition to the N.E.P. signified a repudiation of communism, a surrender of the revolutionary positions, a putting on of the brakes and the restoration of the power of the bourgeoisie.

The fundamental idea running through all the decisions of the Third Congress is that of rallying the great masses of the working class around the Communist Parties.

Along with this, Lenin, in his report on the tactics of the R.C.P. stressed the great importance for the coming battles with imperialism not only of the revolutionary movement in the advanced capitalist countries but of the movement in the colonies as well.

"The movement in the colonies is still regarded as an insignificant national movement of a perfectly peaceful character. But this is not so. Since the beginning of the twentieth century great changes have occurred in this respect, namely, millions and hundreds of millions—in fact the vast majority of the population of the globe—are now coming forward as independent, active, revolutionary factors. And it is perfectly clear that in the coming decisive battles of the world revolution the movement of the majority of the world's population, aiming at first at national liberation, will turn against capitalism and imperialism, and will perhaps play a much greater revolutionary role than we expect. It is important to stress the fact that for the first time in our International we have approached the task of preparing for this struggle. Of course, in this vast field the difficulties are much greater, but at any rate the movement is going forward, and the masses of the toilers, the peasants of the colonial countries, in spite of the fact that they are still backward, will play a very great revolutionary role in the subsequent phases of the world revolution." *

The Executive Committee of the Comintern, developing the points made by Lenin and the decisions of the Third Congress of the Comintern, drafted theses on the tactics of the united front of the working class, and these theses were also adopted by the Eleventh Conference of our Party.

The theses were a logical development of the decisions of

* *Ibid.*

10*

the Third Congress of the Communist International, which set the Communist Parties of Western Europe the task of waging a prolonged day-to-day struggle to win over the majority of the working class in each country. The Eleventh Party Conference recommended the Communist International to accomplish this task by means of the united front of the working class, *i.e.*, by uniting the broad working masses, irrespective of what organisation they might adhere to, around popular slogans, comprehensible to them, for the defence of the elementary political and economic interests of the working class.

In this way, by means of concrete examples, the Communist Parties of Western Europe could expose the Social-Democrats in the eyes of the working masses who still followed them, and show that the Social-Democrats were incapable of defending the most elementary interests of the proletariat. Owing to the delay in the coming of the world revolution, the Communist Parties of the West were confronted with the task of fighting to win over the majority of the working class in their countries by means of slow, persistent work.

The Executive Committee of the Comintern and the Eleventh Conference of our Party deemed it possible to effect this tactic of the united working class front on one condition of struggle—a *sine qua non* condition, namely, the "absolute and complete independence of the Communist Parties" and a relentless struggle on two fronts against opportunist errors and distortions of the tactic of the united front in their own ranks. The theses of the E.C.C.I. and of the Eleventh Conference specifically indicated two possible tendencies, manifestations of which had already appeared in the sections of the Comintern: the tendency on the part of "impatient or sectarian-minded Left elements" to reject or to narrow the base of the united front tactics, and the tendency on the part of Right elements to "diffuse the Communist Parties and groups in an amorphous united *bloc*." A relentless struggle against these tendencies was called for as an absolutely essential part of the struggle for the Leninist tactics of the united working class front.

*The Eleventh Party Conference and the All-Russian Verification
of Party Membership*

In the autumn of 1921, the main tasks which confronted the
Party for economic restoration under the conditions of the N.E.P.
began to take definite shape. The Eleventh Party Conference,
which met at the end of 1921, outlined these tasks. The most
important among them were to establish a stable money system,
a balanced budget, and cost accounting in all enterprises, radically to cut down the staff of the Soviet apparatus, to extend freedom
of trade within the country under state control and to lease out
some of the state enterprises—the small and middle-sized ones—
to private capitalists, co-operatives, etc.

The Soviet government had thus executed a retreat to conditions of money commodity circulation, to conditions of free trade
under state control; it had abandoned the idea of an all-embracing
organisation of production, distribution and consumption.

But the Eleventh Party Conference also defined the limits
of the retreat and pointed out the key positions which were to
be retained at all costs in the hands of the Soviet government.
Retaining these positions in their hands, consolidating them in
every way, the Party and the Soviet government set themselves
the task of preparing for an offensive on the basis of the N.E.P.
The Eleventh Party Conference recognised as such key positions
the nationalisation of the land, of large-scale industry, of transport and of credit and the monopoly of foreign trade. The
nationalisation of the land, of large-scale industry and of transport constituted the principal achievements of the October Revolution. The economic power of the proletarian state was based
upon them. Credit assumed exceptional importance in view of the
transition to cost accounting. The monopoly of foreign trade
was recognised as one of the key positions, ensuring that our
state industry, which was slowly gaining strength, should not be
placed in a position where it would have free competition with
the industry of the stronger capitalist countries, ensuring our
economy from being dominated by that of capitalism.

In connection with the verification and purging of the Party
membership, the Eleventh Party Conference adopted a decision
on the consolidation of the Party. The all-Russian purging of

the Party which the Central Committee ordered in the summer of 1921, in accordance with a decision of the Tenth Party Conference, had only just been concluded. The aim of the purging was to rid the Party of the numerous alien elements which had succeeded in penetrating into its ranks. The Eighth Congress had already introduced certain restrictions with regard to joining the Party, which were designed to keep out these alien elements. But the presence of alien class elements in the Party was particularly dangerous under the conditions of the New Economic Policy, at a time of the economic revival of the petty bourgeoisie and of the capitalist elements who exercised an influence over individual links of the Party.

The Communist Party was now in need of even greater solidarity, discipline and unity, and the situation demanded of the Party membership even more political stamina and capacity to find their bearings in their environment than had been the case in the past. Lenin wrote:

"The Party must be purged of swindlers, of bureaucratised elements, of dishonest people, of unstable Communists and of Mensheviks who have camouflaged their 'facade' but remained Mensheviks at heart."

Two hundred thousand members—almost one third of the Party membership, if we reckon that 730,000 members were represented at the Tenth Party Congress—were eliminated from the Party. It is true, however, that certain excesses were committed during the purging in the provinces.

The Tenth Party Congress had already rendered entrance into the Party considerably more difficult for non-proletarian elements. The Eleventh Party Conference decided that no new members should be accepted into the Party until the next Party Congress. The Conference allowed exceptions only in the case of "workers and peasants who have proved their devotion to the revolution during the Civil War and who have manifested a conscious attitude towards communism."

The Eleventh Party Congress

The Eleventh Party Congress met at the end of March 1922.* This was the last occasion when Lenin delivered the report on

* There were 687 delegates at the Congress, 522 with a decisive vote and 165 with a consultative vote.

behalf of the Central Committee. In his report, Lenin first of all declared that the economic retreat, which we had commenced after the Tenth Congress, was now at an end. We had to set about effecting a re-grouping of forces on the new positions and to entrench ourselves in these positions. Lenin urgently raised the question of the necessity of establishing an alliance with the peasantry by means of organising the industry and the trading apparatus, of securing under the new conditions of peaceful construction a strengthening of the political alliance between the working class and the peasantry which had existed in the period of the Civil War, when the peasants supported the working class as the only class that was capable of liberating them from the landlords. This political alliance now had to be strengthened on a new basis, on the basis of an economic alliance with the peasantry. Either our Party would succeed in establishing an alliance with the peasantry, or the peasantry would turn away from us if it became convinced of our inability to organise the economy of the country. The peasant would now have to decide which power would be of greater advantage to him, which power would give him more—the Soviet power or the bourgeois. The peasant would now have to make his choice. and the choice of the peasant would depend on the successful economic policy of the Soviet government.

"To link up with the mass of the peasantry, the rank and file working peasantry, and to begin to move forward immeasurably, infinitely, more slowly than we ever dreamed, but in such a way that the whole mass will really move forward with us. Then, in time, this movement will begin to accelerate at such a rate as we cannot even dream of at present."

While urging the Party to a slow but unswerving advance together with the mass of the peasantry, Lenin had already foreseen even at that time a tremendous acceleration of our movement in the future.

This acceleration could not come of its own accord. Clearly perceiving the economic consequences of the N.E.P., Lenin foresaw the growth of the capitalist elements, particularly in the countryside, who would carry on a fierce struggle against the Soviet government for the restoration of capitalism. And that is why Lenin at the Eleventh Party Congress spoke of the forth-coming "last decisive battle,"

"not with international capitalism—there we still have many 'last and decisive battles'—no, but with Russian capitalism, with the capitalism which grows out of petty peasant economy, the capitalism which is supported by it. Here a battle is coming in the near future, the date of which cannot be determined exactly." *

Lenin at the same time laid full stress upon the question of the influence exercised on our state apparatus by elements which were alien and hostile to the working class, of their attempts to force it to serve their interests.

"The machine is getting out of hand. It is as if someone were sitting and directing it, but the machine does not move in the direction into which it is guided, but in a direction into which it is guided by somebody, by some lawless, illegal force coming from heaven knows where, by speculators or private capitalists, or by both of these.... The machine does not move quite in the same way—often not at all in the same way—as the person who sits at the wheel of this machine imagines.

"....The contest, the competition, which we placed on the order of the day when we proclaimed the N.E.P. is a serious contest.... It is one more form of the struggle between two classes which are irreconcilably hostile to each other. It is one more form of the struggle between the bourgeoisie and the proletariat. It is a struggle which has not yet been completed, a struggle in which we lag behind them in the sense of culture even in the central institutions in Moscow.

"For it often happens that the bourgeois functionaries know the business better than our best Communists who have all the power and all the opportunities and who with all their rights and with all their power have not been able to advance one single step."**

Here already we may find all the elements of that attitude to the questions of training skilled workers and of mastering technique which was later taken by the Party under the leadership of Comrade Stalin.

Lenin noted that part of the bourgeoisie had changed its tactics, had abandoned the policy of smashing the Soviet government and taken the course of collaborating with it, its ultimate object being to bring about the degeneration in the Soviet govern-

* Lenin, "Political Report of the Central Committee at the Eleventh Congress of the R.C.P.," *Collected Works*, Vol. XXVII.
** *Ibid.*

ment. Lenin spoke of the *"Smenavekh"** tendency, which had shortly before appeared on the scene, of the Ustryalovs who contended that the Soviet government was becoming transformed into an ordinary bourgeois government. While sounding a warning against this danger, Lenin at the same time emphasised that the Party could not abandon the policy of utilising even alien and hostile elements, that it had to find sufficient strength within itself to force them to serve 'the cause of the construction of communism.

"To build up a communist society with the hands of the Communist is a childish, an absolutely childish idea. The Communists are a drop in the ocean, a drop in the ocean of the people. They will only be able to lead the people along their path, if they correctly define this path not only in the sense of a universal historical direction .... We will not be able to direct the national economy, unless the Communists are able to build this economy with other people's hands, unless they themselves learn from this bourgeoisie and direct them along the path they desire." **

Lenin also spoke at the Congress of the organisation of mixed companies into which domestic and foreign private capital was to be attracted. By March 1922, when the Congress met, seventeen such companies had been formed. "There are not many of them," Lenin said. "This small but practical beginning shows that the Communists have met with appreciation, with appreciation from the standpoint of their practical work." The organisation of mixed companies and the attraction of investments by Russian and foreign capitalists, although on a comparatively small scale, into these companies, helped in some degree to restore our industry during that period.

The Eleventh Congress adopted new theses regarding the trade unions—a logical sequence from the New Economic Policy and from the transition of industrial enterprises to the system of cost accounting. Our Party did not adopt the course of investing the trade unions with administrative functions, the course which was urged upon it by Trotsky and the "Workers' Opposition." Quite the reverse, it chose the path of completely relieving

* *Smenavekh,* see pp. 169-70.
** Lenin, Political Report of the Central Committee at the Eleventh Congress of the R.C.P.," *Collected Works,* Vol. XXVII.

the trade unions of administrative duties and of concentrating such duties in the hands of the business organisations, in order that the trade unions, while helping in every way to increase labour productivity and improve the organisation of production by means of educating the working masses, might at the same time systematically defend the interests of the working class against bureaucratic distortions to be met with in the state apparatus and its economic organs, and help to improve the general living conditions of the workers in every respect. The theses adopted by the Eleventh Congress introduced voluntary membership in the trade unions, instead of the virtually obligatory membership which existed before.

The Eleventh Party Congress raised the question of the financial tasks of the Soviet government. In the days of War Communism, the People's Commissariat of Finance had occupied one of the least honoured places in the system of Soviet commissariats. Paper money was steadily declining in value. Money wages were gradually being replaced by wages paid in kind. In his booklet on the question of paper money which was published at the end of 1920, Preobrazhensky wrote that we would soon give up using paper money altogether. But as a result of the transition to the New Economic Policy, the reverse occurred. Paper money, in spite of its continued depreciation, was assuming ever greater importance in the economic life of the Soviet state and of its citizens. The Soviet government had to set about creating a stable unit of currency. For this it had to stop the issue of currency and to make sure that the money which the state expended was received back by it in the form of taxes and through the proceeds of industry, in order to balance the revenue and the expenditure side of the state budget.

The Congress recognised that "the chief measures of financial policy at the present time (including the currency reform) are, firstly, an increase in the volume of commodity circulation, above all through the development of trade both foreign and domestic —state, co-operative and private trade; and, secondly, the reduction and later the elimination of the deficit in the budget, the balancing of the budget by cutting down state expenditures and increasing the state revenues."

*The Struggle Against the Remnants of the "Workers'
Opposition"*

The Eleventh Congress adopted a decision regarding certain members of the former "Workers' Opposition" (Shlyapnikov, Medvedev, Kollontai and others). Although the Tenth Congress had decided that all factions must be dissolved, including the "Workers' Opposition," nevertheless certain members of the latter disregarded this decision and continued to maintain their factional organisation, this time illegally. The practical result of this was that at the Fourth Congress of Trade Unions a considerable number of the Communist delegates who were followers of the "Workers' Opposition" created a very difficult situation for the leadership of the Congress. In spite of the instructions of the Central Committee of the Party, the All-Russian Congress of Metal Workers went so far as to elect a purely factional Central Committee of their Union, composed exclusively of followers of the "Workers' Opposition." The Central Committee of the Party immediately dissolved this committee. The members of the "Workers' Opposition" continued to maintain secret correspondence with one another, continued to maintain factional contact for the purpose of spreading their anti-Party views which had been condemned by the Tenth Party Congress. The fact that they persisted in these views was particularly dangerous for the Party at a time when it was effecting the transition to the N.E.P., when the development of private trade and the outward manifestations of inequality, coupled with the hardships of the workers, provided a certain basis for demagogic criticism and for spreading disintegration in the Party. Meantime, the enemies continued to pin all their hopes on a split in the Party. All the White Guard newspapers wrote that a split in the Communist Party would mean a death blow to the Soviet government.

In the beginning of 1922 a group of twenty-two former members of the "Workers' Opposition," headed by Shlyapnikov, Kollontai and S. Medvedev, submitted a memorandum to the Comintern in which they reiterated the theses of their old platform which had been condemned by the Tenth Congress, declaring that the R.C.P. was carrying on a policy which was alien to the interests of the working class, that the Central Committee was suppressing the Party ,etc. This memorandum provided welcome material to all enemies of the Soviet government, to all anti-Communist elements, to the Second International. It compelled the Eleventh Party Congress to consider very seriously the question of the activities which some members of the former "Workers' Opposition" were carrying on within the Party.*

At the Congress, Shlyapnikov, Kollontai and Medvedev tried to defend their anti-Party memorandum, claiming that the Central Committee had become isolated from the working class, that it was paying quite insufficient attention to our industry and concerning itself more about the peasantry than about the working class. While hesitating to attack the N.E.P. directly, the representatives of the "Workers' Opposition" nevertheless contended that the Party was forced to retreat and to make concessions only because it had become isolated from the working class and did not enjoy its support.

This insolent Menshevik slander against the Party by the former leaders of the dissolved faction of the "Workers' Opposition" caused general indignation and was unanimously repudiated by the Congress.

The resolution on the report of the Central Committee, which was proposed by the representatives of the "Workers' Opposition" at the Congress, did not receive a single vote.

The commission appointed by the Eleventh Congress, upon examining the material regarding the factional activity of the former members of the "Workers Opposition," recommended that Comrades Shlyapnikov, Kollontai and Medvedev, the three comrades who had organised the submission of the memorandum of twenty-two, be expelled from the Party. The Congress decided to let them remain in the Party, but gave them a final warning. Two of those who signed the memorandum (Kuznetsov, who proved to be a former merchant, and Mitin, an old Menshevik who joined the Party in 1920) were expelled. These decisions of the Eleventh Congress were a crushing blow to the factional

* Myasnikov, one of those who signed the memorandum and who went so far that he adyocated freedom of press for all—from the monarchists to the anarchists—had already been expelled before the Eleventh Party Congress.

activity which had been carried on by certain members of the
former "Workers' Opposition." From that time on, this activity
gradually died out, as the last remnants of its former members
broke with the "Workers' Opposition." However, a tiny group
of its leaders continued to organise fresh sallies against the
Party. *

The Eleventh Congress adopted a number of other important decisions on questions of Party organisational and Party
educational work in connection with the final results of the All-
Russian verification and purging of the Party, introducing a
number of new restrictions against the entrance into the Party
of not purely proletarian elements (increasing the number of
Party members required to recommend the applicant, establishing a minimum length of Party membership for those who have
a right to recommend applicants and requiring that admittance
into the Party be approved by higher Party organisations).

The First Results of the New Economic Policy

The Party had to carry out the New Economic Policy,
particularly the first steps of this policy, under extremely difficult conditions. It was extremely difficult to extricate the
country all at once from the severe crisis in which it found
itself, no matter what measures were taken. It was only very
slowly and gradually that the conditions of the working class
improved.

In 1921, the first year of the New Economic Policy, our
country suffered from a very bad harvest. Nevertheless, in his
report at the Congress of Political Instructors, delivered in
November, Lenin was already able to note a definite improvement
in the economic situation of the peasants and simultaneously
an improvement in the state of political feeling among them.
At the time of the Tenth Congress tens of thousands of persons

* It was just at this time that Shlyapnikov began to specialise in writing
slanderous anti-Party memoirs of the Revolution of 1917, and to smuggle
into these memoirs his anarcho-syndicalist views which had been condemned
by the Party, revising a number of programmatic theses of the Party in a
Menshevik-syndicalist spirit and attempting in every way to besmirch the
Party and its leadership. The Party forced Shlyapnikov to admit the slanderous character of his "memoirs."

were participating in political banditry, and this state of things did not disappear all at once. Not until the summer of 1924 was it possible, with great difficulty, to crush the widespread insurrection in the Tambov province which is known under the name of the "Antonov Insurrection" and which was headed by the kulaks and Right Socialist-Revolutionaries.

On August 15, 1921, according to the data of the general staff, there were still fifteen political bands in the region of the western front, including as many as 3,000 bandits. In Western Ukraine, there were 3,260 bandits; in Eastern Ukraine, about 1,500; in the Orlov military district (covering the present Central Black Soil Region), about 1,600; and on the territory of the Northern Caucasus about 4,000 bandits—the total number of bandits in all districts being calculated at 20,000.

These figures refer to August 15, 1921, when only a few months had elapsed since the transition to the New Economic Policy.

The slogan of the Kronstadt rebellion—"Soviets without Communists"—the slogan which figured in almost all of the actions of kulak banditry in that period—was the political banner of the petty-bourgeois anarchic forces which were fighting against the Soviet government and which were headed by the kulaks. Behind these petty-bourgeois anarchic forces loomed the restoration of capitalism.

"When Martov," Lenin wrote, "declares in his Berlin journal that Kronstadt not only put forward Menshevik slogans but even furnished proof that an anti-Bolshevik movement was possible which did not completely serve the White Guards, capitalists and landlords, this is just an example of the self-adoration of a petty-bourgeois Narcissus. Let us simply shut our eyes to the fact that all real White Guards welcomed the Kronstadtites and collected funds through the banks to aid Kronstadt! Milyukov is right, unlike the Chernovs and the Martovs, because he betrays the *real* tactics of the *real* White Guard forces, the forces of the capitalists and landlords: let us support anybody, even the anarchists, let us support any kind of Soviet power, *if only* the Bolsheviks are overthrown, *if only a shifting of power* takes place! It does not matter whether to the Right or to the Left, to the Mensheviks or to the anarchists, if only the power is shifted from the Bolsheviks. The rest 'we,' the Milyukovs, 'we,' the capitalists anl landlords, will do 'ourselves.' As for the anarchists, the Chernovs and Martovs, we will chase them away with a few smacks as was done in Siberia with

Chernov and Maisky, as was done in Hungary with the Hungarian Chernovs and Martovs, as was done in Germany with Kautsky and in Vienna with Friedrich Adler and Co. Such petty-bourgeois Narcissi-Mensheviks, Socialist-Revolutionaries and non-Partyites · have been fooled and driven out scores of times in hundreds, in all revolutions in all countries, by the real business-like bourgeoisie. . . . This has been proven by history. This has been verified by facts. The Narcissi will babble. The Milyukovs and the White Guards will act.

"Provided the power is shifted from the Bolsheviks, no matter whether it goes slightly to the Right or slightly to the Left, the rest will adjust itself. In this Milyukov is perfectly right. This is the class truth, corroborated by the whole history of the revolutions in all countries, by the entire centuries-long epoch of modern history since the Middle Ages. The scattered petty producers, the peasantry, can be united economically *and politically* either by the bourgeoisie (as always happened under capitalism in all countries, in all revolutions of modern times, and as will always happen under capitalism) or by the proletariat (as has occurred in embryonic form for the shortest space of time at the highest point of development of some of the greatest revolutions in modern history, and as has occurred in Russia in a more developed form in 1917-21). Only the self-adoring Narcissi can babble and dream of a 'third' path, of a 'third force.' " *

Gradually, as a result of systematic measures taken by the Soviet government, as a result of the improved situation of the peasantry and the working class and the better state of feeling prevailing among them, an end was put to banditry on the basis of the political isolation of the kulak. The position of the Soviet government was becoming ever more stable and firm.

The Party After the Transition to the N.E.P.

During the Civil War, and more especially after its termination, there was a tremendous increase in the numerical strength of the Party. While on the eve of the October Revolution the membership of the Party was not quite 300,000, at the Tenth Congress, in March 1921, almost 750,000 members were represented. The overwhelming majority of the Party membership on the eve of October was composed of actual workers in industry and of soldiers. After the October Revolution, the composition of the Party membership underwent a considerable change. After the winning of power, scores of thousands of worker members

* Lenin, "On the Food Tax," *Collected Works*, Vol. XXVI.

of the Party were taken away from their work to enter the army or the Soviet apparatus. These were unquestionably the best and most devoted workers who had the greatest influence among the masses. The contact between the Party and the proletarian masses who remained at work in industry was thereby weakened. Moreover, thousands of old Party members from the working class, the Red Army and the intelligentsia perished as victims of the Civil War, of epidemics and of famine.

The longer the war and famine continued, the greater were the ravages which they wrought in the ranks of the Party. Meanwhile the great mass of new members who joined the Party, though consisting of honest revolutionaries, or workers and peasants who were profoundly devoted to the cause of the revolution, were politically immature, inexperienced, untempered in long struggle, prone to commit errors and to fall a prey to demagogy.

The Party, while it continued to receive recruits from the working class, at the same time absorbed a vast number of non-proletarian elements. Along with peasants and farm labourers. elements from among the urban petty-bourgeoisie were also pouring into the Party.

As long as the Civil War continued, Party membership in most cases carried with it the obligation to bear arms in defence of the Soviet country. This to a certain extent served as a barrier against the influx of alien elements into the Party. But the termination of the war removed this barrier.

The Bolshevik Party, as the only legal Party holding the power of the state, was also joined, under false colours, by self-seeking and alien elements. The ideological rout of the conciliatory parties, and the fact that they were later placed in a position of illegality, impelled a large number of former Mensheviks and Socialist-Revolutionaries to join the Communist Party. These included not only workers, but also a great many petty-bourgeois elements. Even if they were sincere in coming over to the side of the Communist Party and the Soviet government, some of them were unable to get rid of their petty-bourgeois ideology.

This makes it quite clear what a tremendous danger the influence of petty-bourgeois environment represented for the Party at a time when the discontent of the peasants with the policy of War Communism was growing especially acute and when a considerable part of the proletariat was becoming declassed.

The transition to the N.E.P. did not improve matters all at once. Bourgeois elements were beginning to grow in both town and countryside and this naturally resulted even in a certain increase of their pressure on certain individual sections of the Party. The complex political manœuvre which the Party carried out in effecting the transition to the N.E.P., the toleration of relative freedom of trade after it had been combated for several years, the growth of a new bourgeoisie in contrast to the desperate want and privations of the masses, were received by individual backward and unstable elements of the Party as the beginning, of the Party's capitulation to the forces of bourgeois counter-revolution, as the prelude to major political concessions and the abolition of the Soviet government. This gave rise to manifestations of a certain degree of panic and demoralisation in individual sections of the Party—tendencies which were utilised in every way by the Mensheviks, who naturally regarded the transition to the N.E.P. as the beginning of the end of the Soviet government. Naturally, what was demanded of the Party at such a moment was tremendous activity in rallying its ranks, in raising the ideological and political level of its members and strengthening Party discipline.

The Party purging helped the Party to get rid of a great part of the degenerate, bureaucratised and politically unstable elements who had entered it under false colours. Entrance of new members into the Party had been almost completely suspended during the period of the purging, and was later allowed only on the basis of a number of serious restrictions. The restrictions even affected the admittance of workers into the Party. They were inevitable at a time when a considerable part of the working class was declassed and in view of those feelings of discontent with the Soviet government which had penetrated into the ranks of the workers from the petty-bourgeois elements which surrounded them. But the restrictions were not enough nor was the purging enough. The situation demanded that Party educational work be developed and extended to the broad Party masses. The Tenth Congress had already outlined a number of measures in this direction. The Eleventh Congress formulated a complete system of Party education. The end of the Civil War, the demobilisation, and the beginnings of an improvement in the situation of the masses produced certain favourable conditions for the development and success of the Party educational activities.

The rallying of the Party's ranks on the basis of the resolution adopted by the Tenth Congress considerably facilitated the struggle of the Party against petty-bourgeois influences and manifestations of degeneration. But these influences persisted. They manifested themselves above all in the views of the former "Workers' Opposition," which virtually joined hands with the Mensheviks. While the Mensheviks tried above all to cause panic among the working masses, attempting to imbue them with the conviction that the Soviet government was bankrupt and that what was taking place was not an organised retreat, but a panic-stricken flight, the representatives of the "Workers' Opposition," who did not abandon their views after the Tenth Congress, were the ones who under cover of "Left" phrases, tried to carry over these Menshevik tendencies into the Party.

Hence Lenin, at the Eleventh Congress, spoke of the panic-mongers who open machine-gun fire when the army is retreating.

The decisions of the Eleventh Congress were a new and crushing blow to the remnants of the "Workers' Opposition."

Somewhat different was the fate of another part of the opposition, at the Tenth Congress—the Trotskyists. We know that on the eve of the Tenth Congress, at the moment of the gravest turmoil and dangers, Trotskyism attempted to carry out an attack on the Leninist Party. It was voicing the sentiments of the turbulent petty-bourgeois forces which surrounded the Party and the Soviet government, particularly of the bourgeois elements which had entered the Soviet apparatus, entrenched themselves there and were already commencing their attempts to direct the machine into another channel. The Tenth Congress dealt a hard blow at Trotskyism, by exposing the essential anti-Leninist character of Trotskyism before the rank and file of the Party. Some of the comrades who had supported the Trotskyists before the Tenth Congress realised their errors and broke with them. But Trotskyism maintained its distinct organisation within the Party even after the Tenth Congress, in spite of all the traditions of the Bolshevik Party which has always fought manifestations of factionalism in its ranks and in spite of the decisions of the Tenth Congress which categorically prohibited all factions and groupings within the Party under threat of expulsion from the Party. This is why our Party mercilessly nipped in the bud all efforts of the Trotskyists to legalise themselves as a faction. It required only a suitable external and internal situation—a new turn, a crisis, difficulties, etc.—for the Trotskyists once more to oppose the Bolshevik line of the Party with their rejected and temporarily concealed 'Menshevik views.

Particularly characteristic of the prominent Trotskyists in the period of the Tenth Congress and after it was a sharply expressed capitulatory and defeatist attitude, a profound mistrust in the ability of the Party to emerge from the crisis by means of the N.E.P., just as previously they mistrusted the ability of the Party to carry the Civil War to a victorious conclusion. In some places, as in the Ukraine, this took the form of definite resistance to the carrying out of the New Economic Policy.

Counting on the failure of the Party in the carrying out of the New Economic Policy, Trotskyism adopted a waiting position. The Party was retreating to the positions of the state regulation of trade and of currency circulation; it was ready to lease or grant as concessions a considerable part of the country's large-scale industry and natural resources. But, while effecting this retreat, the Party and the Soviet government did not for a moment cease to work for the restoration of large-scale industry with their own resources. It was necessary considerably to restrict the supplying of the industrial enterprises and of the workers with raw materials and food through organised distribution of the state resources, and to draw upon the market for this purpose, to begin to learn how to trade, to transfer the enterprises to a cost accounting basis. Of course, we had to learn the methods of trading from the bourgeoisie, but these methods were now being employed, not by a concessionaire or private lessee, but by the socialist state power.

At the time of the Eleventh Congress the Party and the Soviet government were already able to record some progress in the task

11*

of restoring industry, the principal basis of socialist economy, by the methods of the New Economic Policy.

This progress had been made possible to a considerable extent by a regrouping of the forces within the Party, by a shifting of the leading Party cadres, by transferring some of them from military to economic and trade union work. The Party paid particular attention during this period to the strengthening of the leading cadres in the trade unions and to strengthening the contact between the trade unions and the broad working masses.

The Trotskyists and supporters of the "Workers' Opposition," a very considerable number of whom had held leading positions in the trade union movement, were replaced by staunch Leninists. The improvement in the work of the trade unions contributed a great deal to the progress that was made in the restoration of industry. This progress, however, was mainly confined to light industry. Heavy industry, with the exception of the fuel industries, advanced hardly at all from the state of collapse it had been in during the Civil War. Only in the peat industry did we exceed the pre-war level of output, surpassing it as early as 1921. In 1921 the output of coal in the Donbas amounted to 350,000,000 poods* as against 272,000,000 poods in the preceding year and 1,700,000,000 poods prior to the war. There was a slight improvement in the iron and steel industry. In the early months of 1921 the monthly output of pig iron amounted to slightly over 1,000 tons; in October the output was slightly over 2,000 tons; and in November, 4,500 tons. During 1918-19, 51 electric power stations were opened with a total capacity of 3,500 kilowatts, and in 1920-21, 221 stations were put into operation with a capacity of 12,000 kilowatts. Such were the first steps in the realisation of Lenin's electrification plan.

The principal base of the Soviet power and the proletarian dictatorship—large-scale industry—was being restored, although at first but slowly.

In the sphere of industry, the socialist sector had a decisive advantage over the capitalist elements. But the private capitalist elements were developing quite rapidly on the basis of the N.E.P. in the sphere of trade and agriculture. The sphere of

* A pood equals 36 pounds avoirdupois.

trade was becoming a decisive front in the struggle between the socialist and the capitalist elements. Would the Soviet government secure its own apparatus to link up large-scale state industry with the peasantry or would private capital take such an apparatus into its own hands—this was how the question stood at that time. Under these conditions, the problem of restoring a stable currency acquired tremendous importance. Without a stable currency, it was extremely difficult for the socialist state to seize decisive positions in the sphere of trade.

By the time of the Eleventh Congress the main features of the New Economic Policy had already taken shape. The essence of this policy was defined with great precision by Comrade Stalin at the Fourteenth Party Congress:

"The N.E.P. is a special policy of the proletarian state based on the existence of capitalism, while the key positions are in the hands of the proletarian state; based on the struggle between the capitalist and socialist elements . . . based on the victory of the socialist elements over the capitalist elements; based on the abolition of classes and the laying of the foundations of socialist economy."

The first period of the N.E.P., the period of retreat, had come to an end with the Eleventh Congress. The Party was passing over to an offensive on individual sectors of socialist construction, the country was entering upon a period when it could rapidly restore its ruined economy on the basis of the N.E.P. The whole period of the transition to the N.E.P. occupies a very important place in the history of our Party. Lenin attached the highest importance to it. At the Tenth Party Conference, in May 1921, Lenin said:

"If we compare the whole work of the Communist Party to a four-year course of the higher sciences, our situation could be defined as follows: We are now undergoing an examination from the third to the fourth course. We have not yet passed it but, according to all indications, we will pass this examination. If we count by courses, then the first course extended from the seventies of the last century to 1903—the elementary introductory period from the Narodniki, Social-Democracy and the Second International to Bolshevism. This was the first course. The second course was from 1903 to 1917. Here we have serious training for the revolution and the first experience of revolution in 1905. The third course was from 1917 to 1921. Here we have four

* Stenographic Report of the XIV Congress of the C.P.S.U.

years which, in their content, are more than the first forty years. This provided an exceedingly practical test when the proletariat came into power. But it was not yet the decisive test .... And now we are undergoing the examination from the third to the fourth course, after which we will have to make good with the entire fourth course. Then we will really be invincible." *

The end of the retreat at the Eleventh Congress, followed by the socialist offensive on the basis of the N.E.P., signified that the Party had indeed passed the very difficult political examination, graduating from the third course into the fourth.

Immediately after the Eleventh Congress, Comrade Stalin, the closest comrade-in-arms and best disciple of Lenin, was elected General Secretary of the Central Committee.

The election of Comrade Stalin as General Secretary of the Central Committee meant a decided strengthening of the Leninist core of the Central Committee as a result of the victorious struggle against Trotskyism and the "Workers' Opposition." It proved of tremendous importance for securing the firm Leninist line of the Central Committee and of the whole Party.

* Lenin, "Concluding Speech on the Report on the Tax in Kind," *Collected Works*, Vol. XXVI.

CHAPTER XIV

THE PARTY IN THE PERIOD OF THE OFFENSIVE ON THE BASIS OF THE N.E.P.—THE PERIOD OF RESTORATION

The Twelfth Party Conference—The "Smenavekh" tendency exposed by the Party—The international position of the Soviet country—The Fourth Congress of the Comintern—Lenin's last speeches—The Twelfth Party Congress—The Party and the state apparatus—The national question—After the Congress—Trotsky's statement and the "statement of the forty-six"—The economic platform of the opposition exposed by the Party—For Bolshevik organisational principles—What was the opposition aiming at?—The Thirteenth Party Conference—The further strengthening of the proletarian composition of the Party—The Thirteenth Party Congress—The Fifth Congress of the Comintern—The discussion on the "Lessons of October"—The Party in the struggle against Trotskyism

The Twelfth Party Conference

In August 1922, a few months after the Eleventh Congress, the Twelfth Party Conference met. On its agenda were the question of changing the Party constitution, the work of the trade unions, the tasks of the co-operatives and the question of anti-Soviet parties under the conditions of the New Economic Policy. The resolution on the trade unions adopted by the Twelfth Conference summarised the results attained in putting into effect the theses of the Eleventh Congress, approved the work carried on by the Central Committee towards this end (the reinforcement of the trade union organisations by tried and trusted Communists, the reorganisation of the work of the trade unions, etc.) and called for the elimination of the "mutual alienation and antithesis of the Communist trade union leaders and business managers" which was to be observed in certain organisations.

The question of the co-operatives was much more complex. In view of the development of the New Economic Policy and of the significance which was acquired by the market and trade, it is easy to understand why the Party began to devote such great attention to the co-operatives. Our consumers' co-operatives did not cope successfully with the first tasks which were imposed on them in the beginning of the transition to the N.E.P. When, instead of direct commodity exchange, we had to set about adapting ourselves to the conditions of the market, organising purchase and sale, and supplying the working class and the broad masses of peasant consumers by means of trading, the apparatus of our consumers' co-operatives failed to function as effectively as it should have done. The survivals of War Communism were making themselves felt. The apparatus was unelastic, cumbersome, bureaucratic. It was extremely difficult for it to operate in the market, to compete with the private trader, particularly in retail trade, while the trade turnover was increasing month by month. The task of putting fresh life into the co-operative machine depended to a large extent on the independent initiative of the rank and file co-operative members. The Twelfth Party Conference rejected the viewpoint of a section of the trade union workers who urged the separation of the workers' co-operatives from the Centrosoyuz and their formation into an independent organisation. The Conference decided that the separation of the workers' co-operatives would hamper the working class from exerting influence on the peasantry through the general co-operative organisation, would isolate the peasant co-operatives from the workers' co-operatives and would thereby facilitate the activities of all kinds of bourgeois anti-Soviet elements—who were already beginning to assert themselves under the N.E.P.—within the peasant co-operatives. In view of the necessity of learning how to trade and dominating the market, in view of the rapid growth of the market turnover in the country and the growth of private trading capital, the question of organising and strengthening the work of the consumers' co-operatives and of the state trading organisations became a vital question of the economic policy of the Party and of the Soviet government for a number of years.

The Conference considered the question of the work of anti-Soviet counter-revolutionary parties and tendencies under the conditions of the New Economic Policy. The N.E.P. provided a certain temporary opportunity for the development of the capitalist elements in our country, both in the cities and in the villages. This inevitably produced a revival of bourgeois ideology. It found its expression in the endeavours of the old anti-Soviet parties to adapt their activities to the conditions of the N.E.P. Taking advantage of the economic difficulties of the country which affected the conditions of the working class, the Socialist-Revolutionary and Menshevik parties attempted to carry on anti-Soviet agitation and propaganda to the effect that the Soviet government had ceased to be a working class government, that it was degenerating and deserting to the side of the bourgeoisie, that the working class had to carry on its own policy independent of the policy of the Soviet government. This anti-Soviet agitation met with a certain response among individual elements in the Party who were weak and unstable, particularly from among the former "Workers' Opposition."

The Twelfth Party Conference took note of the recrudescence of anti-Soviet activities among the bourgeois intelligentsia, the petty bourgeoisie and the kulaks, of the tendency on the part of their ideologists to adapt themselves to the conditions of Soviet legality and to utilise the opportunities which presented themselves under Soviet law to defend their bourgeois ideas in the press, especially the official papers, in magazines and books, at various public congresses, in the co-operative organisations, particularly in agricultural co-operatives, etc., etc.* The Conference drew two main conclusions from this—on the need to strengthen the work on all ideological fronts and on the need to continue the political repressions against anti-Soviet elements. "Repressions, while they inevitably fail to achieve their purpose when directed against a rising class ... are dictated by revolutionary expediency when it is a question of suppressing the decaying groups which are striving to seize the old positions conquered from them by the proletariat."

The "Smenavekh" Tendency Exposed by the Party

The New Economic Policy compelled a part of the bourgeois intelligentsia to change their tactics. They interpreted the

* In 1922, *The Economist*, a privately owned magazine published in Moscow, openly demanded the de-nationalisation of industry, the transfer of the railways to private companies and predicted the complete collapse of the entire Soviet economy in the near future. Many of the ideas of the Right Opportunists of 1928-30 were first expressed in the columns of this magazine.

N.E.P. as an evolutionary phenomenon of the Soviet government, as the beginning of its organic degeneration, of its transformation into a bourgeois government.

A group of former Cadet professors who had emigrated abroad (Klyuchnikov, Ustryalov, and others) published a collection of articles under the title *Smena Vekh** in which they urged collaboration with the Soviet government, contending that it was becoming transformed into a normal, "national," bourgeois government, that it was becoming a stage on the way to the restoration of the old mighty Russian empire, one and indivisible.

At the Eleventh Party Congress Lenin spoke of the Ustryalovs and Ustryalovism as the class truth of the class enemy, as the new tactics of this enemy against the Soviet government. It was necessary to utilise the *Smenavekh* intelligentsia, just as the Soviet government had hitherto utilised the bourgeois specialists, even those who were hostile in their attitude to it and who did not pin any hopes on its peaceful and organic evolution. But it was also necessary to evince the utmost class vigilance, in order to offer determined resistance to all these tendencies towards degeneration in the Soviet apparatus which the *Smenavekh*-ists were trying to utilise.

Lenin emphasised the fact that our Party considered the New Economic Policy as a tactic of the Party for the construction of Socialism. This tactic, as was noted by the Fourth Congress of the Comintern which met in the autumn of 1922, was not an exception peculiar to our backward country. It would have to be carried out by the working class of the advanced capitalist countries when they, too, came into power. The New Economic Policy was designed to meet the circumstances of the period of transition from capitalism to communism.

Naturally, the difficulties of the transition period were bound to be especially great in a backward country. The strengthening of the bourgeois elements under the N.E.P. brought with it the danger that their influence would increase in individual sections of our apparatus. Another source of danger at the time of the Eleventh Congress was the declassing of the prole-

* *"Smena vekh"* means literally "change of landmarks."

tariat—a fact to which Lenin repeatedly referred at the Congress and which even had its effect on the state of feeling within the Party. The economic situation in the country continued to improve rapidly towards the autumn of 1922. Industry was being restored at an accelerated pace, which meant that the proletarian social base of the Soviet government was growing stronger. Nevertheless elements of alien ideology were penetrating into our Party from the bourgeois environment.   By ideologically strengthening its cadres, by intensifying the Communist education of its members, by improving the whole system of Party education and by mercilessly exposing all those bourgeois views which, though presented under a Soviet flag, tended towards the restoration of capitalism, the Party still further intensified the struggle against these elements, who manifested themselves in the form of various anti-Leninist opposition tendencies and groupings.   The Party was thus strengthening both itself and its influence over the proletarian and toiling masses; it was strengthening the socialist positions in the country against the capitalist elements.

The International Position of the Soviet Country

The international position of the Soviet government underwent some improvement after the transition to the N.E.P. Capitalist Europe was absorbed with its own internal difficulties. In connection with the introduction of the N.E.P., its ruling circles entertained quite strong hopes that the character of the Soviet government would undergo a process of degeneration.   In the beginning of 1922 the Soviet government was invited to take part in the Genoa Conference which was called by the Allied powers.   At this Conference, in connection with the general question of settling the antagonisms between the capitalist nations, the question was raised of the recognition of the Soviet government by the capitalist powers and even of extending credits to the Soviet government on condition that it pay the tsarist debts and compensate the foreign capitalists for the losses incurred by them as a result of the policy of nationalisation.

The negotiations at the Genoa Conference with regard to these questions were fruitless and were postponed to the next conference, at the Hague. Here, too, the Soviet government and the capitalist governments failed to come to an agreement. However, during the Genoa Conference a very important political treaty between the Soviet government and Germany was signed at Rapallo. The German bourgeoisie, under the yoke of the Versailles peace treaty, was compelled to accede to a certain degree of economic and political collaboration with the Soviet government, which from the very outset had been opposed to the Versailles peace and to the despoiling and enslavement of Germany. At Genoa and the Hague, the bourgeoisie of the Allied Powers tried to get the Soviet government to make concessions in principle to international capital, to give up the chief gains of the October Revolution, virtually to place the broad masses of workers and peasants of the Soviet country in bondage to foreign capitalists, to grant the latter such rights and privileges as would have enabled them to dominate our country. The Soviet government definitely rejected the demands of the imperialists, despite the fact that individual elements within the Party showed a tendency to make concessions to the bourgeoisie.

These tendencies to surrender the positions of the proletarian dictatorship and to accept the platform of bourgeois democracy sprang from a lack of faith in the ability of the Party to restore industry with the internal resources of the country. They were to a certain extent reflected in the proposal to abolish the monopoly of foreign trade, which was made by Sokolnikov and defended by Bukharin. Zinoviev and Kamenev supported the proposal that the prominent British capitalist, Urquhart, should be given as a concession those enterprises which he had owned before the Revolution, on terms which were extremely disadvantageous to us. On Lenin's initiative both of these proposals were emphatically rejected by the Political Bureau of the Central Committee.

About this time the Central Committee also rejected Trotsky's proposal to allow our industrial enterprises and trusts to mortgage state property, including fixed capital, to private capitalists. It is not difficult to perceive that this proposal would have enabled foreign capitalists, through their agents in Russia, to get our industry under their control.

In the autumn of 1922, a decision was passed to form the Union of Soviet Socialist Republics, Lenin and Stalin playing a leading part in this. This was one of the most important acts of our international and national policy. It created a form for the union of Soviet states, not only for the present, but for the future as well. It showed that the Soviet government was creating a form for the union of states which could be freely joined by all states in which the toiling masses followed the example of the October Revolution and overthrew the power of their capitalists and landlords.

The Fourth Congress of the Comintern

The Fourth Congress of the Comintern met in the autumn of 1922, at a time when the Soviet government was growing stronger—a fact which both the bourgeois governments and yesterday's open enemies, the apologists of intervention who had now turned to *Smenakh*-ist tactics, were compelled to take into account.

At the Congress a number of reports were presented dealing with the past five years of Soviet government and the prospects of the world revolution, above all a report by Lenin—his last speech before representatives of the international proletariat.

Lenin in his report summarised the good results attained by the New Economic Policy in the country of proletarian dictatorship, stressed the international character of the N.E.P. as a policy of the proletariat in the realisation of its dictatorship, and emphasised the fact that the policy of our Soviet state should serve as a model for other countries, including those that are economically more highly developed than the U.S.S.R. Lenin also dealt with questions concerning the tactics of the Communist Parties in capitalist countries.

In view of the ebb of the revolutionary wave, which had already been noted by the Third Congress of the Comintern, the principal task of the Communist Parties consisted in winning over the majority of the workers, in carefully weighing up the experience of the previous struggle and in preparing themselves in good time for all possible vicissitudes of the struggle in the future.

"I am convinced," Lenin said, "that in this respect we must tell not only the Russian but also the foreign comrades that the most important thing in the period which has now commenced is to learn. We are learning in a general sense. But they must learn in a special sense, so as really to grasp the organisation, structure, method and content of revolutionary work. If this is accomplished, I am convinced that the prospects of the world revolution will be not only good but excellent. . . ."*

"We must not only know how to act when we are going right into an offensive and besides that, are winning. In a revolutionary period, this is not so very difficult nor so important, at least it is not the most essential thing. During a revolution there are always moments when the enemy loses his head, and if we attack him at such a moment, we can easily conquer. But this means very little, since our adversary, if he has sufficient stamina, can mobilise his forces in advance, etc. He can then easily provoke us into an attack and then throw us back for years. That is why I hold that the idea that we ought to get ready so as to be able to retreat is a very valuable one; and not only from the theoretical standpoint but from the practical standpoint as well. All the parties which are preparing to enter upon a direct attack upon capitalism in the near future must now consider also how to secure for themselves the possibility of a retreat."**

In the U.S.S.R. the working class, under the leadership of the Leninist Party, had already completed the most difficult period of the N.E.P., the period of retreat, by the autumn of 1922, and was beginning to take the offensive on individual sectors of the front.

For the principal sections of the Comintern in Western Europe the chief task was that of defence and of preparing for an offensive against the bourgeoisie, which had recuperated its strength after the war and the demobilisation.

The Congress decided that:

"The main demand of the Third World Congress, to achieve the extension of Communist influence over the majority of the working class and to draw the decisive part of this class into the struggle, remains in full force.

"From this follows the necessity of *the tactic of the united front.* The slogan of the Third Congress—'To the masses'—remains in force more than ever at this moment."

* Lenin, "The Fourth Congress of the Comintern," *Collected Works,* Vol. XXVII.
** *Ibid*

The Congress discussed the question of the so-called demands of the transition period, of a workers' or workers' and peasants' government which might serve as a step towards the winning of the proletarian dictatorship, of the situation in individual parties, particularly the question of overcoming the centrist tendencies in the French and Norwegian parties.

The Social-Democratic elements, which had joined the Comintern during the period of revolutionary upsurge, continued to split off from it now that reaction had set in. This process was particularly noticeable in the French Communist Party.

The Congress set the Communist parties of Germany and France the task of fighting together against the Versailles peace. French imperialism was preparing to occupy the Ruhr, while in Germany there was a new and extreme accentuation of the economic and political situation, beginning with the summer of 1923.

The main thing was to win over the masses, to strengthen the Party's influence over them, to organise the struggle for the everyday needs of the workers, to draw away the broad sections of the workers from the reformists by the correct use of united front tactics, to train cadres, and to prepare the forces for an offensive.

Lenin's Last Speeches

Lenin's last speeches were delivered in the autumn of 1922 when he resumed his work in the government for a short time, after his first attack of serious illness in the summer of 1922. During this brief period, Lenin addressed the session of the All-Russian Central Executive Committee, the Fourth Congress of the Comintern and the Plenum of the Moscow Soviet. In these speeches Lenin explained the measures which our Party put into effect on the basis of the decisions of the Eleventh Congress and Twelfth Party Conference. He particularly stressed the necessity of cutting down and simplifying the state apparatus. and also explained the firm stand which had been taken by the Soviet government towards the international bourgeoisie at Genoa and the Hague.

Right up to his death Lenin believed that after the termination of the Civil War the most important task of the Soviet government on the international arena was the preservation of peace. He attached tremendous importance to the breathing space which had at last been secured and considered it necessary to prolong it as much as possible, in order to take full advantage of this breathing space for the building up of socialism.

Lenin did not for a moment allow himself to be deluded by the relative improvement in our international situation as expressed in the fact that peaceful relations had been established during the last few years with the surrounding capitalist states. Lenin continued to regard the danger of war as a very real one. He clearly perceived all the difficulties of the struggle against war, particularly after its outbreak. This can be seen from the famous *Notes on the Question of the Tasks of our Delegation at the Hague*—the delegation which went to a special trade union conference on the struggle against war. The reformists must not be believed when they said they would answer a war with a strike or revolution, that they were opposed to war in general.

"We must explain the real situation to people—in what absolute secrecy war is engendered and how helpless is the ordinary organisation of the workers, even if it call itself revolutionary, in face of an actually approaching war. . . .

"Firstly, an explanation of the question of the 'defence of the fatherland'; secondly, in connection with the first, an explanation of the question of 'defeatism'; and finally, an explanation of the only possible method of fighting against war, namely, the formation and preservation of an illegal organisation for *prolonged* work against war by all the revolutionaries who take part in the war—all this must be placed in the forefront.

"Boycott the war—is a stupid phrase. Communists must take part in every reactionary war.

"We must take examples from the current conflicts, even the most insignificant, and use them to illustrate how a war may arise any day from a dispute between Britain and France regarding some detail in a treaty with Turkey, or between the United States and Japan on account of some petty difference with regard to any question concerning the Pacific, or between any of the great powers as a result of colonial disputes regarding their tariff or trade policy in general, and so forth and so on."*

* Lenin, "The Fourth Congress of the Comintern," *Collected Works*, Vol. XXVII.

In his report to the Fourth Congress of the Comintern on the past five years of Soviet government, Lenin noted that "between last year, when we commenced our New Economic Policy, and today we have already learned to move forward." The alliance with the peasantry on the basis of the N.E.P. had become stronger, the state of feeling among the peasantry had improved, 'some progress was being made in the light industries. But the most important problem, the problem of heavy industry, remained as yet unsolved.

"In a capitalist country a loan of hundreds of millions would be required to improve the state of heavy industry; without this an improvement would be impossible.... We have not got these loans, and our heavy industry continues to remain in a very difficult situation.

"The salvation of Russia lies not only in the yield of a good harvest by peasant farming—that is not enough; not only in the healthy condition of our light industry, which supplies the peasantry with articles of consumption—that also is not enough. We also need heavy industry....

"Heavy industry is in need of government subsidies. Unless we manage to get them, we will perish as a civilised nation, let alone as a socialist nation."*

Thus Lenin, as early as 1922, raised the question of heavy industry as the principal base for our socialist construction.

He constantly returned to this question in his other speeches.

On December 10, 1922, in a telegram of greetings to the All-Ukrainian Congress of Soviets, Lenin wrote:

"The second question to which the Congress should pay special attention [the first question was the formation of the U.S.S.R.—N.P.] is that of our heavy industry. The raising of the Donbas, of the oil and of the iron and steel industries to the pre-war level of production is the main task of our entire economy. All our efforts must be directed towards the solution of this problem."**

In his last speech, at the Plenum of the Moscow Soviet,. Lenin spoke of the task of *transforming the Russia of the N.E.P. into a socialist Russia.*

Lenin's last writings belong to a somewhat later period, when after the second attack of his sickness he was compelled to with-

* *Ibid.*
** Lenin, "The All-Ukrainian Congress of Soviets," *Collected Works,* Vol. XXVII.

draw from government work, this time forever. In his article, *Leaves from a Diary,* published in *Pravda* at the beginning of 1923, Lenin laid great stress on the question of popular education in the villages, this being virtually the question of linking up the socialist transformation of the country with the cultural revolution. In this remarkable article Lenin raised in all its magnitude the problem of a cultural revolution in our country after it had thrown off the yoke of capitalism. Quoting figures to show that in 1897 the level of literacy of the population of Russia was 233 per thousand and in 1920—319, Lenin wrote:

"This shows how much persistent spade-work we still have to carry out in order to reach the level of an ordinary civilised nation of Western Europe. It further shows what a lot of work we now have ahead of us in order really to achieve a certain level of culture on the basis of our proletarian conquests ...

"Nowhere are the masses of the people so interested in real culture as in our country . . . nowhere in no country is the state power in the hands of the working class, the bulk of which perfectly well understands the shortcomings of its, I will not say cultural state, but I will say of its standard of literacy; nowhere is the working class ready to make such sacrifices, nowhere does it make such sacrifices in order to improve its condition in this respect as is the case in our country."[*]

In this article Lenin stressed the tremendous political importance of the work of teachers in elementary schools and the great political significance of the cultural "patronage"[**] of the city workers over the villages.

"Here, the main political question is the relation between town and countryside—a question which is of decisive importance for our revolution as a whole. While the bourgeois state systematically directs all its efforts towards stupefying the workers of the cities, adapting for this purpose all the literature which is issued at the expense of the state, at the expense of the tsarist and bourgeois parties, we can and must utilise our power in order to really make the urban worker a conductor of Communist ideas into the ranks of the agricultural proletariat."[***]

---

[*] Lenin, "Leaves from a Diary," *Collected Works,* Vol. XXVII.
[**] Patronage—the workers in a particular factory became the patrons of a village and provided assistance in the form of lectures, village libraries, radio appliances, etc.—*Ed.*
[***] Lenin, "Leaves from a Diary," *Collected Works,* Vol. XXVII.

In his articles *How We Should Reorganise the Workers' and Peasants' Inspection* and *Better Little but Good*, Lenin most urgently demanded the simplification and improvement of our state apparatus and proposed that for the proper organisation of this work the Workers' and Peasants' Inspection be merged with the Central Control Commission.

"The situation with regard to our state apparatus is so deplorable, not to say disgusting, that we must first of all give serious thought to the question of how to fight its shortcomings, remembering that these shortcomings have their roots in the past, which, although overthrown, has not yet been outlived, has not yet been relegated to the stage of a culture that has receded into the distant past."*

During the period of War Communism our state apparatus became extremely inflated. With the transition to the New Economic Policy, the apparatus, to be sure, was cut down considerably, but its work improved very little. Bureaucracy, isolation from the toiling masses, lack of culture, and all kinds of abuses—these things had not by any means been abolished. In his articles dealing with the Workers' and Peasants' Inspection, Lenin proposed a specific task:

"We must endeavour to build up a state in which the workers may retain their leadership over the peasants, retain the confidence of the peasants towards them and in which they may with the greatest economy banish from their social relations all traces of any sort of extravagance.

"We must cut down our state apparatus so as to effect the greatest possible economy. We must banish from it all traces of extravagance, of which much has been left from tsarist Russia, from her capitalist bureaucratic apparatus.

"Would not this result in the domination of peasant narrow-mindedness?

"No. If we retain for the working class its leadership over the peasantry, then by means of the greatest and greatest economy in the management of our state we will make it possible to secure every possible saving, however small, for the development of our large-scale machine-building industry, for the development of electrification of hydro-peat, for the building of Volkhovstroy, etc."**

Lenin thus saw that the highway to socialist construction lay above all in the direction of the restoration and development of large-scale machine-building industry and electrification;

---

* Lenin, "Better Little But Good," *Collected Works*, Vol. XXVII.
** *Ibid.*

the latter, for him, signified the reconstruction of industry and agriculture on principles of modern technique. The establishment of correct relationships with the peasantry, simplification and retrenchment in the state apparatus, etc., were to contribute to the solution of this basic task. About this time Lenin also wrote his article *On Co-operation* * in which he emphasised the tremendous role which the co-operatives had to play under the conditions of the New Economic Policy as the main lever for effecting the transition of petty peasant farming to socialism.

"It is doubtful," Lenin wrote, "whether everybody understands that our co-operative system has now . . . acquired an altogether exceptional importance. . . . Since the state power is in the hands of the working class, since this state power owns all the means of production, we really have only one task left, namely, to bring the population into the co-operatives. . . . The power of state over all large-scale means of production, the power of state in the hands of the proletariat, the alliance of this proletariat with the many millions of small and very small peasants, the assured leadership of the peasantry by the proletariat, etc.—is not this all that is necessary in order to build complete socialist society from the co-operatives, from the co-operatives alone, which we formerly treated as huckstering and which from a certain aspect we have the right to treat as such now, during N.E.P.? Is this not all that is necessary for the purpose of building a complete socialist society?"**

Lenin said that under the proletarian dictatorship the non-capitalist evolution of the peasantry was possible with the aid of the co-operatives, which would embrace the bulk of the small and smallest farms under our conditions.

"Under private capitalism, co-operative enterprises differ from capitalist enterprises as collective enterprises from private enterprises. Under state capitalism the co-operative enterprises differ from state-capitalist ones, first, as private enterprises and secondly, as collective ones. Under our existing order of society the co-operative enterprises differ from private capitalist enterprises in that they are collective enterprises but they do not differ from socialist enterprises [enterprises of a consistent socialist type, as Lenin points out in a preceding passage.—*N.P.*] if they are founded on land with the means of production belonging to the state, *i.e.* to the working class."**

* The article *On Co-operation* was published in the end of May 1923, when Lenin was already undergoing the last attack of his sickness.
** Lenin, "On Co-operation," *Collected Works*, Vol. XXVII.
*** *Ibid.*

Lenin here emphasised the vast difference in principle between the role of the co-operatives under capitalism and under the Soviet regime and the tremendous part played by the co-operatives in effecting the transition from petty peasant farming to socialism.

By the beginning of 1923, when Lenin wrote this article, we had already achieved considerable success in the restoration of industry, the principal base for the construction of socialism. To be sure, the question of securing the bond between state industry and the millions of peasant farms through the trading apparatus had not yet been completely solved. But besides this, there was already arising the practical question of drawing these scores of millions of peasant farms into the system of socialist economy under the conditions of the N.E.P., not only in the sphere of exchange and trade, but in the sphere of production as well. Lenin's article *On Co-operation* gave the answer to this question.

It pointed the way—the way of co-operative amalgamation for petty peasant farming under the conditions of the N.E.P.—the way by which petty peasant farming might find its way through productive co-operation, through the creation of collective farms, into the channel of socialism. The Party clearly pointed the way for a socialist offensive not only in the sphere of industry but in the sphere of agriculture as well. We have seen that even during the first year of the N.E.P. the Party already attached great importance to the question of the consumers' co-operatives—a question which was discussed at the Twelfth Party Conference. The development of the consumers' co-operatives meant the gradual mastering of the anarchic, unorganised market, which served as the link between the state and scores of millions of scattered peasant farms.

Lenin's co-operative plan now confronted the co-operative system with a new, immeasurably more complex and difficult task of gradually amalgamating these millions of peasant farms on a production basis and thus switching them on to the rails of large-scale socialised economy.

The whole Party was awaiting Lenin's appearance at the Twelfth Party Congress. But shortly before the Congress Lenin underwent the last attack of his illness and lost the power of speech. The Twelfth Party Congress was held without Lenin's leadership. But the questions which were discussed by the Congress had been to a considerable extent dealt with in the last speeches and writings of Lenin, who to the very end reacted with extreme sensitiveness to all the main questions of Party policy.

The Twelfth Party Congress

In connection with the report of the Central Committee, the Twelfth Congress* again dealt with the question of the limits of our concessions to foreign capital. The standpoint of the Central Committee on this question was criticised by L. B. Krassin. He proposed that the Soviet government should agree to the payment of the tsarist debts, contending that the international bourgeoisie wanted only the recognition of these debts in principle and would not insist on their actual payment. Krassin was of the opinion that we had to obtain *de jure* recognition at any price. Subsequent events have shown that Krassin was wrong, that, in spite of our refusing to recognise the old tsarist debts, the Soviet government was recognised by Britain, France and Japan. Krassin argued the necessity of concessions on the grounds that our industry would in any case not be able to extricate itself from its difficult position without large credits and loans from foreign capital, and contended that the credits and loans were a question of life and death for us. This viewpoint reflected the attitude taken by certain of the Party business managers. As subsequent events have shown, Krassin was also wrong in this respect. We achieved tremendous success in the task of restoring industry and of further developing it beyond the pre-war level without any substantial aid from foreign capital. It is very significant that, while offering the Party a programme of concessions in the sphere of foreign policy, Comrade Krassin at the same time strongly opposed the reorganisation of the Central Control Commission and the Workers' and Peasants' Inspection as proposed by Lenin, on the ground that

*Three hundred and eighty-six thousand members were represented at the Congress. The credentials committee reported four hundred and eight delegates with a decisive vote and four hundred and seventeen with a consultative vote.

it would result in the unnecessary tutelage of the Party over the state apparatus and over economic affairs. In this case also, Comrade Krassin reflected the attitude of those groups of business managers and specialists who wanted to free themselves of all Party influence and who quite clearly showed a tendency to direct our economy along a capitalist path of development. In his speech at the Congress, Krassin outlined a consistent Right opportunist programme of capitulation to the bourgeoisie on the external and internal fronts.

The Congress unanimously and emphatically rejected this programme of capitulation.

The second basic question on the agenda of the Twelfth Party Congress was that of the state industry. Almost two years had elapsed since the system of cost accounting had been introduced, when industry, through and by means of the market, had to establish economic contact with the peasantry. To what extent had it succeeded in coping with this task? A certain measure of success had undoubtedly been achieved, particularly in the sphere of light industry which produced consumers' goods. The output of industry and the productivity of labour had increased; a more or less well-arranged system of state trusts had been created; and the first serious steps had been taken towards placing the whole work of industry on a planned basis. But along with this, a whole series of grave defects were making themselves felt in the work of industry—plants operating below capacity, huge overhead expenses, bureaucracy and lack of elasticity in the managing staffs, and finally, low productivity of labour.

The result of all this was excessively high prices on industrial products. And these prices constituted a very real menace to the economic alliance between the working class and the peasantry.

The state industry of our country was the main element of its socialist economy. The future prospects of socialist construction were of necessity linked up with state industry first and foremost. This explains why the Congress devoted so much attention to the report on the condition of industry and adopted a number of practical proposals which aimed at the elimination of the main deficiencies in our industry, above all at the reduction of overhead expenses.

In this connection the Congress was fully aware of the fact that the question of the development of industry could not possibly be considered apart from the general economic situation of the country, particularly the agricultural situation. The peasant market remained under all conditions the principal market for our industry, and the latter had to take its bearings from the former. We could not advance towards socialism save in close contact with the millions of peasants, not allowing any break with them. It would have been fatal for us, in a country with a vast peasant majority, to oppose the interests of industry to the interests of peasant farming, to base the plans for industrial development on a policy of exploiting peasant farming, of transforming it into a colony of the Soviet government and of state industry. Definite tendencies in this direction, however, were manifested by Trotsky and his factional associates.

On the other hand, it was quite obvious that, owing to the low level of technique, the considerable defects in management resulting in high overhead expenses, and the insufficiently high cultural standard of the working masses which affected the productivity of their labour, our industry was not in a position to engage in free competition with foreign industry as regards prices, that its interests had to be guarded by a monopoly of foreign trade as one of the keystones of the policy pursued by the Soviet state.

It goes without saying that this monopoly did not relieve the Party of the duty of carrying on a most intense struggle to reduce the cost of production and the sales prices. This was absolutely necessary in the interests of the alliance with the peasantry, and in the interests of industry itself.

The Party and the State Apparatus

The Twelfth Congress took up the whole question of the relationships between the Party and the state apparatus. This question was raised as a direct result of Lenin's articles concerning the reorganisation of the Workers' and Peasants' Inspection. But whereas Lenin in his articles constantly sounded the alarm against the bureaucratisation of our state apparatus, against its unwieldy character and insufficient contact with the working class and peasantry; whereas the attention of the Party was riveted on the problem of keeping more careful watch over the state apparatus, preventing it from losing contact with the Party and strengthening the guidance of the Party, the oppositionist elements within the Party, yielding to the pressure of elemental petty-bourgeois forces from without, incorrectly attempted to interpret the decision of the Eleventh Congress regarding the demarcation of functions as between Party and state organs in a spirit of severing the state apparatus from the guiding influence of the Party. This tendency was manifested with particular clearness in the anonymous platform which was circulated on the eve of the Twelfth Congress. It was manifested in a more cautious form at the Twelfth Congress itself, where is was upheld by Ossinsky. It was manifested before the Twelfth Congress in Trotsky's theses on the tasks of industry, which he laid before the Central Committee on the eve of the Congress. The discussion of these theses in the Central Committee revealed a number of differences between Trotsky and the Political Bureau. The Politburo adopted amendments to Trotsky's theses, the tendency of these amendments being to stress the need for Party leadership over the state apparatus.

In the organisational report of the Central Committee, Comrade Stalin explained Lenin's scheme for building up the apparatus of the proletarian dictatorship. The most important levers, the driving belts connecting it with the masses, and above all with the working class, are the trade unions, soviets, co-operatives, Young Communist League, etc. The Party is the main guiding force in the system of the proletarian dictatorship, directing the work of all its levers and driving belts. The Party must unquestionably exercise guidance over the state apparatus. The tendencies to separate the state apparatus from the Party— tendencies which were upheld by the authors of the anonymous platform, and by Trotsky and Krassin—were a reflection of bourgeois influence on the Party. Zinoviev, on the other hand, attempted to reduce the proletarian dictatorship to a dictatorship of the Party.

Actually, as Comrade Stalin has explained in detail in his *Problems of Leninism,* the proletarian dictatorship is much broader in its scope and content than a dictatorship of the Party. Although all the most important decisions of the Soviet, trade union and other organs are previously passed upon by the Party, they are afterwards put into effect by the trade unions, the Soviets and the rank and file of these organisations. The Party cannot be identical with, cannot take the place of the whole class, since it constitutes only the vanguard of the class. In carrying out its policy, the Party takes into account the situation of its class, and the state of feeling prevailing within it, without, of course, letting itself be swayed by this state of feeling. The Party, as the vanguard of the working masses, determines its policy in such a way that this policy is supported by these masses. The authority of the Party is based on the confidence of the working class in it.

". . . The Party must closely heed the voice of the masses, must pay close attention to their revolutionary instinct, must study the practice of the struggle of the masses and on this basis test the correctness of its own policy—and must, therefore, not only teach the masses, but also learn from them.

"... The Party must from day to day win the confidence of the proletarian masses; . . . by its policy and its work, it must secure the support of the masses; . . . it must not command, but above all convince the masses and help them to realise by their own experience the correctness of the policy of the Party; . . . it must, therefore, be the guide, the leader, and teacher of its own class."*

The view that the dictatorship of the Party should replace the dictatorship of the proletariat—the view upheld by Zinoviev —would mean replacing persuasion by compulsion, replacing leadership by dragooning methods; it would mean the application of those methods which Trotskyism attempted to enforce in the trade unions and which signified a mistrust in the forces of the working class and of the Party itself, for in reality even the dictatorship of the Party, as conceived by Zinoviev, was transformed into a dictatorship of the "leaders."**

In connection with the need for further improvement in the state apparatus, the Twelfth Congress recognised that the old

* Stalin, "Problems of Leninism," *Leninism,* Vol. I.
** *Ibid.*

administrative division of the country which had been inherited
from tsarism was not conducive to the development of the Soviet
power and socialist construction, and decided to create a new
administrative system based on the organisation of regions (ob-
lasts), changing the boundaries between the previously existing
administrative units (Gubernia, Uyezd, Volost) in accordance
with the economic requirements and the national composition of
the population.

The Twelfth Congress adopted a decision in favour of merging the Central Control Commission with the Workers' and
Peasants' Inspection, as had been proposed by Lenin in his last
articles.*

The National Question

The Congress devoted much attention to the national question.   The decisions of the Twelfth Congress on the national
question still serve even at the present time as guiding principles
in the carrying out of our national policy.   To a considerable
extent they represented a further development of the decisions
previously adopted by the Tenth Congress of the Party.   The
decisions of these two congresses which were adopted on the
basis of Comrade Stalin's reports are an example of the application of the Leninist teachings on the national question under
the conditions of the proletarian dictatorship in a country
whose population comprises many different nationalities at various stages of economic and cultural development.

There were very serious reasons for placing the national
question on the agenda of the Twelfth Congress of the Party.
A considerable period had elapsed since the Tenth Party Congress.   During this period, the New Economic Policy had been
put into effect, accompanied by a growth of capitalist elements
in town and countryside. This created a certain basis for the
development of bourgeois and petty-bourgeois ideology, including the development of nationalism of all forms and shades.

This resulted in the growth of chauvinist tendencies among
the non-Party section of the Soviet apparatus both in the centre
and in the Russian districts and also in the republics inhabited

* V. V. Kuibyshev was placed at the head of the reorganised Central
Control Commission.

by national minorities. This found its reflection among some sections of the Party in the revival and reinvigoration of two deviations noted by the Tenth Party Congress—the deviations towards Great Russian chauvinism and towards local nationalism. Comrade Stalin made the report on the national question at the Congress.

"In connection with the N.E.P.," Comrade Stalin pointed out, "a new force is coming into being in our internal affairs, namely, Great-Russian chauvinism, which is concealed in our institutions, which is penetrating not only into the Soviet institutions but into the Party institutions as well, which is finding its way into all corners of our federation and which is bringing things to such a pitch that, unless we resolutely repulse this new force, unless we cut it off at the root—while the N.E.P. conditions foster it—we run the risk of having to face a rupture between the proletariat of the formerly dominant nation and the peasants of the formerly oppressed nations, which would be equivalent to an undermining of the proletarian dictatorship.

"But the N.E.P. not only fosters Russian chauvinism, it also fosters local chauvinism, particularly in those republics which are inhabited by several nationalities. . . . These local chauvinisms do not constitute in respect of their strength, such a menace as Great-Russian chauvinism. Nevertheless, they constitute a menace, threatening to transform several of our republics into an arena of national squabbles, to disrupt the bonds of internationalism there."*

Russian specialists predominated in the state apparatus, while Russian culture continued to enjoy the privileged position which it had won for itself prior to the Soviet regime. The Party consequently had to take a number of measures in order to create national equality not only in word but in fact. The Twelfth Congress did not confine itself to reaffirming the previous decisions regarding the introduction of the native languages of the population in the Party and Soviet apparatus, and in the whole system of public education. It stressed the need of special measures on the part of the state, aimed at the resuscitation and development of the respective national cultures of the peoples which had been oppressed for centuries under tsarism.

Comrade Stalin in his report, and the Twelfth Congress in its decisions, pointed out the close connection existing in our country between the national question and the peasant

* Stenographic Report of the Twelfth Congress.

question.* If we consider the whole composition of the population of the U.S.S.R., we find that the proletariat of our country, not only in the central parts but in the outlying regions as well, is mainly. Russian or Russianised. And this Russian or Russianised proletariat has to solve the national question in order to strengthen its alliance with the peasantry of the most various nationalities. On the other hand, the Party was still confronted with the urgent problem of creating trained forces from among the proletariat of the national minorities.

The Congress once again strongly emphasised the necessity of developing industry in the backward republics of the Caucasus, Central Asia and the eastern part of the R.S.F.S.R., of developing a proletariat, thereby providing the Communist organisation with a strong and healthy base for securing its influence on the peasant part of the indigenous population. The Congress particularly stressed the importance of the work of training Communist cadres in the national minority republics and regions. While concentrating the chief attention of the Party on the struggle against Great-Russian chauvinism. the Congress at the same time struck a blow at local nationalism which was exercising an influence over certain elements in the Party. Typical representatives of such nationalism at the Congress were the Georgian deviators—a group of members of the Communist Party of Georgia who, under the pressure of the petty-bourgeoisie and the Mensheviks, came out in opposition to the Party with slogans in favour of concessions to the Georgian bourgeoisie and Mensheviks. This group was trying to obtain for Georgia a privileged position in relation to the other Transcaucasian republics, and, in furtherance of this aim, they declared themselves against the creation of the Transcaucasian federation. The Congress emphatically rejected the nationalist pretensions of this group. This deviation, which had affected certain of the leaders of the Party organisation of Georgia, was a sign of the strengthening of the influence of petty-bourgeois ideology

* Connection does not of course mean identity. Those comrades who reduce the whole of the national question to the alliance with the peasantry are greatly mistaken. As was pointed out by Comrade Stalin, in the article *Problems of Leninism*, "the national question is wider and richer in its scope than the peasant question." (Stalin, "Problems of Leninism," *Leninism*, Vol. I.)

on the Party under the conditions of the N.E.P. and the continued growth of the capitalist elements. It was no accident that this influence should have been above all widely manifested in Georgia, where the Soviet government had only been in existence for two years, where there had been no War Communism or the mass expropriation of the bourgeoisie which accompanied it, where there were very few industrial workers as compared with large forces of petty-bourgeois nationalist intelligentsia, and where the old Menshevik traditions still retained considerable force.*

However, the struggle of the Party against the Georgian deviators at the Twelfth Congress proved to be only a vanguard skirmish. It took place a few months before the general battle with the Trotskyist opposition, of which the Georgian deviators, properly speaking, were among the forerunners.**

After the Congress

The Twelfth Party Congress met at the end of April 1923. At this time there were already perceptible indications of those economic difficulties which assumed serious proportions at the end of 1923. These were difficulties connected with the restor-

---

* Not all of the then leaders of our Party at once clearly perceived the petty-bourgeois semi-Menshevik essence of the Georgian deviation. Bukharin and Zinoviev took an altogether conciliatory attitude towards this deviation.

Bukharin, who in the past had run counter to the programme of our Party on the national question and the right of nations to self-determination including secession, now contended that it was only necessary to fight against Great-Russian chauvinism, that local nationalism did not present any danger.

** Shortly after the Twelfth Congress, the Central Committee called a special conference which was devoted to clarifying the situation with regard to the solution of the national question in the various localities and to outlining methods for putting into effect the decision of the Twelfth Congress. At this conference it was found that in the Ukraine and Turkestan particularly poor and inadequate results had been attained in carrying out the national policy, and Comrade Stalin categorically raised the question of the necessity of concentrating attention on Turkestan "in the sense of raising the cultural level of the masses, of nationalising the state apparatus, etc." "I consider that the Ukraine is the second weak point of the Soviet power," said Comrade Stalin. "Yet, the Ukraine is of the same or almost the same significance for the peoples of the West as Turkestan is for the peoples of the East." Stalin pointed out the exceptional importance of the question of cadres for all national minority republics. The conference outlined a number of practical measures for the application of the decisions of the Twelfth Congress on the national question.

ation of the economy of the country, which was then emerging from the depths of privation.

Thanks to the New Economic Policy, agriculture was making quite rapid progress. As a result of a good crop in 1922, a considerable surplus of agricultural products was accumulated, and the Soviet government was enabled to resort to the export of these products. On the other hand, industry was only providing agriculture with a few products and those at high prices. Not the least factor in this situation was the practice of some of our business organisations which, being anxious to accumulate funds for industry (which was badly in need of them) overstepped the mark and sometimes raised the prices of industrial products too high.

The excessively high prices impeded the sales, and to this was added the bureaucratic clumsiness of many of the business organisations. Co-operatives were crammed with goods which could not be sold, while trusts began to experience difficulties. Another exceedingly important factor was that the peasants were very reluctant to accept the depreciated Soviet currency, and this greatly hindered commodity circulation in the country. Difficulties in effecting sales furnished some bureaucrats the welcome excuse of "objective conditions" for delaying the payment of wages to the workers. They did not stir a finger to fight against these conditions, with the result that in the autumn of 1923 there were serious signs of discontent among certain sections of the workers.

Difficulties with the sales, while affecting the state of feeling among the worker and peasant masses, also found their reflection in the internal situation in the Party.

The Georgian deviators were only the harbingers of the oncoming wave of petty-bourgeois opposition within the Party. From the very beginning of the N.E.P. unstable elements began to make their presence felt within the Party—elements which were inclined to criticise the Soviet government from a Menshevik standpoint, alleging that it was a bourgeoisified government which had turned its back on the working class, etc. As a result of this state of feeling, two underground groups were formed in the summer of 1923—the so-called "Workers' Group" and the "Workers' Truth" group. The "Workers' Group" was composed chiefly of followers of the former "Workers' Opposition." It was headed by Myasnikov, who had been expelled from the Party and who even before the Eleventh Congress had already written that it was necessary to allow freedom of the press to all parties, from the monarchists to the anarchists.

The anarcho-syndicalist deviation which the Tenth Congress had noted in the case of the "Workers' Opposition" was further developed by Myasnikov and his associates in the "Workers' Group." It became anarcho-syndicalism pure and simple, rejecting the proletarian dictatorship in principle. This group did not content itself with carrying on its secret propaganda within the Party to the effect that the Soviet government had betrayed the working class. It established contact with the anarcho-syndicalist groups in Western Europe which were trying to organise a Fourth International, got into correspondence with these groups and furnished them with material which the latter utilised in their campaign of calumny against the Comintern and the Soviet government.

The "Workers' Truth" group, which was formed prior to this, was under the ideological inspiration of A. Bogdanov, the former leader of the *Vperyod* group, who had already severed his connection with the Party after the first revolution. What the arguments of this group amounted to was that in the Soviet country the proletarian dictatorship existed only in name. Actually, they alleged, the power was in the hands of the bourgeois intelligentsia who had a monopoly on education. This intelligentsia was carrying out a line of policy in its own interests, exploiting the working class.

The "Workers' Truth" group, even in the composition of its members, had nothing in common with the working class. It was composed of petty-bourgeois elements which were under the direct influence of Menshevism. It was no accident that the *Sotsialistichesky Vestnik (Socialist Herald)** should have been so eager to give space in its columns to the platform of the "Workers' Truth" group and showered whole bouquets of flattering epithets upon them.

---

* Menshevik journal published in Berlin—*Ed.*

The *Sotsialistichesky Vestnik,* in an article by Dan, only urged the "Workers' Truth" group to draw a number of practical conclusions from their premises: Since for the working class the Soviet power is a bourgeois power, the working class should demand of it those liberties which adorned the Menshevik platform, should pursue the same policy towards it as towards a bourgeois government; more than this, they should recognise, as the Mensheviks did, that the Soviet government was even worse for the working class than an openly bourgeois government, since it concealed its social nature from them.

Hostile bourgeois ideology exerted pressure not only on the backward workers who succumbed to the influence of anarchosyndicalist demagogy in the manner of the "Workers' Group" or on the ordinary petty-bourgeois intellectuals who hailed as a revelation the "Workers' Truth" version of Menshevism, slightly retouched by Bogdanov. In the autumn of 1923, an opposition led by Trotsky came out openly against the Party and its policy, raising in its most acute form the question of the future leadership of the Party. The first indications of a new attack by Trotskyism on the Leninist Party were already apparent at the Twelfth Congress. Trotsky's followers, in their speeches on the report of the Central Committee, made attacks on the policy of the Party and particularly on the organisational work in the Central Committee which was carried on under the direct guidance of Comrade Stalin.

The Trotskyists could not reconcile themselves to the selection of Party workers which was made by the Central Committee and which aimed at placing tried and reliable Leninists, capable of fighting Trotskyism, at all the important posts. The Trotskyists were already beginning their attempts to employ arguments about democracy—arguments which were scarcely suited to their leader, who was somewhat later described by Comrade Stalin as "the patriarch of all bureaucrats."

In the original version of Trotsky's theses on industry may be clearly seen the familiar features of Trotskyism of the end of 1920—insistence on a self-contained bureaucratic state apparatus; an endeavour to free this apparatus as far as possible from "Party tutelage" and thereby from the control of the Party and the working class, neglect of the peasantry, and a supercilious and disdainful attitude towards the working class, which found its expression in the proposal to close a number of the largest plants. In the autumn of 1923 Trotsky demonstratively walked out of the session of the Plenum of the Central Committee, and on October 8 he presented a statement to the Politburo, declaring that, thanks to the incorrect leadership of the Central Committee, the country was going to ruin.

Trotsky's Statement and the "Statement of the Forty-Six"

Trotsky's statement was immediately followed by the "statement of the forty-six," who came out in opposition to the Central Committee under the banner of Party democracy and a struggle against its suppression.* The group of "the forty-six" consisted mainly of individuals who had been at the head of the Trotskyist faction during the discussion on the trade unions. Most of the former leaders of the "Democratic Centralism" group made common cause with the Trotskyists.

These two groups, which in 1920-21 had opposed the Central Committee from different standpoints and which had fought against each other on a number of questions, were now united in one anti-Leninist *bloc*. We have already noted that in 1920-21 Trotsky's group had shown clear signs of a tendency towards the excessive use of administrative methods, favouring methods of compulsion as an infallible panacea, pleading for a policy of "shaking up" the trade unions, etc. The very same Trotskyists who actively opposed the Central Committee at the end of 1923, accusing it of a retreat from democracy, had occupied leading posts in some of the Party organisations in 1920, when the Party organisation was militarised, and firmly adhered to military methods even after the termination of the Civil War.

Now this group, which had defended Trotsky's platform on the trade unions in 1921, opposed the Central Committee, charging it with insufficient democracy. In close contact with them were people who in 1920-21 had subjected them to the most

---

* At the Plenum in September 1923, one month before the "statement of the forty-six" was submitted, the Central Committee raised the question of extending Party democracy. This fact alone is evidence of the lying and slanderous character of the "statement of the forty-six."

severe criticism and denounced them as "militarisers." The leaders of the former "Democratic Centralism" group were Sapronov, V. M. Smirnov and others. As to the former "Workers' Opposition" group, in so far as this group still remained in existence, it only formally refrained from joining the opposition *bloc,* while participating in this *bloc* in actual fact.

. The opposition of the end of 1923 was thus composed of quite diverse elements, who this time acted together, uniting against the Central Committee and the line of its policy, which. had already been laid down in Lenin's time. The following is a characteristic passage from the "statement of the forty-six": ·

"The regime which has been set up within the Party is absolutely intolerable. It destroys the initiative of the Party, replacing the Party by a selected bureaucratic apparatus, which does not fail to function in normal times, but which inevitably misfires at moments of crisis and which threatens to prove absolutely bankrupt in the face of the serious events which are approaching. The present situation is due to the fact that the regime of factional dictatorship within the Party which objectively developed after the Tenth Congress has outlived its usefulness."

The authors of this statement were here aiming first and foremost at the decisions of the Tenth Congress, adopted on Lenin's initiative, concerning the prohibition of factions and groupings, and at the members of the Central Committee who had been elected at that Congress under the direct guidance of Lenin and who consisted in their overwhelming majority of firm supporters of the Leninist line. Why did the Trotskyists in this connection lay stress on inner-Party democracy? They had in mind a change in the Party leadership. It seemed easiest to fight for a change in the Party leadership under the guise of democratisation. The Trotskyists hoped that this bait would be the easiest with which to catch the Party rank and file. But they wanted a change in the Party leadership in order to change the political line of the Party. The central point in Trotsky's statements to the Politburo and of the memorandum of "the forty-six" was the declaration that the Central Committee, through its incorrect economic policy and by its lack of a plan, had brought the country to the verge of ruin. On this point all the supporters of the opposition were more or less in agreement, though this could not be said of them with regard to their own practical programmes. Indeed, what programme could have been seriously proposed in opposition to the line of the Leninist Central Committee, except a programme of bourgeois restoration?

The moment which the Trotskyists chose for their attack on the Party was one when there were quite serious economic difficulties within the country and when the revolution in Germany had undergone defeat.

The Fourth Congress of the Comintern, which met in the latter part of 1922, had already noted the tense economic and political situation in Germany. Germany was not in a position to pay the gigantic indemnity which had been imposed on her by the Allied Powers. French imperialism accordingly sent its troops to occupy the Ruhr coal-basin. This resulted in an extreme accentuation of the economic crisis in Germany and caused the collapse of the currency system. The broadest masses of the workers and petty bourgeoisie were in the mood for revolution, but the opportunist leadership of the German Communist Party, which was headed by the Luxemburgists Brandler and Thalheimer, proved absolutely incapable of utilising the situation which had arisen, let themselves be taken in tow by the "Left" Social-Democrats, and thus enabled the German bourgeoisie to extricate itself from the acute political crisis.

In spite of the fact that the Trotskyists maintained factional contact with the Brandler group, they attempted to saddle the Central Committee with the responsibility for the crass opportunist errors of the Brandlerists.

The Economic Platform of the Opposition Exposed by the Party

Not until considerably later did the opposition put forward its economic platform. On the one hand, it contained the standpoint which Trotsky had enforced in the business organs, the standpoint of "the dictatorship of industry" or of "super-industrialisation." The gist of this policy was to enforce commercial accounting of the most vulgar bourgeois kind in the industries and completely to ignore the interests of the peasant consumer in the price policy, regarding the peasantry as a "colony" to be exploited by industry. On the basis of this premise, Trotsky proposed plans for ruthless concentration, for the closing of a large number of plants (in Petrograd), completely disregarding political considerations. The Trotskyist theory of "the dictatorship of industry" gave every encouragement to individual business managers to indulge in a reckless raising of prices.   ,

The policy of raising prices on industrial products at all costs might have resulted in very grave political consequences, and threatened to disrupt the political alliance between the working class and the peasantry. In the case of Trotsky, this policy was connected with a habit of ignoring the peasantry, which was characteristic of him even after he joined the Bolshevik Party and which came out with particular clearness at the time of the Brest Peace Treaty and during the discussion on the trade unions. It is significant that during the Revolution of ·1905-07, Trotsky wrote that the working class after seizing power would come into hostile relations with the peasantry. On the other hand, there were elements in the opposition who showed that they were actually ready to make the most sweeping concessions to the kulaks. No doubt this explains why the opposition theses also contained the idea of "commodity intervention." How could the prices on commodities be reduced? By allowing large imports of foreign commodities, disregarding all considerations of a favourable trade balance. The fact that large imports of foreign commodities, even if they had resulted in a reduction of prices, would have seriously affected our still insufficiently strengthened industry, was of small concern to the opposition, although they themselves advocated high prices on industrial products on the plea that this was in the interests of industry. Factionalism led the Trotskyists to forget the first elements of logic. Inasmuch as the opposition was composed of the most heterogeneous elements which were under the influence of different bourgeois and petty-bourgeois groups, its economic theses incorporated absolutely conflicting tendencies and contradictory demands. Another characteristic peculiarity of the economic platform of the opposition was also a bureaucratic attitude to the problem of planning in economy. The cpposition 'insisted on such strict and all-inclusive planning as was quite beyond the power of our business organs to attain, owing to the weak state of industry and in view of the tremendous role which was still played by scattered peasant farming. This was another example of the opposition's anti-Bolshevik tendency to ignore the peasantry.

For Bolshevik Organisational Principles

The opposition's attempt to use the demand of inner-Party democracy as its trump card was of a thoroughly hypocritical and anti-Party character. The Bolsheviks have always regarded the Party as a solid centralised organisation, closely connected with the masses. For this reason democratic centralism was the fundamental organisational principle of the Party. The Party has never taken the standpoint of broad democracy at any price. It held that the extent to which, and the form in which, democracy can be applied depends on the specific conditions, that these things have to be subordinated to the principle of strength and fighting capacity in the Party organisation, to the general interests of the revolutionary struggle of the working class. At the time of the Revolution of 1905-07, as we have seen, inner-Party democracy was considerably extended, while during the years of reaction it was greatly reduced. After ceasing to be illegal, the Party built up its organisation on the principles of broad democracy. In 1920, when the policy of War Communism was applied in our country, extremely great limitations of democracy were tolerated in the organisational practice of the Party.

In 1920-21, the Party adopted decisions regarding inner-Party democracy, but in view of the objective conditions it appended a number of restrictions to these decisions. By the autumn of 1923, however, the objective conditions had already become different. The social composition of the Party had improved. It was gradually purging itself of alien elements. As a result of planned and systematic educational work, the ideological and political level of the rank and file of the Party was gradually being raised. The objective conditions had thus become more favourable for the practice of Party democracy. The decision of the Central Committee of December 5, 1923, on the realisation of inner-Party democracy, was adopted prior to the discussion. The decision pointed out the objective conditions which created a basis for the development of inner-Party democracy, as well as a number of factors which hindered this development and which the Party must concentrate on overcoming. These included survivals of the war period, bureaucratic influence in the state apparatus, the still low cultural level of some of the Party units, etc.

What Was the Opposition Aiming At?

But no sooner did the Politburo, with Trotsky's participation, pass this decision, than Trotsky gave the signal to his followers to launch an attack on the Party leadership, above all in the Moscow districts. What did the Trotskyist opposition want? It wanted to smash the existing Party apparatus, to disrupt the Leninist Party cadres. While the Party was guided by the existing Leninist cadres, the opposition could not put its policy into effect. The Central Committee stood for the preservation and strengthening of the cadres which had been formed and had grown up under Lenin's leadership.

All the other differences of opinion were subordinate to this fundamental difference. Trotsky wrote of the danger of the degeneration of the cadres, because he wanted to "shake them up," as he wanted to shake up the leading cadres of the trade unions in 1921. Trotsky speculated on finding support among the youth, pleading the need to "rejuvenate" our Party cadres, arguing that the Party ought to give heed to the voice of the student youth and to look upon it as a barometer. This was but another instance of the desire to change the Party line by thoroughly demolishing the leading apparatus of the Party. In order the more easily to win the central Party leadership, the opposition demanded that the freedom of ideological groupings (really equivalent to freedom of factions) be restored in our Party, though this had been categorically forbidden by the Tenth Congress.

What can be said on behalf of people who now laid claim to the leadership of the Party while they had spent the last few

years in a continuous struggle against Lenin? To be sure
Lenin gave them the chastisement they deserved. It was Lenin
and no other who at all congresses attacked the "Democratic
Centralism" group and the "faction which out-shouted all
shouters"; it was Lenin who, spoke in the severest possible
manner against the main Trotskyist group on the eve and during the course of the Tenth Congress; it was Lenin who carried
on a systematic struggle against Trotsky after the latter had
joined the Party, not to mention the struggle before he joined
the Party.

What would have been the effect of the policy of the 1923
opposition? It would have resulted in the weakening of the organisational apparatus of the Party, in the weakening of the
firm leadership of the Party in the. Soviet apparatus and hence
in the strengthening of those bourgeois tendencies in the Soviet
apparatus which Trotskyism supported in the period of 1920-23,
and, in the last analysis it would have resulted in the disintegration of the Party and the collapse of the proletarian dictatorship.

The "criticism" of the opposition, which was directed in all
its venom against the Party apparatus, against its leading cadres
and against the Party regime which had been established by
Lenin, facilitated the process of degeneration of individual links
in the Soviet apparatus and its liberation from Party influence,
the danger of which had been pointed out by Lenin on the eve
of the Twelfth Congress. In the lower ranks, those who associated themselves with the opposition were primarily all those
strata who were discontented with the policy of the Party, the
petty-bourgeois elements who had penetrated into the Party, who
felt very uncomfortable in the grip of proletarian discipline and
who had not been assimilated by the Party; by all those who
differed with the Party on points of principle, who declared at
meetings that we had a dictatorship over the proletariat, that
the Party nuclei should decide and the Central Committee only
carry out the decisions without discussion. All this motley throng
of diverse petty-bourgeois anarchic forces were aroused and taken
in tow by the Trotskyist opposition.

On questions of Comintern policy the leaders of the opposition (Trotsky, Radek) tended to support the Rights within the
Comintern, particularly in the German Communist Party. On

questions concerning the foreign policy of the U.S.S.R. they were in favour of making decisive concessions to foreign capital in the negotiations regarding loans and concessions.

The economic policy of the Trotskyist opposition would have led to a rupture between the working class and the peasantry, towards capitulation to the new bourgeoisie and the enslavement of the country by foreign capital. The organisational policy of the opposition would have led to the collapse of the Party, to giving free rein to the anti-Soviet activity of the petty-bourgeois elements in the country, for whom the "Party regime," which was being assailed with such venom by the opposition, was synoriomous with proletarian dictatorship. Finally, the policy of the opposition in the Comintern would have led to the support of Right Social-Democratic deviations.

The Thirteenth Party Conference

But the Party was able decisively to repulse the opposition. During the discussion the vast majority of the workers' nuclei supported the line of the Central Committee. This line was endorsed by an overwhelming majority at the Thirteenth Party Conference. At the same time the Conference, after hearing Comrade Stalin's report, characterised the line of the opposition as a petty-bourgeois deviation which, objectively considered, would lead to a weakening of the Party, to a weakening of the Leninist leadership given by the Party to the Soviet apparatus. There can be no doubt that the disruptive anti-Party activity of the opposition would have been utilised by our enemies had not the Party been able by quick and decisive measures to strengthen its unity and to repulse the petty-bourgeois deviation of the opposition.

"The opposition headed by Trotsky," reads the resolution adopted by the Thirteenth Party Conference on Comrade Stalin's report, "put forward the slogan of breaking up the Party apparatus and attempted to transfer the centre of gravity from the struggle against bureaucracy in the state apparatus to 'bureaucracy' in the Party apparatus. Such utterly baseless criticism and the downright attempt to discredit the Party apparatus cannot, objectively speaking, lead to anything but the emancipation of the state apparatus from Party influence. The tendency to divorce the state organs from the influence of the Party was already manifested by Trotsky before the Twelfth Congress of the R.C.P. The opposition has attempted to set the younger Party generation against the main cadres of the Party and its Central Committee. The Party's doctrine has been that it must gauge its policy by its basic proletarian core, by the worker Communists who work at the bench; the opposition headed by Trotsky has begun to contend that the student youth should serve as a barometer for the Party."

"Trotsky," the resolution continued, "has given vague hints of the degeneration of the main cadres of our Party, thereby attempting to undermine the authority of the Central Committee, which is the sole representative of the whole Party between Congresses. . . . Trotsky has not only attempted to set himself against all the rest of the Central Committee, but has resorted to such charges as could not but arouse anxiety among the broad circles of the working class and stormy protests in the ranks of the whole Party.

"In economic questions the opposition has manifested complete bankruptcy. It has been absolutely unable to support its charges against the Central Committee of the Party and has not even attempted to put forward any kind of systematic proposals on questions of economy as an alternative to the policy of the Party.

"In its criticism of the economic policy of the Party the opposition has manifested two shades of opinion. One part of the opposition pays ample tribute to 'Left' phrases against the N.E.P. in general, making such statements as could only have a meaning if these comrades were proposing to abandon the N.E.P. and return to War Communism. . . . Another and much more influential part of the opposition has, on the contrary, reproached the Central Committee with not going far enough towards meeting the demands of foreign capital, with not making sufficient concessions to the imperialist powers, etc. This part of the opposition (Radek) proposed outright that the terms which the Party had outlined in connection with the Genoa Conference be revised and that great economic concessions be made to international imperialism with the aim of strengthening business relations with foreign capital. The Party has had no hesitation whatever in rejecting both of these errors.

"The opposition in all its shades has revealed absolutely un-Bolshevik views with regard to the significance of Party discipline. The actions of a large number of representatives of the opposition constitute a gross violation of Party discipline, recalling the times when Lenin had to fight against 'the anarchism of the intellectuals' in organisational questions and to defend the principles of proletarian discipline in the Party [against the Mensheviks—N.P.].

"The opposition has clearly violated the decision of the Tenth Congress of the R.C.P. prohibiting the formation of factions within the Party. For the Bolshevik conception of the Party as a monolithic whole the opposition has substituted a conception of the Party as an agglomeration of all possible tendencies and factions. These tendencies, factions and groupings, according to the new views of the opposition, should have equal rights in the Party, and the Central Committee of the Party should act not so much as the leader of the Party, but rather simply as a register of and mediator between the various tendencies and groupings. This conception of the Party has nothing in common with Leninism. The factional activities of the opposition could not but become a menace to the unity of the state apparatus. The factional actions of the 'opposition' have revived the hopes of all the enemies of the Party, including the bourgeoisie of Western Europe, for a split in the ranks of the Russian Communist Party. As a result of these factional actions the Party has again been confronted in all its acerbity with the question of whether the R.C.P., being in power, can allow the formation of factional groupings within the Party.

"Drawing the balance of these differences of opinion and analysing the whole character of the actions of the representatives of the 'opposition,' the All-Union Party Conference concludes that the present 'opposition' represents not only an attempt to revise Bolshevism, not only an outright departure from Leninism, but a clearly expressed *petty-bourgeois deviation*. There can be no doubt that this 'opposition,' objectively considered, reflects the pressure of the petty bourgeoisie on the positions held by the proletarian Party and the policy pursued by it."*

Thus the Thirteenth Party Conference, in its resolution on Comrade Stalin's report, characterised the essence of Trotskyism as a petty-bourgeois deviation within the Party.

Objectively reflecting the pressure of the petty-bourgeoisie on the positions of the proletarian dictatorship, refraining as yet from stating its views explicitly and fully, confining itself at times, from purely tactical considerations, to "vague hints," Trotskyism even at that time was already revealing all its profound and irreconcilable hostility to Bolshevism, was already well on the way to becoming the vanguard of bourgeois counter-revolution.

One factor which made it especially necessary to strengthen the unity of the Party was the need to overcome the economic difficulties, which found their reflection in the increased activity of the opposition. The opposition had the backing of hostile forces, and to struggle against these the Party had to rally still more closely around its Leninist Central Committee. These hos-

* Resolution of the Thirteenth Party Conference on the results of the discussion and on the petty-bourgeois deviation in the Party.

tile forces were attempting to drive a wedge between the working class and the peasantry, and between the working masses and the Party. The struggle against the opposition was organically connected with the task of overcoming the difficulties, with the solution of a number of important economic questions. It was precisely the difficulties which spurred on the forces hostile to the Party and the working class, and which intensified their struggle against the proletarian dictatorship. The Thirteenth Party Conference endorsed the Central Committee's policy of lowering the prices of industrial products, to which the opposition objected. The Thirteenth Party Conference outlined the main task with which the further development of industry was connected, namely, the carrying out of the currency reform. The *chervonetz*,* which was introduced in the end of 1922, was gradually becoming the basic medium of money circulation. The' Conference recognised the necessity of establishing a stable currency on the basis of the *chervonetz* and of discontinuing further issues of currency. This was the most important means for strengthening and rectifying the system of commodity circulation. During the discussion the spokesmen of the opposition predicted that our currency reform would meet' with all sorts of mishaps. The currency reform which was put into effect immediately after the Thirteenth Party Conference, replacing the non-guaranteed currency with the *chervonetz*, clearly proved that the predictions of the opposition were without foundation. The currency reform was carried through, the country received a stable currency, and thereby much more favourable conditions were created for the further strengthening of the socialist elements in our economy.

The Further Strengthening of the Proletarian Composition of the Party

The Thirteenth Party Conference also called attention to the need of changing the social composition of our Party. This change in the social composition, coupled with the raising of the political level of its members, constituted important conditions for the extension of Party democracy.

* A ten-ruble gold coin. *Ed.*

At the time of the Thirteenth Party Conference only slightly over 40 per cent of all Party members were workers by origin, while the proportion of workers from the bench was still less —only 17 to 18 per cent. Such a state of things was very abnormal in a proletarian party.

Why did the Party bring this matter to a head at the Thirteenth Conference and not before? Lenin spoke of it at the Eleventh Congress. The explanation lies in the fact that our proletariat had not yet outlived its declassed condition, in the powerful influence exercised over it by anarchic petty-bourgeois forces which were imbued with feelings of discontent against the Soviet government during the interval between the Civil War and the N.E.P.

But in proportion as the declassed elements of the proletariat returned to the mills and factories, in proportion as industry revived and the economic condition of the proletariat improved, the political temper of the proletariat also underwent a change for the better. This fact was proved afresh in the discussion which was held on the eve of the Thirteenth Party Conference. The discussion showed that the working class section of the Party was the soundest of all, while during the discussion on the eve of the Tenth Congress some of the working class nuclei showed signs of sympathy towards the "Workers' Opposition."

In view of this situation, the question of drawing the broad working masses into the ranks of the Party could now be tackled in a different way. According to a decision of the Central Committee, adopted by the Thirteenth Party Conference, no less than one hundred thousand workers from the bench were to be recruited into the Party within the next few months.

This was an absolutely correct political step, dictated by the situation at home and abroad. The ensuing days showed that this was a step to meet that tremendous urge towards the Party which had developed by this time among the working masses and which was manifested with especial force in the unforgettable days after the death of Lenin. This was the result of all the previous work done by the Party and of the correct policy pursued by it.

The Thirteenth Congress

The Thirteenth Congress of the Party,* held in May 1924, unanimously approved the policy of the Central Committee. The Congress, in particular, endorsed the international policy pursued by the Central Committee—a policy which had led to the recognition of the U.S.S.R. by a number of capitalist states, including Britain. The Congress approved the policy of extreme caution pursued by the Central Committee in giving out concessions and authorised it to develop further our connections with capitalist states on the basis of the monopoly of foreign trade and of a favourable trade balance. This favourable balance secured for the Soviet government a certain reserve of foreign currency, thus enabling it to manoeuvre more easily on the foreign market. During the discussion the Trotskyist opposition attacked the policy of a favourable balance, arguing that the U.S.S.R. must inevitably become increasingly dependent on capitalist countries.

The Trotskyists in general looked upon our economic system as a part of world capitalist economy, distinguished from its other sectors chiefly by its backwardness. In their opinion the same laws held good for Soviet economy as for capitalist economy. From the Trotskyist standpoint there could be no question of our socialist industry surpassing the industry of capitalist countries, particularly of such advanced countries as the United States. They saw no other prospect save the increasing dependence of our country upon capitalist countries, save an increase in the distance which separated us from them in technical and economic respects.

This state of things was to go on, in the opinion of the Trotskyists, until the coming of a socialist revolution in the countries of advanced capitalism.

The Congress noted with satisfaction the considerable success which the Party had achieved in carrying out the decisions of the preceding Twelfth Congress on the national question. The

* The delegates to the Congress represented 736,000 members and candidates, including 241,000 candidates accepted during the period of enrolment after Lenin's death and 127,000 who were already candidates before this period.

Thirteenth Congress was likewise able to record considerable progress by the Soviet power in the task of economic restoration. By 1923, the area under cultivation had increased to 80 per cent· of the area of 1916. Production of coal and oil for the year reached about 50 per cent of the pre-war output. By the middle of 1924, the daily loadings of freight averaged about 40 per cent of the 1913 level and were 14 per cent higher than in the preceding year. After the prolonged crisis in the iron and steel industry, which had almost ceased to operate in 1920-21, this very important industry also showed considerable improvement. Production of pig iron in the first half year of 1923-24 showed an increase of 203 per cent as compared with the first six months of 1922-23. The output of the open hearth furnaces during the same period showed an increase of 204 per cent, while the output of rolled metal increased by 176 per cent. In spite of these figures, however, the output of our iron and steel industry was still very small, reaching only about 10 to 15 per cent of the pre-war level.

The situation was only slightly better in the metal working industry. Much more rapid was the recovery of light industry, whose output in the spring of 1924 had already reached 70 per cent of the pre-war level. The productivity of labour, owing largely to the worn-out condition of the equipment, was only 60 per cent of what it had been before the war. However, this marked a great advance as against the period of War Communism. Wages reached approximately 65 per cent of the pre-war level. In general, as a result of the correct policy of the Party, the process of the economic recovery of the country and the restoration of its economy to approximately pre-war level was proceeding quite rapidly.

The resolution of the Thirteenth Congress on the report of the Central Committee noted the great achievements of the Party in the restoration of state industry. Of the immediate economic tasks, the main one confronting the Party was the further improvement of the iron and steel industry. Referring to the currency reform which had been put into effect, the resolution pointed out the particular importance·for that period of internal trade and systematic improvement in the sphere of agriculture. The resolution devoted considerable attention to the question of

improving the quality of the organisational and educational work
of the Party, in view of the fact that almost a quarter of a
million candidates had joined the Party during the period of enrolment after Lenin's death.

The Congress dealt specially with the problems of trade and
of the co-operative system, this being connected with the question of eliminating hitches in the marketing of commodities. The
reason why the peasants had to pay a high price for our industrial products was not only because the cost of production
was too high, but also because, after leaving the syndicates and
trusts, they passed through a very long and complicated path
before reaching the consumer, because our state trading organisations and co-operatives operated with wretched inefficiency.
The private trader was quite successfully competing with the co-
operatives, in some sectors even gaining the upper hand. Private
trade constituted 64 per cent of the total trade turnover in the
country, as against 36 per cent by the government and co-
operative organisations. Inasmuch as the co-operatives sold the
commodities at prices which were considerably higher than the
original cost of production, the private trader was able to sell
his commodities at the same prices, enriching himself at the expense of industry and the state as well as at the expense of the
peasantry. This put the broad masses of the peasantry in a
relation of still greater economic dependence to the private trader
and thus enabled the latter to influence them in a political sense
as well. In view of this, the Thirteenth Congress, while noting
the considerable achievements of the Soviet government in the
field of the restoration of industry, also set the Party certain
urgent tasks in the domain of trade. Without mastering this
domain, without seizing the key positions in it, without drawing
the great mass of the peasantry into the co-operatives (in accordance with Lenin's co-operative plan), the Party could not
count on sure success in the further construction of socialism.
The successful carrying out of the currency reform created favourable conditions for a broad offensive of the socialist elements in the sphere of trade and in that of the co-operatives.

The Thirteenth Congress confirmed the resolution of the
Thirteenth Conference on the petty-bourgeois deviation in the
Party. Speaking on the report of the Central Committee, the

leaders of the opposition, Trotsky and Preobrazhensky, took exception to this resolution. Trotsky, however, declared that he quite categorically condemned freedom of factions and groupings (as later events have shown, this statement was nothing but a hypocritical manoeuvre).

A detailed resolution was adopted by the Thirteenth Congress on the organisational work of the Party under the new conditions. At the time of the Congress almost 250,000 workers had already joined the Party during the period of enrolment after Lenin's death, and the Party was carrying on a great deal of ideological educational work among these recruits. The Congress called for the further recruiting of a large number of workers from the bench into the Party, so that within a short time this type of member might constitute a majority in its ranks.

The tremendous urge towards the Party felt by the 'workers was splendid evidence of the correctness of the Party's general line and of its increased influence, while at the same time it was no less strong and clear evidence of the isolation of the opposition from the Party. The more violent and rabid the attacks launched by the petty-bourgeois opposition on the Party and its Leninist leadership, the stronger was the urge to join the Party ranks felt among the broad proletarian masses. This urge had become most clearly apparent since the beginning of 1924. It was given a powerful impetus by the death of Lenin. But it was the result of all the previous work done by the Party.

After hearing the report of the Central Committee, the Thirteenth Congress approved the measures taken to effect a much needed reorganisation of the army. As head of the war department, Trotsky systematically tried to pursue a policy of divorcing the army from the Party, relying on those elements among the old specialists who were alien to the working class and the Party and on their outworn routine methods of organising the armed forces of the republic. This policy had had very evil effects on the state of the army, the war industry and the Party organisation in the army.

During the discussion in the autumn of 1923, the Trotskyists made every effort to set the Party organisation in the army at odds with the Central Committee.

After the Thirteenth Party Conference the Central Committee

took a number of decisive measures to strengthen the army with tried Party workers. Comrade Frunze was appointed vice-chairman of the Revolutionary War Council. Under his guidance and in accordance with the direct instructions of Comrade Stalin, a reorganisation of the army was put into effect. The most essential feature of the reorganisation was the formation of so-called territorial divisions with small permanent cadres. This system, allowing much larger masses of the population than heretofore to pass through the army and receive military training, became a powerful factor in strengthening the defensive capacity of the Soviet country. But it presupposed one essential political factor, the policy of an alliance of the working class with the broad masses of the peasantry, the policy which was pursued by the Party and which the Trotskyists rejected.

The Thirteenth Party Congress had to devote much attention to Comintern questions, since in certain Comintern parties about this time there was an active growth of oppositional tendencies which tried to unite around the banner of Trotskyism. In the foreign parties the petty-bourgeois make-up of the opposition was even more glaringly apparent. This opposition which now appeared in the Comintern and which reflected the tendencies of Trotskyism in the ranks of the R.C.P., approached the position of Social-Democracy on all questions. While paying lip service to revolutionary tactics, the opposition in actual fact fought hard against the policy of bolshevising the Communist Parties of Western Europe which was being carried out by the Comintern. The Thirteenth Congress condemned the deviations of the opposition in the Comintern which were actively defended by Radek and others.

It is significant that in almost all the fairly large Communist Parties of Western Europe the representatives of the Right tendencies, which clearly deviated towards the side of Social-Democracy, lined up with the Trotskyist opposition. This was done by Brandler and Thalheimer in Germany; by Rosmer, Monatte and Souvarine, all of whom had subsequently to be expelled from the Communist Party, in France; by Tranmel, who was also subsequently expelled from the Comintern, in Norway. The then Central Committee of the Communist Party of Poland, which was headed by Warski and Kostrzewa, and which had committed a number of opportunist errors, likewise adopted quite a friendly attitude towards Trotskyism.

The Thirteenth Congress also considered questions connected with the work in the countryside and the Young Communist League. The Y.C.L. at the time of its Fifth Congress (in April 1922) had a membership of 247,000. By May 1, 1924, its membership had already increased to 595,000. The Y.C.L. extended the influence of the Party to ever larger masses of workers and peasants. The role of the youth was acquiring increased importance in connection with the training of skilled labour for the rapidly growing industries; and in view of this, correct guidance of the Y.C.L. by Party organisations was becoming an exceptionally important factor.

The Fifth Congress of the Comintern

The Thirteenth Party Conference and the Thirteenth Congress resolutely repulsed the efforts of Trotskyism to undermine the unity and strength of the Leninist Party. The Fifth Congress of the Comintern represented a very important stage in the ideological rallying and consolidation of the Communist ranks on the international arena in the struggle against Trotskyism, which became a rallying point for all opportunist semi-Social-Democratic elements. It is highly significant that during this period it was mainly the open Right opportunists whom Trotskyism rallied around itself in the ranks of the Comintern. Their opportunism found its expression first and foremost in a dogmatic interpretation of the decision of the Third Congress of the Comintern regarding the winning over of the masses. This decision was misconstrued into meaning that the Communist Party could not undertake any offensive action until it had rallied around itself practically 90 per cent of all the toilers. The tactic of the united front was interpreted as a tactic of co-ordinated action with the leaders of Social-Democracy. The slogan of a workers' and peasants' government was misinterpreted in the sense of a coalition of the Communists with the Social-Democrats on the basis of winning a parliamentary majority. This was approximately the line followed in Saxony by Brandler, Thalheimer and Co. in the autumn of 1923, and

14*

essentially, it was not far removed from the position of Mac-Donald's "Labour" government.

It is characteristic that the German Brandlerites combined a direct lapsing into Social-Democratic positions with expressions of solidarity with the Russian Trotskyists, who in 1923 made ample use of "Left" phrase-mongering.

Along with Right opportunist deviations, there were also signs of "Left" deviations in the Comintern. The latter deviations found their expression in a tendency to disregard the slogan of winning over the masses. The "Left" sectarians pictured the Communist Parties as parties of a terrorist minority which were able to lead the masses into struggle at any given moment when they so desired. This gave rise to a negative attitude towards work in the reformist trade unions.

The theses on tactics which were adopted by the Fifth Congress squarely raised the question of the bolshevisation of the Communist Parties abroad, of their mastering the strategy, tactics and organisational methods of the C.P.S.U.

This was a continuation of the political line which had been carried out by Lenin from the very beginning of the formation of the Comintern and which found particularly clear expression in the Twenty-One Conditions adopted by the Second Congress in order to prevent centrist and semi-centrist elements from obtaining access to the Comintern.

The decisions of the Fifth Congress particularly stressed the need of changing the organisational methods in the work of the Communist Parties, which retained numerous vestiges of Social-Democratic methods.

The experience of unsuccessful class battles in various countries, particularly in Germany where the leaders had committed a number of crass opportunist errors in the autumn of 1923, made it a matter of urgent necessity to tackle the tremendous task involved in the bolshevisation both of the German and of other Communist Parties. The Congress emphasised that a workers' and peasants' government cannot be brought into being as a result of any parliamentary combinations and bargains with Social-Democracy, but only as a result of the overthrow of the bourgeoisie by means of an armed uprising of the proletariat leading the broad toiling masses.

The Congress drew the attention of all Parties to the paramount importance of work in trade unions and pointed out the need to organise shop nuclei as the basic units of the Party organisations. Until then some of the Communist Parties, retaining Social-Democratic traditions, had been organised chiefly on a territorial principle, according to electoral divisions.

The Congress endorsed the decision of the Thirteenth Conference and the Thirteenth Congress of the R.C.P. regarding the opposition, condemning the petty-bourgeois deviation of the latter and recognising its actions as a menace to the unity of the Party and consequently to the proletarian dictatorship in the U.S.S.R.

The resolution on the Russian question, which was moved at the Congress by the German, French, British and American delegations, emphasised that the sections of the Comintern

"have followed the Russian Party discussion with the greatest attention and grave anxiety and have unanimously expressed themselves in support of the Central Committee of the R.C.P.

"They have done this because they saw in the proposals of the opposition a threat to the stability of the proletarian dictatorship and the unity of the R.C.P. Owing to this, the action of the Russian opposition was not only directed against the Central Committee of the R.C.P., but objectively, in its consequences, was directed against the interests of the Communist International."

Trotsky, who was invited to attend the Congress and state his views, refused to appear, hypocritically pleading Party discipline as his reason. Party discipline, however, did not prevent him at this very time from delivering a report on the international situation at a congress of veterinaries—a report which radically differed from the line of the Comintern and the Party. In this report Trotsky, among other things, declared that the world was entering into a prolonged era of democratic pacifism in connection with the policy of the United States, whose influence would assist the recovery of European capitalistic economy. The sharpening of all the contradictions of capitalism, the growth of fascism, the world economic crisis which started in 1929 in no other country than the United States, the transition to a new round of wars and revolutions, have utterly smashed all Trotsky's forecasts.

The Fifth Congress of the Comintern placed on record that the general crisis of capitalism was continuing. Of how protract- ed a character this crisis would be, and when its revolutionary solution would take place, would depend on the activity, deter- mination and fighting capacity of the Communist Parties.

The keynote of the entire Fifth Congress was a general struggle against opportunism, the firm Bolshevik direction given to the work of the Communist Parties abroad, and a fight against Social-Democracy.

The revolutionary battles in Germany had ended in failure, but the mood of the masses remained a militant one. The elec- tions held in the spring of 1924 were very successful for the Communist Party. However, the revolutionary wave, following the sharp economic and political upheavals in individual coun- tries, was ebbing. Capitalism, while continuing to pass through a general crisis, had entered upon a period of partial stabil- isation.

The Discussion on the "Lessons of October"

A few months after the Thirteenth Congress the Party had to go through another discussion, which was organically con- nected with the discussion of 1923. In the autumn of 1924 Trotsky published a new polemical work against the Central Committee in which, under the guise of analysing the "lessons of October" of 1917, he tried to take his revenge for the dis- cussion of 1923.

In his *Lessons of October* Trotsky again openly propounded his old theory of permanent revolution, representing things as though Lenin and the Bolsheviks had adopted this theory in 1917, thereby taking up new ideological weapons and renounc- ing the views which they held during the first revolution and after. . . Trotsky attempted to belittle, to minimise the role of the Party and of the Central Committee in preparing for the October Revolution, depicting the course of events as though Lenin had almost had to drag the Party towards the October uprising by the scruff of the neck and representing himself, Trotsky, as the principal inspirer and organiser of the October uprising, since Lenin, of course, was in hiding. The main object of the *Lessons of October* was to compromise the Party leadership.*

Trotsky's assertions naturally met with a lively rebuff from the members of the Central Committee who had taken part in the October events, and subsequently also, from the whole rank and file of the Party. The overwhelming majority of the Party, including many of the former rank and file followers of the opposition, rallied around the Central Committee, in order to repulse the new attempts to shake the unity of the Party and to replace Leninism by Trotskyism.

What was the essence of this attempt? As was pointed out by Comrade Stalin in his report to the Party fraction of the Plenum of the All-Union Central Council of Trade Unions, the old Trotskyism (before 1917, before Trotsky joined the Bolshevik Party), was characterised by:

1) The theory of permanent revolution, connected with a tendency to underrate the peasantry and the ability of the proletariat to lead the peasantry;

2) Lack of faith in the Bolshevik Party and a tendency to consort with opportunists;

3) Lack of faith in the leaders of Bolshevism and a desire to discredit them in every way.

The new Trotskyism (already within our Party), offers us, as Comrade Stalin pointed out:

1) The theory of bisecting Leninism into two periods. According to this theory the Bolsheviks were on the wrong track up to 1917, when they allegedly adopted Trotsky's viewpoint of permanent revolution;

2) The theory of bisecting the history of the Party. According to this theory the whole history of the Party up to October is of no significance, its real history not commencing until after October;

* The "strike-breaking" action of Zinoviev and Kamenev in October was turned to especially good account by Trotsky, who attempted to create the impression that the semi-Menshevik opportunist views of Kamenev and Zinoviev were shared by the Central Committee. Trotsky did not at all suspect that about a year and a half later he would find himself in a close political *bloc* with Zinoviev and Kamenev.

3) A struggle against the organisational principles of Bolshevism, continued effort to transform the Party into an agglomeration of groupings;

4) A theory which would depose Lenin under the guise of extolling him.

Comrade Stalin in his report drew the conclusion that the Party must stand guard over Leninism and bury Trotskyism ideologically once and for all.

In January 1925, the Plenum of the Central Committee, upon considering the numerous resolutions from local organisations regarding Trotsky's *démarche*—including resolutions which demanded his expulsion from the Party—decided to give emphatic warning to Trotsky, pointing out that efforts to revise Leninism and to undermine the unity of the Party were incompatible with membership of the Bolshevik Party. The Plenum at the same time expressed itself in favour of the removal of Trotsky from his post of Chairman of the Revolutionary War Council, while allowing him to remain, conditionally, a member of the Politburo.

The Party in the Struggle Against Trotskyism

The Eleventh Party Congress had officially declared, in its resolution on the report of the Central Committee, that the retreat was at an end. At the conclusion of the retreat the Party had entrenched itself in the key positions, retaining in the hands of the proletarian state the principal means of production, circulation and transportation (the land, large-scale industry, the banks, and the monopoly of foreign trade). Private capital was concentrated primarily in the sphere of trade, where it was quite successfully competing with the co-operatives and state organs. Private capital, including foreign capital, scarcely penetrated into the sphere of industry, concessions, leases, etc. In the countryside, the N.E.P. was again giving rise to a certain differentiation and growth of capitalist elements, who joined hands with the N.E.P. bourgeoisie of the towns.

Such was the economic disposition of the forces at the end of the retreat. Having completed this retreat and carried out the necessary regrouping of forces, the Party gradually passed over into an offensive on the basis of the N.E.P., this offensive commencing on the most important sector, on the front of the state socialist industry.

We have seen in what a sorry state industry was at the beginning of the N.E.P., when its output scarcely exceeded 20 per cent of the pre-war level, coupled with the fact that both the productivity of labour and the wages were extremely low, while the equipment was suffering terribly from excessive wear and tear. During the first three years of the N.E.P., however, the Party had already succeeded in making decisive progress on this all important sector of the front. Light industry, which worked for the peasant market, had reached 70 per cent of the pre-war level; production of coal and oil had reached about 50 per cent of this level, and only in the case of the iron and steel industry was the process of restoration still at its very beginning. Considerably worse was the situation in the sphere of trade. The market had become the principal means of contact between the state industry and peasant farming. And the proletarian state had not secured full control of this means of contact. Private wholesale and retail trade, which had caused a considerable inflation in prices, was undermining the policy of the state organs and reaping large profits at the expense of the state and above all at the expense of the peasantry, among whom the high retail prices were evoking feelings hostile to the Soviet government. Following the Thirteenth Congress, the Party adopted a number of decisive measures aimed at bringing the market under control. The development of agriculture during the first years of the N.E.P. took the form almost exclusively of the restoration of individual peasant farming; the process of drawing peasant farming into co-operative production in the spirit of Lenin's co-operative plan was still in its first, weak rudimentary beginnings, while Soviet and collective farms were as yet a quite insignificant factor.

The successes achieved by the Party in economic restoration were secured at the price of great efforts. The restoration curve moved upward with marked zigzags. In this respect the economic difficulties encountered at the end of 1923 are particularly significant.

The effects of these difficulties on the Party, however, will not be quite clear, unless they are considered in connection with the world situation. We know how high the revolutionary wave had risen in western and central Europe in 1918-19. In 1920 and particularly in 1921 (the March defeat in Germany) it began to ebb. The defeat of the German revolution in 1923, which coincided in point of time with our economic difficulties of the end of 1923, signalised the further ebb of the revolutionary wave.

This gave rise to a number of happenings of a critical character in certain Communist Parties. In 1918-20, a considerable number of socialist parties and groups had made common cause with Communism. In Europe a process was going on analogous to that which Russia began to experience somewhat earlier and which manifested itself in the passing of Menshevik, particularly "Left" Menshevik elements (Trotskyism), into the camp of Bolshevism. Now, however, the ebb of the revolutionary wave in Europe gave rise to an opposite process—the return of a part of the "Communists-for-an-hour" into the camp of Social-Democracy. This gave our enemies a pretext for loud outcries about the dissolution of the Communist International. Actually, it meant a great step towards transforming the main sections of the Comintern into real, genuine Bolshevik parties, capable of really leading the revolutionary movement of the working masses. The Fifth Congress of the Comintern, meeting after the Thirteenth Congress of the R.C.P., gave a decisive rebuff to the Trotskyist opportunist elements within the various parties of the Comintern and outlined a number of measures for the further bolshevisation of these parties.

The very same questions were dealt with in a more extended form by the Fifth Plenum of the E.C.C.I. after the discussion on *Lessons of October.*

The Plenum declared that Trotsky's action which gave rise to a new discussion in the ranks of the R.C.P., signified an attempt to revise Leninism and to disorganise the leadership of the R.C.P.

Detailed theses were adopted by the Plenum on the bolshevisation of the Comintern sections, impressing upon them the necessity of a most resolute struggle against all deviations from Leninism, including the historic errors of Luxemburgism.

"This action was supported by all the forces which are hostile to Bolshevism. Within the Comintern it was supported by the Right sections of the Communist Parties, namely by those elements in them whose tactics have repeatedly been condemned by the international congresses as semi-Social-Democratic. Outside of the Comintern this action was supported by a number of persons who have been expelled from the Communist ranks (Levi, Rosmer, Monatte, Balabanova, Hoeglund, etc.). Lastly, all sorts of attempts were made by the Social-Democratic and bourgeois press to take advantage of this action."

It was no accident that Trotskyism should have received its most active support in 1923-24 from those elements of the Comintern that had not outlived the semi-Menshevik errors and tendencies of Luxemburgism (in Germany and Poland).

"Real assimilation of Leninism and its application in practice in the construction of the Communist Parties throughout the whole world," reads the Plenum resolution, "is impossible without registering the errors of a number of outstanding Marxists who have tried to rise to the level of applying Marxism under the conditions of the new epoch but have not been able to attain this level in all respects.

"Among these are the errors of the 'Left' Communists in Russia, of a group of Dutch Marxists (Gorter, Pannekoek) as well as the errors of Rosa Luxemburg. . . .

"Developments have been such that a number of Comintern Parties cannot now become really bolshevised unless they overcome the errors of Luxemburgism, which owing to historical conditions play a considerable role in the movement of these countries. Among the most important errors of Luxemburgism which are of actual, present-day significance are:

"a) A non-Bolshevik approach to the question of 'spontaneity' and 'consciousness', of 'organisation' and the 'masses.' The incorrect estimations arrived at by the Luxemburgists, who at that time had before them the experience of the German Social-Democratic Party which was frequently a downright hindrance to the revolutionary sweep of the class struggle, prevented them from correctly understanding the role of the Party in the revolution in general.

"b) An underestimation of the technical factor in preparing for an uprising has hindered, and in some cases still partly hinders, the correct approach to the question of 'organising the revolution.'

"c) Errors on the question of the attitude towards the peasantry. Rosa Luxemburg in her last article, written after the suppression of the Spartacist uprising in January 1919, came close to sensing her own error, expressed in an underestimation of the role of the peasantry. However, in a number of her earlier writings Rosa Luxemburg underestimated the role of the peasantry, *i.e.*, did not present the peasant question in a Bolshevik spirit, thereby making a number of ideological concessions to Social-Democracy.

"Such Social-Democratic errors on the peasant question were also committed in practice by the Hungarian Communists when they were in power, by the Polish Communist Party, by the Bulgarian Communist Party in 1923, by the Italian Maximalists and by the pseudo-Left ideologists of the 'Communist Labour Party' in Germany, and are committed even now by several sections of the Comintern.

"d) No less serious were the errors of Rosa Luxemburg and of a number of Polish, Dutch and Russian Marxists on the national question. The rejection of the slogan of the self-determination of nations (the right to form an independent state) on the grounds that under imperialism 'it is impossible' to solve the national question, has in fact led to an attitude of complete negation on the national question, greatly hindering the work of the Communists in a number of countries.

"e) The propaganda in favour of making the trade unions Party organisations, defended as it was for a number of years by the Polish Party under the leadership of Rosa Luxemburg, was a grave error which testified to a failure to understand the role of the trade unions as an organisation comprising all wage workers without exception. This error has seriously hindered and still hinders the vanguard from making the correct approach to the whole class.

"The error which was committed by a part of the German Communists prior to the the Frankfurt Party Congress in 1924 on the question of trade unions was of an analogous character....

"Without overcoming the erroneous aspects of Luxemburgism, real bolshevisation is impossible. Only Leninism can serve as the guiding star for the Communist Parties the world over. Everything which deviates from Leninism is also a retreat from Marxism."

The strengthening of the bourgeois elements in the Soviet Union, the strengthening of their pressure on the Soviet state and on the Communist Party, the economic embarrassments of the Soviet power, reflecting as they did both international and internal difficulties, and, lastly, the ebb of the revolutionary wave in the West and the critical phenomena which it occasioned in some of the Communist Parties—these were the three groups of phenomena which precipitated the Trotskyist assault on the Party policy at the end of 1923, signifying the beginning of the complete rupture of Trotskyism with Bolshevism, with which it had temporarily joined hands in 1917. In this assault, particularly in the *Lessons of October* Trotskyism openly attempted to re-establish its ideology—the theory of permanent revolution; dating from 1905, the rejection of the proletarian dictatorship, of the alliance of the working class with the peasantry, and of the organisational principles of Bolshevism. It meant the downright revision of Leninism, the replacement of Leninism by Trotskyism. In taking this course, Trotsky clearly revealed his inner Menshevik nature, which had been temporarily concealed.

At the present time it has already become perfectly clear that the action of Trotsky and his associates in 1923 was a decisive step towards a complete breach with Bolshevism, that the Trotskyists were voicing the sentiments of the bourgeois environment which surrounded the Party and the Soviet government. Not long before, we have seen how Trotskyism acted as the mouthpiece of the bourgeois elements in the state apparatus who longed to see the weakening of Party control, which would, in fact, have meant the weakening of the control of the masses. Now Trotskyism changed its methods and again, as in 1918, began to employ "Left" phrases; besides this, it had also mastered all the demagogic manoeuvres of the "Workers' Opposition" of 1920-21. It employed "Left" phrases in its endeavours to conceal its Right programme of support to the Social-Democratic deviations in the Comintern, of concessions to the foreign bourgeoisie, of weakening the dependence of the state apparatus, which was choked with alien elements, on the Party. Not hesitating to resort to the most vile and lying demagogy and speculating on the difficulties of the N.E.P., Trotskyism in 1923 was already trying to imbue the Party rank and file with the conviction that the Party leadership was retreating, that it was surrendering positions, that it was allowing the bourgeoisie to grow rich. Trotskyism continued to employ these demagogic methods, adding strength and fury to its fight against the Bolshevik Party, until it found itself outside of its ranks. Of course, the Party was not deceived by the "Left" phrases of the Trotskyists. It understood that shifting of the Soviet power (and Trotskyism, in striving to get control of the Party, was also fighting for power) ever so slightly to the "Left" or to the Right would signify the beginning of the end of the Soviet power, the beginning of the victory of bourgeois counter-revolution.

At the end of 1923 the Party victoriously repulsed the on-slaught of Trotskyism. The economic difficulties of the restoration period, which the Trotskyists tried to take advantage of, had been overcome, thus removing the basis for further Trotskyist assaults upon the Party. When Trotsky attempted a new sally against the Party by publishing his *Lessons of October,* the conditions were so hopeless for a successful struggle against the Party that even. Trotsky's closest associates hesitated to join in the struggle.

Towards the middle of 1924, the country entered into a phase of the most intense industrial upswing.

Trotskyism found itself compelled to refrain from further onslaughts on the Party and to adopt an attitude of "wait and see." In taking this stand, it remained ready to strike, hoping for new difficulties, for crises, and fresh allies. But the Party as it emerged from the discussion of 1923-24 was not the same as when it entered the discussion. It had grown tremendously in ideological stature. The struggle against Trotskyism impelled thousands and scores of thousands of young Party members to read the works of Lenin, to study the history of the Party.

The assimilation of the lessons of this history, the assimilation of the principles of Lenin's teachings and of Leninist tactics by the broad masses of young Party members was one of the positive results of the discussion against Trotskyism in 1923-24.

Having gained in ideological strength, having grown organisationally, having drawn into its ranks hundreds of thousands of advanced proletarians, having won a decisive victory over Trotskyism in 1923-24, the Party extended the front of the offensive of the working class against the capitalist elements, attaining a tremendous speeding up of the rate of socialist construction, of the preparations for its radical reconstruction on socialist lines.

CHAPTER XV

THE PARTY DURING THE TRANSITION FROM THE PERIOD OF RESTORATION TO THAT OF RECONSTRUCTION

Overcoming the difficulties of the restoration period—The decisions of the Fourteenth Party Conference on the peasant question—The Fourteenth Party Conference on the working class and industry—On building socialism in one country—The beginning of the "New Opposition"—The anti-Leninist platform of the "New Opposition" prior to the Party Congress—The October Plenum of the Central Committee—The opposition against the Party—The report of the Central Committee at the Fourteenth Party Congress—The Party exposes the manoeuvres of the Opposition—The Congress of industrialisation—The problem of reconstruction—The Party in the struggle against agrarianisation and super-industrialisation—The Party exposes the "New Opposition" which is forming a bloc with Trotskyism

Overcoming the Difficulties of the Restoration Period

The Thirteenth Party Congress was able to note the great achievements of the Party in the task of industrial restoration. As had been foreseen by the Party with Lenin at its head when the New Economic Policy was begun, the rise of agriculture in the first years of the N.E.P. was followed by a similar rise in the field of industry. True, it was at first only light industry that was affected, but heavy industry afterwards followed suit.

Considerable resources were required for the complete restoration of heavy industry. At the Twelfth Congress, Comrade Krassin expressed the opinion that this task could not be carried out without foreign credits. We did it by mobilising our internal resources. But this involved certain difficulties. Wages rose but slowly and prices were too high.

In 1923 the Party was compelled to strike hard against attempts to raise prices excessively and took steps to have them lowered to some extent. Nevertheless the level of prices continued to remain considerably higher than it had been before the war. Without this it was impossible to secure the rapid restoration of industry and to create the necessary conditions for the reconstruction of the whole economy of the country on socialist lines. Our agriculture made enormous strides during 1922 and 1923. But the crop failure of 1924, coupled with the excess labour power which had accumulated in the countryside owing to inability to find sufficient employment in industry, retarded the further development of agriculture.

Besides this, the steady growth in the cultural and political development of the peasant masses was making them more and more sensitive to the shortcomings in our state apparatus in the rural districts.

The arbitrary methods which were employed in some places in dealings with the peasantry, the failure to observe revolutionary law, the insufficient attention paid by some of our local organs to the wants and needs of the peasantry—all this had an adverse effect on the temper of the peasant masses.

The Soviet government steadfastly enforced the policy of restricting the exploiting tendencies of the kulaks. This was effected by the government's taxation and credit policy, by protecting the agricultural labourers against direct kulak exploitation and by the firm enforcement of the Soviet constitution which deprived the kulak of political rights.

Nevertheless, kulakdom undoubtedly grew stronger during the first years of the N.E.P., in comparison with the period of War Communism. Gradually the anti-Soviet activity of the kulaks again began to grow. While constituting only a very small percentage of the rural population, the kulaks endeavoured to influence the temper of the middle peasant and even of the poor peasant masses, making use of every opportunity to stir up discontent against the Soviet government among certain groups of the middle and poor peasants.

At the beginning of the N.E.P. the countryside had already become predominantly middle peasant. The N.E.P. itself was clearly bound to serve as a new stimulus to the process of differentiation among the peasantry. But this process of differentiation was retarded by the nationalisation of the land and by the various measures which the Soviet government took to assist the poor peasants and restrict the kulaks. At the end of 1925 over 60 per cent of the rural population were middle peasants, about 35 per cent poor peasants and 5 per cent kulaks. In spite of a certain process of differentiation, the middle peasantry continued to remain the central figure in the countryside both in numbers and above all in point of economic importance.

The change for the worse in the state of feeling among individual sections of the rural population had already been manifested in the early autumn of 1924 by a number of serious symptoms.

The first of these was the August insurrection in Georgia. This insurrection, which was suppressed in a few days, was the result of provocation by foreign imperialists and was organised by the Mensheviks with money supplied by these imperialists. It was supported by the former nobility and part of the petty bourgeoisie. But a small part of the peasantry also manifested a sympathetic attitude towards the insurrection. Particularly dangerous was the fact that this attitude was manifested in the poor, semi-proletarian districts of Georgia (Guria and Mingrelia).

There were three main factors which account for a part of the peasantry having been drawn into the insurrection: (1) extreme over-population and shortage of land, coupled with the fact that the local population of these regions now had little or no opportunity for outside earnings, as it had had in the past; (2) the fact that industrial commodities, owing to their high prices, were beyond the reach of the population (the Mensheviks took advantage of this, spreading rumours that if they came into power the British government would supply Georgia with cheap goods); (3) The fact that the population had but weak contact with the local Soviet apparatus, which was not working satisfactorily.

Almost immediately after the Georgian insurrection new elections to the rural soviets were held throughout the whole Union, and in some districts the participation at these elections was very weak.

In some districts the activity of the peasants, which was undoubtedly on the increase, found other channels for itself than the soviets. The Soviet government could not under any circumstances reconcile itself to such a state of things, the more so as the enemy without might immediately take advantage of the slightest internal difficulty in our country. The international position of the U.S.S.R. continued to grow stronger. It was in this very autumn of 1924 that the Soviet government was recognised by the governments of France and Japan. But on the other hand, the Conservative government which had come into power in Britain launched a most intensive diplomatic campaign against the Soviet Union. The pretext for this campaign was the infamous forgery known as the Zinoviev letter, which was designed to serve as evidence of the interference of the U.S.S.R. in the internal affairs of Britain. Despite the fact that this forgery was immediately exposed, the die-hard government continued to use it as a pretext, launching a venomous campaign against the U.S.S.R., and openly took the lead in promoting anti-Soviet intervention both in Poland, the Baltic countries and Rumania and in the near and middle East (through Persia, Afghanistan, etc).

From this time on, the method of forging documents as a means of political struggle against the Soviet power, as a means of organising anti-Soviet intervention, came into especially widespread use.

The Decisions of the Fourteenth Party Conference on the Peasant Question

The question of the Party's policy in the countryside from the standpoint of the further development of productive forces in agriculture was raised at the Plenum of the Central Committee in October 1924. A number of practical proposals which were discussed at this Plenum received their final formulation in the decisions of the Fourteenth Party Conference, which met at the end of April 1925.

The result of the hitch that had occurred in the rise of agriculture was that, although industry was being rapidly restored, there appeared a certain discrepancy between the rise of industry and the rise of agriculture, which threatened to obstruct the further development of the former.

It was a case of difficulties of growth. The winter of 1924-25 was characterised by a rise in the price of grain and an acute shortage of industrial raw materials, due to the extremely slight increase in the area planted with industrial crops.

It was necessary to provide a stimulus for the development of the productive forces in agriculture. The general rise of agriculture in 1924-25 was only possible provided there was a growth in the individual farming of the poor and middle peasants and provided this type of farming was to a large extent drawn into the sphere of the co-operative system. The level of the development of industry, which was not yet fully restored to the pre-war level, made it quite impossible to contemplate a widespread development of state and collective farming.

This was why the Fourteenth Party Conference, in aiming to raise the productive forces in agriculture by utilising the old technical equipment to the maximum degree and introducing new technical equipment, pursued a policy of rigorously obliterating all remnants of War Communism in the countryside, both in the sphere of economic relations and in the political sphere, and proposed that a number of concessions be made to the middle peasants with a view to encouraging the development of individual peasant farming and its further inclusion in the co-operative system. By means of a considerable reduction in the agricultural tax, peasant farming was assured greater freedom for the accumulation of capital. This provided an incentive for more intensive labour, for improved methods of farming and for the introduction of crops requiring a high degree of cultivation. The conditions for leasing land were made easier, thus making it possible to cultivate unused land; and in addition to this, conditions were made easier for the hiring of agricultural labourers, the interests of the hired labourers at the same time being strictly safeguarded. Besides this, the position of domestic handicraft workers was rendered considerably easier in economic and legal respects, which naturally opened a certain channel for the employment of surplus labour power and created an additional source for the production of commodities needed to supply the rural districts. This was a factor of great importance in view of the marked shortage of commodities.

The conference definitely adopted the policy of removing restrictions upon trade in the rural districts—a policy designed to promote the well-being of the peasantry and to increase the total volume of commodity circulation in the country. This naturally involved the danger of a further growth of kulakdom, of a further acceleration in the process of differentiation among the peasantry. There could be no doubt that the kulaks,

15*

too, would take advantage of the freedom which had been granted for the accumulation of capital, of the removal of the restrictions on the leasing of land and the hiring of labourers. But, while perfectly clear about the political consequences which must ensue from the growth of the kulak element, the Party took into account the fact that, as against the first period of the N.E.P., we had a strong state industry, a system of state credit, a stable currency and, lastly, the co-operative organisations which had already developed a quite extensive network in the countryside.   •

At this time the Soviet government, relying on a powerful industry, the financial apparatus and the credit system, was already able to a large extent to restrict the accumulation of capital by the kulaks. The task of fighting the kulaks continued to confront the Party in its full scope and urgency. Comrade Stalin dealt with it in his speech at the Sverdlov University, in which he explained the decision of the Fourteenth Party Conference.

"We can and must revive the soviets, win over the middle peasants and organise the poor peasants in the soviets in order to relieve the main masses of the peasantry of the burden of taxation and shift the main burden of taxation to the shoulders of the kulaks. . . .

"The state can and must have at its disposal a sufficient reserve of food to be able to bring pressure to bear upon the food market, to have the power of intervening when necessary, to keep prices at a level which is acceptable to the toiling masses and thus to thwart the machinations of the kulak speculators. . . .

"In this case it is a matter of direct exploitation of wage-labour or semi-wage-labour by the peasant *enterpreneurs*. We cannot, therefore, here adopt a policy of abating or of moderating the fight. *Our task is to organise the struggle of the poor peasants and guide the struggle against the kulaks*."*

Now that the land was nationalised and the power was in the hands of the working class, the kulaks could not develop rapidly. The middle peasant remained the main economic force in the countryside. The decisions of the Fourteenth Conference were aimed first and foremost at improving the position of poor and middle peasant farming, which also involved the necessity

* Stalin, *Leninism*, Vol. I

of developing those branches of industry which used agricultural products as raw materials. The co-operatives acquired tremendous significance. It was not for nothing that Lenin described the co-operatives as a form of socialist construction in which every rank and file peasant could take part. According to Lenin's co-operative plan, the development of commodity production in the rural districts and the growth of peasant accumulation had to be utilised, first and foremost for the purpose of strengthen-.ing the co-operatives.

"Under conditions when there is freedom of commodity circulation and a predominance of petty commodity production in the country-side," reads the decision of the Fourteenth Party Conference, "the co-operatives constitute the main social and economic form of the bond between state economy and the petty commodity producer of the village. The co-operatives alone can secure for the state the greatest possibility of controlling and regulating both petty agricultural production and commodity circulation in the country."

It was just at a time when large-scale industry was successfully developing that co-operatives offered an opportunity of directing the development of trade in the countryside along socialist channels and not along kulak-capitalist ones. This was why the Fourteenth Party Conference, while pursuing a policy of developing the individual farming of the poor and middle peasantry and reckoning on the inevitable growth of the capitalist elements in the countryside in the immediate future, at the same time set the Party the task of strengthening the co-operatives, which were to serve not only as a counterbalance to the kulaks but also as a highway to socialism for the poor and middle peasant masses. Various forms of co-operatives came under consideration—consumers' co-operatives, sales co-operatives, credit co-operatives, and also production co-operatives, notably collective farms (though at that time it was chiefly the primary form of collective farm—the association for joint tilling of the soil—which came under consideration).

In the main, it was a question of the first phase in the realisation of Lenin's co-operative plan, when the co-operatives in the countryside acted principally as a force linking up petty peasant farming with socialist industry, as a force regulating the

development of petty peasant farming and preparing it for the
transition to the system of large-scale socialist agriculture.

However, in order to render the co-operatives capable of
carrying out the great tasks which Lenin designed for them
and which now acquired the greatest practical significance, it
was necessary to raise the prestige of the co-operatives, to rid
them both of the remaining traces of War Communism and of
those distortions of the New Economic Policy to which Stalin
later applied the term "the Nepman spirit." The resolution on
the co-operatives which was adopted by the Fourteenth Party
Conference emphasised the necessity of stimulating individual
initiative among the rank and file co-operative members, of enforcing democracy within the co-operatives, of placing representatives of the non-Party peasantry in the leading organs
of the co-operatives, of waging a merciless struggle against
embezzlement, abuses, bureaucracy, inefficiency and the kulak
influence.

The decisions of the Fourteenth Party Conference at the same
time called for the abolition of all remnants of War Communism in the political sphere, since these likewise hindered the
development of individual peasant farming. This involved two
main tasks—to put fresh life into the soviets and to strengthen
revolutionary law.

To put fresh life into the soviets meant to make them the
centres of public life in the countryside, to get the peasantry
interested in them—not only the poor but also the middle peasants, who in some places were virtually being ousted from the
soviets—to put a stop to the illegal deprivation of electoral
rights, to set the local soviets specific practical tasks so that the
peasantry, by helping to carry out these tasks, might improve its economic position and better organise local affairs.
To strengthen revolutionary law meant to guarantee the toiling peasant against all manifestations of arbitrary action, to
see that the government organs strictly carried out the laws
and finally to give every peasant a clear idea of what he might
and what he might not do under the Soviet government.

The resolution adopted by the Fourteenth Party Conference
on the report of Comrade Molotov regarding Party construction
outlined a number of measures for the strengthening of the

Party organisations in the rural districts, for enlarging their membership, improving the quality of their work and purging them of kulak elements.

The Fourteenth Party Conference on the Working Class and Industry

The Fourteenth Conference took note of a tremendous growth of activity among the working masses as a result of the restoration of industry and the improved material conditions of the workers. In view of this it became particularly necessary to abolish those methods of arbitrary command and petty tutelage which were still being practised here and there in city soviets, trade unions and co-operatives. The influx of workers into the Party continued at a quite rapid rate after the Thirteenth Party Congress. The number of Party nuclei and of their members was increasing, while new forms of organisational and Party educational work continued to develop. The resolution of the Fourteenth Conference on Party construction took note of the fact that, thanks to the numerical growth of the Party and to the growth of political activity among the workers and among the Party rank and file, the work of our Party was gathering momentum, and called for the further development of inner-Party democracy.

The Thirteenth Congress had confronted the Party with the urgent task of raising the level of the metal industry. The Fourteenth Party Conference was able to note tremendous achievements in this field. Production in the metal industry had risen by 72 per cent as compared with the preceding year. A number of very large plants, which had been standing idle, had commenced operation or were shortly about to do so. The task of attaining the pre-war level of production was for the first time becoming an immediately practicable one; and this was true precisely of those branches of industry which were of vital significance for the economy of the country and which heretofore had been lagging far behind.

The Conference outlined a number of practical measures for the further development of the metal industry, the leading branch of our heavy industry. The development of this industry was gradually creating the necessary conditions for the mechanisation and tractorisation of our agriculture, for the widespread development in the forthcoming period of the socialist reconstruction of agriculture.

In his report on the work of the Fourteenth Party Conference at a meeting of the active Party members in Moscow, Comrade Stalin emphasised the tremendous significance of the achievements of our metal industry as noted by the Fourteenth Party Conference:

"*The output of our metal industry this year is almost double the output of last year....*

"What does ... this prove?

"It proves that as far as the organisation of industry is concerned, which constitutes the main basis of socialism, we have already entered the broad highway of development. As for the metal industry, which is the mainspring of industry in general, we may say that the period of stagnation has passed, and that our metal industry has now every opportunity of advancing and flourishing. Comrade Dzerzhinsky is right when he declares that our country can and must become a land of metal.

"I need hardly prove the tremendous significance of this fact both for the internal development of our country and for the world revolution.

"From the point of view of internal development, the development of our metal industry, the significance of its growth, is undoubtedly enormous, for it implies the growth of the whole of our industry, of the whole of our economy; for the metal industry is the main basis of industry in general; for without a powerfully developed metal industry we cannot hope to put our light industry, transport, fuel, electrification and agriculture on their feet. The growth of our metal industry is the basis for the growth of the whole industry in general, of the whole of national economy in general....

"As for the international significance of the development of our metal industry, we can say that this significance is incalculable. For what is the surging growth of the metal industry under the dictatorship of the proletariat if not direct proof that the proletariat is not only capable of destroying the old but also of constructing something new, that it is competent to build up by its own efforts a new industry and a new society free from the exploitation of man by man? To be able to prove this in actual fact and not in books, is to advance the cause of the world revolution."[*]

- * Stalin, *Leninism*, Vol. I.

We were approaching the end of the restoration period. The Party and the country were squarely confronted with the question: What next?

On Building Socialism in One Country

In giving an answer to this question, the Party had carefully to consider not only the situation within the country but the international situation as well. The chief resolution of the Fourteenth Party Conference, that on Party construction, spoke of a turning point in the situation.

"The chief and basic features of this turn can be summarised in the following facts: the absence of a revolutionary upsurge in Central Europe, with a simultaneous development of the revolutionary movement against imperialism in the colonies and dependent countries and with a certain temporary stabilisation of the capitalist regime as a whole: the quite rapid economic growth of the U.S.S.R. and the consolidation of the Soviet power; the changed interrelation between the U.S.S.R. and the capitalist world, which found its expression in the form of 'recognitions'; the development within the U.S.S.R., on the basis of its economic growth, of new processes, which create new difficulties for the strengthening of the workers' and peasants' *bloc*."

An enlarged Plenum of the Comintern was held shortly before the Fourteenth Party Conference. The Plenum took note of the relative stabilisation of capitalism and the absence of an immediate revolutionary situation in the most important capitalist countries. Such a situation was still present in Germany in the autumn of 1923. In the spring and summer of 1924, when the Thirteenth Party Congress and the Fifth Congress of the Comintern met, it was still impossible to declare with certainty whether the situation of the autumn of 1923 would not recur in the near future.

In March and April 1925 there could no longer be any doubt that the relative stabilisation of capitalism had set in, nor of the fact that it might last some years. To be sure, Comrade Stalin even at that time pointed out that this stabilisation could not be either prolonged or settled.

"In what ways has the stabilisation of capitalism found concrete expression?

"First, in that America, England and France have temporarily succeeded in coming to an understanding as to how and to what extent they will despoil Germany. In other words, they have managed to reach an understanding, which they call the 'Dawes Plan' for Germany. Can this understanding be considered to be at all durable? Not For, in the first place, it was brought about without 'reckoning with the master,' namely, the German people; in the second place, this understanding means the subjection of the German nation to a double yoke: the yoke of its own bourgeoisie, and the yoke of the foreign bourgeoisie. We should certainly have to believe in miracles to think that a cultured nation like Germany, and a cultured proletariat like the German proletariat, would consent to bear this double yoke without making a number of serious attempts at a revolutionary upheaval. . . .

"Secondly, the stabilisation of capitalism has found expression in the fact that British, American and Japanese capital has temporarily managed to come to an understanding as to the allotment of spheres of influence in China, the vast market for international capital, as to the ways of plundering it. Can this understanding be considered to be at all durable? Once again, no! In the first place, because the contracting parties are fighting and will fight to the death among themselves over the division of the spoils. In the second place, because the pact was concluded behind the back of the Chinese people, who do not want to, nor will they, submit to the laws of alien robbers. Does not the growth of the revolutionary movement in China prove that the machinations of alien imperialists are doomed to failure?

"Thirdly, the stabilisation of capitalism has found expression in the fact that the imperialist groups of the advanced countries have managed for the time being to come to an understanding mutually to refrain from interfering in the plunder and oppression of 'their' respective colonies. Can such an understanding or this attempt to come to an understanding be considered to be at all durable? No, it cannot! In the first place, because each group of imperialists is striving, and will continue to strive to grab a portion of its rivals' colonies. In the second place, because the policy of opression pursued by the groups of imperialists in the colonies serves merely to steel and revolutionise these colonies, thereby intensifying the revolutionary crisis. The imperialists are trying to 'pacify' India, to bridle Egypt, to tame Morocco, to bind Indo-China and Indonesia hand and foot; and they resort to every imaginable device and machination to achieve this purpose. Perhaps they will succeed in securing certain temporary 'results' in this respect; but there is hardly any doubt that these machinations will not be successful for long.

"Fourthly, capitalist stabilisation may find expression in an attempt on the part of the imperialist groups in the advanced countries to reach an understanding concerning a united front against the Soviet Union. Let us suppose that they succeed in patching up this understanding, and that by resorting to every possible stratagem, including scoundrelly forgeries, like those used in connection with the explosion in Sofia, they succeed in forming something in the nature of a united front. Is there any reason to believe that an understanding against our country or stabilisation in this field can be at all durable, at all successful? I think there is no such reason. Why? Because, in the first place, the effect of the threat of any such united front and concerted capitalist attack would be to rally the whole of our country as never before around the Soviet government, thus making it an even more impregnable fortress than it was, for example, in the days when the country was invaded by the armies of 'fourteen states'.... Because, in the second place, the march against the Soviet Union would unravel a series of revolutionary skeins in the enemies' rear, and thus disintegrate and demoralise the ranks of imperialism. There can hardly be any doubt that a whole heap of such knots have accumulated of late and that they bode no good to imperialism. Because in the third place, our country no longer stands alone, for it has the workers of the West and the opressed peoples of the East for its allies. There can hardly be any doubt that a war against the Soviet Union would also be a war waged by imperialism against its own workers and colonies. There is no need for me to show that should our country be attacked, we would not stand by with folded arms but would use any and every means to unleash the lion of revolution in all countries of the world. The rulers of capitalist countries cannot but know that we have some experience in this domain.

"Such are the facts and the considerations which go to prove that the stabilisation of capitalism cannot be durable; that this stabilisation implies the creation of conditions which will lead to the defeat of capitalism."*

This factor alone—the stabilisation of capitalism, however relative it might be—meant that the question of the future prospects of socialist construction in the U.S.S.R. had to be squarely faced and a clear, direct answer given to it. When the October Revolution had been accomplished, Trotsky and his followers believed the Soviet government would perish, unless the proletariat of Western Europe, organised as a state power, came to its aid in the near future. Trotsky also said that the epoch of genuine socialist construction in our country would not commence until the power in Western Europe passed into the hands of the proletariat, that the contradictions between the interests of the proletariat and the peasantry could only be solved on the,

---

* Stalin, "Work of the Fourteenth Conference of the Communist Party of the Soviet Union," *Leninism,* Vol. I.

arena of the international Communist revolution, and that these contradictions would otherwise prove insurmountable.

This recalls Preobrazhensky's amendment to the resolution of the Sixth Congress, in which Preobrazhensky tried to express the idea that it was impossible to build socialism in our country until the coming of the revolution in Western Europe. The desertion of Kamenev and Zinoviev in the days of the October Revolution was likewise caused by their lack of faith in the success of socialist construction in our backward country. The "Left" Communists, who proposed to declare war on Germany in the beginning of 1918, were also of the opinion that only an international revolution could save us from destruction.

Contrary to all the predictions and prognostications of Trotsky, Zinoviev, Kamenev and of the "Left" Communists, the Soviet government did not collapse. The international revolution being delayed, the Soviet government commenced the New Economic Policy, or as Lenin put it, changed its tactics from storm to siege. The N.E.P. at first meant a retreat, which was followed, however, by a regrouping of forces and by a transition to the offensive. And since, in the spring of 1925, the relative stabilisation of capitalism had definitely set in, the question arose as to whether the U.S.S.R., in view of the delay in the coming of the international revolution, was not destined to degenerate into a capitalist country.

The Party gave one answer to this question, the Trotskyists another.

But the question had to be faced squarely and allowed of no ambiguity or equivocation.

Was it possible or impossible to build socialism in one country, particularly in such a country as ours, a country of enormous territory, of unbounded economic resources, but at the same time, a backward country, encircled by capitalist states, while the international revolution was being delayed?

A reply to this question had been given in the previous works of Lenin, but it had to be applied to a new specific situation.

As early as 1915, during the world imperialist war, Lenin wrote that, in view of the law of the uneven development of capitalism in the period of imperialism, the victory of socialism in one country was possible.

Later, in one of his last articles, *On the Co-operatives,* Lenin expressed the thought that it was possible to build socialism in one country, referring directly to the U.S.S.R. Lenin wrote that, with the power and the means of production in the hands of the working class and with the co-operative organisations, we had in our hands all that was necessary and sufficient for the building of socialism.   At the Sixth Party Congress, Comrade Stalin said that Russia could become the country which would break the road to socialism.   The Party set about the task of building socialism immediately after the victory of the October Revolution, which was achieved under the leadership of the Leninist Central Committee, despite the deserters and capitulators.

What could stand in the way of the consummation of this task?   Our economic and cultural backwardness?   The existence of certain contradictions between the interests of the working class and the main middle mass of the peasantry?

As for economic and cultural backwardness, the Soviet government had been fighting it successfully for a number of years.   As regards the contradictions between the interests of the workers and peasants, Lenin categorically stated, in his articles on the Workers' and Peasants' Inspection, that in our social order there were no insurmountable contradictions between them, that the existing contradictions could be overcome and eliminated, provided our Party pursued a skilful policy in this matter and provided the leadership of the working class was maintained.

These opinions of Lenin were fully corroborated by the entire experience of socialist construction. The elements of socialism in our economy, which had completely collapsed during the Civil War, developed at a rapid rate.   Our industry was already close to its pre-war level of production, and was now based on socialist lines.   The situation of the working class and peasant masses was one of increased well-being.

There was no such direct threat to the alliance of the working class and peasantry as had existed in 1920-21.

On the appearance of any distortions of Party policy, adversely affecting the attitude of certain groups of the poor and middle peasants towards the Soviet government, the Party, under the firm leadership of its Leninist Central Committee, resolutely overcame these distortions. This was the case in particular in the autumn and spring of 1924-25. The New Economic Policy had fully justified itself as a method of laying the foundations of socialist economy.

Now the retarded tempo of the revolution made it essential

"to adopt the less painful, although slower, methods of enlisting the peasantry in the work of building socialism, of constructing socialism together with the peasantry."*

In view of this, the question of strengthening the alliance with the middle peasantry became one of particular urgency.

And for this reason, Comrade Stalin, in his report on the Fourteenth Party Conference, emphasised:

"The main task at present is to rally the middle peasants around the proletariat, to win them over to our side again. The main task at present is to link up with the main masses of the peasantry, to raise their material and cultural level, and to move forward together with these main masses along the road to socialism. The main task is to build socialism together with the peasantry, absolutely together with the peasantry, and absolutely under the leadership of the working class; for the leadership of the working class is the fundamental guarantee that our work of construction will proceed along the path of socialism."*

On the international arena, the growth of the contradictions in the capitalist world and the accumulation of the forces of revolution fully justified the hope that the Soviet government would be able, at any rate during the next few years, to avoid war and intervention.

On the basis of all these factors, the Fourteenth Party Conference deemed it necessary for the Party to adopt a detailed resolution on the question of whether it was possible to build socialism in our country under conditions when the international revolution was being delayed and in the concrete situation which had been created as a result of several years of the N.E.P.

Comrade Stalin, in his *Questions and Answers*, formulated this point of view as follows:

* *Leninism*, Vol. I.

*"Is the building of socialist economy in our country possible without the victory of socialism being first achieved in the principal countries of Europe, without direct assistance.... from the victorious proletariat of Europe?....

"Yes, it is possible. And it is not only possible, but necessary and inevitable. For we are already building socialism by developing nationalised industry and linking it up with agriculture, by implanting co-operation in the countryside and bringing peasant economy into the general system of Soviet development, by reviving the soviets and merging the state apparatus with the vast masses of the population, by building a new culture and fostering new social activity. Undoubtedly, there are very many difficulties on this road, we shall have to pass through a number of trials. Undoubtedly, the matter would have been greatly facilitated had a victory of socialism in the West managed to come to our assistance. But,' in the first place, the victory of socialism in the West is not 'made' as speedily as we might wish; besides, in the second place, these difficulties are surmountable and we are already surmounting them, as you know. ...

"To deny the socialist possibilities of construction in our country amounted to 'liquidationism,' which leads to the degeneration of the Party."*

This point of view encountered no objection at the Conference. In the Politburo of the Central Committee, however, Zinoviev and Kamenev disputed the possibility of building socialism in our country, referring to the—in their opinion—insurmountable obstacle of our economic and technical backwardness. The Conference drew a clear distinction between the building of socialism and its final victory, pointing out that the final victory of socialism in our country, in the sense of the complete elimination of the danger of intervention, would come about as a result of the victory of the revolution in a number of countries. However, this was not the question under dispute.

The resolution of the Fourteenth Conference on the tasks of the Comintern, containing as it did the decision on the building of socialism in our country as the main outline for future work, was of historical significance for our Party. The Party set itself a clear aim. The road to the realisation of this aim led through the further development of state-owned (socialist) industry, through the development of peasant farming

* *Ibid.*

on a co-operative basis, through the transformation of the middle peasant into our firm and reliable ally, while maintaining and strengthening the Party's connection with the poor peasant, and through the socialist reconstruction of the whole national economy. The Fourteenth Conference outlined the immediate tasks on this road. They involved a number of concessions to the middle peasantry, necessitated by the needs of the construction of socialist economy. However, an obstinate struggle against the line of the Fourteenth Conference was immediately started by a new opposition which had sprung up.

The Beginning of the "New Opposition"

The first signs of this struggle had already appeared a few months before the Conference. However, the opposition which had sprung up within the Politburo in the persons of Zinoviev and Kamenev did not at once bring to light the fundamental political questions that were involved. At first, the opposition tried to create the impression that it was fighting against any concessions to Trotskyism and continued to characterise the latter as a petty-bourgeois deviation, as a lapse into social-democracy. At the January Plenum of the Central Committee, Zinoviev and Kamenev demanded the expulsion of Trotsky from the Politburo.

The leaders of the "New Opposition" tried to secure a majority on this question at the Plenum, in order to create the impression that they had the Party behind them and thereby to secure a base for further offensive action.

When this failed, Zinoviev and Kamenev tried to transfer the organisational struggle to the Young Communist League and to place the Central Committee of the Y.C.L. in opposition to the Central Committee of the Party. When this, too, failed, they attempted to create a second centre of the Y.C.L. in Leningrad. But this attempt also was nipped in the bud. Zinoviev and Kamenev, who were preparing to capitulate to Trotskyism on such a vital and fundamental question as the building of socialism in our country, carried on their preparations under cover of "Left" phrases about a struggle against Trotskyism, allegedly more determined and consistent than the struggle which was being waged by the Central Committee. The Fourteenth Conference came, and Zinoviev and Kamenev did not reveal their differences with the Politburo, voting, without voicing the slightest objection, for the resolution of the conference on the international situation. This resolution contained a point regarding the possibility of building socialism in the U.S.S.R., which subsequently became the principal point of difference between the Zinoviev-Trotskyist opposition and the Party. Zinoviev and Kamenev deemed it more advantageous to postpone their attack until the Fourteenth Congress; they wanted to utilise the time which remained until the Congress in order to popularise their views among the rank and file of the Party, and to appear at the Congress with an already prepared platform.

In the meantime, there were symptoms in the Party of a tendency to give a Right opportunist interpretation to the decision of the Fourteenth Party Conference. This tendency, represented by the so-called Bukharin school, headed by Slepkov, Maretsky and Astrov, was manifested in attempts to draw general theoretical conclusions from the concessions to the middle peasantry decided upon by the Fourteenth Conference, interpreting these concessions as an extension of the N.E.P., as the beginning of an entire policy of making concessions and removing restrictions, as the beginning of a new policy of "face towards the kulak" and towards a capitalist way of development for agriculture.

These obvious opportunist distortions of the policy of the Party which had been made in a number of articles were aggravated by Bukharin, who in one of his reports put forward the slogan "Enrich yourselves." Addressed to the peasantry, this slogan of Bukharin's could only mean that the Party's policy was one of developing kulak farming and not one of socialist accumulation, or of the reconstruction of peasant farms. The natural outcome of this was to lapse into the theory of the kulak and the Soviet government peacefully existing side by side with one another, of the kulak peacefully growing into socialism.*

---

* "... The kulak co-operative nests will, in exactly the same way, through the banks, etc., grow into the same system, but they will be to a certain extent alien bodies.... The kulak co-operative, if it desires to flour-

The Central Committee proposed to Bukharin that he repudiate this clearly anti-Party slogan, while Slepkov, the closest adherent of Bukharin and principal organiser of his "school," was removed from the position of responsible editor of the *Komsomolskaya Pravda,* where he had been systematically trying to propound the opportunist method of misinterpreting the decisions of the Fourteenth Party Conference.

Nevertheless, the errors of Bukharin's disciples and of Bukharin himself were ascribed by Zinoviev and Kamenev to the Central Committee and its line. Zinoviev delivered a number of speeches and wrote a number of articles on the peasant question, in which he posed as the defender of the poor peasants, while frantically exaggerating the kulak menace. In these speeches and articles, Zinoviev obscured as much as possible the slogan of actively winning over the middle peasantry to the side of the Soviet government, systematically replacing it by the slogan of neutralisation, which had already been characterised as inadequate by Lenin at the time of the Eighth Congress. This amounted to a repudiation of the slogan of an alliance with the middle peasantry. Lenin's co-operative plan was also completely glossed over. Zinoviev described the situation as if the overwhelming majority of the peasantry were composed of poor peasants and kulaks. "The peasant, as a toiler, is our friend," said Zinoviev, inaptly paraphrasing the words of Lenin, "while the peasant as a seller of commodities is our enemy." Thus, the middle peasants, who sold their grain, *i.e.,* the vast majority of the middle peasants, were completely identified with the kulaks. If this standpoint were adopted, it would have been ridiculous to speak of the middle peasant farms united on a co-operative basis as a factor in socialist construction. From Zinoviev's standpoint, the only course left open to the Party was that of *dekulakisation.*

---

ish, must inevitably be connected, just as all other co-operatives, with the state economic organs. It will, for instance, deposit its spare cash in our banks, in order to obtain a certain percentage of interest. Even if co-operatives of this type were to develop their own banking organisations, they would in any case inevitably have to be connected with the powerful credit institutions of the proletarian state, which have the main credit resources of the country at their disposal." (Bukharin, *The Path to Socialism.)*

But the policy of dekulakisation, which was presupposed in the standpoint of the opposition, could not under the then existing conditions have enabled us to replace the produce of the kulak by that of the Soviet and collective farms.   It would have been a blow to the middle peasant, and would have deprived him of all incentive to enlarge the scale of his individual farming; while 'a mere equalitarian division of the kulak farms could not have resulted in any perceptible improvement in the situation of the poor peasants.

As against the line of the Fourteenth Conference, the opposition could offer nothing but demagogy.   The conditions were obviously not yet ripe for the extensive organisation of Soviet and collective farms.

Comrade Stalin, in his speech at the Conference of Marxist Agrarians in 1929, gave an exhaustive explanation of why the Party could not apply the policy of liquidating kulakdom in 1925:

"... Could we have counted on such an attack being successful at that time? No, we could not. That would have been the most dangerous adventurism! That would have been playing a dangerous game. We would certainly have come to grief and thereby strengthened the position of the kulaks. Why? Because we had not yet at our disposal those strongholds in the countryside in the shape of a broad network cf Soviet and collective farms upon which to rely in the decisive attack on the kulaks. Because at that time it was not possible for us to *substitute* the capitalist production of the kulak by socialist production in the shape of the collective and Soviet farms.

"In 1926-27, the Zinoviev-Trotsky opposition *wanted at all costs* to force upon the Party the policy of an immediate attack on the kulaks. The Party did not enter on this adventure, as it knew that serious people could not permit themselves to play at attacks. The attack on the kulaks is a very serious matter. One must not confuse it with declamation against the kulaks. One must not confuse it with a policy of scratching the kulaks, which the Zinoviev-Trotsky opposition energetically endeavoured to force upon the Party. To attack the kulaks means to smash the kulaks, to liquidate them as a class. Without these aims, attack is a declamation, mere scratching, empty noise, anything but a real Bolshevik attack. To attack the kulaks means to make proper preparations and then deliver the blow, a blow from which they could not recover. That is what we Bolsheviks call a real attack. Could we have undertaken such an attack five, or three years ago with any prospect of success? No we could not."*

* Stalin, *Leninism*, Vol. II

What Comrade Stalin said here regarding the Zinoviev-Trotskyist opposition of 1922-27 is even more true of the Zinoviev-Kamenev opposition of 1925.

The Anti-Leninist Platform of the "New Opposition" Prior to the Party Congress

In the autumn, with the approach of the Party Congress, the opposition intensified its activities. The difficulties experienced in the grain collections, the oscillations in the price of grain, the fact that here and there the kulak and well-to-do upper section of the peasantry refused to sell their grain, the threat to the stability of the *chervonetz,* etc.—all this was regarded by the opposition as offering a favourable occasion for an attack on the Party.

At the Plenum of the Moscow Committee of the Party, Kamenev made a report on the political situation in the country, while Zinoviev sent an article to the *Pravda,* "On the Philosophy of the Epoch."

The gist of Kamenev's report was contained in the following celebrated computation: the kulaks, constituting 14 per cent of the peasantry, hold in their hands · 61 per cent of the grain surplus. This meant that the dominant force in the countryside was no longer the middle peasant but the kulak, and that all the talk about an alliance with the middle peasant was quite without foundation. . . . Kamenev's report was substantially an indictment of the Party for underrating the kulak menace.

Zinoviev's article also contained two demagogic slogans, designed to serve as a bait for the rank and file of the Party as well as for the non-Party workers. We refer to the slogans of "equality" and the alleged danger of "the degeneration of the Party."

The toiling masses, Zinoviev argued, fought and died in the October Revolution for the sake of equality. It was now time for the Party to set about realising this slogan.

On the question of equality, Zinoviev was violating the fundamental proposition of Marxism-Leninism that the realisation of complete equality is possible only as a result of the complete elimination of classes, as a result of the transition to the highest phase of communism. Essentially, what Zinoviev had in mind was not equality, but petty-bourgeois equalitarianism.

As regards the degeneration of the Party, Zinoviev did not go beyond very cautious hints. He cited extensive quotations from the articles of Ustryalov, the *Smenovekh*-ist, which referred mostly to the degeneration of the Central Committee. He cited Bukharin's erroneous slogan, "Enrich yourselves," which had already been condemned, and made a direct comparison between this and the policy of Stolypin. From all of this the conclusion was to be drawn that the Central Committee was leading the Party towards degeneration and that the Party must mobilise against this danger.

Zinoviev's book, *Leninism,* published in the autumn of 1925, provided a theoretical basis for the platform of the opposition.

Confusing the task of building socialism in one country with the question of its final victory, Zinoviev in this book disputed the decision of the Fourteenth Party Conference, which was adopted, it is worth noting, on the basis of his report. He interpreted the N.E.P., not as a road to socialism but as a continuous retreat, as the most widespread retreating movement of Leninism. From this it followed that we could only set about the work of socialist construction by giving up the N.E.P. Lenin himself said, at one time, that we had to commence the N.E.P. with a retreat. But less than one year after the beginning of the N.E.P., Lenin had already declared, first at the Congress of Metal Workers and later at the Eleventh Party Congress, that the retreat was at an end and that we must set about the re-grouping of forces. Following this re-grouping of forces we started an offensive on the basis of the N.E.P. It was quite impossible to compare the condition of our state industry in the spring of 1922 with its condition in the autumn of 1925. But the point is that the opposition completely denied the fact of our offensive on the basis of the N.E.P. For the opposition did not consider our state industry, which was unquestionably being restored and developed, as an element of socialism.

The workers in our state enterprises are placed in a very difficult situation, Zinoviev repeatedly stated in the pages of his *Leninism.* They receive wages, they conclude collective agreements. This is not socialism, but state capitalism. With regard to the kulak, Zinoviev demanded a renewal of the policy of 1918, when a revolution against the kulak was going on in the countryside. This revolution was at that time characterised by Lenin as a socialist revolution in the countryside. For it not only expropriated the kulaks' means of production but destroyed what had been the virtual power of the kulak in the countryside and created a real Soviet power there. By urging a renewal of the policy of 1918, Zinoviev was thus suggesting that in some way or other the kulak had again managed to become the dominant class in the countryside. However, dekulakisation alone could not possibly have raised our productive forces, and consequently it did not offer a solution of the situation. By rejecting Lenin's co-operative plan, by reducing the co-operative system to state capitalism and thereby denying the possibility of a non-capitalist path of development for the petty commodity producer, the opposition took the standpoint that there were no prospects for the policy of the Party in the countryside. Our technical and economic backwardness was an insurmountable obstacle to the construction of socialism in our country— so Zinoviev and Kamenev declared in the Politburo on the eve of the Fourteenth Party Conference. Where was salvation to be found? From the standpoint of the opposition, salvation could come only from without, from an international revolution.

It is obvious that this approach to the question showed a lack of faith in our socialist construction.

But the Party had by now matured to a sufficient extent to prevent the success of these efforts on the part of the opposition to win it over by its methods of fawning demagogy. The chatter about equalitarianism and dekulakisation, designed to hook the backward working class members of the Party and the village organisations, was of no avail. The Party was able to expose the anti-Leninist demagogy of the opposition. The opposition later played its third demagogic card when it came out with the slogan: "Proletarianise the Party." Since the Party, according to the opposition, was confronted with the danger of degeneration, it was necessary to enlist the masses of non-Party workers in its ranks. Some of the Leningrad Party functionaries, who constituted Zinoviev's staff, proposed to accept into the

Party within one year several million workers, *i.e.,* practically the entire working class which we then had in the country. They contended that 90 per cent of the Party membership must consist of workers at the bench. This proposal was in sharp divergence from all Bolshevik traditions regarding the relation between the class and the Party. The Party is the *vanguard* of the class, the leader of the class. If the Party, at the given stage of the political and cultural development of the working class, were to merge with the proletariat as a whole, dissolve among the proletariat, it would cease to be a Party in the Bolshevik sense. Such views recall the memorable declaration of the Mensheviks that every striker should declare himself a Social-Democrat and the famous Menshevik plans for the creation of a broad labour party.

The October Plenum of the Central Committee

At the October Plenum of the Central Committee the leaders of the opposition urgently raised the question of opening a Party discussion. This was the gist of the memorandum "of four," submitted by Zinoviev, Kamenev, Sokolnikov and Krupskaya. The majority of the members of the Central Committee categorically rejected this proposal. At the same time the Plenum adopted the theses of Comrade Molotov on the question of work among the poor peasants, which contained practical proposals for increased economic aid to the poor peasants from the state and on the need to organise the poor peasants, for the defence of their interests, in the rural soviets, co-operatives, etc., in the form of so-called groups of poor peasants. The task of these groups of poor peasants, as outlined in the theses, was not to place themselves in opposition to the middle peasantry, but to work hand in hand with the middle peasants against the kulak.

A number of previous decisions of the Party, including the decisions of the Fourteenth Party Conference, pointed out that more work was needed among the poor peasants and agricultural labourers and that it was necessary to strengthen the village Party organisations, above all by enlisting poor peasants and agricultural labourers in them.

Molotov's theses pointed out the existence of two deviations in the Party with regard to the policy on the peasant question —the deviation which tended to underrate the kulak menace and the deviation which tended to underrate the importance of the middle peasant. The local Party organisations were urged to combat both deviations. Comrade Molotov's theses completely exposed the demagogy of the opposition, which charged the Central Committee with underrating the kulak menace.

The Opposition Against the Party

At the Plenum the opposition was exposed and was forced to withdraw a number of its accusations against the Party. The leaders of the opposition undertook not to start a struggle against the Party. The opposition, however, saw fit to violate this pledge in Leningrad, where it controlled the Party apparatus. All the preparations for the pre-Congress conference of the Leningrad Gubernia were marked by a secret mobilisation against the Central Committee. However, fearing to repel the rank and file of the Party by coming out openly against the Central Committee, the opposition did not show all its cards at the conference but proposed a resolution endorsing the political and organisational line of the Central Committee.

But the speeches which were delivered in the discussion on the report of the Central Committee made it obvious that preparations were being made for an attack on the Central Committee at the Congress. The delegation chosen for the Congress was made up of "reliable" followers of the opposition, saturated in the ideas of their faction. This was why the conference of the Moscow Gubernia, which was held at the same time as the Leningrad conference, deemed it necessary, in its resolution on the report of the Central Committee, to give a proper political appraisal of the campaign which had been launched against the Central Committee in Leningrad. About the same time several articles were published in *Pravda* exposing the opposition.

By exerting incredible pressure and by misleading the lower ranks of the Leningrad organisations, the opposition succeeded in packing almost the entire delegation from the Leningrad conference to the Fourteenth Congress with its supporters. This, however, was its first and only victory.

A large number of gubernia Party conferences and almost all the regional Party conferences were held in time to respond to the factional struggle which had been launched against the Central Committee in Leningrad. These conferences adopted resolutions severely condemning the "New Opposition." The delegations from those conferences which closed too early to express their opinion on this matter also took a firm and definite stand in defence of the Party. When the Leningrad delegation, consisting of adherents of the opposition, arrived at the Congress, it found that it had all the other delegations against it. There was still time to call a halt. The Central Committee, supported by representatives of all the delegations, made every effort to induce the opposition and its leaders to renounce their erroneous views, to stop setting themselves up as a faction against the whole Party and its Central Committee. But the opposition would not give way. The Congress opened in the middle of December 1925 in such a tense atmosphere as had not been witnessed at our Party Congresses for many years.

The Report of the Central Committee at the Fourteenth Party Congress

Comrade Stalin's political report at the Fourteenth Congress gave an analysis of the international and internal situation of the country which contained answers to all the questions under dispute.

In the capitalist world which encircled the Soviet Union, Comrade Stalin noted five groups of contradictions—between the bourgeoisie and the working class, between the imperialist states and the colonial and semi-colonial peoples subject to them, between the countries victorious in the World War and those defeated in it, between the victorious countries themselves, and, finally, between the capitalist world and the U.S.S.R. Most of these contradictions, in view of the strengthening of the proletarian dictatorship and the growth of socialism, made it easier for the U.S.S.R. to prolong its existence within the ring of encircling capitalist states, and prevented the hostile bourgeois forces from throttling the Soviet republics. Referring to the Locarno Conference which had ended shortly before the Congress, Comrade Stalin pointed out how utterly futile this conference had been in furthering the cause of European peace, emphasising that for us the Locarno Conference was of significance solely as a new attempt to create an anti-Soviet *bloc*.

The task which Comrade Stalin set our Party was to take every possible advantage of the contradictions of international imperialism in order to secure for our country the opportunity to continue peaceful socialist construction.

The report pointed out the intensive growth of the socialist elements in our economy in relation to the elements of private capitalism. In the first category Comrade Stalin definitely included our state industry, which is owned by the working class and in which there are no exploiters and exploited, as is the case under all forms of capitalism, including state capitalism. Unquestionably there were many distortions within our state enterprises, just a within our state apparatus. Our industry, therefore, could not be considered as the complete embodiment of socialism. Nevertheless, both our state apparatus and our state industry were key positions of the proletarian dictatorship and of socialism.* Our main task was to facilitate the further growth of the socialist elements, unswervingly pursuing a policy of the industrialisation of the country. This was the basic general line of our development, which went beyond the task of restoring our economy to its pre-war levels, envisaging a radical transformation of the economic character of our country and the building of socialism.

The policy of industrialisation was a necessary consequence of the task of building socialism which the Party had set itself. The immediate objective of industrialisation was to secure the technical and economic independence of our country from the bourgeois countries which surrounded it. This was one of the decisive conditions for the successful construction of socialism.

---

* The most widespread forms of state capitalism in our economy of that time were the concessions, mixed companies and enterprises leased out to private capitalists. None of these played any important role in our economy. It goes without saying that we were interested in directing the development of capitalism, which was inevitable within certain limits at that stage of the N.E.P., into the channels of state capitalism.

The slogan of industrialisation, in view of the lack of large foreign credits, naturally demanded the straining of all the country's economic forces and involved the surmounting of very serious difficulties. But the path of industrialisation was at the same time the sole path which would protect our country from becoming a colony for foreign capital, a plaything of international imperialism, which would make it an invincible base and fortress of the international revolution and would ensure that the work of socialist construction was carried to completion.

Comrade Stalin, following in the footsteps of Lenin, held that for the economy of the small and smallest peasants the highway to socialism lay in the merging of the peasant farms in production co-operatives, which were subsequently turned into the channels of collectivisation.

Passing to the question of class relationships, Comrade Stalin dealt with the different stages in the relation of the working class to the peasantry during the course of our revolution: 1) with the peasantry as a whole against the landlords; 2) with the poor peasants against the urban and rural bourgeoisie, while neutralizing the middle peasants; 3) relying on the poor peasantry, in alliance with the middle peasantry, for socialist construction, against the kulak and the nepman.

Comrade Stalin clearly proved that the opposition absolutely denied the third stage. Comrade Stalin analysed the two deviations which had been noted by the October Plenum of the Central Committee—the deviation which tended to underrate the kulak danger and the deviation which tended to underrate the importance of the middle peasant.

"The first deviation consists in underestimating the role of the kulak and, in general, of the capitalist elements in the countryside, in obscuring the kulak danger. It proceeds from the premise that the development of the N.E.P. does not lead to a revival of the capitalist elements in the countryside, that the kulak and the capitalist elements in general are passing, or rather, have already passed into history in our country, that there is no process of differentiation going on in the countryside, that the kulak is only an echo of the past, only a bugaboo.

"What does this deviation lead to?

"This deviation virtually leads to a denial of the class struggle in the countryside.

"The second deviation consists in exaggerating the role of the kulak and, in general, of the capitalist elements in the countryside, in panic in the face of these elements, in a denial of the fact that an alliance of the proletariat and the poor peasantry with the middle peasantry is possible and expedient. This deviation proceeds from the premise that a simple restoration of capitalism is taking place in our country-side, that this process of the restoration of capitalism is an all-absorbing process, embracing even our co-operatives in their entirety or in their overwhelming majority, that the result of this development must be a continually increasing differentiation on a large scale, that the extreme groups, i.e., the kulaks and the poor peasants, must grow stronger and increase from year to year, that the middle groups, i.e., the middle peasants, must grow weaker and become effaced from year to year....

"You ask, which deviation is the worse? This is not the way to approach the question. They are both worse, both the first and the second deviation. If these deviations develop, they are capable of dis-integrating and ruining the Party. Fortunately, we have forces in the Party that can cut off both the first and second deviation. (Applause.) Although both deviations are worse and it is foolish to ask which of them is more dangerous, there is another standpoint from which these two deviations should be approached. Against which of these devia-tions is the Party better trained to fight, against the first or against the second deviation? That is how to approach the question, in a practical way....

"If Communists were asked the question, for what is the Party more ready—to strip the kulak naked, or to refrain from doing this and form an alliance with the middle peasant—I believe that ninety-nine out of a hundred Communists would answer that the Party is best prepared for the slogan 'Attack the kulak.' Give the signal, and they will strip the kulak naked in the twinkling of an eye. But as to refraining from expropriating the kulak and pursuing a more complex policy of isolating the kulak through an alliance with the middle peas-ant, this task is not so easily assimilated. This is why I believe that in its struggle against both these deviations the Party must neverthe-less concentrate its fire on the struggle against the second deviation." (Applause.)

The strengthening of the alliance with the middle peasant was the urgent task of the day. The necessary objective condi-tions for the widespread organisation of collective and Soviet farms were not yet present. The country could not yet provide the necessary number of machines and tractors and the neces-sary quantity of funds. It was still premature to raise the ques-tion of intensifying the offensive against the kulak and of liquidating kulakdom. This being so, it was necessary to turn our main fire against the deviation which rejected and slurred over the slogan of an alliance with the middle peasant. With regard to the Party, the task set it by Comrade Stalin was to increase its contacts with the toiling masses, to make more flexible the leadership which they received through the transmission belts of the trade union and other Soviet organisations.

Reverting at the end of his report to the contradiction between the socialist and capitalist elements in our economy, Comrade Stalin expressed confidence that we would overcome these contradictions with our own forces.

"He who has no faith in this task is a liquidator, has no faith in socialist construction. We will overcome, we are already overcoming these contradictions. Of course, the sooner help comes from the West, the better it will be, the sooner will we overcome these contradictions in order to put an end to private capital and to achieve the complete victory of socialism in our country, the construction of a complete socialist society. But even without help from outside, we will not become downhearted, we will not despair, will not give up our work *(applause)* and will not be scared of difficulties. Those who are tired, who are frightened of difficulties, who have lost heart, must make way for those who have kept their courage and determination. *(Applause.)* We are not people to be scared of difficulties. We are Bolsheviks, we underwent Leninist tempering, and because of this, we do not evade difficulties, but tackle them and overcome them." *("Correct," Applause.)*

The Party Exposes the Manoeuvres of the Opposition

After the reports of Comrade Stalin and Molotov, the opposition demanded the right to submit a co-report. There was no precedent in our Party for such co-reports. The opposition, however, did not hesitate at such a flagrant violation of Bolshevik traditions.

How did the opposition act during the discussion on the report of the Central Committee? The leaders of the opposition did not dare to carry to a logical conclusion their contentions regarding the alleged state capitalist character of our industry, regarding the N.E.P. as a continuous retreat, regarding the hopeless prospects of socialist construction in our country. On these fundamental and decisive questions, the leaders of the opposition tacked and manoeuvred, offering conflicting formulations. Nor did they as yet dare to speak outright of the degeneration of the Party, preferring to confine themselves to hints, to beat about the bush. These manoeuvres, however, failed to deceive the Party and were resolutely exposed by the Congress. Sokolnikov upheld his theory of the agrarianisation and "Dawesisation" of the country, which was altogether inconsistent with the "Left" demagogy of the opposition. Briefly stated, the gist of Sokolnikov's theory was that, since we had no means to develop large-scale industry, all our attention should be directed towards the development of agriculture and the export of agricultural produce, while manufactured articles should be imported from abroad. Sokolnikov made certain reservations to his proposal But, in spite of these, the proposal, against which not a single one of Sokolnikov's associates in the opposition raised any objection, would have meant transforming our country into a agrarian colony of world imperialism.

Sokolnikov, who was more consistent and resolute than the other spokesmen of the opposition, attempted to prove that our industrial enterprises and the Soviet apparatus (the Commissariat of Foreign Trade, the State Bank, etc.) were of a state capitalist character.

The opposition tended to give a Menshevik interpretation of our Soviet state and of our socialist industry, to deny that our industrial enterprises were of a consistent socialist type. Comrade Stalin exposed this Menshevik interpretation in his concluding speech at the Fourteenth Congress.

In one respect, there was a striking resemblance to the opposition of 1923. In both cases, the attack against the Central Committee was carried on under the banner of democracy and with the slogan of "organisational guarantees," which meant the legalisation of factions and groupings. But the democratic toga was just as unbecoming to the leaders of the "New Opposition" in 1925, as it had been in 1923 to Trotsky—the patriarch of all bureaucrats, as Comrade Stalin then called him. Not that this diminished in any degree the boldness of the opposition leaders. Zinoviev went so far as to demand that all former opposition groupings should be drawn into Party work (apparently on the

basis of their legalisation). At this time the outlines of the future
bloc of the "New Opposition" with the fragments of all former
oppositions under Trotskyist leadership could already be clearly
discerned.

At the Plenum of the Central Committee, the Trotskyists, together with the leaders of the "New Opposition," opposed the
removal of the editors of the *Leningradskaya Pravda,* which
had become the factional organ of the "New Opposition" and
which openly attacked the line of the Party.

The Congress of Industrialisation

After the co-report and the discussion, the opposition, following the example of the "Workers' Opposition" at the Tenth Congress, voted against the resolution approving the report of the
Central Committee (which was adopted by a vote of five hundred and fifty-nine in favour and sixty-five against). In the
sphere of international relations, the resolution thus adopted
against the votes of the opposition instructed the Central Committee:

"a) To strengthen by all means the alliance of the proletariat of the
U.S.S.R., as the base of the world revolution, with the proletariat of
western Europe and the oppressed peoples, aiming at the development
and victory of the international proletarian revolution;

"b) To pursue a policy of peace, since this is the core of the
foreign policy of the government and should determine all its principal actions;

"c) To carry on economic construction with a view to transforming
the U.S.S.R. from a country importing machinery and equipment into
a country producing machinery and equipment, so that the U.S.S.R.,
surrounded as it is by capitalist countries, may not on any account
become an economic appendage of the capitalist world economy, but
may form an independent economic unit, developing along socialist
lines and able, as a result of its economic growth, to serve as a
powerful means of revolutionising the workers of all countries and the
oppressed peoples of the colonies and semi-colonies;

"d) As far as possible to prepare economic reserves capable of
securing the country from all accidents of any kind whether on the
internal or the external market;

"e) To take all measures to consolidate the defensive capacity of
the country and to strengthen the power of the Red Army and Red
Fleet, both naval and air."

The section of the Congress resolution containing directives in the sphere of internal policy recommended the Central Committee:

"a) To give first place to the task of securing by every means the victory of socialist economic forms over private capital, the strengthening of the monopoly of foreign trade, the growth of the socialist state industry and, under its guidance and with the aid of the co-operatives, of drawing an ever larger number of peasant farms into the channel of socialist construction;

"b) To ensure the U.S.S.R. economic independence, so as to protect the U.S.S.R. from becoming an appendage of capitalist world economy, and for this purpose to pursue a policy aimed at the industrialisation of the country, the development of the production of means of production and the formation of reserves for economic manoeuvring;

"c) On the basis of the decisions of the Fourteenth Party Conference, to facilitate in every way the growth of production and of commodity circulation in the country;

"d) To make use of all resources, observe the strictest economy in the expenditure of state funds and to accelerate the turnover of state industry, trade and the co-operatives with a view to increasing the tempo of socialist accumulation;

"e) To develop our socialist industry on the basis of a higher technical level, but in strict conformity with the capacity of the market, as also with the financial possibilities of the state;

"f) To do everything to assist in every way the development of the local Soviet industry (in the various districts, areas, gubernias, regions and republics), giving every incentive to local initiative in the organisation of such industry which should aim at satisfying the diverse needs of the population in general and of the peasantry in particular;

"g) To support and push forward the development of agriculture by introducing improved agricultural methods, developing the cultivation of industrial crops, raising the technique of agriculture (tractorisation), industrialising agriculture, properly organising land allotment and giving all possible support to the different forms of the collectivisation of agriculture.

"The Congress holds that one of the essential conditions for the solution of these tasks is a struggle against the lack of confidence in the cause of socialist construction in our country and against the attempts to characterise our enterprises, which are of 'a consistent socialist type' (Lenin), as state capitalist enterprises. Such ideological tendencies, rendering impossible a conscious attitude on the part of the masses towards the construction of socialism in general and of socialist industry in particular, can only retard the growth of the socialist elements in economy and make it easier for private capital to struggle against them. The Congress, therefore, holds that widespread educational work is needed for the purpose of overcoming these distortions of Leninism.".

In the resolution on the report of the Central Control Commission the Congress fully endorsed the position taken by the Central· Control Commission on the question of preserving the unity of the Party and supporting the Leninist line of the Central Committee.

In the resolution on the report of the delegation of the R.C.P. to the Comintern, the Congress instructed the delegation to continue the struggle both against the Right and against the "Left" deviations, to intensify the struggle for the trade unions and their unity and for winning over the broad masses of non-Party and Social-Democratic workers, and also to secure the strengthening of the apparatus of the Comintern, at the same time increasing the influence of foreign Parties in the leadership of the Comintern.

The theses adopted by the Congress regarding the work of the trade unions pointed out that

"with the growth of our industry, the proletariat of the U.S.S.R. is growing and becoming stronger, not only quantitatively but also qualitatively. The difficulties connected with the proletariat's becoming declassed have been left behind. The power of the working class is growing, its activity is increasing. In proportion as our industry develops further, the activity of the working class of the U.S.S.R. and its consciousness of its own strength will grow to an even larger degree."

The theses adopted by the Congress were a further. development of the decisions of the Eleventh Congress with special reference to the need for developing trade union democracy and initiative on the part of the masses and for extending the work of 'the trade unions to the new cadres of workers who were coming in from the countryside.

The theses on the work of the Y.C.L. took note of the further achievements which had been made in this work since the Thirteenth Congress. During this period, the Y.C.L. organisation had almost trebled its membership, its numbers having increased from 600,000 to 1,633,000. The Pioneer organisation had also increased from 200,000 to 1,500,000. About 50 per cent of the working class youth were in the ranks of the Young Communist

League. The Leningrad opposition was against admitting the middle peasant youth into the Y.C.L., proposing that they should be organised into a special delegate organisation outside of the Y.C.L. The Congress, however, decided in favour of admitting the middle peasant youth, emphatically repudiating the anti-Leninist tendencies of the opposition. The principal tasks of the work of the Y.C.L. as outlined in the theses adopted by the Congress, were the strengthening of its organisation, the struggle against pessimistic moods, improving the mode of living of the youth, establishing correct forms of inter-relationship between the Y.C.L. and the Party and finally, widespread enlistment o the youth in the work of economic construction and the bettering of their material conditions.

Taking into consideration the fact that the old name of the Party—the R.C.P.—had now ceased to conform to the structure of the Soviet state, which had become a Union of Soviet Republics, the Congress passed a decision in favour of changing the Party's name from that of the Russian Communist Party (Bolsheviks) into that of the Communist Party of the Soviet Union (Bolsheviks), without creating a special Party for the R.S.F.S.R. and preserving the old names for the Communist Parties of the national minority republics (the Ukraine, White Russia, Georgia. etc.).*

This decision was of great significance from the standpoint of the national policy. The old colonies of tsarist Russia had become Soviet Republics, where national culture was strongly developing, where industry was being created, and where new forces of the proletariat were springing up. The Congress gave recognition to this important fact.

"Lack of faith in the victory of socialist construction is the basic mistake of the new opposition," Stalin wrote after the Congress, ... "because all the other mistakes of the new opposition spring from it ... on the question of the new economic policy, state capitalism, the nature of our socialist industry, the role of co-operation under the dictatorship of the proletariat, the methods of the kulaks, the role and importance of the middle peasants—all these mistakes are the outcome of this basic mistake of the opposition, of their lack of faith

---

* According to the data of the Credentials Commission, there were 643,000 Party members and 445,000 candidates represented at the Fourteenth Congress. The Party membership had thus exceeded the million mark.

in the possibility of constructing socialist society with the efforts of our own country. . . .

"The historical significance of the Fourteenth Congress of the Communist Party of the Soviet Union lies in the fact that it was able to expose, to the very roots, the mistakes of the 'New Opposition,' that it threw aside its lack of faith and snivelling, clearly and distinctly indicated the path of the further struggle for socialism, gave the Party prospects of victory and thereby armed the proletariat with invincible faith in the victory of socialist construction.'*

The Problem of Reconstruction

The violent struggle with the opposition which took place at the Fourteenth Party Congress did not cease after the Congress itself was over. Although it was condemned by the Congress, the "New Opposition" did not lay down its arms, despite the fact that it was at odds with the Leningrad organisation which it had claimed to represent at the Congress, despite the fact that the Leningrad organisation, after the issues which divided the opposition from the Party had been explained to its membership, lined up with the Central Committee, just as did all the other organisations of our Party.

The "New Opposition" did not discontinue its struggle. Its anti-Party activities were given an incentive by the economic difficulties which were somewhat aggravated during the autumn of 1925. In part, these difficulties were rooted in the general conditions of the development of our economy, in the fact that we were already approaching the end of the restoration period, while in part they were the result of errors and miscalculations committed by the leading economic organs. The resolution of the Fourteenth Party Congress on the report of the Central Committee pointed out that

"the Soviet Union has proved capable of securing a stable state budget, of promoting the rapid development of industry, coupled with a simultaneous general rise in the wages and labour productivity, and the further development of agriculture, bringing their output almost up to the pre-war level and securing the growing role of the socialist elements in the whole of our national economy."

But the very same resolution pointed out

* Stalin, *Leninism*, Vol. I.

"errors in the sphere of grain collections and foreign trade, which resulted in endangering our stable currency, this essential condition for our economic development "

The months which followed the Fourteenth Congress were characterised by a certain accentuation of the scarcity of commodities and of the consequent rise in the prices of industrial and agricultural products, and by further fluctuations in the purchasing capacity of the *chervonetz*, which also affected the wages. This was the result of the increased activity of the capitalist elements in town and countryside, who were attempting to accumulate capital in quick time at the expense of the toiling masses. The main attention of the April Plenum of the Central Committee, the first Plenum after the Fourteenth Congress, was devoted to questions concerning our Party's economic policy.

"Industry has utilised almost to the full the fixed capital inherited from the bourgeois epoch, and its further development depends upon the re-equipment of the enterprises and upon the construction of new mills and factories; this in turn depends wholly upon the extent of the accumulations which could be invested for the purpose of industrial expansion."

Such was the conclusion drawn by the Plenum of the Central Committee in its resolution on the economic situation and the economic policy of the Party. This meant that in a number of industries we had already completed the restoration period. Previously it was necessary to set the existing enterprises in operation with the equipment which was available. Now it was necessary to find funds for the construction of new enterprises, of new industries, for the further industrialisation of the country in accordance with the decisions of the Fourteenth Party Congress.

At the Twelfth Party Congress, Comrade Krassin had declared that we would not succeed in putting industry on its feet without large foreign credits. People who had no faith in our socialist construction, who had no faith in the strength of the Party and the working class, were inclined to interpret the difficulties of the autumn of 1923 as a confirmation of Comrade Krassin's views.

Closely connected with these difficulties was the furious attack which was launched by the Trotskyist opposition on the Central Committee elected by the Twelfth Congress. And it was no accident that some of the leaders of this opposition followed Comrade Krassin in demanding that further concessions be made to foreign capital, that concessionaires be attracted into the country on a large scale, etc.

The Party emphatically rejected the capitulationist proposals of the opposition and under the firm leadership of its Leninist Central Committee succeeded in coping with the difficulties of the restoration period. In the economic year 1924-25 our industry showed an increase in production of 60 per cent, while the next year, 1925-26, showed a further increase of 40 per cent. We had thus come close to the end of the restoration period, but for all that we were coming up against new difficulties, for we were brought face to face with the problem of capital construction and of re-equipping our industry, with the necessity of investing hundreds of millions of rubles for this purpose.

Since our foreign credits were extremely limited, the internal resources of the country remained the sole source from which these hundreds of millions could be obtained. The tempo of socialist accumulation, the tempo of our country's industrialisation could be accelerated only through the mobilisation of our internal resources.

The Party in the Struggle Against Agrarianisation and Super-Industrialisation.

There were two main dangers confronting the Party and the country in this connection.

The first danger was that of capitulating before the difficulties of industrialisation, of renouncing this policy on some plausible pretext or other and of taking the line of least resistance in the economic construction of the country. This course would have meant the domination of peasant narrow-mindedness; it would have meant transforming the U.S.S.R. into an agrarian kulak state of the type of Esthonia or Latvia, into an agrarian appendage of international imperialism. It is hardly necessary to prove that to take this course would have meant to pursue a policy the aim of which, objectively speaking, was the abolition of the Soviet power and the restoration of capitalism. It was precisely towards such a policy that Comrade Sokolnikov's theory tended, the theory which was defended in the columns of our economic magazines by Shanin and which was pulled to pieces by Comrade Stalin at the Fourteenth Party Congress. The basic idea of this theory was to speed up the development of agriculture (for export purposes) and of the light industries, and to import manufactured goods from abroad. Such a policy was to be combined, according to Comrade Sokolnikov, with the abolition, or at any rate with a restriction, of the foreign trade monopoly. This was an unconcealed Right opportunist way of thinking, although Sokolnikov was in one *bloc* with Zinoviev and Kamenev and later also with Trotsky, who posed as "Lefts."

The second danger was that of forgetting the political circumstances in which we were carrying out the industrialisation of our country, of forgetting that the Soviet power was strong only so long as it based itself on the alliance of the workers and peasants, of forgetting that to pursue a kind of colonial policy of exploitation towards the mass of the peasantry, even if this were done under the name of primary socialist accumulation, would have meant endangering the existence of the proletarian dictatorship. This was the policy of super-industrialisation advocated by Trotsky—an attempt to impose upon the Party an adventurist policy towards the peasantry.

The Central Committee was equally resolute in rejecting both the policy of agrarianisation and the policy of super-industrialisation. It outlined a number of practical measures for the enforcement of a regime of rigorous economy, doing everything to cut down all the unnecessary and superfluous expenditure and raising the productivity of labour to the maximum degree. Having established the connection between the economic difficulties and the rise in the prices of commodities, the Party set itself the shock task of lowering the price of commodities at all costs, thereby securing the stabilisation of the *chervonetz* and of real wages.

The Party Exposes the "New Opposition," Which Is Forming a Bloc With Trotskyism

The anti-Party action of the "New Opposition," headed by Zinoviev and Kamenev, on the eve of the Fourteenth Party Congress caused great jubilation in the camp of our enemies and was hailed by them as the beginning of the complete collapse and disintegration of our Party's old Bolshevik cadres. The enemies of the Communist Party and of the Soviet power, both inside and outside of the country, pinned all their hopes on the success of the "New Opposition." These enemies, however, were badly mistaken this time, as they had been badly mistaken on previous occasions. The Party calmly but firmly and decisively gave a rebuff to Zinoviev, Kamenev and their associates.

The Party knew from the experience of its previous history that at certain times individual Party leaders, and even whole groups of leaders, who had once quite correctly expressed the Party line, later diverged from and even broke with the Party, some temporarily, others forever. But the Bolshevik Party, in spite of the errors of these leaders, moved forward, rallying around itself the working class, organising it for victorious struggle and becoming steeled in successes and defeats.

Indeed, did not Lenin, one year after the Second Congress, break with several members of the Central Committee—Noskov, Krassin, Dubrovinsky and others, who had capitulated to the Mensheviks? Some of them (such as Krassin and Dubrovinsky) deserted Lenin only for a short time, while others (such as Noskov, who played a very important part during the *Iskra* period) left him forever. During the Revolution of 1905-06, we find a large number of new people in the leading staff of the Bolshevik Party (Bogdanov, Lunacharsky, Rumyantsev, Bazarov, Rykov, Desnitsky-Stroyev, Postalovsky, Lalayantz, Rozhkov. Lyadov, S. Volsky). During the years of the reaction many of these people joined the *Vperyod* group, or came close to the Mensheviks (as did Bazarov and Rozhkov), or withdrew from Party work. Only a few of them remained in the Bolshevik ranks.

In his struggle for the re-establishment of the Party against the liquidators and against the "Left" Otzovists, Lenin relied on such tried professional revolutionaries as Comrades Stalin, Kalinin, Sverdlov, Orjonikidze, Voroshilov and others. It was on these leading cadres and on the basic masses of the Bolsheviks who were firmly linked up with them that Lenin relied in his struggle against the liquidators from the Right and from the "Left."

Since that time the Party had grown tremendously and acquired a colossal fund of experience. A firm Leninist core, headed by Comrade Stalin, had been formed in the Central Committee.

Of course, the action of the "New Opposition" was no accident nor can it be attributed to personal factors. The opposition was an expression of the pressure brought to bear on the Communist Party by the petty-bourgeois anarchic forces. It was these petty-bourgeois forces that were behind the opposition. But the opposition was also trying to take advantage of a feeling of discontent to be met with among certain groups of workers and poor peasants. The discontent among individual groups of workers was due to the slow increase in the wages and to unemployment. The discontent among the poor peasants was in its turn due to the fact that the aid extended to them by the Soviet government was not yet particularly great.

Why should it have been precisely Zinoviev and Kamenev who, at this difficult moment through which the Party was passing, succumbed before the onslaught of the petty-bourgeois forces? Lenin wrote that the desertion of Zinoviev and Kamenev during the October Revolution was no accident. At that time they also wavered. Faced with the supreme difficulties and dangers of October 1917, Zinoviev and Kamenev yielded to the influence of forces alien to the Party and to the proletarian revolution and attempted to restrain the Party from setting up the dictatorship of the proletariat in a backward peasant country, fearing a defeat which was in their opinion inevitable. Eight years later, faced with the difficulties and dangers which our Party had to cope with, Zinoviev and Kamenev virtually arrived at the liquidationist conclusion that the construction of socialism in our country was impossible, that the collapse of the proletarian dictatorship was inevitable, unless it were quickly aided by the arrival of the international proletarian revolution.

Certain difficulties which our Party had to cope with in the
countryside in the autumn of 1924 brought Zinoviev into such
a state of panic that he went so far as to propose the formation
of non-Party peasant fractions in the soviets.

This state of mind found a peculiar reflection even in the
theoretical works of Zinoviev, who about this time wrote that
the main point in Leninism was not the dictatorship of the proletariat, but the peasant question. Leninism itself Zinoviev defined as

"Marxism of the epoch of imperialist war and of the world revolution, which began directly in a country where the peasantry pre-
dominates."

In this connection Comrade Stalin wrote that

"To introduce the backwardness of Russia, its peasant character,
into a definition of Leninism means the transformation of Leninism
from an international proletarian doctrine into a specifically Russian
product.

"It means playing into the hands of Bauer and Kautsky, who deny
that Leninism is suitable to other countries, which are capitalistically
more developed."*

In the spring of 1925, when the situation in the countryside
had improved, Zinoviev executed a right-about turn and went
so far as to repudiate the Leninist slogan of an alliance with
the middle peasant.

As Comrade Stalin said at the Fourteenth Party Congress,
this was not a line but a seesaw.

But this seesaw conformed to a certain rule of its own. Its
premise was the old philosophy of lack of faith in the Party
and working class of our country, in the internal forces of our
revolution. It was this philosophy that made Zinoviev and Kamenev the strike-breakers of the October Revolution. It led
them to the defeatist, liquidationist, semi-Menshevik position of
Trotskyism on the question of the victory of Bolshevism in the
U.S.S.R. and on other fundamental questions of Leninism.

The result was that Zinoviev and Kamenev with a group
of their associates found themselves occupying the position of
Trotskyism, against which they had previously fought together

* Stalin, "Problems of Leninism," *Leninism,* Vol. I.

with the Party in 1923-24. Instead of turning back in time, loyally submitting to the decisions of the Fourteenth Party Congress and loyally working for the carrying out of these decisions, Zinoviev and Kamenev completely capitulated to Trotsky and formed one anti-Party *bloc* together with him.

Their long record as Bolsheviks and the prestige which the Party gave them despite their numerous errors which it did not forget—all this Zinoviev and Kamenev placed at the service of the old Menshevik, Trotsky, using it as a screen under cover of which to clear a path for him to the rank and file of the Party. But Zinoviev and Kamenev were badly deceived by their presumption. The Party was able to expose the essential Menshevik nature of Trotskyism, while Zinoviev and Kamenev, having broken with Bolshevism and continued on the downward path, failed to justify the hopes reposed in them by all the enemies of the Party and the working class.

With the aid of the "New Opposition" of Zinoviev and Kamenev, Trotskyism, which was shamelessly speculating on the difficulties and which was emboldened by the increased discontent among bourgeois circles against the Soviet government, launched its last attack against the Party in the summer of 1926. The attack, which was prolonged for a year and a half, ended in the crushing defeat of Trotskyism and in its being definitely thrown overboard by the Communist Party.*

The Fourteenth Party Congress, in striking this blow at the "New Opposition," was at the same time striking a decisive blow at the anti-middle-peasant deviation from the Leninist line —the deviation which employed "Left" phrases to cover up its policy of defeatism and capitulation, although the opposition

---

* In the early autumn of 1925, a few months prior to the Fourteenth Party Congress, Trotsky, addressing a general meeting of the Zaporozhye Party organisation, spoke of the necessity of developing the productive forces of the countryside, even though this might mean employing capitalist methods, "until we can collectivise agriculture with the resources of our industry." Trotsky also declared at this meeting that the term "kulak" was out-of-date under Soviet conditions and should be replaced by the more euphonious term "farmer." His report at the Zaporozhye meeting was published in pamphlet form by Trotsky as early as 1926—only a very short while prior to the time when he became the leader of the opposition *bloc*, one of whose chief "trump cards" was to charge the Central Committee with a kulak deviation.

also included some open opportunist elements such as Sokolnikov. This blow had to be struck because it was necessary at
all costs to strengthen the alliance with the middle peasant,
whom the "New Opposition," following in the footsteps of
Trotskyism, was in fact attacking. The strengthening of the alliance with the middle peasant was an essential condition for
the carrying out of that tremendous work of reconstructing industry and agriculture with which the Party was confronted at
the conclusion of the restoration period. But besides the "Left"
deviation, the Fourteenth Congress also took note of an open
Right opportunist deviation within the Party. In the beginning
of 1925, Comrade Stalin, in his *Questions and Answers,* pointed
out that bourgeois influence on the Party creates the danger of
"losing the international revolutionary perspective" and of "the
conversion of the Party into an appendage of the state apparatus." Open Right opportunism was manifested in several
articles written and speeches made on the eve of and during the
Fourteenth Party Conference,and this danger was noted in the
decisions of the Plenum of the C.C. held in October 1925 and
in those of the Fourteenth Party Congress.

"The Congress emphatically condemns the deviation which consists
in an underestimation of the differentiation in the countryside, which
fails to perceive the dangers connected with the growth of kulakdom
and of various forms of capitalist exploitation, which refuses to comprehend the full necessity of repulsing kulakdom and of restricting its
exploiting aspirations, and which does not perceive that the party of
the proletariat is in duty bound to organise and rally the poor peasants and agricultural labourers against the kulak and in the struggle
against him."

This was how the resolution of the Fourteenth Congress
characterised the open Right opportunist deviation. The Right
opportunist elements were against the "New Opposition" and
favoured the alliance with the middle peasant. But to them this
alliance only served as a screen for a policy based on a capitalist course of agricultural development. They exhorted the
Party not to be afraid of the kulak menace. They welcomed
Bukharin's slogan "Enrich yourselves," which was addressed to
all sections of the peasantry, the kulaks first and foremost. They
were inclined to favour changing the Soviet constitution so as
to give the peasantry equal suffrage rights with the working

class and to extend the suffrage rights in favour of those sections of the population who were deprived of such rights by the Soviet constitution as exploiters of hired labour. They were willing to make political concessions to the new bourgeoisie .

They were trying to replace the slogan of fighting the kulak with the slogan of collaborating with the kulak, advancing as a basis for this slogan a whole theory to the effect that the kulak would grow into socialism. At the Fourteenth Conference the Party made a number of serious concessions to the middle peasantry, aiming at the development of the productive forces of the countryside, pursuing a policy of developing the individual farming of the poor and middle peasants, of attracting the latter into the co-operatives and of restricting the kulak. However, even as early as 1925, the Right opportunist elements or those who tended towards Right opportunism attempted to interpret these temporary concessions as "the path to socialism." Even at that time they were already attempting to obscure the basic factors of productive co-operation in Lenin's co-operative plan; even at that time they were trying to supplement this plan with "kulak co-operative nests."

On the question of the tempo of industrialisation, Bukharin made a statement at the Fourteenth Party Congress which was in glaring contradiction to the whole policy of the Party and the decisions of the Congress:

"We can build socialism," said Bukharin, "even on this miserable technical base. . . . This growth of socialism will be many times slower. . . . We shall creep at a snail's pace, but . . . we are building socialism and . . . we shall complete the building of it."

This policy of moving towards socialism at a snail's pace would have led essentially towards capitulation to the bourgeois elements within the country and to the international bourgeoisie.

Later developments clearly showed that Bukharin's reference to a snail's pace was no accidental slip of the tongue.

It was just at this time that certain groups of bourgeois specialists—Menshevik, Socialist-Revolutionary and Cadet—who had found their way into a number of our most important state institutions (State Planning Commission, Commissariat of Agriculture, Commissariat of Finance) became particularly active,

These so-called specialists of the type of Groman, Kondratyev and Yurovsky, having gained influence over some individual Communists who held responsible posts and who had lapsed into Right opportunism, tried to carry out certain measures the aim of which was to extend and strengthen capitalist elements in the towns and, more especially, in the countryside.

The Bolshevik vigilance of the Central Committee, however, nipped these attempts in the bud.

But at that particular stage, the chief way in which those class elements hostile to the proletarian dictatorship carried on their anti-Soviet struggle was by directly and indirectly utilising the "New Opposition" and the Trotskyist *bloc* which was in the process of formation, as a faction within the C.P.S.U. which essentially assisted "the third force" in its struggle for the overthrow of the proletarian dictatorship in the U.S.S.R.

"The schismatic activity of the opposition," said Comrade Stalin, "leads to an alliance with bourgeois intellectuals, and the alliance with bourgeois intellectuals makes it easier for all kinds of counter-revolutionary elements to entangle the opposition—that is the bitter truth . . .

"Thus Lenin's prediction was justified, the prediction which he made at the Tenth Congress of our Party (see the resolution of the Tenth Congress 'On the Unity of the Party.'), stating that a third force, *i.e.*, the bourgeoisie, will inevitably endeavour to insinuate itself into a struggle within our Party in order to utilise the activity of the opposition for its own class ends."*

The decisions of the Fourteenth Congress were aimed chiefly at the "New Opposition," which employed "Left" phrases to cover up its defeatist-capitulationist position. But these decisions at the same time constituted a serious blow at the open Right opportunist deviation, whose chief laboratory of ideas was the "school" of Bukharin (Slepkov, Maretsky, etc.) which even at that time had already begun to cultivate an attitude of factional aloofness and which was making its first attempts to bring the line of the *Pravda* and of the *Bolshevik* into conflict with the line of the Central Committee. Less than three years were to pass before the Party, after inflicting a crushing defeat upon pseudo-"Left" Trotskyism, would have to concentrate its main attention on the open Right deviation.

* Stalin, *On the Opposition.*

THE PARTY EFFECTS THE TRANSITION TO THE PERIOD OF RECONSTRUCTION—THE ROUT OF TROTSKYISM

The formation of an opposition "bloc"—The opposition staff without an army—The Party exposes the platform of the united opposition at the July Plenum of 1926—On the building of socialism in our country—The slanderous charge that the Party had degenerated—The attitude of the Trotskyist opposition towards the peasantry—Questions concerning the international situation—The anti-Leninist groupings follow in the footsteps of the August "bloc"—The decisions of the July Plenum of 1926—The opposition attempts to force a discussion upon the Party—The double-faced manoeuvres of the Opposition Bloc—The Fifteenth Party Conference—The Fifteenth Party Conference on the work of the trade unions—The Social-Democratic deviation of the opposition exposed at the Fifteenth Conference—After the Fifteenth Conference—The Party exposes the further manoeuvres of the opposition—The Plenum of the Central Committee in July 1927—Trotskyism becomes the vanguard of the counter-revolutionary bourgeoisie—The decision of the Fifteenth Congress to expel the opposition from the Party—The Fifteenth Congress on the new tasks of the Party—Work in the rural districts.

The Formation of an Opposition "Bloc"

The decisive successes achieved by the Party on the economic front in 1924-25 clinched the victory of the Party over the Trotskyist opposition which had attempted to take advantage of the economic difficulties of the autumn of 1923. Owing to this, Trotsky's action in publishing his *Lessons of October* was not supported even by his closest friends. It was clearly not a favourable moment for an attack on the Central Committee. There was not the slightest chance of such an attack finding any response among more or less wide sections of the Party.

Moreover, in the beginning of the autumn of 1925, the country's economic outlook was also a favourable one. And Trotsky, who two years earlier had contended that the country was moving towards disaster, deemed it possible to write of the music of socialism in construction and to speak, in an address delivered at a session of the Kislovodsk Soviet, in quite laudatory tones of the results of our economic policy. At the

Fourteenth Party Congress, Trotsky, as is known, kept silent, and all of his associates, too, kept silent, awaiting a favourable moment. Zinoviev, the leader of the "New Opposition," in his concluding speech on the report of the Central Committee, made a direct appeal for aid to all of the old opposition groupings (and that meant to the Trotskyists, first and foremost), thereby indicating that he was ready to form any kind of a *bloc* with them. And when the Party and the country were faced with new economic difficulties, the Trotskyists, speculating on these difficulties, deemed the moment suitable for a resumption of their attack on the Party which had been interrupted in 1924. The first indications of a *bloc* between the "New Opposition" and the Trotskyists were already observable at the Plenum of the Central Committee held at the time of the Fourteenth Party Congress. The Trotskyists, on the plea of "inner-Party democracy," came out in defence of the anti-Party, factional activities of the "New Opposition."

At the April Plenum of 1926, the *bloc* of the Trotskyists and the representatives of the "New Opposition," who did not give up the struggle after the Fourteenth Congress, took on more definite shape. To be sure, Trotsky and Kamenev each proposed his own separate amendment to the theses of the Central Committee. Kamenev stressed the question of differentiation in the countryside. By a malicious distortion of the facts, he tried to prove that what was taking place in the countryside was capitalist differentiation. Trotsky proposed that the past economic policy of the Party be recognised as erroneous. But for the time being they were in agreement on the practical programme of super-industrialisation, *i.e.,* on the economic programme of Trotskyism. The "New Opposition" capitulated completely to this programme, justifying their action by the assertion that, while formerly this programme was incorrect, the conditions had now changed. And in order demagogically to deceive the broad Party masses, evidently having in mind the discussion which they were preparing to force upon the Party, the opposition put forward the demand for an increase in wages as against the lower price policy which the Party was putting into effect and which gave the workers a real improvement of their conditions. This irresponsible demand, put forward in a time of economic difficulties, showed that the opposition *bloc* which was in the process of uniting would not stop at any demagogic means in its struggle against the Party and would seek allies even among the remnants of the "Workers' Opposition," who retained their old views of drawing a Menshevik-syndicalist antithesis between the interests of the working class and those of the Soviet state. Indeed, at this very same April Plenum of the Central Committee, Zinoviev, shamelessly distorting the programme of the Party, reproached the Central Committee for the fact that the Party had hitherto refrained from handing over the management of industry to the trade unions, *i.e.*, directly defended the demands of the former "Workers' Opposition" which had been categorically condemned and rejected by the Tenth Party Congress.

The Opposition Staff Without an Army

The opposition *bloc* took definite shape between April and July, when the next Plenum of the Central Committee met. The *bloc* included the remnants of all factions and groupings which from the time of the Tenth Party Congress had put forward a line of their own in opposition to the Party line and which had stuck to their former ideological positions. The main core of the *bloc* was the group of Trotskyists who had signed the "Declaration of Forty-six" in 1923 (Preobrazhensky, Pyatakov, L. Serebryakov and others). These were joined by the "New Opposition," headed by Kamenev, Zinoviev and the former leaders of the Leningrad organisation (Yevdokimov, Zalutsky, Bakayev and others), the remnants of the "democratic centralism" group, represented by Sapronov, and finally the representatives of the former "Workers' Opposition" (Shlyapnikov, Medvedev) who had not only stuck to their old positions but had lapsed even further in the directions of Menshevism. Very considerable cadres of former leaders of various anti-Party factions and groupings were thus gathered in the ranks of the opposition *bloc*. The only thing which this motley and multifarious staff lacked was an army.

During the discussion of 1920-21, the "Workers' Opposition" was supported by some workers' nuclei. However, by the time the discussion of 1923-24 took place, as a result of the tremendous growth and the ideological unification of the whole Party, the overwhelming majority of the workers' nuclei had already lined up with the Central Committee. Not only did the former rank and file members of the "Workers' Opposition" renounce their views which had been condemned by the Tenth Congress, but a considerable number of their former leaders also definitely adopted the Party standpoint at this time. Suffice it to mention A. Kiselev, Tolokonzev, Kubyak, Perepechko.

In 1923-24, the Trotskyist opposition had a considerable number of supporters in the Party nuclei of the Red Army and of Soviet and higher educational institutions. But the tremendous work which the Party had done after the Thirteenth Conference and the Thirteenth Congress to explain the petty-bourgeois deviation of Trotskyism was bearing fruit. In the autumn of 1924, when the broad Party masses discussed the *Lessons of October* at the meetings of the nuclei and of the active Party workers, only isolated voices were raised in defence of Trotsky's position. The majority of those young Party members who had previously supported Trotskyism lined up with the Central Committee.

And finally, the "New Opposition" at the Fourteenth Congress still had a formal right to speak in the name of scores of thousands of Leningrad Communists and was, moreover, in a position to utilise the apparatus of the Leningrad organisation for its factional ends. Following the Fourteenth Congress, as a result of the tremendous work which the Central Committee performed within the Leningrad organisation in explaining the decisions of the Fourteenth Party Congress—work which met with a lively response and support among the masses of the Leningrad Communists—the new elections to the Leningrad Committee, the district committees, and the bureaus of the nuclei resulted in the complete elimination of the adherents of the opposition. The overwhelming majority of the Leningrad Communists lined up with the Central Committee.

Thus, none of the factions which joined the united opposition *bloc* brought with it an army with which it might have been possible to advance against the Party and win the Party leadership in battle. All the efforts of the opposition *bloc* after

April were aimed, at recruiting such an army at all costs. Feverish activities were started in order to create secret factional groups and establish contact between them. The groups thus formed developed intensive activities designed to work up public opinion among the rank and file members of the Party by distributing suitable literature. With an eye to the fact that the Party during the last few years had been joined by hundreds of thousands of workers who not long ago were non-Party, all the literature distributed by the opposition stressed the question of the material conditions of the working class, making the most generous promises in the name of the opposition. It should be noted that no opposition in the past had resorted to such irresponsible methods of influencing the rank and file of the Party, if we except the completely anti-Party "Workers' Group" and "Workers' Truth" group in 1923, and certain spokesmen of the "Workers' Opposition" in 1921. This was a symptom of the steady evolution of Trotskyism towards a complete return to its old Menshevik positions.

The Party Exposes the Platform of the United Opposition at the July Plenum of 1926

The formation of the opposition *bloc* was fully completed before the July Plenum of the C.C. of the C.P.S.U. It developed secret factional activities on a large scale. The July Plenum had to face outrageous facts of such activities as the organising of an illegal meeting in the woods by Comrade Lashevich, a candidate for membership of the Central Committee and vice-chairman of the Revolutionary War Council. At this meeting he related the plan of the united opposition "to bring the Central Committee to its knees," urging his hearers to pay special attention to the need of organising activities in the Red Army. By this time the united opposition already had a definite plan of fighting against the Party. According to this plan, the opposition, relying on the illegal apparatus which was being created within the Party, was to force a new discussion upon the Party within a short time and to win over the Party rank and file by means of demagogic promises. The opposition utilised the July Plenum as an occasion for making a declaration expounding its views, on the basis of which it had united.

What was the basis on which the opposition had united? But a short time previously Kamenev and Zinoviev were fighting against the economic platform of Trotskyism of 1923, against the attacks on the Party apparatus, against the tendency to' regard the Party as a conglomeration of factions and groupings—the view which was upheld by the opposition of 1923. Yet at the April Plenum the "New Opposition" had already virtually subscribed to the economic platform of Trotskyism. At the July Plenum it went a step further. A statement which Trotsky read in the name of the whole *bloc* declared outright that the opposition of 1923 was correct in its organisational views, in its criticism of "Party bureaucracy." Thus, Kamenev and Zinoviev, for the sake of a union with Trotsky in the common struggle against the Central Committee, deleted from the history of the Party the whole struggle waged by them against the ideological and organisational views of Trotskyism, which they had then characterised as a revision of Leninism. In return for this, Trotsky, in a statement included in the minutes of the July Plenum, characterised as a gross error the direct charge of opportunism which he had made against Zinoviev and Kamenev in his *Lessons of October*. In this reciprocal amnesty both sides manifested a supreme lack of principle, amounting to nothing more nor less than ideological self-castration. This lack of principle was particularly glaring in the case of Kamenev . and Zinoviev. In the beginning of 1925 they demanded that extreme organisational measures be taken against Trotsky and accused the Central Committee of semi-Trotskyism; whereas about a year later Zinoviev decided to withhold his book *Leninism*, to which at the time of its publication (in the autumn of 1925) he attached the greatest importance, from translation into foreign languages, since it contained passages which were directed against Trotsky and against the substitution of Trotskyism for Leninism.

On the Building of Socialism in Our Country

But lack of principle was not the only characteristic of the opposition *bloc*. The platform of Trotskyism on which the *bloc* united was not only an unprincipled but also a clearly liquid-ationist one, which represented a direct retreat from Lenin's views. The main proposition on which the *bloc* united was *the denial that it was possible to build socialism in our country.*

We have already pointed out above that the prospect of building socialism in our country was presented to the Party by Lenin. To deny that such a prospect existed meant to con-sign the Soviet power either to collapse or to gradual degenera-tion, loss of its proletarian character, which denoted essentially the same thing. Both the Mensheviks and the Social-Democrats of all countries were constantly pointing out this dilemma to our Party. Trotskyism's denial of the possibility of building socialism in one country, namely in our country,* constituted indubitable proof of the Menshevik character of its ideology. No one was as persistent as the Mensheviks in trying to prove that the building of socialism in one country, particularly in so backward a country as ours, was out of the question. The resolution adopted by the Fourteenth Party Conference on this question reads as follows:

"An essential part of the Trotskyist theory of permanent revolution is the contention that 'a real rise of socialist economy in Russia would not become possible *until after the victory* of the proletariat in the most important countries of Europe' (Trotsky in 1922)—a contention which condemns the proletariat of the U.S.S.R. in the present period to fatalistic passivity. Against such 'theories' Lenin wrote: 'Infinitely hackneyed is their argument which they have learned by heart during the development of Social-Democracy in Western Europe and which consists in declaring that we are not ripe for socialism, that we lack, as various 'learned' gentlemen among them declare, the objective prerequisites for socialism." (Notes on Sukhanov.)

The resolution of the Fourteenth Conference of the R.C.P. "On the Tasks of the Comintern and of the R.C.P. in Connec-tion with the Enlarged Plenum of the E.C.C.I." gave a definite characterisation of the Trotskyist viewpoint on the building of socialism in one country, placing Trotskyism on this question

---

* Of course the question under dispute was not whether socialism could be built up in any country, irrespective of its size and level of economic development. It was precisely a question of our country, with its territory, natural resources, and the stage of economic development already attained by it, which was typical also of other countries with an average level of capitalist development.

completely on a par with Sukhanovism, *i.e.*, with Menshevism. This resolution was unanimously adopted by the Fourteenth Party Conference on the basis of a report by Zinoviev. Now the "New Opposition," under the leadership of Trotsky, did not hesitate to come out in opposition to this very resolution.

As was later pointed out by Comrade Stalin at the Seventh Plenum of the E.C.C.I., the lack of faith in the possibility of building socialism in our country, which had reached a certain stage of capitalist development, had gone through the imperialist phase of capitalism and had experienced three revolutions under the leadership of the working class, meant lack of faith in the power and capacity of the proletarian dictatorship to cope with the bourgeoisie within the country.

The Slanderous Charge That the Party Had Degenerated

Lack of faith in the success of socialist construction in our country, in case the international revolution should be delayed —this was what characterised Trotsky's position throughout the entire period during which he was in the ranks of the Bolshevik Party. It was clearly manifested during the disputes concerning the Brest Peace and at the time of the Tenth Congress. It was just in connection with this that Trotsky in 1923 directly raised the question of the degeneration of the leading cadres of our Party. And at the Fourteenth Congress, the "New Opposition," once again in close connection with the lack of faith in our socialist construction, also put forward the idea of the degeneration of the Party (Zinoviev's article, *The Philosophy of the Epoch*, Zalutsky's letter concerning a "Thermidor"). Now, at the July Plenum, during the discussion of the results of the new elections to the Soviets, the united opposition *bloc* advanced the charge of degeneration in a much clearer and more definite form against the Party and the Soviet government.

Our state is far from being of a proletarian character— Trotsky declared, lapsing into a position of out-and-out Menshevism. The policy of the Party runs counter to the interests of the toiling masses—he was echoed by Kamenev. The lower storeys of the edifice of the Soviet state apparatus are being flooded by the kulak element in the countryside and the petty-bourgeois element in the towns—such was the slanderous manner in which the united opposition summed up the results of the elections to the lower Soviet organs—while the intellectual-specialist bureaucracy, allegedly connected with the growing bourgeoisie, was entrenching itself in the upper storeys of this edifice, crowding out the workers from thence. As for the Party and the Y.C.L., bureaucracy and oppression had established themselves there since the death of Lenin. None of the previous oppositions had gone so far with such insolent slander against the Party, with such shameless distortion of the real facts—namely, that the influence of the Party over the peasant masses had strengthened as had also the contact of the state apparatus with the vanguard of the working class.

What was the conclusion to be drawn from such premises? Only this, that in view of the unquestionable degeneration of the Soviet power and of the Communist Party it was necessary for the working class to create a new proletarian party. One of the supporters of the opposition, Ossovsky, actually went so far as to draw this conclusion.

Was this idea of bourgeois degeneration in our Party a new one? No, it was no new idea.

The father of this idea was Axelrod, the Menshevik patriarch. In his articles, published in 1904 in the Menshevik *Iskra,* Axelrod covered scores of pages in trying to prove the petty-bourgeois character of Bolshevism and withal the truly proletarian character of Menshevism. Axelrod even predicted that Lenin would play a role analogous to that of Struve—as the latter turned from a Marxist into a liberal, so Lenin would become the leader of a party of petty-bourgeois revolutionaries. The whole Menshevik literature of the epoch of the first revolution was replete with charges that Bolshevism was of a petty-bourgeois character. When Menshevism turned into liquidationism, the main reason advanced by the liquidators in favour of breaking with the old party and creating a new Stolypin labour party was precisely the view that the old Party had lost its proletarian character, that it had become hopelessly isolated from the working class. In his notorious and despicable pamphlet *Saviours or Abolishers,* published in 1911, L. Martov plainly wrote that "the official Party organisation had degenerated and become wild" and defended liquidationism as "the liquidation of the rule of anti Social-Democratic, anti-proletarian elements in the Party."

Finally, we may recall what was written in 1917 on the occasion of the October Revolution to the effect that Bolshevism was being swallowed up by petty bourgeois, peasant and soldier, elemental forces. This was written by Mensheviks of all shades as well as by former Bolsheviks who had lapsed into Menshevism (Bogdanov, V. Bazarov, B. Avilov, S. Volsky and others). They tried to justify their desertion of Bolshevism on the plea that Bolshevism had undergone petty-bourgeois degeneration. For this reason, when the "Left" Communists spoke of the degeneration of the Party and of the Party leaders in 1918, saying that the latter had turned from proletarian into petty-bourgeois leaders, it was neither new nor original.

At the beginning of the period of the New Economic Policy the *Smenavekh* intellectuals spoke without restraint of the future prospects of the degeneration of the Soviet government. Lenin then said at the Eleventh Party Congress:

"This frank statement of the *Smenavekh*-ists should be welcomed. The enemy speaks the class truth in pointing out the danger confronting us. The enemy is striving to make this inevitable. The *Smenovekh*-ists are expressing the feelings of thousands and tens of thousands of all kinds of bourgeois, or of Soviet employees who participate in our New Economic Policy.... And that is why our main attention must be devoted to this question: really and truly who will win? I spoke of competition—there is no direct attack on us, no attempt is being made to get us by the throat. What will happen tomorrow, we have yet to see, but today they are not attacking us with arms in their hands, and, nevertheless, the struggle with capitalist society has become a hundred times more violent and dangerous.... This is not competition; it is a desperate, ferocious struggle, if not the last, then one close to the last struggle, a life and death struggle between capitalism and communism." *

The correct Leninist policy of our Party, the resolute struggle against opportunism on two fronts which it has carried on throughout the entire history of Bolshevism, was a mighty weapon for overcoming every danger of degeneration. As a

* Lenin, "A Liberal Professor on Equality," *Collected Works,* Vol. XVII.

result of the carrying out of this policy, Bolshevism has not only not degenerated, as the enemies slanderously tried to assert, but has steadily and systematically strengthened its connection with the proletarian masses, purging itself of opportunists and degenerated elements.

And at the beginning of the New Economic Policy, when a considerable part of our industry was at a standstill, and a considerable part of the proletariat was scattered and declassed, when in purging the Party of alien class elements and decadent elements, it was necessary to expel many scores of thousands from the Party—at that time also the Party was successfully overcoming and overcame the danger of degeneration.

Between 1922 and 1926 we achieved new and gigantic successes. By 1926, we had restored industry almost to the prewar level and recruited into the Party several hundred thousand workers at the bench. The policy of further industrialisation of the country and the further strengthening of the Party's contact with the proletarian masses was the best guarantee against any danger of degeneration. And it was just this policy that our Party was pursuing with Leninist consistency and determination. The slanderous chatter of the opposition about the degeneration of the Party only testified to the complete isolation of the opposition from the Party and to the Menshevik degeneration of the opposition itself.

The Attitude of the Trotskyist Opposition Towards the Peasantry

In 1923, the Trotskyists demanded high prices on industrial products and unlimited issues of currency (at the Thirteenth Party Conference the Trotskyists warned us against the proposed stabilisation of the currency, asserting that it was premature). Both these demands in substance meant forcibly pumping out money from the peasantry and thereby undermining the political alliance of the proletariat with the basic section of the peasantry—the middle peasants. The natural result of such a policy would only have been to ruin the broad masses of poor and middle peasants, and to embitter them against the Soviet government.

The splendid success achieved by the Party in the restoration of industry caused utter confusion in the ranks of the Trotskyist opposition, but the new economic difficulties which arose during the transition from the period of restoration to that of reconstruction gave it fresh encouragement.

The "New Opposition" which attacked the Party in 1925 renounced the Leninist view on the alliance of the working class with the peasantry, depicting the kulak, instead of the middle peasant, as the central figure in the countryside. While ostensibly fighting against the kulaks, the "New Opposition" actually adopted a policy hostile to the middle peasantry. It thus paved the way for its complete ideological capitulation to Trotskyism on the peasant question as well. The Party continued to hold the view that the industrialisation of our country could only be effected on the basis of a firm alliance with the middle peasant, by promoting the well-being not only of the workers but of the poor and middle peasants as well, by gradually transferring these masses to socialised economy through the co-operative system. Trotskyism contrasted the peasantry to the proletariat as two mutually hostile forces. It could not see any other way to industrialisation than through the exploitation and ruin of peasant farming. Trotskyism proposed to fashion our economic relationships with the peasantry on the model of the relation of a capitalist "mother country" towards its colonies. Hence we have the two main economic demands of the opposition *bloc*—the raising of the retail prices of industrial commodities and the raising of the taxes on the middle peasants. |

Owing to the Menshevik character of its position, the opposition *bloc* was unable to comprehend the role and significance of the middle peasant as an ally of the proletariat under the conditions of socialist construction. What lay at the root of this was once again the old Trotskyist lack of faith in the ability of the proletariat to lead the peasantry. It was not so long ago that Zinoviev and Kamenev had written and spoken most eloquently of this organic Menshevik ailment in Trotskyism. Now they themselves adopted the Trotskyist point of view.

Questions Concerning the International Situation

But it was the question of Comintern tactics which the oppo-sition *bloc* made one of the chief points in its attack on the Party at the July Plenum of 1926. The premise from which these tactics proceeded was the fact of the relative stabilisation of capitalism and the absence of an immediate revolutionary situation. Hence it followed that the task of the Communist Parties.was to gather and accumulate forces, to strengthen the Communist influence in the mass labour organisations, above all in the trade unions.

It was just for this reason that the Fifth Plenum of the Comintern, which met on the eve of the Fourteenth Party Con-ference, already recognised that:

"In view of the slow and protracted rate of development of the revolution, the slogan of Bolshevisation acquires not less but greater significance. . . .

"Under the present conditions, the Communist Parties must take into account two main dangers—on the one hand, the danger of turn-ing into small sects of 'pure' Communists, possessing 'good' principles but unable to get into touch with the mass labour movement of the given period; on the other hand, the danger of turning into an amorphous semi-Social-Democratic party in those cases where the Party is unable to combine the struggle for winning over the working masses with faithfulness to the principles of Communism."

Our Party could not but take into account the delay in the coming of the international revolution and the relative stabil-isation of capitalism, but the Party firmly adhered to the point of view that, even despite the delay in the coming of the inter-national revolution, we were in a position to build socialism in our country with our own forces.

With the opposition it was otherwise. In view of their lack of faith in our socialist construction, in the internal forces of our revolution, the delay in the coming of the international revolution meant for them the degeneration of the Party and of the Soviet government. The sole road to salvation, in their opinion, was to hasten on the coming of the international rev-olution. In its spirit of panic capitulation, the opposition pro-posed skipping over the prolonged and difficult work of win-ning over the proletarian masses and their organisations; they were inclined to deny the fact of even a partial stabilisation of capitalism, and in the absence of a revolutionary situation in the actual state of economic and political affairs, they created such a situation out of their own imagination. This gave rise to the tendency somehow or other to explain away and to reduce to nought (of course, only in words) the stabilisation of capitalism, a tendency, in the words of Marx, to substitute revolutionary phrases for revolutionary development. Finally, this gave rise to the *bloc* of the united opposition with the "Left" opportunist groups in the Communist International.

It was precisely at this time that the Communist International urged all its sections to concentrate their attention on intensifying the work in the trade unions, on activising in every way the revolutionary elements within the reformist trade unions for the purpose of carrying out the tactics of a united front, in order to isolate the leadership of the Amsterdam International and to strengthen the influence of the Communist Parties among the masses.

As a result of the Left swing among the trade union masses—a factor which the reformist leaders were forced to take into account, particularly in Great Britain which was going through a prolonged period of depression which was reflected in the state of mind of the workers—as a result of the achievements of socialist construction in the U.S.S.R., which enhanced the feeling of sympathy towards the U.S.S.R. among the broad masses of the British proletariat, the so-called Anglo-Russian Trade Union Unity Committee was formed.

The Soviet trade unions made extensive use of this committee in order to combat the leaders of the Amsterdam International, to further popularise the achievements of socialist construction in the U.S.S.R. among the masses of the British workers and to mobilise them in defence of the U.S.S.R. against the policy of intervention.

"On May 1, 1926, the coal barons declared a lockout to enforce a reduction in wages and a lengthening of the working day.

"The miners responded to this with a general strike in the coal industry, which later developed into a general strike of the British proletariat.

"The British workers had to smash the obstinate resistance of the trade union bureaucrats and of the leaders of the Labour Party, who were later forced into hypocritical and treacherous manoeuvres, formally taking over the leadership of the general strike in order to leave it without leadership later on.

"From a struggle against the reduction of the miners' wages, the general strike developed into a political battle. The general strike showed that there was real proletarian solidarity among the entire British proletariat."*

The Soviet proletariat, under the leadership of the C.P.S.U. and of the Comintern, showed an example of international proletarian solidarity by holding gigantic meetings and demonstrations and collecting funds of many millions and food supplies to aid the British miners.

The Comintern and Profintern immediately issued an appeal to the international proletariat to give all possible support to the workers of Great Britain by collecting funds, holding mass meetings and demonstrations, preventing the shipping of coal to Great Britain, declaring strikes, etc.

The treacherous conduct of the leaders of the General Council of the Trades Union Congress in Great Britain during the general strike in May 1926, and the sharp criticism of this conduct on the part of the Soviet trade unions resulted later in the Anglo-Russian Trade Union Unity Committee being dissolved on the initiative of the British trade union bureaucrats.

The Trotsky-Zinoviev opposition *bloc* developed a furious demagogic agitation in the summer of 1926, demanding that the Soviet trade unions immediately withdraw from the Anglo-Russian Committee. They took the same stand of rejecting the united front and refusing to work in the reactionary trade unions which was taken by the "Left" phrasemongers in Germany, Poland and other countries.

Together with these "Left" phrasemongers, the Trotsky-Zinoviev *bloc* tried to reduce to nought the whole of Lenin's policy of working in the reactionary trade unions, which had been expounded with such classic clarity in Lenin's *"Left-Wing" Communism—an Infantile Disorder.*

"To be afraid of *this* 'reactionariness,' to attempt to dispense with it, to skip over it, is the greatest stupidity, for this means to be afraid of that role of the proletarian vanguard which consists of teaching,

* Theses of the Agitprop Section of the C.C. of the C P.S.U. and of the C.C. of the E.C.C.I. on the tenth anniversary of the Comintern.

educating, training, drawing into a new life the most backward sections and masses of the working class and peasantry."

The "Left" deviations in the Comintern mainly took the form of refusing to work in the reformist trade unions, rejecting the tactics of the united front with the Social-Democratic workers, and also that of *putschism* and individual terrorism.

They were particularly clearly manifested in the German and Polish parties.

As the decision of the Sixth Plenum of the E.C.C.I. points out:

"The Communist International was forced, following the defeat of 1923 [in Germany—*N.P.*] and the bankruptcy of the Brandlerite Central Committee, to let the leadership pass into the hands of the 'Lefts,' despite the fact that it knew that Maslov, Fischer and Scholem were capable of committing the greatest ultra-Left errors. The Comintern resolutely fought, at the Frankfurt Congress, against the errors of the above-named group (on the questions of the trade unions, the tactics of the united front, etc.). From the very first minute after the leadership passed into the hands of this group, the Comintern warned the Party against its errors."

When it became clear that this group was incapable of getting rid of its deviations, when a group of the best workers had been formed within the Central Committee who were capable of taking matters into their own hands, the Comintern, on the initiative of the Bolshevik core of the Central Committee of the German Communist Party headed by Comrade Thälmann, supported the removal of the Maslov-Fischer group from the leadership.

The vicious factional struggle which was carried on by the group of Maslov and Ruth Fischer after it had been removed from the leadership, forced the Central Committee of the German Party to expel Maslov, Ruth Fischer and their closest associates.

In Poland, the leading group in the Central Committee, which was headed by Domski (who in 1920 opposed the advance of the Red Army on Warsaw) also committed a number of crass "Left" errors, which were almost disastrous for the Party, and was removed from the leadership in the latter part of 1925.

In the Communist Parties of Western Europe (just as in the case of our "Otzovist-Ultimatumists" in 1907-11), the "Left" opposition, despite the revolutionary phrases which were used to justify it, signified first and foremost a refusal to perform the day-to-day work in the mass organisations. As was most strikingly proved by the experience of the German Communist Party in 1924-25, under the leadership of Maslov and Ruth Fischer, what it meant for the Communist Parties was virtually a voluntary surrender of their positions in the labour movement to the Social-Democrats. There is nothing surprising in the fact that Social-Democracy as one man did everything in its power to support the "Left" liquidators as against the Bolshevik elements who carried out the line of the Comintern.

But there was yet another reason why the Social-Democrats supported the Leftists. The "Lefts" were waging a bitter struggle against the U.S.S.R. and the C.P.S.U. Some of them, such as Professor Korsch, went so far as to declare that the U.S.S.R. was a country of developing capitalism and that the C.P.S.U. was a kulak Party, bringing about the dictatorship of the bourgeoisie. It was the task of the working class, according to Korsch, to overthrow this dictatorship by armed force, and in case of war, to adopt a defeatist attitude. Korsch, who expressed these out-and-out counter-revolutionary views, occupied a position close to that of Maslov and Ruth Fischer. Close contact with the latter was maintained by Urbans and Weber, who had not yet been expelled from the Party at the time and who on every occasion advertised themselves (just as did Maslov and Ruth Fischer) as supporters of the opposition *bloc* in the ranks of the C.P.S.U.

A distinguishing characteristic of the opposition *bloc* of 1926 was the fact that it not only united in its ranks the fragments of the opposition groups within the C.P.S.U. who fought against the Leninist line of the Party, but that it also attempted to draw over to its side the anti-Leninist elements in the international movement who were hiding behind the Communist flag, who proclaimed themselves as "Lefts" (though they sometimes upheld open Right opportunist views, as did Souvarine, who was expelled from the French Party), but who had virtually become out-and-out henchmen of the counter-revolution and who were being expelled by the Comintern from its ranks.

The Anti-Leninist Groupings Follow in the Footsteps of the August Bloc

The groups of former leaders, who united in the opposition *bloc* in 1926, renounced with a complete lack of principle the differences which had formerly divided them, and found common ground upon the platform of Trotskyism. Besides the main groups of Trotskyists and of the so-called "New Opposition," the *bloc* also included the remnants of the former "Workers' Opposition" headed by Shlyapnikov and Medvedev.

What was the political make-up of Shlyapnikov and Medvedev at the time when they joined the opposition *bloc?* Following the Tenth Party Congress, they did not renounce those views the defence of which the Congress had recognised as incompatible with membership of the R.C.P. and continued to carry on factional activities behind the back of the Party, despite the decision of the Tenth Congress regarding the dissolution of factions and groupings. The Eleventh Congress accordingly discussed the question of these activities and decided to give a final warning to Shlyapnikov, Medvedev and Kollontai. Though compelled for the time being to discontinue their factional activities after the decision of the Congress, Shlyapnikov and Medvedev continued to hold their former views. During the discussion in 1923, Shlyapnikov once more upheld his old programme in opposition to the Central Committee.

In 1925, a letter of Medvedev's fell into the hands of the Central Control Commission. It was addressed to his associates in Baku and contained a peculiar platform for the creation of a faction. The contents of this letter clearly showed that the ideas of the "Workers' Opposition," which had been condemned by the Tenth Congress, tended to develop in the direction of utter and obvious Menshevik degeneration. In this letter Medvedev expressed himself in favour of an extension of the concessions policy, which he envisaged as the sole means for the further development of industry. The policy of an alliance of the working class with the middle peasantry he regarded as fundamentally incorrect. As regards the international labour movement, he described the foreign Communist Parties as petty-bourgeois rabble gangs, at the same time singing the praises of the Social-Democratic parties and the Amsterdam trade unions and advocating that the Profintern be immediately dissolved and that the Soviet trade unions be affiliated to the Amsterdam International.

The remnants of the former "Workers' Opposition" who stuck to their anti-Leninist views had thus come to anchor in the haven of Menshevism. All the more insolent did they become in their attempts to accuse the Party of betraying the interests of the working class. And all the more joyfully did the leaders of the opposition *bloc* welcome with open arms the remnants of the former "Workers' Opposition." As for the former "Democratic Centralism" group, which Lenin resolutely fought in 1920-21, the Trotskyists had already established close connections with the remnants of this group in the autumn of 1923.

This *bloc* of all the anti-Leninist groups not only within the ranks of the C.P.S.U. and the Comintern but even of those who had been expelled from the ranks of the Comintern (such as Maslov, Ruth Fischer, etc.) was thus distinguished by two main characteristics. It was unprincipled and it was liquidationist. In these respects it very strongly resembled the notorious August *Bloc* of 1912. The August *Bloc* was formed to fight Lenin and the Leninist Party and it, too, was headed by Trotsky. It, too, included the most diverse elements—open liquidators of the type of Chatsky-Harvy,* Ezhov, Levitsky; not quite so frank but no less harmful and vicious liquidators such as Martov, Dan and Axelrod; the Bundists and Georgian Mensheviks of the type of Lieber and Noah Jordania whose liquidationism was flavoured with a strong dose of diehard petty-bourgeois nationalism; and finally the "non-factional" Social-Democrats of Trotsky's group who were extremely "revolutionary" in words but who in reality supported the liquidators. What was it first and foremost that

* Who now advocates the overthrow of the Soviet government by armed force.

united all these multifarious groups and groupings?* They
were united by a hatred of the "Leninist regime" in the Party,
by a passionate desire to replace it by complete freedom of factions and groupings, by freedom for all kinds of opportunism.
But the mountain brought forth a mouse. The August *Bloc* in-
gloriously disintegrated. It did not succeed in creating any sort
of a party on the basis of freedom and factions and groupings.
And now, almost fifteen years later, the opposition *bloc* of 1926,
headed by Trotsky, likewise unfurled the banner of struggle
against the "regime," "the banner of inner-Party democracy."
For the Trotskyists and their allies, inner-Party democracy
meant, just as in 1923, freedom of factions and groupings, freedom for all opportunism including that of the Menshevik-syndicalist "Workers' Opposition." They attempted to realise this
freedom on the sly by carrying on factional activities, trying
everywhere to organise nuclei, virtually building up a new party
within the existing one. However, the anti-Party work of the
opposition *bloc* encountered a crushing repulse at the hands of
the whole Party, of all the Party organisations. This repulse
frustrated the attempts of the opposition to create a new Party.
The opposition did not succeed in uniting anybody, except some
pitiful groups of decayed and degenerated elements who had become isolated from the working class or who had never had
any contact with it.

The Decisions of the July Plenum of 1926

The July Plenum was able to note considerable successes
won by the Party in the struggle against economic difficulties.
The Party had achieved a certain reduction in the prices of
agricultural products and stabilised the prices of industrial goods.
The fluctuation of the *chervonetz* had ceased. The determined
struggle for a regime of economy and for raising the efficiency
of labour was also productive of results. The hopes of the opposition for an accentuation of the economic difficulties proved
vain. On the contrary, the improved economic condition of the

* The "Left" *Vperyod*-ists (the otzovists and ultimatumists), who had tried
to describe Lenin as an opportunist, did not formally join the *bloc*, but,
essentially, acted in full contact with it.

country rendered it possible to raise the question not only of securing the wage level already reached but even of raising wages to a certain extent.

Following a discussion on the results of the elections to the lower Soviet organs, the Plenum pointed out the indisputable fact that the political activity of the masses of workers and peasants had further increased. The results of the elections to the rural Soviets testified quite clearly to the fact that, apart from the kulak stratum, the rest of the peasant masses supported the policy of the Party. The elections of 1925-26 were a clear proof of the successful results of the policy of strengthening the alliance of the working class with the peasantry which the Party was putting into effect. One of the main factors in the execution of this policy was the putting into effect of the slogan "to put fresh life into the Soviets."

But side by side with these indisputable achievements, the Plenum took note of the fact that the activity of the poor peasantry was still inadequate as compared with that of the middle peasantry. The reason for this was that some of the local organisations did not carry out the Party directives regarding work among the poor peasants. The Plenum also noted that in a number of cases the rights of suffrage had been distorted in violation of the Soviet constitution, and that some of the local organisations did not show sufficient flexibility and skill in guiding the elections.

The Plenum gave practical instructions aimed at removing these shortcomings.

Following a prolonged discussion on questions concerning the international situation, the Plenum endorsed the line of the Comintern, particularly with regard to the British general strike and the miners' strike, emphatically rejecting the opposition's proposal that the Soviet trade unions should withdraw from the Anglo-Russian Trade Union Unity Committee and the entire Trotskyist interpretation of the international situation.

The Plenum outlined a plan for a new grain collections campaign. The principal task of this campaign, according to the decision of the Plenum, was:

"To secure for the peasantry the possibility of disposing of their surplus on such conditions as may not in any way undermine the peasantry's interest in further extending the scope of their economy, in extending the area under cultivation, etc., while at the same time securing the possibility for the speediest development of the national economy as a whole on the road of industrialisation, facilitating the accumulation of funds by the socialist elements of our economy and making exports pay with a view to importing equipment and raw materials which are essential for our entire economy, including peasant farming."

The whole practical policy of our Party was adapted to the task of carrying out the basic decision of the Fourteenth Party Congress regarding the industrialisation of the country.

The Plenum in its resolution took note of the errors which had been committed in the preceding grain collections campaign (excessive overhead expenses, the absence of a reserve which could be used to force down the market prices, etc.). During the discussion on the question of the grain collections, the opposition again attempted to start a general discussion on economic policy, charging the Central Committee with lack of firmness in carrying out the policy of industrialisation. The opposition was decisively repulsed by a brilliant speech from Felix Dzershinski, who exposed the whole demagogic mendacity of the opposition and vividly delineated the tremendous work done by the Central Committee in carrying out the decisions of the Fourteenth Congress for the industrialisation of the country.*

The July Plenum adopted a detailed resolution concerning housing construction, thus linking up the carrying out of the policy of industrialisation with the utmost possible improvement of the living conditions of the working masses.

The Plenum pointed out that the growing housing crisis was hindering the further development of industry; that it constituted a considerable obstacle in the way of attracting labour forces into industry and retarded the growth of labour productivity.

The Plenum called for new large appropriations for housing

* Felix Dzerzhinski died a few hours after delivering this speech. Dzerzhinski, who held the post of chairman of the Supreme Council of National Economy for two and a half years, carried through a tremendous work for the restoration of industry. Following his death, Comrade Kuibyshev was appointed chairman of the Supreme Council of National Economy while Comrade Orjonikidze became chairman of the Central Control Commission.

construction both in the state budget and in local budgets, outlined a number of measures for improving the work of the housing co-operatives and deemed it necessary:

"That the State Planning Commission, in drawing up the Five-Year Plan for the development of industry, shall also take into account a prospective plan for the construction of workers' houses over the same period, so that housing construction may be brought into line with the plan for restoring industry in the largest industrial centres and that there may be a more even distribution of housing space among these districts."

Finally, the July Plenum, on the basis of the report of the Central Control Commission, adopted a resolution concerning the unity of the Party in connection with the case of Lashevich. This resolution pointed out that:

"The opposition did not confine itself in its struggle to lawfully upholding its views within the bounds of the Party constitution and of late has passed over to direct violations of the decisions of the Tenth and Fourteenth Congresses regarding the preservation of unity within the ranks of the C.P.S.U., having resorted in its struggle against the Party to attempts to create an illegal factional organisation opposed to the Party and directed against its unity."

The holding of an "illegal factional meeting in the woods near Moscow," the circulation of secret documents of the Politburo etc., "all the threads of these factional steps of the opposition lead towards the apparatus of the E.C.C.I., at the head of which is a member of the Politburo, Comrade Zinoviev."

The practical political conclusion drawn from the above was the expulsion of Zinoviev from the Politburo and of Lashevich from the Central Committee, as well as instructions to the local organisations to carry on the most relentless struggle against all manifestations of factionalism and against attempts to undermine the unity of the Party. The resolute measures taken by the July Plenum to safeguard the unity of the Party met with the unanimous support of all local Party organisations.

The Opposition Attempts to Force a Discussion Upon the Party

However, the factional activities of the opposition under the direct guidance of Trotsky, Zinoviev and others who headed the opposition *bloc,* were not discontinued but proceeded on the contrary with gathering speed. From occasional factional meetings and correspondence, the opposition everywhere proceeded to extensive activities aimed at the creation of a complete centralised apparatus. The contents of the literature circulated by the opposition acquired an ever more demagogic and anti-Party character, and was already scarcely distinguishable from the appeals of the Mensheviks and other counter-revolutionary groups.

Finally, in the end of September, the representatives of the opposition started a simultaneous campaign throughout the entire country at nuclei meetings with the purpose of forcing a discussion upon the Party regarding fundamental questions of policy which had been decided on by the Fourteenth Congress. The initiative was taken by the leaders of the opposition *bloc* themselves, headed by Trotsky and Zinoviev, who appeared at a meeting of the nucleus at the Aviopribor Factory in Moscow. These actions constituted a violation of discipline by members of the Central Committee unprecedented in our Party. However, the worker Communists, rank and file members of the nuclei, to whom the leaders of the opposition appealed after several months of preliminary work, gave a resolute rebuff to the attack on the Leninist line and the Leninist leadership of our Party. The entire Party unanimously supported the decision of the Central Committee not to open a general Party discussion merely on the demand of the leaders of the opposition who did not have a single Party organisation on their side. The resolute rebuff which the opposition received was a clear proof of the fact that the improved social composition of the Party, which began with the period of enrolment after Lenin's death and which was achieved by admitting hundreds of thousands of the best workers at the bench into the Party—that the genuine enforcement of inner-Party democracy, the tremendous educational activities carried out since then in the sense of explaining the foundations of Leninism to the broad Party masses—that all this had helped to rally the Leninist ranks of the Party even more closely around the Central Committee. The leaders of the opposition, who in their blind self-adoration expressed themselves confident up to the very last moment that the working class section of the Party would follow them as soon as they took action, thus received a severe and well-earned lesson from the Bolshevik Party.

The crushing defeat which the opposition met with at all Party meetings in Moscow at which its representatives appeared, was a bitter disappointment to all anti-Soviet elements both at home and abroad, from the monarchists to the Mensheviks, who confidently hoped that the victory of the opposition *bloc,* which they expected, would become the first stage towards the disintegration and collapse of our Party and following this, also of the Soviet government, that it would play a similar role in our revolution as was played by the victory of the Thermidor *bloc* during the great French Revolution.*

The leaders of the opposition could now see with their own eyes how insignificant was the "army" which they had succeeded in launching against the Party at the decisive moment. This was why on October 4, only a few days after they had commenced an open struggle, the leaders of the opposition submitted a statement to the Politburo, declaring their readiness to discontinue the factional struggle. However, immediately after submitting this statement they made an attempt to utilise their last means of struggle, namely, to incite the Leningrad organisation against the Central Committee at the Party meetings held on October 7. This last move was beaten too. The Leningrad Communists, by an overwhelming majority, expressed themselves in favour of the Party line, although the united opposition had pinned its chief hopes on Leningrad.

The Double-Faced Manoeuvres of the Opposition Bloc

On October 16, the *Pravda* published a declaration by six members of the Central Committee who had adhered to the opposition *bloc* (Zinoviev, Kamenev, Trotsky, Pyatakov, Sokolnikov and Yevdokimov). In this declaration, which was a direct result of the catastrophic defeat suffered by the opposition when it attempted to come out in the open before the Party masses,

* As is well known, the Thermidor *bloc* which brought about the triumph of the bourgeois counter-revolution in France was also composed of the most diverse elements, a prominent place among whom was occupied by the "extreme Lefts."

the leaders of the opposition renounced all solidarity with the theory and. practice of factions and groupings, fully acknowledged the incorrectness of upholding their views ' by factional methods, called upon their followers to dissolve the factional organisations created by them, dissociated themselves from the "Left" opportunists in the Comintern (Weber, Urbans, Bordiga), who were attacking the U.S.S.R. and the C.P.S.U., as well as from. Korsch, Souvarine, Ruth Fischer and Maslov, who had been expelled from the Comintern, dissociated themselves from the Menshevik-liquidationist views of the remnants of the former "Workers' Opposition" (Medvedev, Shlyapnikov), and pledged themselves in the future to submit without reservation to the decisions of the Party Congresses, of the Central Committee and of the Central Control Commission. However, in addition to this the authors of the declaration also stated that they continued to hold the same views as before on matters of principle and would uphold these views, though henceforth only within the bounds of the Party constitution.

The Central Committee noted with satisfaction that the opposition had thus publicly renounced factional methods of struggle, but, naturally, neither the Central Committee nor the Party as a whole could be satisfied with the fact that the opposition adhered to its anti-Leninist opinions and would continue, as before, to try to force them upon the Party. Although this forced self-condemnation of the opposition constituted a proof of its new moral defeat, nevertheless, all members of the Party were confronted by the following obvious facts:

1) The opposition did not renounce factional methods of struggle until after they had made 100 per cent use of these methods and until the opposition had suffered a crushing defeat in its attempts to force a discussion upon the Party.

2) The extremely small forces of the oppositionists would have inevitably been placed outside the ranks of the Party, had they continued the factional struggle. By publishing their declaration, the leaders of the opposition saved these extremely small forces of theirs from an unquestionably hopeless and disastrous struggle.

3) At the Thirteenth Congress the Party had already heard from the lips of Trotsky, the leader of the opposition *bloc*, a

hypocritical condemnation of the theory and practice of factions and groupings. This utterance, however, did not prevent Trotsky from renewing the factional struggle as soon as he found a suitable moment to do so.*

In view of all these circumstances the Party had absolutely no assurance that the opposition would not take advantage of the first opportune situation to resort to factional methods for the defence of their anti-Party, anti-Leninist views. One of the guarantees against this was the decision of the Joint Plenum of the Central Committee and Central Control Commission of October 22-26, removing Trotsky from membership of the Politburo and Kamenev from the position of candidate to that body, and removing Zinoviev from work in the Comintern. The Plenum also adopted the theses of Comrade Stalin's report regarding the opposition *bloc.* These theses were submitted to the Fifteenth Conference of the C.P.S.U. which opened on October 26, 1926.

The Fifteenth Party Conference

There were four questions on the agenda of the Conference—the international situation; the economic situation of the country and the tasks of the Party; the results of the work and the immediate tasks of the trade unions; and, finally, the inner-Party situation and the opposition *bloc.*

After listening to and discussing the report on the international situation, the Conference

"fully and unreservedly endorsed the fundamental line of the delegation of the C.P.S.U. and its work in the Communist International."

The Conference instructed the delegation

"to pursue in the Communist International the policy of the further bolshevisation of the Communist Parties, which precludes the theory and practice of the so-called 'freedom of factions and groupings' as a principle sharply hostile to the organisational principles of Leninism."

The Conference emphatically condemned the factional work which the opposition of the C.P.S.U. had carried on in the Communist International.

* Subsequently Trotsky himself admitted that the declaration of October 16 was nothing but a manoeuvre.

The Conference unanimously endorsed the theses of the report regarding the economic situation. The basic point from which .these theses proceeded was the fact that we had in the main completed the restoration of the country's economy and that we were now passing to a new period of economic development, to a period of the reconstruction of the whole economy along socialist lines and on the basis of a new and higher technique. The first period, which we had already · passed in the main, was not only one of restoration, since during this period a firm foundation had also been laid for the · socialist reconstruction of our entire economy. The period. which was now at an end was customarily called a restoration period, inasmuch as we had approached the pre-war level of production in industry and agriculture. However, the process of restoring agriculture

"was accomplished under the conditions of the nationalisation ·of the land, of the removal of the whole landlord stratum, of dividing up the land among the propertyless, of implanting in the countryside the rudiments of a new system in the organisation of agricultural production (collective farms, Soviet farms, etc.) with a differently organised system of taxation and a different organisation and different policy in respect of agricultural credits."

As regards large-scale industry, which had been taken over by the socialist state and had thereby become transformed from capitalist into socialist industry, at present

"almost the sole consumer [of its products—N. P.] is the mass consumer, the worker and peasant, to whose needs our industry is adapting itself. A considerable stratum consisting of the former landlords and. nobles, the highly paid section of government officials, etc., had dropped out of the number of consumers. The rise of industrial production has been accompanied by the realisation of the electrification plan, for example, by a development of the electrical engineering industry already considerably exceeding the pre-war level, and by the rise of a number of new industries."

Passing on to the outlook for the further industrialisation of the country, the theses specified the following basic-sources for the development of industrialisation: accumulation within industry itself; utilisation of the revenues derived from other branches of national economy by means of redistribution of funds through the state budget and the credit system; and the utilization of the savings of the population.

The opposition was seized with panic because, with the transition to the new reconstruction period in the development of our national economy, there was a certain slackening in the tempo of industrial development. In 1925-26, industrial production increased by 40 per cent, while in 1926-27, it was to have an increase of 19.7 per cent. The slower rate in the growth of industry was due to the fact that we had already made full use of the old equipment, which had previously been lying idle. Now it became necessary, not merely to put into operation old plants with already existing equipment, but to build new plants. Nevertheless, this slower tempo of growth far exceeded the highest tempo attained by capitalist countries. In the U.S.A., industry's average rate of growth between 1910-13 did not exceed 3.5 per cent, while in the European countries it was even less.

In the field of industrial management the report of the Central Committee, which emphasised the necessity of securing concrete guidance, set the Party the task of decentralising the management to a certain degree and of guaranteeing local organs as well as individual enterprises a certain degree of independence —the task of attaining an increased measure of planning and rationalisation and of fighting harder against excessive expenditure.

The opposition envisaged agriculture as an inexhaustible source of funds for the development of industrialisation.

The opposition continued to contend that an intensified process of capitalist differentiation was taking place in the countryside and that the tendency of this process remained the same as before the war, i.e., in the direction of the gradual elimination of the mass of middle peasantry. Trotskyism based itself on the process of capitalist differentiation in the countryside, on the ruination of the peasant masses.

However, the assertions of the Trotskyists were refuted by the existing statistical data. In reality

"we had a growth of all groups of farms, and a reduction in the number of farms which had no cattle, and of those which cultivated little or no land. The main stratum of the middle peasantry has not only not disintegrated but has grown and acquired greater importance, since the poor peasant strata in the countryside, whose position has improved as a result of our policy, have reinforced the middle stratum."

The opposition exaggerated to a hysterical degree the growth of private capital. In reality, the part played by the private trader had been further diminished both in the wholesale and retail trade. The Party was confronted with the task of continuing to fight with its whole energy for the further lowering of prices. Every success achieved in this direction helped to strengthen the economic and political alliance of the working class with the peasantry, whereas the policy of high prices, which the opposition proposed, meant, objectively speaking, an alliance with the kulak and nepman.

In the sphere of the labour question, the tasks confronting the Party were those of a determined struggle against all attempts to enforce a regime of economy at the expense of the vital interests of the working class, the tasks of raising the productivity of labour and strengthening labour discipline. Of particular significance was the task of meeting the needs of the working class in respect of housing and of fighting against unemployment.

During the course of the previous few years, the opposition had been indulging in the most gloomy forecasts regarding the success of our construction. But the actual facts invariably refuted these forecasts. All the acts and words of the opposition were characterised by a lack of faith in the forces of the working class and of the Party. And all the opposition's practical proposals were dictated by the interests of bourgeois groups, hostile to the Soviet government.

The Fifteenth Party Conference on the Work
of the Trade Unions

The theses on the work of the trade unions adopted by the conference took note of a certain accentuation of the class struggle in the country during the given period, while the proletariat continued to consolidate the economic and political positions which it had won. The theses emphasised a number of achievements in the work of our trade unions under the guidance of the Party. Besides the general increase in the number of workers and employees engaged in our industry, an uninterrupted growth was taking place in the number of trade union members, above all in the sphere of industry.

The growth of the trade unions reflected the growth of the working class and of the entire economy of the country as a result of the correct policy of the Party.

At the end of 1920, on the eve of the transition to the New Economic Policy, the production of our industry was equivalent to only about 20 per cent of the pre-war output. By the end of 1926, industrial production had almost reached the pre-war level, having thus increased fivefold.

During the period since the Fourteenth Party Congress, the work of the active groups of trade union members had considerably revived and extended its scope. There was an increased percentage of non-Party workers on the factory committees and on various commissions. The very composition of the factory committees was more than 50 per cent new as a result of new elections—a fact which testified to the proper realisation of democracy. The finances of the trade unions were in a sounder state. Considerable progress had also been made in the cultural fields.

Among the chief defects in the work of our trade unions, the theses mentioned the inadequate care for and protection of the economic interests of the working class, particularly in those cases where the policy of enforcing a regime of economy had been distorted, as well as weakness in the work of production conferences.

On the question of wages, the Conference endorsed the decisions adopted by the Plenum of the Central Committee of April 1926, which rejected the noxious and demagogic proposals of the opposition with regard to wages. It was in strict conformity with the rise in the labour productivity, the growth in the harvest and the development of the entire national economy, which became apparent in the autumn of 1926, that the Fifteenth Party Conference adopted a decision in favour of raising wages.

The Social-Democratic Deviation of the Opposition Exposed at the Fifteenth Conference

Comrade Stalin's report characterised the views of the opposition *bloc* as a manifestation of a Social-Democratic deviation in the ranks of the C.P.S.U.

Comrade Stalin commenced by describing the various stages in the development of the opposition *bloc*, incidentally exposing the attempts of the leaders of the opposition to screen themselves behind the authority of Lenin, who, they alleged, looked with favour upon all kinds of *blocs*. In reality it was only *blocs* based on revolutionary principle that Lenin recognised, such as, for example, the bloc of the Bolsheviks with the Menshevik supporters of the Party, which was formed in defence of the Party against the liquidators.

Lenin had always fought with the utmost determination against unprincipled, adventurist, and liquidationist *blocs* of the type of the August *Bloc*. And the opposition *bloc* in all its features had an exact resemblance to the August *Bloc*, while it bore no resemblance whatever to the *bloc* of Lenin with Plekhanov (1907-11) against the liquidators. Comrade Stalin in his report focused his main attention on the question of building socialism in our country, since this was the starting point of the whole liquidationist philosophy of the opposition *bloc*.

.‟We cannot move forward," said Comrade Stalin in his report, "without knowing where we have to move to, without knowing the aim of the movement. We cannot build without perspectives, without confidence that, having started to build a socialist economy, we can complete the building of it. Without clear perspectives, without clear aims, the Party cannot guide construction. We cannot live according to the recipe of Bernstein: 'The movement is everything, the aim is nothing.' On the contrary, we, as revolutionaries, must subordinate our movement forward, our practical work, to the fundamental class aim of proletarian construction. Or else—into the swamp of opportunism, inevitably and unconditionally....

"Without clear perspectives for our construction, without the confidence of being able to complete the building of socialism, the working masses cannot *consciously* take part in this construction, they cannot *consciously* lead the peasantry. Without the confidence of being able to complete the building of socialism, there can be no will to build socialism. Who wants to build, knowing that the building will not be completed? The lack of socialist perspectives for our construction, therefore, leads to the enfeebling of the will of the proletariat for this construction, inevitably and unconditionally.

"Further. The enfeebling of the will of the proletariat for the construction of socialism cannot but cause a strengthening of the capitalist elements in our economy. For what does it mean to build socialism, if not to overcome the capitalist elements in our economy? Pessimistic and defeatist moods in the working class cannot but encourage the hopes of the capitalist elements for the restoration of the old order. He who underrates the decisive signifcance of the socialist perspectives of our construction is helping the capitalist elements in our economy, cultivating capitulation.

. "Finally, the enfeebling of the will of the proletariat for victory over the capitalist elements in our economy, by retarding our socialist construction, cannot but delay the outbreak of the international revolution in all countries. It should not be forgotten that the world proletariat is watching our economic construction and our achievements on this front with the hope that we will emerge victorious from this struggle, that we will succeed in completing the building of socialism. The infinite number of worker delegations coming to us from the West and probing every corner of our construction shows that our struggle on the front of construction is of immense international significance in the sense of its revolutionising importance for the proletarians of all countries. He who tries to narrow the socialist perspectives of our construction is trying to extinguish the hopes of the international proletariat for our victory, and he who extinguishes these hopes violates the elementary requirements of proletarian internationalism "

After analysing the basic propositions of the ideological platform of the opposition *bloc,* Comrade Stalin came to the conclusion that we undoubtedly had to do with a Social-Democratic deviation. This conclusion was identical with the decision which the Central Committee adopted in January 1925 following the discussion on the *Lessons of October.*

"Essentially, modern Trotskyism is a falsification of Communism in the spirit of approaching the European models of pseudo-Marxism, *i.e.,* in the final analysis, in the spirit of the European Social-Democracy."

The views of the opposition *bloc,* as represented by its basic group, coincided with those of Trotskyism on all the most important questions. And between January 1925 and the autumn of 1926, Trotskyism, while still acting as a faction within the Communist Party, had taken a gigantic stride in the direction of open Menshevism.

The leaders of the opposition who spoke in the discussion following Comrade Stalin's report once more confirmed their anti-Leninist views. They did not follow the example of Shlyapnikov and Medvedev, who in a statement addressed to the Central Committee and Central Control Commission, dated October 29, 1926, declared that the notorious letter of Medvedev "contains a number of grossly erroneous views directed against some of the theses of the Party and conflicting with Leninism and the principles of the Communist International."

While they could not make up their minds openly to reiterate their previous accusations in which they charged the Party with degeneration, Thermidorism, kulak deviation, etc., the leaders of the opposition *bloc* strove their hardest to prove that the charge made against them by the Party that they were guilty of a Social-Democratic deviation was unjustified. But the Conference mercilessly exposed this other double-faced manoeuvre of the leaders of the opposition *bloc,* who hypocritically tried to represent themselves as loyal members of the Party in order to lull its vigilance.

Comrade Stalin in his report showed that from the law of uneven development of capitalism in the epoch of imperialism it followed that it was possible to build socialism in one country.

The leaders of the opposition, concentrating their fire against this fundamental proposition of Leninism, contended that the law of uneven development of capitalism had undergone no changes under imperialism, that on this point Lenin had contributed nothing new to the doctrines of Marx and Engels.

In reality, imperialism has intensified to an extraordinary degree the unevenness of economic development in individual countries and has accentuated to an extreme the contradictions of their conflicting interests.

It was just from this that Lenin drew the conclusion that the victory of socialism in one country is possible in the imperialist epoch.

The October Revolution and the victorious work of socialist construction in the U.S.S.R. have brilliantly confirmed Lenin's point of view.

"What are the basic elements of the law of uneven development under imperialism?

"First, the fact that the world has already been divided up among the imperialist groups, that there are no more 'free,' unoccupied territories in the world, and that in order to occupy new markets and sources of raw materials, in order to expand, it is necessary to take such territory from others by force.

"Secondly, the fact that the unprecedented development of technique and the increasing uniformity of the level of development in capitalist countries have enabled and assisted some countries spasmodically to overtake others, have enabled the less powerful but rapidly developing countries to crowd out the more powerful ones.

"Thirdly, the fact that the old division of spheres of influence between individual imperialist groups is always coming into conflict with the new correlation of forces on the world market, that for the establishment of equilibrium between the old distribution of spheres of influence and the new correlation of forces on the world market, periodic redivisions of the world are necessary by means of imperialist wars.

"Hence the intensification and accentuation of the unevenness of development in the period of imperialism.

"Hence the impossibility of settling the conflicts in the camp of imperialism in a peaceful manner.

"Hence the bankruptcy of the Kautskyist theory of ultra-imperialism—the theory which preaches the possibility of a peaceful settlement of these conflicts.

"The fundamental error of the opposition lies in the fact that it fails to perceive the difference between two phases of capitalism or avoids emphasising this difference. And why does it avoid this? Because this difference leads to the law of uneven development in the period of imperialism.

"The second error of the opposition lies in the fact that it does not comprehend or underrates the decisive importance of the law of uneven development of capitalist countries under imperialism. And why does it underrate this? Because a correct appraisal of the law of the uneven development of capitalist countries leads to the conclusion that the victory of socialism is possible in individual countries.

"Hence the third error of the opposition, consisting in the denial of the possibility of the victory of socialism in individual capitalist countries under imperialism.

"What is the practical significance of this question?

"From the standpoint of practice, two lines arise before us.

"One line is the line of our Party, which calls upon the proletarians of individual countries to prepare for the coming revolution, vigilantly to watch the course of events and to be prepared, under favourable conditions, independently to break through the front of capital, to seize power and to shake the foundation of world capitalism. The other line is the line of our opposition, which sows doubt regarding the expediency of independently breaking through the capitalist front and calls upon the proletarians of individual countries to await the moment of 'general climax.'

"While the line of our Party is a line of intensifying the revolutionary pressure of the proletariat on its own bourgeoisie and of giving rein to the initiative of the proletarians of individual countries, the line of our opposition is a line of passive waiting and of shackling the initiative of the proletarians of individual countries in their struggle against their own bourgeoisie.

"The first line is a line of activising the proletarians in the individual countries.

"The second line is a line of enfeebling the will of the proletariat to revolution, a line of passivity and waiting."*

On this point, which most clearly and distinctly revealed the chasm that divided Leninism from Trotskyism, all the leaders of the united opposition came out before the Party in defence of Trotskyism.

Kamenev contended that the quotation from Lenin on the possibility of the victory of socialism in individual countries could not even refer to Russia since Lenin during the war did not, he alleged, even entertain a thought of the possibility of a socialist revolution in Russia within the near future, believing that Russia would not go beyond the bounds of a bourgeois-democratic revolution.

The quite obvious conclusion from this contention of Kamenev's was that Trotsky, according to Kamenev, was correct in his *Lessons of October* and in his other writings, in which he asserted that Bolshevism in its strategic theses prior to 1917 did not go beyond the bounds of a bourgeois-democratic revolution, that it denied the possibility of such a revolution immediately growing into a socialist revolution, that it was not until 1917 that it re-equipped itself, availing itself of Trotsky's theory of permanent revolution.

This interpretation was a glaring distortion and castration of Bolshevism. But we have already seen it in the case of the *Novaya Zhizn* group in 1917 (Bazarov, Avilov and others), who showed themselves to be of the same breed as the Mensheviks

* Stalin, *On the Opposition*. In the same passage Comrade Stalin writes: "The law of uneven development in the period of imperialism means the spasmodic development of some countries in relation to others, the rapid crowding out of some countries from the world market by others, periodic redivisions of a world that has *already been divided*, through armed clashes and armed catastrophes, the deepening and accentuation of the conflicts in the camp of imperialism, the weakening of the front of world capitalism, the possibility of proletarians of individual countries breaking through this front, the possibility of the victory of socialism in individual countries."

by upholding the view that the October Revolution was of a
bourgeois-democratic character.

Exposing Kamenev's distortion of the position taken by Lenin in 1905—a distortion so indispensable for Trotsky—Comrade
Stalin pointed out:

"Both in 1905 and in 1915, Lenin equally proceeded from the
premise that the bourgeois revolution must grow in Russia into a
socialist revolution, that the victory of the bourgeois-democratic revolution in Russia was the first stage of the Russian revolution which
was necessary in order to pass immediately to its second stage—to the
socialist revolution."

Zinoviev and Trotsky, in trying to substitute Trotskyism for
Leninism on the question of the building of socialism in our
country, based themselves on similar distortions of Lenin's views
as those of which Kamenev was guilty.

At the Fifteenth Conference, the opposition *bloc,* in the face
of the whole Party, upheld the Trotskyist view that it was impossible to build socialism in our country and in doing this
they did not hesitate to employ out-and-out Menshevik arguments. Thereby the opposition *bloc,* in spite of all its phrases
about loyalty, reserved the right to draw all kinds of liquidationist conclusions of degeneration, of Thermidorism, of pettybourgeois backslidings, of a kulak deviation in our Party, etc.
It retained in its hands this weapon for the ideological corruption of the Party ranks. The Conference unanimously adopted
Comrade Stalin's theses regarding the Social-Democratic deviation of the opposition; these theses set the Party the task, of
which Comrade Stalin spoke in his concluding speech, of ideologically finishing off the opposition.*

As Comrade Stalin pointed out:

"The Conference drew the balance of the inner-Party struggle since
the Fourteenth Congress, set the seal on the victory which the Party

---

*The opposition leaders, in their speeches at the Fifteenth Conference,
took advantage of the Right errors committed by Comrade Bukharin on the
kulak question in 1925, of his statement that it was possible for our country to develop towards socialism "at a snail's pace" and of his assertion,
made as early as 1926, that we would be able to build socialism in our
country without regard to the international situation. This was,
of course, absolutely impossible. The international situation was a
very vital factor affecting the tempo of our industrialisation. The crass
Right errors of Bukharin, committed by him in 1925-26, subsequently developed into a whole system of Right opportunist views.

had won over the opposition, and, by isolating the opposition, put an end to the factional bacchanalia which the opposition had forced upon the Party in the preceding period....

"The Conference rallied our Party together, more than ever before, on the basis of the socialist perspective of our construction, against all oppositionist tendencies in our Party, against all deviations in our Party. The most burning question of the day in our Party at present is the question of building socialism in our country.

"Lenin was right when he said that the whole world is watching us, watching our economic construction, our achievements on the front of construction. But in order to attain success on this front it is necessary that the basic instrument of the dictatorship of the proletariat, our Party, shall be ready for this task, that it shall be able to serve as a lever for the victory of socialist construction in our country.

"The meaning and significance of the Fifteenth Conference lies in the fact that it crowned and set the seal on the task of arming our Party with the idea of the victory of socialist construction in our country."*

In his speeches at this conference, as well as in a number of his speeches and articles prior to and after the Fifteenth Conference, Comrade Stalin gave circumstantial proof of, and further developed, the Leninist doctrine of the uneven development of capitalism and of the victory of socialism in individual countries.

After the Fifteenth Conference

The decisions of the Fifteenth Conference at the end of 1926 completed the first stage of the open struggle of the united opposition *bloc* against the Party. After sustaining a crushing defeat both ideologically and organisationally, and having been disappointed in its hopes of economic difficulties which the Trotskyist magicians predicted for the country for the autumn of 1926 in the hope that their demagogy would convince the rank and file of the Party of the correctness of Trotskyism, the Trotskyist opposition pretended to have renounced the factional struggle. But this double-faced manoeuvre of the Trotskyist opposition was also mercilessly exposed by the Party.

At the Enlarged Plenum of the Comintern at the end of 1926, following Comrade Stalin's report on the Social-Demo-

* Stalin, *On the Opposition.*

cratic deviation in the C.P.S.U., Zinoviev, Kamenev and Trotsky spoke in defence of their anti-Party views, protesting against the charge of a Social-Democratic deviation made against them by the Fifteenth Conference. Kamenev even went so far as to accuse our Party, before the representatives of the international proletariat, of national reformism. Needless to say, these demagogic charges met with a unanimous rebuff from the Enlarged Plenum of the Comintern.

In the resolution adopted on Comrade Stalin's report, the Seventh Plenum of the E.C.C.I. declared:

"The opposition in the C.P.S.U. in its ideological content, represents essentially a Right danger within the C.P.S.U., screened by Left phrases.... The C.P.S.U. by all its work past and present, has proved its internationalism not in words but in deeds and has given the finest examples of this internationalism."

The Enlarged Plenum characterised the charge of national narrow-mindedness as a slander against the C.P.S.U. The C.P.S.U. quite correctly carries out the policy of socialist construction with the full conviction that the U.S.S.R. has within the country "everything that is essential and adequate for the building of a complete socialist society." The Enlarged Plenum placed the obligation upon

"all sections of the C.I. to wage a determined struggle both against all attempts of the opposition in the C.P.S.U. and of its supporters in the other parties to undermine the ideological and organisational unity of the ranks of the Comintern and also against the extremely harmful consequences and influences which the propaganda of the opposition, utilised by our enemies, might have on the work of our parties towards winning over the broadest masses of the international proletariat for the revolution and for socialism. This struggle against the opposition is particularly necessary at the present time, when the imperialist states are attempting to encircle the U.S.S.R., when Social-Democracy is supporting these tendencies under cover of pacifist phrases and when the renegades from Communism (Korsch, Schwartz and others) are openly preaching the harmfulness of defending the U.S.S.R. against the imperialist states."

The Enlarged Plenum also summed up the results of the period during which the Comintern had been waging a widespread struggle against the supporters of the opposition *bloc* in the international field. Their basic organisational nucleus was the group of Ruth Fischer and Maslov in Germany. This group of petty-bourgeois "fellow-travellers" had joined the Party at the time when the revolutionary struggle was at its height. It succeeded in adroitly taking advantage of the discontent prevailing among the rank and file of the Party with the Right opportunist leadership of Brandler and Thalheimer during the events of 1923, and in 1924 it appeared at the head of the Party. However, the "Left" sectarian line of the Maslov-Fischer group, which it pursued in spite of the directives of the Comintern and which was manifested above all in the refusal to work in the reformist trade unions, very soon proved its bankruptcy and brought heavy defeats upon the Party. The Maslov-Fischer group which was disappointed with the difficulties of the struggle and demoralised by the temporary stabilisation of capitalism which was setting in, was removed from work in the Central Committee and, on account of the factional activities which it carried on against the Party and the Comintern, was expelled from the Communist International.

The Seventh Enlarged Plenum definitely endorsed the expulsion of Maslov, Ruth Fischer and their closest associates. At the same time the Plenum declared that the Communist Party of Germany, in its struggle against the "Left" deviations which had joined forces with the Trotskyist opposition *bloc*, must not for a moment forget the existence of Right tendencies, which were again reviving under the influence of the partial stabilisation of capitalism.

"The Party should confront the former supporters of the Right groupings with the clear and unequivocal choice between the opportunist deviations and errors of Brandler-Thalheimer and the policy of the Central Committee and the Comintern."*

At the Seventh Plenum, Souvarine, a former member of the French Communist Party who was close to Trotsky, was finally expelled from the ranks of the Comintern for counter-revolutionary propaganda, while the organ of the French Trotskyists, Rosmer and Monatte, was also characterised as counter-revolutionary by the Plenum.

* Theses and resolutions of the Seventh Plenum of the E.C.C.I.

The Plenum clearly demonstrated the unity of all sections of the Comintern in the struggle against Trotskyism both in the ranks of the C.P.S.U. and in the international field.

A new Plenum of the Central Committee of the C.P.S.U. was held in February 1927. It was marked by the growth of rock-like unity in the Party and the slackening of activity on the part of the opposition leaders. The bankruptcy of the opposition platform became quite evident. The opposition was unable to offer anything as against the vast programme of capital con- struction (the building of the Stalingrad Tractor Plant, of the Rostov Agricultural Machinery Plant, etc.) proposed by the Politburo, to the Plenum of the Central Committee. When the question of reducing retail prices on commodities within the near future by at least 10 per cent was raised at the Plenum by the Politburo, the opposition could not summon up enough political courage to oppose this demand. Assuming that the Party had already forgotten about the writings of Smirnov, Smilga, and Preobrazhensky on the necessity of raising prices, that it had forgotten what a prominent place this demand oc- cupied in the opposition programme for the super-industrialisa- tion of the country, the opposition was even insolent enough to criticise the Central Committee for—not lowering prices enough. At any rate, the new feature of the February Plenum, as com- pared with the bitter factional struggle in the preceding period, was the fact that the opposition did not offer a platform of its own, but voted, with certain reservations, for the proposals of the Politburo. Some of its supporters (K. Nikolayeva, Badayev) renounced their oppositionist views at this Plenum. The leaders of the opposition, however, had no intention whatever of work- ing honestly in the ranks of the Party. They only wanted to lull the vigilance of the Party, in order to make a surprise attack as soon as a propitious occasion arose.

The Party Exposes the Further Manoeuvres of the Opposition

The betrayal of the Chinese revolution by Chiang Kai-shek, the shooting down of the Shanghai workers, the bloody suppres- sion of Chinese proletarians and peasants by the Kuomintang bourgeoisie which deserted to the side of counter-revolution, were used by the opposition as a pretext for coming out against the Party with new accusations of the incorrect leadership of the Comintern in the Chinese revolution.

For several years past the opposition leaders had raised no objections to the Chinese Communists having to form a *bloc* with the Kuomintang against the foreign imperialists, while at the same time organising the worker and peasant masses. strengthening their influence in the national army, etc. Despite this, however, when at a certain stage of the revolution the bourgeoisie which was organised in the Kuomintang began to swing round towards imperialism, the opposition leaders, wise after the event, raised a desperate howl about the "betrayal" of the Chinese workers and peasants by the Comintern. The severe defeats which the Chinese revolution sustained at the hands of "its" bourgeoisie and of the foreign imperialists, as well as the opportunist errors committed by the leadership of the Chinese Communist Party, were utilised by the leaders of the opposition for a stab in the back at the Comintern and our Party.

In opposition to the appraisal of the Chinese revolution and of its dynamic forces given by the Comintern, the Trotskyists put forward their own anti-Leninist appraisal. The Trotskyists denied the anti-imperialist, anti-feudal character of the Chinese revolution; they denied the revolutionary role of the peasantry in this revolution.

In opposition to the task of effecting a revolutionary-democratic dictatorship of the proletariat and peasantry, directed against imperialism, national oppression and against the vestiges of feudalism, they put forward slogans based on the Trotskyist theory of permanent revolution.

This was a Chinese edition of the Trotskyist theory of permanent revolution of 1905, and essentially it differed in no way from the Russian edition of this theory.

While being "Left" in its outward appearance, it was defeatist and capitulationist in actual fact.

This explains why Trotsky, who began with propaganda for soviets as the organs of the socialist dictatorship of the proletariat, with "Left" criticism of the Comintern line, very quickly revealed his real Menshevik colours, declaring that the Chinese revolution had been defeated once and for all and advising the Chinese Communists to put forward the slogan of a national (constituent) assembly.

The severe defeat suffered by the Chinese revolution, diminishing as it did the tremendous menace which the spread of this revolution had created for the imperialists, enabled international imperialism to intensify its aggressiveness towards the U.S.S.R. There began a series of raids on Soviet institutions abroad, directly inspired by British imperialism; after which preliminary artillery barrage, the British Conservative government announced the breaking off of diplomatic relations with the U.S.S.R. White Guard agents of the British government assassinated Comrade Voykov, the Soviet ambassador in Warsaw, under the eyes of the Polish authorities. Following this assassination, they proceeded to organise a number of explosions and murderous attempts within the U.S.S.R. There arose an almost direct menace of war. This situation the Trotskyist opposition deemed a most favourable one for the commencement of a new attack against our Party, virtually hand in hand with British imperialism. Zinoviev, speaking at a non-Party meeting in celebration of the *Pravda* jubilee, charged the Central Committee with concealing the truth in regard to the Chinese revolution. Trotsky, speaking at the Plenum of the Comintern, went even further and, not contenting himself with demagogic and hysterical talk about the "betrayal" of the Chinese revolution, slanderously charged the Party leadership with pursuing the policy of the Amsterdam and Second Internationals. About the same time a large number of opposition platforms were presented to the masses. A statement published by eighty-three Trotskyists attempted to draw a picture of the bankruptcy of the Party's home and foreign policy. A declaration signed by fifteen supporters of Sapronov went even further, declaring that the Soviet government had degenerated into an anti-proletarian one. The Sapronovists, quite in the spirit of the *Sotsialistichesky Vestnik,* described the G.P.U. as an organ for the suppression of the labour movement. This was precisely at the time when the secret agents of Wrangel tried to put an infernal machine in the G.P.U.

headquarters. The Sapronovists declared that the commanding staff of the Red Army was composed of kulak elements. The programmatic part of the Sapronov platform (as also the Trotskyist "statement of eighty-three") was full of the most irresponsible demagogic demands, plainly designed to incite the most backward sections of the workers against the Soviet government. The Sapronovists demanded an immediate rise in wages, an appropriation of hundreds of millions for labour protection, the immediate solution of the housing problem, etc. At the same time, the state was to supply the poor peasants with implements and with money, to finance the agricultural co-operatives, etc. The Sapronovists of course did not offer any clue as to where such colossal funds were to be obtained from. Evidently they approved of all means for inciting the masses against the Party, particularly when we were faced with the danger of war. This moment the Sapronovists (together with the Trotskyists) deemed the most suitable one for discrediting the Central Committee and the Soviet government in the eyes of the masses. Trotsky hastened to justify these tactics in an article which he sent to the *Pravda*. In this article, Trotsky called upon the opposition to follow the example of the well-known French bourgeois parliamentary leader, Clemenceau, who, in the autumn of 1914, when the Germans were approaching Paris, carried on agitation for the overthrow of the cabinet and for its replacement by a new cabinet. In just the same way, the opposition, not regarding the war danger but, on the contrary, taking advantage of it, was to strive to effect a change in the government and the Politburo of the Central Committee. This was how the Trotskyist opposition was preparing to "defend" the Soviet power.

The Trotskyists in the struggle against the Party employed an entire arsenal of the most slanderous accusations against the Central Committee—Thermidorism, degeneration, Menshevism, betrayal, treachery, kulak-nepman policy against the workers, against the poor peasants, against the Chinese revolution—accusations that were monstrous in their insolence and obvious falsehood. There was a recrudescence throughout the entire country of the most unbridled factional activities,

· The Plenum of the Central Committee in July 1927

The Plenum of the Central Committee which met in July 1927 gave a detailed appraisal of the international position of the U.S.S.R. and of the attacks of the opposition on the Party in this field. The resolution adopted by the Plenum declared:

"The tendency to the Right among the leaders of the labour aristocracy and bureaucracy was reflected also in the treacherous conduct of the leaders of the General Council and of their representatives on the Anglo-Russian Committee. The Communists in the All-Union Central Council of Trade Unions on the whole correctly criticised the treacherous actions of the General Council. At the same time they acted correctly in not allowing themselves to be made responsible for disrupting and splitting the Anglo-Russian Committee, thereby fully exposing the treacherous tactics of the leaders of the General Council. While utilising the 'legal opportunities' for contact with the British trade unions, the All-Union Central Council of Trade Unions should consistently condemn every treacherous, conciliationist and social-imperialist step taken by the leaders of the General Council. At the same time it is necessary to make every effort to put fresh life into the international work of the All-Union Central Council of Trade Unions with a view to a struggle against war, against the offensive of capital and for the unity of the trade union movement both in the West and in the East . . . It is equally necessary for the Central Committee to make every effort to ensure more vigorous work on the part of the Profintern in the same direction."

The same resolution gave a detailed analysis of the Chinese revolution. The resolution pointed out that:

"While the Chinese revolution, in spite of the correct tactics of the Comintern, has suffered a great defeat, this can be explained first and foremost by the correlation of the class forces within the country and also from the international standpoint; this defeat was further due to the fact that the worker and peasant masses had not yet had time to organise sufficient forces in order to win a victory over the united or co-ordinated forces of the enemy, namely, foreign imperialism, the feudal gentry headed by Chang Tso-ling and the counter-revolutionary national bourgeoisie; finally, it was due to the fact that the working class had not yet had time to create a solid well-organised mass political party. On the other hand, it is necessary to recognise that the leadership of the Chinese Communist Party, which systematically rejected the directives of the Communist International, bears its share of the responsibility for the defeat of the working class and peasantry in China. . . .

"The present period of the Chinese revolution is characterised by its severe defeat and simultaneously by a *radical* re-grouping of forces, in which a *bloc* of the workers, peasants and urban poor is being organised against all the ruling classes and against imperialism. In *this* sense the revolution is passing to a higher phase of its development, to the phase of the direct struggle *for the dictatorship of the working class and peasantry.* The experience of the preceding development has clearly shown that the bourgeoisie is incapable of carrying out the tasks of *national liberation* from the yoke of the imperialists, since, while waging war against the workers and peasants, it is unable to wage a consistent struggle against foreign imperialism and tends ever more towards a compromise with it—a compromise, moreover, which virtually leaves the imperialist domination almost in full force. Nor can the national bourgeoisie carry out the *internal tasks* of the revolution, for it not only does not support the peasants but actively opposes them, thus tending more and more towards a *bloc* with the feudal gentry and failing to solve even the elementary problems of the *bourgeois democratic revolution.* On the other hand, it is almost impossible for the national bourgeoisie to compromise with the peasantry, since it is impossible to carry out even the most puny land reform in China without undermining the gentry and the small landlords, for which task the bourgeoisie is absolutely incapable. Thus the probable outlook is that the *temporary defeat of the revolution will give way in a comparatively short time to a new revolutionary upsurge.*"

This forecast was brilliantly corroborated by the subsequent course of revolutionary events in China, particularly by the development of the revolutionary peasant movement under the leadership of the proletariat and the formation of Soviet districts.

These districts, with a population of over sixty million, have now for a number of years been under the power of the Soviets with their heroic Red Army, which has successfully repulsed all the campaigns of the counter-revolutionary armies of the Kuomintang and of the imperialists against the Soviet districts and is waging a successful offensive against the Kuomintang and world imperialism.

In a special resolution dealing with the violation of Party discipline by Zinoviev and Trotsky, the Plenum analysed the various stages in the development of the opposition *bloc* and exposed their capitulationist nature, thus placing them on the brink of expulsion from the Party.

The resolution emphasised that

"of late, in connection with the special difficulties in the international position of the U.S.S.R. and the partial defeat of the Chinese Revolution, the opposition has concentrated its attack against the Party along the line of our international policy (in China and Great Britain). In response to the increased war danger confronting the U.S.S.R., the opposition came out with such statements as undermine the work of the Party in mobilising the masses for a struggle against the war danger and for strengthening the defence of the Soviet country.

"The statements regarding the Thermidorian degeneration of the Central Committee, the policy of conservative nationalism, the ·kulak-Ustryalov line of the Party, the declaration that 'the greatest of all dangers is the Party regime' and not the menace of war—all of these statements, tending as they did to weaken the will of the international proletariat for the defence of the U.S.S.R., were characterised by the Plenum of the E.C.C.I. as 'a means, in the face of the war danger ... of camouflaging their desertion before the workers.' "

Having, moreover, enumerated a number of gross violations of Party discipline by the leaders of the opposition, and having taken cognisance of the formation of secret groups and of the illegal distribution of literature, the resolution declared that

"owing to all these crimes against the Party and the proletariat, the leaders of the opposition (Trotsky and Zinoviev) drove themselves into a blind alley, came into hostile relations with the Party and confronted the latter with the necessity of applying to them the decision of the Tenth Party Congress regarding the unity of the Party."

Zinoviev and Trotsky pledged themselves at this Plenum to unreserved defence of the U.S.S.R.; condemned the slander about the Thermidorian degeneration of the Party and undertook to sever their connections with groups hostile to the Comintern. In view of this the Plenum, having enjoined the opposition to dissolve the illegal anti-Party groups created by them, decided to give Zinoviev and Trotsky a severe reprimand coupled with a warning, without, however, expelling them from the Central Committee.

The leaders of the opposition once more signed a statement pledging themselves to refrain from factional activity, only to begin violating it on the very next day in the most cynical fashion.

Trotskyism Becomes the Vanguard of the Counter-
Revolutionary Bourgeoisie

Scarcely a month had elapsed after the Plenum when the leaders of the opposition presented their pre-congress platform to the Politburo, once again repeating their slanderous charges against the Party and its leadership. In this platform the Politburo of the Central Committee was accused of the intention to dissolve the Comintern, to betray the Chinese revolution, to recognise the tsarist debts, to abolish the foreign trade monopoly, to adopt a policy favouring the kulak in the countryside and similar insolent nonsense.

All this despite the fact that the opposition leaders were well aware of the directives which the Comintern gave to the Chinese Communist Party, long before Chiang-Kai-shek's act of betrayal, to organise the masses on its own initiative, independently of the Kuomintang, to strengthen its influence over the working class and peasantry, to develop the strike movement among the workers, to arouse the peasant masses for a struggle against the landlords and to consolidate its positions in the army.

The leaders of the opposition knew just as well that Shlyapnikov and Medvedev, who adhered to the opposition *bloc,* had proposed to dissolve the Comintern, that in the foreign Communist Parties a rapprochement with the Social-Democrats was favoured by those very Right elements who had followed Trotsky prior to the Fifth Congress of the Comintern, that essentially there was very little difference between these Rights and the "Left" supporters of the opposition *bloc* of 1926-27, many of whom after their expulsion from the Comintern found refuge in the haven of Social-Democracy.

The opposition leaders were likewise aware that the abolition of the foreign trade monopoly was demanded by Sokolnikov, their recent comrade-in-arms, that Zinoviev and Kamenev had proposed to accept Urquhart's terms for a concession, that the Politburo of the C.C. of the C.P.S.U. had invariably rejected both these and all similar capitulationist proposals.

Finally, the opposition leaders could not but know that Zinoviev, as late as the autumn of 1924, had proposed to form non-Party peasant fractions in the soviets, which would undoubtedly have been utilised by the kulak elements for attempts to set the peasantry against the Soviet government. The Politburo of the C.C. of the C.P.S.U. was steadfastly pursuing a policy of restricting and squeezing out the kulaks, of isolating them completely from the mass of the middle peasantry, while carrying on a determined struggle against Trotskyism.

When the Central Committee decided that the platform of the opposition was an anti-Party document and refused to publish it, the opposition began to circulate this platform with the aid of its factional apparatus (printing it in illegal printshops) not only among members of the Party but among non-members as well. And the supporters of the opposition abroad published the platform in foreign languages.

Following this, the October Plenum of the Central Committee expelled Trotsky and Zinoviev from the Central Committee and decided to submit for consideration to the Fifteenth Congress of the Party all the evidence concerning the schismatic activities of the leaders of the Trotskyist opposition.

For the tenth anniversary of the October Revolution, the Central Committee passed a decision in favour of adopting the seven-hour working day and of exempting the poor peasantry from taxation. These measures of the Party clearly indicated that it would utilise every forward step of socialist construction, in spite of all difficulties, to improve the situation of the worker and peasant masses. The representatives of the opposition clearly showed that they had taken up a counter-revolutionary, anti-Soviet and anti-proletarian position by voting at the session of the Central Executive Committee of the Soviets against the manifesto proclaiming the seven-hour working day. A few days later, on the tenth anniversary of the October Revolution, the opposition, to the joy of all secret and open counter-revolutionary elements, made an attempt to lead its supporters out on to the streets for a demonstration against the Central Committee of the Party and the Soviet government.

The foreign correspondents of the bourgeois press, however, were obliged to report to their papers that this attempt of the opposition had met with complete failure. The tiny groups of oppositionists were lost among the hundreds of thousands of proletarians who demonstrated their inflexible will to defend the achievements of the October Revolution under the leadership of the Communist Party and its Central Committee.

By its anti-Soviet demonstration on the streets on November 7, following its action in voting against the seven-hour working day, the opposition broke the last thread which connected it with the Party. Openly, in the face of the whole country, it had taken the path of counter-revolution.

The counter-revolutionary action of the Trotskyist opposition came at a time when the Party was in the midst of its preparatory work for the Fifteenth Congress. During the process of this work it had already become clear that the opposition was but an insignificant force within the ranks of our Party. Among the hundreds of thousands of Party members who at the meetings of their nuclei discussed the theses of the Central Committee for the Fifteenth Party Congress, the opposition was unable to mobilise even one per cent in favour of its views.

The rank and file of the Party thus pronounced an annihilating verdict against the whole activity of the Trotskyist opposition. By coming out on to the streets on November 7, the opposition passed an even more annihilating verdict upon itself. It signed its own death warrant. The opposition showed that, after resorting to fighting against the Soviet government on the streets, it could no longer be tolerated in the Party. And although the immediate answer to the action of the opposition on November 7 was only the expulsion of Trotsky and Zinoviev from the Party and the expulsion from the Central Committee of those oppositionists who still remained in it, it was already quite clear that the Fifteenth Party Congress would adopt a resolution declaring adherence to the Trotskyist opposition to be incompatible with membership of the Party.

. For a number of years after 1917,

"inasmuch as the Trotskyists broke organisationally, even though temporarily, with Menshevism, put away even though temporarily, their anti-Bolshevik views, were admitted into the C.P.S.U. and Comintern and submitted to their decisions, Trotskyism was undoubtedly a part, a faction of Communism. . . .

"The C.P.S.U. does not tolerate factions and cannot consent to their legalisation? No, it does not tolerate them and cannot consent to their legalisation. But this does not mean that the Trotskyists did not in reality constitute a faction. It was just because the Trotskyists in reality had their own faction, for the legalisation of which they fought, it was just for this reason—for this reason among others— that they were later expelled from the Party. . . .

"What was the characteristic feature of the Trotskyists when they constituted a faction of Communism? It was that the Trotskyists 'permanently' vacillated between Bolshevism and Menshevism, these vacillations reaching their highest point with every turn in the policy of the Party and the Comintern and breaking out into a factional struggle against the Party. What does this mean? It means that the Trotskyists were not *real* Bolsheviks, although they were in the Party and submitted to its decisions, nor could they be called *real* Mensheviks, although they frequently wavered towards Menshevism. These vacillations were at the bottom of the inner-Party struggle between the Leninists and the Trotskyists during the period when the Trotskyists were in our Party (1917-27). And the basis of these same vacillations of the Trotskyists was the fact that, although they had put away their anti-Bolshevik views and thus made their way into the Party, the Trotskyists nevertheless *did not give up* these views, as a result of which these views made themselves felt with particular force at every turn in the policy of the Party and the Comintern. . . .

". . . Trotskyism was a faction of Menshevism until the Trotskyists joined our Party. It temporarily became a faction of Communism after the Trotskyists joined our Party. It again became a faction of Menshevism after the Trotskyists were driven out of our Party. 'The dog returns to his vomit.' " *

Why did the Party in the autumn of 1927 squarely raise the question of expelling the Trotskyists? Because they again brought out those Menshevik views which they had temporarily put away. Because they ceased to submit to the decisions of the Party and to Party discipline and began to 'create their own special Menshevik-Trotskyist·Party.

Between the Fourteenth and Fifteenth Congresses, the Party made great strides in the work of socialist construction. The policy of industrialisation, which was firmly adopted by the Fourteenth Congress, was resolutely put into effect. Industry exceeded its pre-war level, and in some branches (electrical engineering, oil and others) went far beyond it. The measures taken by the Fourteenth Conference, and which were endorsed by the Fourteenth Congress, helped the Party to consolidate the alliance with the middle peasantry. Following the Fourteenth Congress, there was a further intensification of the work done

* Stalin, *Letter to Comrade Olekhnovich,* published in *The Bolshevik.* No. 16, 1932.

to rally the poor peasantry around the Party and the Soviet government. Increased economic aid was extended to the poor peasants and they were exempted from payment of the agricultural tax. The elections to the soviets in 1927 were marked by an increase in the activity of the poor peasants such as had not been seen for years. The manifesto of November 7 gave them new privileges. In spite of all difficulties, the Party had already achieved a considerable rise in the workers' wages in the summer of 1926. In the summer of 1927, the retail prices of consumers' commodities were lowered, thus reducing the household expenses of the workers. The manifesto of November 7 announced that preparatory measures had been begun for the introduction of the seven-hour working day. Plans had been outlined for an intensified offensive against the capitalist elements, and they were beginning to be put into effect.

It is sufficient to recall the years of civil war and economic collapse to see that there were times when the Party, however much it might desire to, however great its efforts, could not do much to improve the material conditions of the worker and peasant masses. In 1926-27, the picture had changed altogether. The economic policy of the Party and of the Soviet government, while giving the working class and poor peasantry a real improvement in their position, was striking ever harder and harder against the nepman and the kulak, against the bourgeois elements, causing increasing discontent among them. And nothing served to expose the petty-bourgeois nature of Trotskyism so much as the fact that just at this time Trotskyism reacted to the Party's intensified offensive against the bourgeois elements by new attempts 'to attack the Party. Gradually severing the last threads which still bound it to the Bolshevik Party and Leninism, Trotskyism was becoming an out-and-out, hundred-per-cent weapon of the bourgeois anarchic forces, and its hysterical "revolutionary" phrases took on a striking resemblance to those employed by the Left Socialist-Revolutionaries in 1918. The absurd calumny that the Party was subordinating the Soviet power to the interests of the kulak and of international imperialism could only be compared to the foul counter-revolutionary demagogy of the Left Socialist-Revolutionaries on the subject of Lenin's alliance with Wilhelm Hohenzollern.

. The "Left" phrases employed by Trotskyism in 1926-27 became, even more than in 1923-24, a means for hoodwinking and confusing the masses. The representatives of bourgeois counter-revolution listened with relish to these "Left" phrases, bearing only one thing in mind—an inch to the "Left" or an inch to the Right, it was all one so long as a shifting of power was effected, so long as the existing government was shaken to its foundations. The rest would follow of its own accord.

But the rank and file of the Party had sufficiently matured and developed during the preceding years. In 1923-24, Trotskyist demagogy could still find a certain response among individual groups of backward Party members. In 1926-27, it found no, or almost no response. The appeal to the non-Party working masses, whom the Trotskyists tried to set against the Party, was absolutely fruitless. In the autumn of 1927, on the streets of Moscow and Leningrad the only sympathetic spectators of the counter-revolutionary street sallies of Trotskyism were the representatives of defeated counter-revolution who longed for the downfall of the Soviet government. They hailed Trotskyism as the force which, for the first time after a number of years, dared to come out on the streets against the Soviet government.

By the autumn of 1927, Trotskyism, from a faction within the Communist Party, a faction which held anti-Leninist and semi-Menshevik views, had turned into the vanguard of the counter-revolutionary bourgeoisie.

"Who gave the counter-revolutionary bourgeoisie its intellectual weapon against Bolshevism, in the form of the thesis of the impossibility of building socialism in our country, in the form of the thesis of the inevitability of the degeneration of the Bolsheviks, etc.? That weapon was given it by Trotskyism. It is not an accident that all anti-Soviet groupings in the U.S.S.R. in their attempts to give grounds for their argument for the inevitability of the struggle against the Soviet government referred to the well-known thesis of Trotskyism of the impossibility of building socialism in our country, of the inevitable degeneration of the Soviet government, of the probable return to capitalism.

"Who gave the counter-revolutionary bourgeoisie in the U.S.S.R. its tactical weapon in the form of attempts at open attacks on the Soviet government? This weapon was given to it by the Trotskyists, who tried to organise anti-Soviet demonstrations in Moscow and Leningrad on November 7, 1927. It is a fact that the anti-Soviet actions of the Trotskyists raised the spirit of the bourgeoisie and let loose the work of counter-revolutionary sabotage of the bourgeois specialists.

"Who gave the counter-revolutionary bourgeoisie an organisational weapon in the form of attempts at organising underground anti-Soviet organisations? This weapon was given to it by the Trotskyists who founded their own anti-Bolshevik illegal group. It is a fact that the underground anti-Soviet work of the Trotskyists facilitated the organised formation of the anti-Soviet groups within the U.S.S.R." *

In the autumn of 1927, on the eve of the Fifteenth Congress, Trotskyism virtually returned to the bosom of Menshevism, completing the cycle of its counter-revolutionary degeneration.

This confronted the Party with the question of expelling the Trotskyists from the ranks of the C.P.S.U.

The Decision of the Fifteenth Congress to Expel the Opposition From the Party

The Party had already inflicted a decisive defeat on the Trotskyist opposition prior to the Fifteenth Congress.** Before the opening of the Fifteenth Congress the Party had already exposed once and for all the anti-Party and anti-Soviet character of Trotskyism. The largest Party organisations had declared at their pre-Congress conferences that the defence of Trotskyist views was incompatible with membership of the C.P.S.U.

During the discussion in the ranks of the Party which preceded the Congress, the opposition received about 6,000 votes as against 725,000, who voted for the theses of the Central Committee. The appeal of the opposition to the non-Party working masses against the Party resulted in a no less crushing defeat. The more the opposition resorted to demagogic arguments in the style of pure Menshevism, the clearer became the anti-Communist, essentially Menshevik character of the opposition not only to the members of the Party but to non-Party workers as well.

---

* Stalin, *Leninism*, Vol. II.
** The Fifteenth Congress opened on December 2, 1927. It was attended by 898 delegates with a decisive vote and 771 with a consultative vote. The delegates represented about 890,000 members and about 350,000 candidates. The Congress was in session for over two weeks.

Under such conditions, faced with the prospect of inevitable expulsion, there was nothing left for the opposition to do but to repeat the manoeuvre which they had resorted to on the eve of the Fifteenth Conference—to withdraw from battle and to declare once more the cessation of the factional struggle, while contemplating a new attack on the Party as soon as a more or less suitable situation would arise.

However, the Party could not allow the Trotskyists to continue their unprincipled factional game *ad infinitum*. Much water had flown under the bridges from the end of 1926 to the end of 1927. During this time the views of the opposition had continued to develop uninterruptedly in the direction of Menshevism. They lapsed more and more into a standpoint of completely denying the existence of a proletarian dictatorship in our country, the socialist character of our revolution, the alliance with the middle peasantry. More than that, the opposition had virtually set about creating a second party which was trying to wrest the non-Party working masses from the influence of the C.P.S.U. Could the Fifteenth Congress, under these conditions, allow the Trotskyists to continue to screen themselves behind formal adherence to the C.P.S.U., purchasing their membership at the price of utterly worthless and obviously deceitful pledges?

When the representatives of the opposition once more submitted a statement in which, in a formula which had already become stereotyped, they promised to dissolve their faction and to uphold Trotskyist views in the future only within the limits of the Party constitution, it was quite natural that the Congress should have emphatically rejected this new and glaringly obvious manoeuvre.

In the political report of the Central Committee, Comrade Stalin pointed out the radical differences of principle which existed between the Trotskyist opposition and the Party on the most fundamental questions.

"The opposition," said Comrade Stalin, "denies the possibility of the victorious construction of socialism in our country... You know that Kamenev and Zinoviev went to the uprising only when shown the rod. Lenin drove them with a rod, threatening to expel them from the Party, and they were constrained to drag their feet to the uprising. Trotsky went to the uprising voluntarily. However, he did not just go, but went with a slight reservation, which already at that time brought him near to Kamenev and Zinoviev. It is of interest that it was precisely before October, in June 1917, that Trotsky deemed it appropriate to republish in Leningrad his old pamphlet *The Peace Programme,* as if he wanted to say by that that he was going to the uprising under his own flag. What does he say in this pamphlet? He enters into a polemic there with Lenin on the question of the possibility of victory for socialism in a single country, considers this thought of Lenin's wrong and asserts that power will have to be seized, but that unless assistance from the victorious West European workers will arrive in time, it is a forlorn hope to imagine that revolutionary Russia can hold its own in the teeth of a conservative Europe, and whoever does not believe in Trotsky's criticism suffers from national narrow-mindedness . . .

"Here, comrades, you have the Trotskyist slight reservation, which largely helps us to understand the roots and the subsoil of his present *bloc* with Kamenev and Zinoviev."

The opposition denied the fact of the dictatorship of the proletariat in our country, slanderously accusing the Party and the Soviet government of Thermidorian degeneration. This was a purely Menshevik standpoint.

The opposition rejected the idea of a *bloc* of the working class with the middle peasantry. The only road to "salvation" (for a short time), which it proposed, was based on a break with the middle peasantry (super-industrialisation). Here, too, the opposition shows the cloven hoof of Menshevism.

The opposition denied the socialist character of the October Revolution. The proletariat, they maintained, had simply carried the bourgeois revolution to its conclusion. Now the peasantry, having received the land, had turned away from the proletariat. The only thing left for the Soviet government to do was to withdraw, or to degenerate.

The opposition, in glaring contradiction to the teachings of Lenin, refused to see any difference between the policy of the Communist Party in imperialist countries and in colonial countries.

Lenin said that the idea of "the defence of the fatherland" is fully acceptable for Communists in colonial countries when they wage war against imperialism. For this reason, Lenin, under certain conditions and within certain limits, conceded the possibility of forming a *bloc* with the nationalist bourgeoisie or with a part of it, if it were waging war against imperialsm and did not persecute the Communist parties in their work among the proletarian and toiling masses. The opposition discarded this argument of Lenin's and descended to the standpoint of repudiating the revolutionary wars of colonies against imperialism.

The opposition rejected the tactic of the united front in the international labour movement. The opposition had virtually broken with the Leninist idea of the unity of the Party and the Comintern, having set about creating a second party in the U.S.S.R. and in other countries.

The Menshevik views of the opposition were incompatible with the ideology, programme, tactics and organisational principles of our Party and of the Comintern.

The Congress, in its resolution on the report of the Central Committee, declared:

"The opposition has ideologically broken with Leninism, has degenerated into a Menshevik group, has taken the path of capitulation to the forces of the international and internal bourgeoisie and has become, objectively, a weapon of the third force against the regime of proletarian dictatorship."

For this reason

"bearing in mind that the differences of opinion between the Party and the opposition have developed from tactical into programmatic differences... the Fifteenth Congress declares that adherence to the Trotskyist opposition and propaganda of its views is incompatible with membership in the ranks of the Bolshevik Party."

The Congress unanimously adopted the resolution on the report of the Central Committee, from which it clearly followed that the expulsion of the Trotskyist opposition was inevitable, unless at the last moment it renounced its anti-Party views. This caused a split in the ranks of the opposition *bloc*. The old basic Trotskyist core and the Zinoviev group which had joined hands with Trotskyism could not come to an agreement as to how further to manoeuvre against the Party and the Party Congress. Zinoviev and Kamenev decided to alter their tactics. A few days after the Congress had adopted the resolution on the report of the Central Committee they addressed a statement to the Congress, promising to submit to its decision and to refrain from propagating their views not only outside the Party but within the Party as well, they themselves however still retaining their views. The Congress naturally could not accept this thoroughly hypocritical statement of bankrupt politicians.

On December 18, 1927, following a report by a specially elected commission of which Comrade Orjonikidze was the chairman, the Congress reaffirmed the thesis previously adopted as a matter of principle in regard to the Trotskyist opposition and on this basis expelled from the Party seventy-five leading members of the opposition (including Bakayev, Zalutsky, Yevdomikov, Kamenev, Muralov, Rakovsky, Safarov, Smilga, I. N. Smirnov, L. Sosnovsky, Kharitonov and others).*

The Congress at the same time decided to "instruct the Central Committee and Central Control Commission 'to take all measures to bring ideological influence to bear on the rank and file members of the Trotskyist opposition so as to persuade them, while at the same time purging the Party of all clearly incorrigible elements of the Trotskyist opposition." **

By the same decision the Sapronov group (V. M. Smirnov, Khorochko and others) were expelled from the Party by the Congress as clearly anti-revolutionary. On the day following the adoption of this decision the Zinoviev group (Kamenev, Yevdokimov, Zinoviev, Bakayev, Zalutsky, Kharitonov and others) submitted a new statement to the Congress, in which they recognised as incorrect and, in acordance with the Congress resolution, condemned as anti-Leninist the views which denied the possibility of victorious socialist construction in the U.S.S.R., denied the socialist character of our revolution, denied the socialist character of our state industry, denied the socialist path of development of the countryside under the conditions of the proletarian dictatorship and the policy of the alliance of the proletariat with the great masses of the peasantry on the basis of socialist construction, and denied the proletarian dictatorship in the U.S.S.R. ("Thermidor.")

* Several prominent representatives of the Trotskyist opposition had already been expelled prior to the Congress (E. A. Preobrazhensky, L. Serebryakov, Sharov, Beloborodov, Mrachkovsky and others).
** In accordance with this decision the local control organs expelled about 1,500 Trotskyists from the Party after the Congress. Over 2,500 submitted statements declaring that they repudiated the opposition.

However, the statement of the Zinoviev group did not say the main thing, that precisely these were the views of the opposition.

The statement spoke very mildly of the violation of Party discipline.

"As our basic error we consider the fact that, in the struggle against the Central Committee of the Party, we entered upon activities which made the danger of a second Party a real one. We must recognise as an error the action of November 7, the seizure of premises (those of the Moscow Higher Technical School), the organisation of illegal printshops, etc."

The authors of the statement also recognised as an "error" the "maintainance of contact with the Ruth Fischer-Maslov group." Outright and obvious counter-revolutionary activities were thus described as "errors" in the statement of the Zinoviev group.

In reply to this last statement the Fifteenth Congress decided:

"Not to consider the statement submitted on December 19, 1927, by Kamenev, Zinoviev and others who have been expelled from the Party, in view of the fact that the Fifteenth Congress has already dealt exhaustively with the question of the opposition in the resolution of December 18.

"To instruct the Central Committee and Central Control Commission not to accept applications from leading members of the former opposition who have been expelled from the Party unless submitted individually and not to make decisions on such statements until at least six months after their submission, provided that: 1) the conduct of those submitting the statements has conformed to the pledges made by the authors of these statements; 2) the statements themselves of the former oppositionists are fully in accord with the demands of the Fifteenth Congress ... and hence are based on a repudiation of the platform of the eighty-three, of the platform submitted on September 3' and of the platform of the fifteen."

Thus the Trotskyist opposition *bloc* ended its inglorious existence under the blows of the Leninist Party. Its definite ideological bankruptcy resulted in complete organisational collapse. Part of the *bloc* turned back, capitulating to the Party at the Fifteenth Congress.*

* After the Fifteenth Congress, Kamenev, Zinoviev, Yevdokimov, Bakayev, Zalutsky, Lashevich, Kharitonov and others submitted individual statements (in accordance with the provisions of the Fifteenth Congress) for readmission to the Party. As subsequent events showed, however, the state-

Another part, headed by Trotsky himself, quickly lapsed into counter-revolution after being expelled from the Party. Its attempts to carry on illegal anti-Soviet activities were of course repressed by the organs of the Soviet government. The latter were obliged to treat the illegal Trotskyist groups as identical with the Mensheviks, since the Trotskyists came to occupy the place in anti-Soviet conspiratorial circles which had been vacated by the decayed and disintegrated Menshevik Party.

After the Trotskyists had been expelled from the Party, Trotskyism even more rapidly denuded itself of the last vestiges of Bolshevik phraseology. In the letters, articles and pamphlets written by Trotsky in 1928-29 this process was reflected with extraordinary clarity. Finally, after the expelled Trotskyists began to form their underground counter-revolutionary groups, their activities proceeded along the well-known Menshevik track, quite clearly opposing the working class to the Soviet government, speculating on every difficulty, repeating the outworn Menshevik charges against the Soviet government that it was exploiting the proletariat, etc.

Vivid evidence of the complete ideological self-exposure of counter-revolutionary Trotskyism was furnished by the literary productions of Trotsky, particularly after he had been banished abroad. These writings above all restored the notorious "theory" of permanent revolution to its original Menshevik form. In spite of all his diplomatic declarations during the period of the *bloc* with Zinoviev, Trotsky, stating explicitly what he only hinted at in his *Lessons of October,* now attempts to prove that he was correct in his theory of permanent revolution which he opposed to Lenin, that all Lenin's objections to this theory were based on misunderstanding or lack of knowledge and that the time has come to apply this Trotskyist theory to all Eastern countries,

ments of Zinoviev and Kamenev were nothing but a new lying manoeuvre. Although they presented these statements, they continued to maintain contact with the Trotskyists.

At the present time (1932) the Central Control Commission has expelled Zinoviev and Kamenev from the Party. They obtained readmission to the Party through deception, for they claimed to have renounced the Trotskyist views but actually continued to maintain political contact with the Trotskyists and Rights and ended by maintaining contact with the open counter-revolutionary group of Ryutin. (See also *Biographical Notes.*)

including China. Thereby Trotsky resurrected in their original nakedness his views on the peasant and national-colonial questions, against which Lenin fought so relentlessly in his day.

Even during the years when Trotskyism was still a faction of Communism it carried on a factional struggle against Leninism and the Bolshevik Party, but it did not always do this openly, usually camouflaging itself with "Left"-adventurist phrasemongering.

Having lapsed into a definitely counter-revolutionary standpoint, Trotskyism—immediately after the expulsion of Trotsky from the Party and from the Soviet Union—launched an open frantic struggle against Leninism, against the Bolshevik Party, against the victorious socialist construction in the Soviet Union.

It is both curious and repellent that Trotsky, while taking up his rusty Menshevik arms, indulges at the same time in rabid anti-Menshevik declamation. Defying all historical facts, Trotsky solemnly declares that neither in 1905 nor later on did he have anything in common ideologically with Menshevism. All he condescends to do is to confess a certain tendency to conciliate with Menshevism on organisational questions—as if this conciliationist attitude on organisational points could have existed without an ideological base. The Party knows and remembers full well that both at the Second Congress and after it Trotsky adhered to the organisational principles of Menshevism, and that he did not only take a conciliationist attitude towards them. The Party knows well that in 1905, when we had two parties in existence not only in actual fact, but in the formal sense as well, Trotsky was a collaborator in the Menshevik newspapers and participated in the Menshevik organisations; that he developed his theory of permanent revolution in the columns of the Menshevik press (*Iskra* and *Nachalo*); that during the period of reaction, on all the fundamental questions which divided the Bolsheviks from the liquidators (the petition campaign, freedom of coalitions and "uncurtailed slogans," the split of the fraction in the Fourth Duma, the shameful platform of the August Conference) Trotsky was with the liquidators and against the Bolsheviks; that he wrote a letter to Chkheidze in which he referred to Lenin as a professional exploiter of everything that was backward; that he,

Trotsky, mobilised all the leading lights of international opportunism and centrism, with Kautsky at their head, against the
Bolsheviks in defence of the liquidators' proposal to curtail the
slogans and to replace the demand for a democratic republic
by the demand for freedom of coalitions; that during the years
of the World War, he, Trotsky, formed a *bloc* with part of the
Mensheviks and with the Bolshevik conciliators against Lenin,
that at Zimmerwald he lined up with the Kautskyists, that he
defended the faction of Chkheidze which held a semi-Defencist
position with regard to the war, etc., etc. Truly, paper will bear
everything.

In the autumn of 1928, Trotsky authoritatively declared that
the Soviet Union was going through a period of Kerenskyism
reversed—a stage leading from the October Revolution towards
a fascist dictatorship. It was at the same time that he expressed
himself in favour of the Chinese Communists putting forward the
slogan of a constituent assembly.

The banishing of Trotsky from the Soviet Union, his articles
in the bourgeois yellow press and his self-advertising auto-
biography did their work. The disintegration of the Trotskyist
forces reached catastrophic dimensions. Almost all of the more
or less outstanding representatives of Trotskyism have dissociated
themselves from their leader. A large part of them (Radek,
Preobrazhensky, Smilga, I. N. Smirnov) have returned to the
ranks of the Party.

The "leader" is followed only by the most embittered *en-
ragés,* by those who were least closely connected with the Party
in the past, by a handful of petty philistines, absolutely alien to
the working class, who join hands with all those disappointed
remnants of defeated classes and parties who hate the Soviet
power.

But they march at the head of the fragments of the counter-
revolutionary bourgeoisie at a time when the class struggle in
our country is growing more acute, and therefore

"liberalism with regard to Trotskyism, even though it has been
smashed and wears a disguise, is pigheadedness bordering on crime,
on betrayal of the working class." (Stalin.)

The Trotskyist headquarters abroad, as Stalin said at the

Sixteenth Party Congress, has become an intelligence bureau for the foreign bourgeoisie regarding the affairs of the C.P.S.U.

The Fifteenth Congress on the New Tasks of the Party

The Fifteenth Congress inflicted the final blow, the death blow, on the Trotskyist opposition in the ranks of the Party. And this congress, in its resolutions on the report of the Central Committee, Central Control Commission and the delegation to the Comintern, on the Five-Year Plan and on work in the rural districts, gave the Party the tactical line for the new period, which is characterised by a considerable change both in the international and in the internal situation as compared with the period of the Fourteenth Congress.

What had been happening since the Fourteenth Congress in the capitalist world surrounding the U.S.S.R.? The partial character of capitalist stabilisation, its internal antagonisms and decay became more clearly outlined. In his report at the Fourteenth Congress, Comrade Stalin enumerated five kinds of contradictions within the system of international capitalism, having in view also the relation of the latter towards the U.S.S.R. These were: the contradictions between the victorious countries and the countries defeated in the World War; the contradictions among the victorious countries themselves; the contradictions between the bourgeoisie and the working class, between the imperialist countries and the colonial countries, and finally between capitalist imperialism and the Soviet Union.

What was the situation with regard to all these contradictions? Had the contradictions within the dominant imperialist system grown more acute or had they diminished? Unquestionably, they had become considerably more acute. The axis of all these contradictions was becoming, ever more clearly and definitely, the antagonism between the United States and Great Britain. The world was becoming too small for these two giants. Hence the growing menace of a new imperialist war, which must unquestionably be much more terrible and destructive than the last. Hence the ever more obvious shattering of the pacifist illusions which had been fostered by Social-Democracy and which disarmed the working class for the struggle against the menace of imperialist wars. Had the contradictions between the working class and the bourgeoisie grown more acute or had they diminished? The British general strike and the miners' strike of 1926, the events in Vienna in 1927, the change for the worse in the conditions of the working class in all capitalist countries without exception, the unceasing offensive of capital on the economic and political front, the spreading of the fascist regime to new countries—all this taken together testified, not to the mitigation, but to the accentuation of class antagonisms.

Had the contradictions between the imperialist countries and colonial countries grown more acute or had they diminished? The years 1926-27 'marked the crest of the wave of Chinese revolution. Its temporary defeat had not by any means removed the questions raised by this revolution from the order of the day. A revolutionary explosion in India was steadily continuing to mature. The movements in Latin America and in the Negro countries were making themselves felt ever more strongly. The sharper the clashes became between the imperialist countries as a result of the lack of markets, the stronger was the pressure which they naturally had to exert upon the colonial countries.

And finally, in view of the growth of production in the principal capitalist countries beyond the pre-war level, in view of the development of capitalist industries in a number of new countries (Canada, Australia, South Africa), in view of the change for the worse in the conditions of the working class and the ruin of the middle strata of the population, the fact that the U.S.S.R. had been eliminated from the system of world capitalism 'and the desire of the capitalist countries to conquer our market were bound to find their expression in ever more perceptible forms. This was why the period following the Fourteenth Congress brought with it a considerable growth of the war danger for the U.S.S.R.

At the time of the Fourteenth Congress it was still possible to speak of a period when the U.S.S.R. and the capitalist countries existed side by side on relatively peaceful terms. Now this period was already retreating into the past. In May 1926, the

Sixteenth Party Congress, has become an intelligence bureau for the foreign bourgeoisie regarding the affairs of the C.P.S.U.

The Fifteenth Congress on the New Tasks of the Party

The Fifteenth Congress inflicted the final blow, the death blow, on the Trotskyist opposition in the ranks of the Party. And this congress, in its resolutions on the report of the Central Committee, Central Control Commission and the delegation to the Comintern, on the Five-Year Plan and on work in the rural districts, gave the Party the tactical line for the new period, which is characterised by a considerable change both in the international and in the internal situation as compared with the period of the Fourteenth Congress.

What had been happening since the Fourteenth Congress in the capitalist world surrounding the U.S.S.R.? The partial character of capitalist stabilisation, its internal antagonisms and decay became more clearly outlined In his report at the Fourteenth Congress, Comrade Stalin enumerated five kinds of contradictions within the system of international capitalism, having in view also the relation of the latter towards the U.S.S.R. These were: the contradictions between the victorious countries and the countries defeated in the World War; the contradictions among the victorious countries themselves; the contradictions between the bourgeoisie and the working class, between the imperialist countries and the colonial countries, and finally between capitalist imperialism and the Soviet Union.

What was the situation with regard to all these contradictions? Had the contradiction within the dominant imperialist system grown more acute or had they diminished? Unquestionably, they had become considerably more acute. The axis of all these contradictions was becoming, ever more clearly and definitely, the antagonism between the United States and Great Britain. The world was becoming too small for these two giants. Hence the growing menace of a new imperialist war, which must unquestionably be much more terrible and destructive than the last. Hence the ever more obvious shattering of the pacifist

illusions which had been fostered by ....
which disarmed the working class for the ...
menace of imperialist wars. Had the ...
working class and the bourgeoisi grown ...
diminished? The British genera strike ...
of 1926, the events in Vienna in 1927, the ...
in the conditions of the working class in all ...
without exception, the unceasing offensive of ...
nomic and political front, the speading of the ...
new countries—all this taken togther testified ...
tion, but to the accentuation of class antagonisms.

Had the contradictions betwen the imperialist ...
colonial countries grown more cu... they di...
The years 1926-27 marked the res... e of Chi...
revolution. Its temporary defeat had n... ns remov...
the questions raised by this revoltion fro... of the da...
A revolutionary explosion in Idia was... nuing...
mature. The movements in Latin Americ... Neg...
countries were making themselvs felt ever... T...
sharper the clashes became bween the im... r...
as a result of the lack of marets, the stron...
sure which they naturally had o exert upon th...
tries.

And finally, in view of the gowth of productio...
cipal capitalist countries beyord the pre-war leve...
the development of capitalist industries in a num...
countries (Canada, Australia, South Africa), in vi...
change for the worse in the coditions of the working...
the ruin of the middle strata of the population, the fact...
U.S.S.R. had been eliminated fom the system of world...
ism and the desire of the captalist countries to conque...
market were bound to find thr expression in ever more...
ceptible forms. This was why the period following the Fou...
teenth Congress brought with't a considerable growth of t...
war danger for the U.S.S.R.

At the time of the Fourteeth Congress it was still possib...
to speak of a period when the U.S.S.R. and the capitalist cou...
tries existed side by side on retively peaceful terms. Now th...
period was already retreating nto the past. In May 1926, t...

fascist *coup* in Poland brought the Pilsudski government into power, and this government, under the direction of British imperialism, began the most intensive preparations for a war against the U.S.S.R. A year later, in May 1927, the British Conservative government broke off diplomatic relations with the U.S.S.R. Even before this the French government had virtually broken off the negotiations with the U.S.S.R. regarding the debts and credits. For the international policy of the U.S.S.R. with regard to the capitalist countries, the situation at the time of the Fifteenth Congress was considerably less favourable than at the time of the Fourteenth Congress.

The menace of war had become considerably more real.

What changes had occurred in the internal situation of the country? The socialist sector in industry and trade had become considerably stronger. Industry itself had grown, a great number of industries having exceeded the pre-war level of production. But its further growth was encountering a number of serious difficulties.

The organisation of new enterprises required large capital investments. The increase in the output of industry was not enough to cover the demand for commodities. Agriculture was developing at a comparatively slow rate, and its lagging behind the development of industry made itself felt ever more strongly. The relatively slow development of agriculture placed a number of industries depending upon agricultural raw materials in a difficult position. It threatened to undermine the export trade and hence also to jeopardize the imports of industrial equipment into our country.

The squeezing out of the capitalist elements in the towns in the field of industry and trade had gone quite far by the time of the Fifteenth Party Congress.

The achievements of socialist construction in the U.S.S.R. at a time when there was an increasing menace from the imperialist countries naturally impelled the class elements that were hostile to the proletarian dictatorship to take the line of furious resistance to the growth of socialism. This applied above all to the kulak section of the peasantry, which had had time to grow considerably stronger and consolidate itself during the years of the N.E.P. and also to the urban petty-bourgeoisie which was being squeezed out of economic life, the intelligentsia connected with it, etc.

This complicated and intensified the class struggle. But it was precisely the Leninist general line of our Party in this bitter class struggle which facilitated the extension and consolidation of all the positions of the proletarian dictatorship.

Comrade Stalin, in his political report to the Fifteenth Congress on the work of the Central Committee, also pointed out the

"dark sides of our economic construction" (a certain commodity shortage, the slow progress made in reducing the cost of production in industry and in lowering retail prices, the inadequate growth of reserve funds, the partial growth of kulakdom and of capitalist elements in the country, etc.) "to which attention must be paid and which must be liquidated at all costs, in order to be able to move forward at a more rapid rate."

An accelerated tempo of industrialisation, with special emphasis on the development of heavy industry—such was the slogan issued by the Fifteenth Congress of the Party.

The basis of this slogan was the whole general line of the Party, and the decisions of the preceding Fourteenth Congress. To carry out this line, to secure a Bolshevik tempo in the industrialisation of the country, was the best means of overcoming the difficulties—of eliminating unemployment, increasing the country's commodity supplies, of isolating, further restricting and squeezing out the kulak.

The Fourteenth Congress had squarely raised the question of industrialisation, of freeing the country from economic dependence on abroad, of building socialism.

The Fifteenth Conference raised the question of the tempo of industrialisation in a more acute form. The partial stabilisation of capitalism had by that time made certain advances in Europe and America, and this was bound to lead to the capitalist countries increasing their economic pressure on us. In our relations with them the question of "Who would win?" was arising ever more clearly and definitely.

The Fifteenth Conference confronted the Party and the country with the slogan which Lenin had already put forward on the eve of the October Revolution—to catch up and then to outstrip the advanced capitalist countries in technical and economic respects.

The Fifteenth Congress had to present this slogan in an even more concrete form, since the time was fraught with grave and clearly outlined difficulties, involved in the tremendous growth of socialism. This slogan was imperatively dictated by the whole international and internal situation. The Fifteenth Congress laid particular stress on the need to develop heavy industry, since only a highly developed heavy industry could secure a firm foundation for the genuine industrialisation of the country in all fields.

By the time of the Fifteenth Congress we had won great achievements in the sphere of industry:

"The surpassing of the pre-war levels by industry, the renewal of the fixed capital in socialist industry, the beginning of a radical technical-industrial reorganisation, the considerable achievements in electrification, the creation and development of entire new branches of industry (machine building, machine tool, automobile, turbines, aviation, chemical industry), the construction of new plants, of large constructions and installations and the radical re-equipment of old plants —such are the substantial achievements of the Party and the working class on the path of the industrialisation of our country as called for by the Fourteenth Congress." *

But these achievements were inadequate. Our iron and steel industry was in a very backward state, continuing to remain somewhat behind the pre-war level. And the backwardness of the iron and steel industry retarded the development of transport, of machine building and of other industries.

The question of speeding up the development of agriculture had of course been raised before. This question, as is well known, was urgently presented to the Fourteenth Party Conference. The Fourteenth Conference adopted a policy the aim of which was the maximum development of the productive forces of the countryside and the obliteration of the last vestiges of War Communism while doing everything to strengthen the connection of socialist industry with poor and middle peasant farming.

* Resolution on the report of the Central Committee to the Fifteenth Congress of the C.P.S.U.

This policy was fully endorsed by the Fourteenth Congress. It was productive of great results. The Fifteenth Conference was able to note a general rise in agriculture, an increase of the middle peasantry with a corresponding diminution in the number of poor peasants. This was accompanied, however, by a certain growth of well-to-do and kulak elements.

What distinguished the decisions of the Fifteenth Congress from those of preceding Congresses was the urgent manner in which they raised the question of the socialist reconstruction of agriculture, of developing the socialist sector (Soviet and collective farms) within agricultural economy—a sector which had remained almost stationary during the previous few years, producing a comparatively insignificant part of the total agricultural output—and of switching scores of millions of small and dwarf peasant farms on to the rails of large-scale socialised agriculture.

It was in just such urgent fashion that Comrade Stalin raised this question in his political report to the Congress:

Where is the way out? The way out is in transforming the small disintegrated peasant farms into large-scale amalgamated farms, on the basis of communal tillage of the soil, in adopting collective tillage of the soil, on the basis of the new higher technique. The way out is to amalgamate the small and tiny peasant farms gradually but steadily, not by means of pressure, but by example and persuasion, into large-scale undertakings on the basis of communal co-operative, collective tillage of the soil, applying agricultural machinery and tractors, applying scientific methods for the intensification of agriculture. *There is no other way out.*

Without this agriculture can neither catch up with nor surpass those capitalist countries which are most highly developed in agricultural respects (Canada, etc.). All our measures for restricting the capitalist elements in agriculture, for developing the socialist elements in the countryside, for drawing the peasant farms into the channel of co-operative development, for bringing the influence of the state to bear on the countryside in a planned manner by extending its scope over peasant farming both through supply and sale and also through production—all these measures are, to be sure, decisive measures, but none the less preparatory to switching agriculture on to the rails of collectivism."

The Fifteenth Congress inaugurated a new epoch in the history of our socialist construction. As Comrade Stalin later declared:

"The new thing in the decisions of the Fifteenth Congress as compared with the Fourteenth Congress lies in the fact that the Fifteenth Congress defined the development of the collective farm movement to the utmost, as one of the most important tasks of the present day." *

The slogan of an intensified offensive against the capitalist elements was of course not a new or unexpected one at the Fifteenth Congress. At the Fourteenth Congress, the Party had emphatically rejected the view of the "New Opposition" that the N.E.P. meant only a retreat. Starting with the Eleventh Congress, when Lenin declared that the retreat had come to an end, the Party had been carrying on an offensive on the basis of the N.E.P.

This offensive had produced great results. In industry the socialist sector was already providing the overwhelming bulk of the output, and it was gradually occupying the dominant positions in trade by systematically squeezing out the capitalist elements.

The ideological and organisational rout of Trotskyism, which was completely smashed at the Fifteenth Congress, was not only an act of purging the Party of degenerated elements who had become agents of the bourgeoisie. It also signified a victory over the efforts of the bourgeoisie to undermine socialist construction.

In putting forward the slogan of the socialist reconstruction of agriculture, the Fifteenth Party Congress naturally had to raise more sharply the question of an offensive against the capitalist elements in the field where they were strongest, namely, in that of individual farming.

It was just here, among the scores of millions of small and dwarf peasant farms, that the roots of capitalism were particularly deeply embedded, while the kulak class remained the representative and the most rabid defender of the capitalist system of production in agriculture.

Noting the tremendous progress that had been made in the field of the socialist industrialisation of the country, in the struggle to strengthen the alliance of the working class with the peasantry and to enlist the great masses of the peasantry in the work of socialist construction, in the struggle against the kulak on the

* Stalin, *Leninism*, Vol. II.

basis of "restricting him and squeezing him out" (in trade, in the grain collections, in the co-operatives, in the first stage of the organisation of tractor squads, etc.); taking note also of the partial growth of kulakdom (the inevitability of which had been foreseen by the Fourteenth Party Conference and the Fourteenth Congress), the Fifteenth Congress recognised that it was necessary, on the basis of the achievements already attained, to commence widespread activities for the socialist reconstruction of agriculture (Soviet farms, collective farms, tractorisation, etc.) and for an intensified offensive against the kulak.

The speeding up of the tempo of industrialisation, the urgency of the question of the socialist reconstruction of agriculture, the intensified offensive against the capitalist elements, particularly against the kulak—all this demanded a tremendous increase in the activity and class-consciousness of the toiling masses, headed by the proletariat, and a considerable improvement in the quality of the work of the entire state and economic apparatus of the Soviet government.

The Fifteenth Congress put forward the slogan of a cultural revolution, in all its urgency. It was impossible to carry out those colossal changes in all our economic relations which were envisaged by the Fifteenth Congress without raising tremendously the cultural level of the masses. The task of improving the work of the state and economic apparatus was indissolubly linked up with the more active participation of the broad proletarian masses in this work and for this (as also for speeding up the rate of industrialisation, increasing the productivity of labour, etc.) it was necessary to raise the cultural level of the working masses. But improving the work of the state apparatus meant at the same time a more widespread and intensive struggle against bureaucracy within this apparatus, against the backwardness and lack of culture which fostered this bureaucracy and which impeded the further advance of the Soviet country along the road to socialism.

The growing activity of the anti-Soviet elements led them to make increased use of their connections in the state, economic and co-operative organisations in order to undermine our policy. Contact with an alien and hostile environment, coupled with the fact that this environment was displaying an increased activity, also resulted in cases of the decay of individual elements of our Party who fell under the influence of the alien forces. The struggle against bureaucracy, against lack of culture, against alien influences and elements of decay urgently demanded of the Party the strengthening of healthy proletarian self-criticism, a question which was sharply raised by Comrade Stalin in the report of the Central Committee:

"If we, Bolsheviks, who criticise the whole world, who, in the words of Marx, are storming heaven, if we were to discard self-criticism for the sake of leaving some comrades undisturbed, is it not clear that the only result of this could be the ruin of our great cause? ('*Correct.*' *Applause.*) Marx said that the proletarian revolution is distinguished from all other revolutions, among other things, by the fact that it criticises itself and, by criticising itself, grows stronger."

Work in the Rural Districts

The task of the socialist reconstruction of agriculture which the Party first set itself as an urgent practical task at the Fifteenth Congress, was of course bound to rivet the concentrated attention of the whole Party for a considerable period. It demanded a detailed practical study and a concrete approach.

The Party Congress devoted a special discussion to the question of work in the rural districts employing all the transmission belts connecting the Party with the peasant masses, paying special attention to the village organisations of the Y.C.L., the co-operatives and the Soviet apparatus.

The resolution on work in the rural districts adopted by the Congress on the basis of Comrade Molotov's report pointed out that since the Fourteenth Congress, as a result of the policy pursued by the Party in this matter, a number of great changes had occurred:

"1) The area under cultivation has increased and the area of uncultivated land has sharply decreased, a fact connected with the general advance in the economy of the main masses of the peasantry; 2) In the political field, there has been an increased dissociation of the middle peasants from the kulaks, the alliance of the working class with the masses of the middle peasantry has become stronger and a decisive turn has become apparent towards the isolation of the kulak.

"Thus the aims which the Party set itself in the period of the Fourteenth Conference and the Fourteenth Congress may be considered as in the main attained. The Party has won these successes by waging a struggle both against the tendency to underrate the kulak menace and in particular against the anti-middle peasant deviation of the opposition. The Party could not have won these successes if it had not concentrated its fire against the opportunist anti-middle peas· ant deviation of the opposition, since this deviation, by undermining the alliance of the proletariat with the middle peasant masses and making it more difficult to sever the middle peasant from the kulak; leads in reality to a strengthening of the kulak influence in the coun· tryside. It is essential to continue the Leninist policy of an alliance with the middle peasant which the Party has been carrying out."

In addition to this the resolution also noted a number of Right opportunist distortions of the policy of the Party in the countryside, in the practical work of the land departments, of the co-operatives, of the Soviet apparatus and of individual Party organisations.

These distortions found their expression in some places in insufficient resistance to kulak encroachments in the field of credit, machinery supply, and land allotment, in the fact that the financial organs in a number of cases imposed excessively low taxes on the incomes of the kulak groups, in the failure to enforce the Party's instructions not to permit kulaks to pene-trate into the elective organs of the co-operatives, in allowing the existence of kulak pseudo co-operatives, in insufficient atten-tion on the part of certain local organisations to the task of organising the agricultural labourers and the poor peasants.

The resolution declared:

"The successes achieved by the policy of the Party in the country-side and the new situation which has arisen as a result of this enable the Party of the proletariat, by utilising the full power of the eco-nomic organs and relying as before on the poor and middle peasant masses, further to develop the offensive against the kulak and to adopt a number of new measures restricting the development of cap-italism in the countryside and leading peasant farming in the direction of socialism."

Of great importance was the emphasis which the resolution placed on the alliance with the peasantry based on production.

Heretofore, the alliance with the peasantry had been effected by the Party chiefly and primarily through the connection be-tween state industry and the peasantry in the sphere of trade. For the Party it was a question of extreme importance, who would directly supply peasant farming with industrial products —the proletarian state itself through the co-operatives or the private capitalist. But even if this question were answered in the affirmative, in favour of the proletarian state, this did not directly affect the extremely primitive, backward technique of peasant farming. It was only possible to set about transforming this technique by the widespread application of the contract system,* by supplying peasant farms with machinery on a mass scale, by the organisation of tractor squads, by the utmost possible development of production co-operatives, particularly of special kinds of co-operatives, by collective farms.

It was precisely these methods which were outlined in the resolution adopted by the Fifteenth Congress on the report of Comrade Molotov.

In this article *On Co-operation,* Lenin had already clearly stated that the highway of socialist transformation of peasant farming leads through the co-operatives.

"The experience of past years, particularly of recent years," says the resolution of the Fifteenth Congress on Comrade Molotov's report, "has fully confirmed the correctness of Lenin's co-operative plan according to which it is precisely through the co-operatives that socialist industry will lead small peasant farming on to the road to socialism, transforming the individual and scattered productive units—both through a process of circulation and also to an ever greater extent through the reorganisation and amalgamation of production itself—into large-scale socialised farming on the basis of new technique (electrification, etc.)."

On the basis of the general policy aiming at the practical realisation of the socialist reconstruction of agriculture, the resolution outlined a number of concrete tasks with regard to the Soviet apparatus, to the rural co-operative and trade union bodies and finally with regard to the Party organisations.

The resolution laid particular stress on the question of extending the work among agricultural labourers and poor peasants.

The decisions of the Fifteenth Congress on speeding up the

---

* Contract system: the system by which the peasants used to conclude contracts with the state to grow and deliver certain quantities of certain crops at a given price in compensation for credits and agro-technical assistance rendered by the state. In 1933 this system was abolished, except for certain industrial crops.—*Ed.*

tempo of industrialisation of the country, on special attention to heavy industry, on the socialist reorganisation of agriculture, on an intensified offensive against the capitalist elements, on a determined struggle against bureaucracy, on the cultural revolution, and on the enforcement of self-criticism, determined the character of the Party's work for a considerable time to come.

The realisation of these decisions, in view of the international situation which was characterised by increased pressure on the Soviet state on the part of imperialism and by growing danger of war, could not but encounter considerable difficulties. The Fifteenth Congress, in its resolution on the report of the Central Committee, sharply emphasised the fact of the intensified class struggle within the country during the reconstruction period:

"In spite of the leading and ever increasing role of the socialist economic kernel, the rise of the productive forces in the economy of the U.S.S.R. is inevitably accompanied by a partial growth of class contradictions. The private capitalist strata of town and countryside, which are linked up with certain bureaucratic elements in the Soviet and economic apparatus, strive to strengthen their resistance to the offensive of the working class, and attempt to exercise an influence hostile to the proletarian dictatorship over certain sections of the employees and intelligentsia and the backward sections of the handicraftsmen and artisans, peasants and workers. This influence is also manifested in the cultural, political and ideological fields (propaganda of Smenovekhism, the slogan for a kulak 'peasant union,' chauvinism, anti-Semitism, propaganda in favour of bourgeois democratic 'liberties' and, in connection with this, the petty-bourgeois oppositionist slogan of two parties)."

The intensified offensive of the working class, under the leadership of the Party, along the road outlined by the Fifteenth Congress was naturally bound to cause even more bitter resistance on the part of the counter-revolutionary elements, particularly of the kulaks.

The difficulties involved in overcoming this resistance led to the formation of an open opportunist opposition with regard to the line of the Fifteenth Congress.

CHAPTER XVII

THE PARTY DURING THE RECONSTRUCTION PERIOD OF SOCIALIST CONSTRUCTION (FROM THE FIFTEENTH TO THE SIX-TEENTH CONGRESS OF THE PARTY)

The struggle of the Party for a Bolshevik solution of the grain problem—The Shakhty case and the problem of cadres—The Party in the struggle against the Right deviation as the main danger—The Comintern in the struggle against the Right deviation as the main danger—The Sixth Congress of the Comintern —The C.P.S.U. and the Comintern expose the anti-Leninist platform of the Rights and conciliators and suppress their factional struggle—The mobilisation of the masses for a Bolshevik overcoming of difficulties—The struggle against the revision of Leninism, the anti-Party slander and the kulak platform of the Rights—The Sixteenth Party Conference—The struggle of the Party against bureaucracy—The general purging of the Party ranks and the enrolment of workers—The Party in the struggle on two fronts in the period of the extended socialist offensive—The struggle against Right opportunism and against the conciliators in the Comintern—The Plenum of the Central Committee in November 1929—From restricting and squeezing out the kulak to the liquidation of kulakdom—The Party in the struggle against anti-middle peasant excesses—The Sixteenth Party Congress—The socialist offensive along the whole front—The national question at the Sixteenth Congress—After the Sixteenth Congress

The Struggle of the Party for a Bolshevik Solution of the Grain Problem

The Fifteenth Congress took note of the great achievements of the Party on all fronts of socialist construction—the development of industry, which had surpassed the pre-war level, the consolidation of all the other economic key positions of the proletarian state (transport, state budget, trade apparatus) the strengthening of the leading rôle of socialist industry in relation to agriculture, etc. The Congress decided that

"with respect to the elements of private capitalist economy which have increased absolutely, although to a lesser degree than the socialist sector of economy, a policy of even more determined economic squeezing-out can and must be pursued."

In accordance with the task set by the Congress for the social-ist reconstruction of agriculture, the principal blow of this offensive had to fall on the kulak. In view of the insignificant rôle played by private capital in industry, and since the proletarian state had conquered the key positions in the domain of commodity circulation and trade, the kulak remained the strongest exploiting class, the main bulwark of capitalist exploitation in the country.

The kulak offered systematic resistance to the policy of the Party—a policy which aimed at restricting and squeezing out the kulak, and which the Party pursued even before the Fifteenth Congress.* The intensification of our socialist offensive was bound to encounter intensified resistance on the part of the kulak.

This made itself felt above all on the front of the grain collections. By January 1, 1928, the deficit in the amount of grain collected, as against the preceding year, reached the considerable figure of 21,000,000 centners.**

What was the reason for this deficit? The crop of 1927, although somewhat worse than that of the preceding year, was by no means bad. The grain collection plan was designed not only to satisfy the demand within the country but also to permit the export of several tens of millions of centners. Why, then, were we confronted with the fact that at the beginning of 1928, although there was unquestionably enough grain in the country, there was, nevertheless a considerable under-fulfilment of the plan which not only obliged us to abandon the exports but even endangered the supplies of the industrial centres?

The shortage of marketable grain increased in proportion as the land was divided up and the average size of peasant farms was reduced. In 1927, the number of these peasant farms reached 25,000,000 as against 15,000,000 in 1917. This reduction in the size of the peasant farms undoubtedly resulted first and foremost in decreasing the marketable portion of their produce.

In pre-revolutionary Russia hundreds of millions of centners

---

* "This was the policy [of restricting and squeezing out the kulak—N.P.] we conducted not only during the restoration period, but also during the reconstruction period, in the period following the Fifteenth Congress (December 1927), during the period of the Sixteenth Party Conference (April 1929), and in the period following that conference right down to the summer of 1929, when the phase of mass collectivisation began and when the swing towards the policy of *liquidating* the kulaks as a *class* commenced." (Stalin, *Leninism*, "On the Policy of Liquidating the Kulaks as a Class," Vol. II.)

** Centner—one-tenth part of a metric ton, equal to 220.46 lbs.—*Ed.*

of marketable grain were supplied by the landlord estates. These estates now existed no longer. Kulak farming also occupied an incomparably more modest position, in spite of the fact that the kulak became somewhat stronger during the first years of the N.E.P.

The table cited by Comrade Stalin in his article *On the Grain Front* shows that prior to the war the landlords supplied 28,600,000 poods of marketable grain, or 22 per cent of the total, the kulaks 650,000,000 poods, or 50 per cent, and the middle and poor peasantry 369, 000,000 poods, or 28 per cent.

In 1926-27, the Soviet and collective farms supplied 38,000,000 poods, or 6 per cent of the total,* the kulaks 126,000,000 poods, or 20 per cent, and the middle and poor peasants 466,000,000 poods, or 74 per cent of the total of marketable grain.**

Comrade Stalin analysed these figures, as follows:

"What does this table show?

"It shows, first of all, that the production of the overwhelming proportion of grain products has passed from the hands of the land-lords and kulaks into the hands of the small and middle peasants. That means that the small and middle peasants, having completely emancipated themselves from the yoke of the landlords, and having, in the main, broken the strength of the kulaks, thereby obtained the opportunity of considerably improving their material well-being. That was the result of the October Revolution. It is primarily an expression of the important gains which accrued to the great mass of the peasantry as a result of the October Revolution.

"It shows, secondly, that the chief holders of marketable grain are the small, and primarily, the middle peasants. That means that as a result of the October Revolution, the Soviet Union has become a country of small peasant farming not only from the point of view of the gross output of grain, but also from the point of view of the production of marketable grain, and that the middle peasant has become the 'central figure' in agriculture.

"It shows, thirdly, that the abolition of landlord (large-scale) production, the reduction of kulak (large-scale) production to less than one-third and the transition to small peasant production, with a marketable output of only 11 per cent, accompanied by the absence of any degree of developed large-scale social production of grain

---

* These 38,000,000 poods of marketable grain constituted 47.2 per cent of the total production of the Soviet and collective farms.
** Four hundred and sixty-six million poods amounted to 11.2 per cent of the total production of the poor and middle peasant farms, which reached 4,052,000,000 poods.

(collective and Soviet farms), must lead, and in fact has led, to a drastic reduction in the output of marketable grain as compared with pre-war days. It is a fact that although we have reached the pre-war level in respect of the gross production of grain, the output of marketable grain has been reduced to one-half.

"Therein lies the basis of our difficulties on the grain front."*

On the other hand, the demand for grain on the part of the towns increased year by year as a result of the improved conditions of the broad working masses and the general rapid growth of industry and of the urban population. And in addition to this, the quantity of industrial commodities which were sent to the countryside was absolutely insufficient to meet the rapidly growing demand. The middle peasant, who had a surplus of grain, had no particular incentive to exchange it for money, because he could not purchase with this money a sufficient quantity of the commodities of which he was in need. Moreover, since the prices on industrial crops had been raised during the preceding years a very unfavourable ratio was established in the market between the prices on grain and those on industrial crops; in view of which, the peasant preferred to sell the industrial crops and to hold the grain crops.

If we further bear in mind that the well-to-do and kulak upper stratum of the peasantry offered every kind of resistance, for political reasons, to surrendering their grain surplus at the fixed government price to the organs of the Soviet government which had charge of grain collections, that the kulak systematically withheld his grain surplus and incited the upper stratum of the middle peasantry to follow his example, the causes of our difficulties in the field of grain collections in the winter of 1927-28 become perfectly clear.

The Party, while developing an intensified offensive against the capitalist elements in town and countryside, was confronted with the necessity of taking the most determined measures to avert the threat of a general food crisis in the country.

"Only two or three months remained before the roads became impassable owing to the spring thaws. We were therefore faced with the choice: either to make up lost ground and secure a normal rate of grain collection for the future, or to face the inevitability of a profound crisis in the whole of our national economy. What had to

* Stalin, *Leninism*, Vol. II.

be done in order to make up lost ground? It was necessary, first of all, to strike hard at the kulaks and the speculators who were screwing up the price of grain and creating the danger of famine in the country. Secondly, it was necessary to pour the maximum amount of goods into the grain-producing regions. Finally, it was necessary to rouse all our Party organisations and bring about a decisive turn in the whole of our work on grain collection, by rooting out the practice of waiting for grain to come automatically. We were consequently obliged to resort to emergency measures. The measures adopted were effective, and by the end of March we had collected 275,000,000 poods of grain. We not only made up for lost ground, we not only prevented a general economic crisis, we not only caught up with the rate of grain collection of the previous year, but the possibility was created for us to emerge painlessly from the grain collection crisis, provided a normal rate of grain collection was maintained in the succeeding months."*

Thus Comrade Stalin, in his report to a meeting of the active members of the Leningrad organisation on the July Plenum of the Central Committee of the C.P.S.U., characterised the situation with regard to grain collections in the winter and spring of 1928.

A few months before this, the April Plenum, in its resolution on the grain collections, unanimously declared, after referring to the emergency measures which had been taken:

"Without the enforcement of these and similar measures, the very serious difficulties in the field of grain collections could not have been removed...

"These measures made it possible to diminish and later to overcome the interruptions in supplying the cities, the Red Army and the workers' districts, thus preventing a decline in the real wages, to do away with the shortage in the supply of grain to the cotton and flax raising districts as well as to the districts supplying the state with timber, and finally to create a certain minimum reserve of grain."

While pointing out the great success achieved in the grain collections by mobilising the forces of the whole Party on the grain collections front and by the application of the emergency measures, the April Plenum at the same time declared that:

"In proportion as the difficulties in the grain collections are overcome, it is necessary to drop those of the Party's measures which were of an emergency character."

* Stalin, *Leninism,* Vol. II.

However, the failure of the winter crops in the Ukraine and to some extent also in the Northern Caucasus again radically changed the situation, resulting in the complete discontinuance of any further grain collections in these most important districts. This not only reduced the potential extent of state grain collections but necessitated even larger grain supplies from the state for re-sowing purposes. In order to secure the food plan, it became necessary to increase the collections quota for other districts.

"This circumstance, combined with the fact that we had permitted an over-expenditure of grain, imposed on us the necessity of pressing more heavily on the remaining regions, thereby breaking in on the emergency reserves of the peasantry, which could not but make the situation worse. . . . Hence the repeated relapse to emergency measures, administrative arbitrariness, violation of revolutionary law, raids on peasant houses, illegal searches and so forth, which affected the political condition of the country and created a menace to the *smychka* between the workers and the peasants."*

The July Plenum of the Central Committee, which met after the conclusion of the grain collections campaign, had to face the grain question once again in all its urgency. The Plenum argued that the country's grain difficulties were without doubt neither accidental nor periodic; that they were rooted, on the one hand, in the backward and diffused state of peasant farming and, on the other hand, in the increased resistance of the kulaks, who had accumulated considerable reserves of grain and were using them as a weapon with which to bring pressure to bear on the Soviet government; that the successful socialist industrialisation of the country and the enlistment of the main masses of the peasantry in the co-operatives had created the necessary conditions for the socialist reconstruction of agriculture. The Plenum, therefore, emphasised the great importance and urgency of carrying into effect the measures outlined by the Fifteenth Congress for the socialist reconstruction of agriculture, while continuing to exert determined pressure on the kulak. The Plenum declared that "the grain problem is one of the most serious problems of economic policy."

In his report "On the Results of the July Plenum of the Central Committee of the C.P.S.U.," Comrade Stalin pointed out

* *Ibid.*

that the solution of "our difficulties on the grain front" lies in correctly combining three tasks:

1) ". . . Raising the level of small and middle peasant farming, lending it every assistance in raising its yield and productivity. . . . To replace the *sokha* by the plough, to provide sorted seed, to supply fertilisers and simple machines, to cover the individual peasant farms with a wide network of co-operative organisations and to conclude contracts with whole villages (the contract system).

2) ". . . Gradually amalgamating individual small and middle peasant production into large-scale collective and co-operative, entirely voluntary, associations, working on the basis of modern technique, on the basis of tractors and other agricultural machinery.

3) "... Improving the old Soviet farms and creating new large-scale farms."*

Comrade Stalin in his report also exposed those who believed that "individual production is at the end of its tether and is not worth supporting," as well as those who believed that "individual, peasant production is the *alpha* and *omega* of agriculture."

"We need neither decriers nor boosters of individual peasant production. We need sober statesmen capable of getting the best out of individual peasant economy, but who at the same time will be capable of gradually transferring individual economy to the lines of collectivism."*

Prior to the July Plenum, the Central Committee, on the initiative of Comrade Stalin, had already adopted a most important decision to enlarge the old Soviet farms and to organise large new Soviet farms in districts where there was free land not cultivated by the peasants. These farms were to yield from thirteen to eighteen million centners of marketable grain within three or four years.

"The new Soviet farms should be organised on such a plan as may enable them in the future to become industrial centres using the agricultural products of the surrounding agricultural population as raw material and to become powerful levers for the socialisation of peasant farming (as was the case with the Shevchenko Soviet Farm in the Ukraine)."

The Plenum emphasised that:

"The development of socialist forms of economy on the basis of the N.E.P. leads not to the weakening but to the strengthening of the resistance of capitalist elements. Simultaneously, however, there

* *Ibid.*

is an even greater strengthening of the Soviet power and of its mass basis, though this does not preclude certain vacillations on the part of some sections of the population in case of an aggravation of the general situation. The basic class policy of the Party in the country-side should be 'the policy of relying on the poor peasant, of a firm alliance with the middle peasant and of an offensive against the kulak' (Fifteenth Congress). While the development of the socialist forms leads to the intensified resistance of the capitalist elements, the errors in planning and the shortcomings of our policy raise the degree of this resistance, enabling these elements to take in tow the wavering sections of the urban and rural petty bourgeoisie."*

Among the shortcomings referred to were the violation of revolutionary law, arbitrary administrative action, etc. These shortcomings, along with the errors in planning, were secondary but not unimportant causes of our grain difficulties. The elimination of these shortcomings, the elimination of the errors in planning and a certain increase in grain prices, which varied according to the districts and the kind of grain, were of great significance for the success of the struggle for grain.

The Shakhty Case and the Problem of Cadres

Even prior to the July Plenum, the Fifteenth Congress had already noted the fact that the class struggle in the country was growing more acute. The Party could feel the resistance of the kulak with especial force during the grain collections campaign. The discovery of a wrecking organisation at Shakhty, in the Donets coal basin, and later of a number of similar organisations, brought to light "new forms and new methods of the struggle of bourgeois counter-revolution against the prole-tarian state, against socialist industrialisation." The bourgeois counter-revolution, in the form of kulakdom, not only made every effort to throttle the Soviet power by the bony hand of famine; it also succeeded in obtaining a firm foothold in the Soviet state and economic apparatus, organising a widespread system for the undermining of socialist construction from within by means of wrecking. It was no accident that the Fifteenth Congress, on the basis of the report of the Central Control Com-mission, urgently raised the question of a struggle against

*Resolution of the Plenum of the Central Committee on the policy of grain collections in connection with the general economic situation, July 1928.

bureaucracy in the state apparatus, of effecting improvements and economies in this apparatus, of getting the broad proletarian and toiling masses to play a more active part in its work, of promoting new cadres from the ranks of the working class. The masterful insight of Lenin was again and again most strikingly revealed; in his report at the Eleventh Party Congress and in his articles regarding the reorganisation of the Workers' and Peasants' Inspection, he mercilessly exposed all the ulcers of bureaucracy and the distortions of the class line in our apparatus, all the dangers for the proletarian state arising from the presence of alien and hostile elements in this apparatus. The Party drew the political conclusions from the Shakhty case at the April and July Plenums of the Central Committee. These conclusions called not only for increased vigilance against the counter-revolutionary activities of hostile forces, for an intensified struggle against manifestations of bureaucracy both in the state and economic apparatus and also in individual trade unions and even in Party organisations, and for an even more resolute enforcement of the slogan of self-criticism, to which Comrade Stalin devoted so much attention in his report at the Fifteenth Party Congress. They also sharply raised the question of training new cadres of Soviet specialists, above all in the economic field.

"The essence and significance of the Shakhty case," said Comrade Stalin in his report to the active members of the Leningrad organisation on the July Plenum, "consists in the fact that we proved to be almost unarmed and entirely backward, monstrously backward, in the matter of providing our industry with a certain minimum of experts loyal to the cause of the working class. The lesson of the Shakhty case is that we must accelerate the pace of educating and creating a new technical intelligentsia from among members of the working class, devoted to the cause of socialism and capable of technically guiding our socialist industry."*

The Party in the Struggle Against the Right Deviation As the Main Danger

The Fifteenth Congress revealed the complexity of the tasks which confronted the Party under the conditions of the recon-struction period—tasks which called for pushing forward the industrialisation of the country (at a rate which would permit

* Ibid.

us to overtake and outstrip the advanced capitalist countries in the shortest historical time-limit) under conditions of growing external dangers and intensified resistance of the capitalist enemies within the country, which called for carrying out the work of the socialist reconstruction of agriculture, of rallying the working masses even more closely around the Party, of mobilising the tremendous reserves of the proletarian and semi-proletarian section of the rural population, of strengthening the alliance with the middle peasant and suppressing with an iron hand the resistance of the nepman and kulak. Even at the time of the Fifteenth Congress it had already become perfectly clear that the Party would only be able to cope with all the new and complex tasks which had arisen with the beginning of the reconstruction period by reorganising the whole system of its work, by strengthening all the transmission belts linking it up with the worker and peasant masses, by raising the class fighting capacity and solidarity of its ranks, by a determined struggle against opportunism on two fronts.

This was why Comrade Stalin, in his political report to the Fifteenth Congress, emphatically warned some of the comrades who failed to perceive all the dangers and difficulties which were awaiting the Party, who were inclined to relax and to rest on their laurels after the rout of the Trotskyist opposition, who were inclined to believe that the further construction of socialism would take place "of its own accord."

Not without reason did Comrade Stalin, at the Fifteenth Congress, speak of

"The desire of a number of our comrades to drift quietly and smoothly with the current, without perspectives, without looking at the future, so that a holiday and festive mood should prevail around us, that we should have celebration meetings every day, nay, that there should be applause everywhere and that each one of us should have his turn as an honorary member of all kinds of presidiums.

"This unrestrained desire to see everywhere a holiday mood, this urge towards decorations, towards all kinds of jubilees, useful or useless, this desire to drift at random without looking whither the current is carrying us—all this constitutes the essence of the third defect of our Party practice, the basis of our shortcomings in our Party life. . . . Have you seen rowers who row hard, in the sweat of their brow, but who do not see whither the current is carrying them? I have seen such rowers on the Yenisei. They are honest, tireless rowers. But the trouble with them is that they do not see, nor do they wish to see, that a wave may throw them on the rocks, where destruction threatens them. This also happens with some of our comrades. They row hard, without resting for a moment, they drift along smoothly, surrendering to the current, but whither they are being carried they not only do not know, but do not even want to know. Work without perspectives, work without rudder and sails —this is what the desire to drift with the current at all costs leads to. And the results? The results are clear: at first they go mildewed, then they go a little gray, then they are sucked into the slime of philistinism and then they become ordinary philistines themselves. This is indeed the road of real degeneration "

In speaking thus, Comrade Stalin had in mind certain moods of complacency and self-satisfaction which were to be met with among opportunist elements in our Party, particularly among the then leaders of the Moscow organisation (*e.g.*, Uglanov), and which had become noticeable by the time of the Fifteenth Congress. Such moods could not, of course, serve as a weapon to fight difficulties. They were very dangerous symptoms of degeneration, of a refusal to fight difficulties, of capitulating to them, of succumbing to the influence of the class enemy.

The slogan of intensifying the offensive against the capitalist enemies, which was put forward by the Fifteenth Congress, the slogan of actively fighting to overcome difficulties—slogans which the Party was most determinedly carrying into effect—could not be to the taste of such elements. This was clearly revealed when, owing to the difficult situation which arose with regard to the grain collections immediately after the Fifteenth Congress, it became necessary to mobilise the entire Party organisation.

The Right opportunist elements in the higher ranks of the Party and Soviet organisations adopted a definitely hostile attitude to the emergency measures, believing that it would have been better to raise the prices on grain at the expense of slowing down the tempo of industrialisation.

The April Plenum was obliged to point out that:

"Individual elements of the Party, particularly in the countryside, did not prove capable of giving an adequate rebuff to the kulaks and thus rousing the poor and middle peasant strata of the rural population to an active role."

The April Plenum also pointed out that, in order to secure the success of the grain collections, the Party had to carry out a verification of the Soviet, co-operative and Party apparatus in the grain collection districts, purging them "of the clearly degenerated elements, who do not see classes in the country and who do not want 'to quarrel' with the kulak." This was the case not only in the countryside. The resolution of the April Plenum regarding the Shakhty case pointed out that, in individual sectors and in individual branches, there was also to be observed "a blunting of the Communist vigilance and revolutionary intuition of our workers with regard to class enemies" in the field of economic control and in the work of the trade unions. The political conclusions drawn from the Shakhty case spoke of the need of radical changes in the whole system of work of the economic, trade union and other organisations and of radical measures in the field of training specialists. The Right opportunist elements were of the opinion that everything could remain as of old; they were ready to continue drifting with the current. Their attitude of "dragging at the tail" of events was essentially an attitude of capitulation, making them virtually agents of the class enemy.

The threat to the *smychka* with the middle peasantry, which became apparent in the course of the grain collections, they attempted to interpret as an actual rupture, for the obviation of which the Rights proposed to introduce higher prices on grain and freedom of speculation, striving to avoid a battle with the kulak. Their attitude was clearly taking the form of an open retreat from the line of the Fifteenth Congress, the form of an open opportunist, kulak deviation. The Fifteenth Congress, and before it the Fifteenth Conference pointed out the fact that the class struggle in the country was growing more acute. This accentuation of the class struggle was a result of the intensified offensive of socialism on the capitalist elements and of the intensified resistance of the latter.

The Right opportunists considered this fundamental thesis of the Party to be incorrect. They had forgotten about the last decisive battle with capitalism (arising out of petty-peasant economy), of which Lenin had spoken as long ago as the Eleventh Congress. To this thesis of Lenin's Bukharin opposed

23*

his theory of the dying out of the class struggle under the Soviet system. If the facts testified eloquently against this theory of Bukharin's these facts signified, in his opinion, that our policy was incorrect, that we should not have irritated the kulak for nothing and that we were driving him to "excesses." This was how Bukharin argued.

The line of the Rights—a policy of passivity in the struggle against the kulak and the wrecker—was turning into a very live and active policy of making concessions to the kulak and refusing to carry out the line laid down by the Fifteenth Congress, giving up the idea of industrialisation or at least retarding its tempo to the utmost. The Right opportunists sought a solution for the food difficulties along the line of concessions to the kulak, describing the measures outlined by the Party at the Fifteenth Congress for the socialist reconstruction of agriculture (collective and Soviet farm construction) as "music of the future," for the present, at best, an expensive plaything.

This attitude was expressed with especial clarity in a letter written by Comrade Frumkin on the eve of the July Plenum, in which the Party line in the countryside since the Fifteenth Congress was subjected to opportunist criticism.

Frumkin put forward the slogan—"Back to the Fourteenth Congress"—which in his mouth could mean nothing but a revision of the policy adopted by the Fifteenth Congress for the socialist reconstruction of agriculture and for an intensified offensive against the kulak.

Owing to the attitude which found its expression in the letter of Comrade Frumkin, the Plenum of the Central Committee in July 1928 had to call attention once again to the influence of alien ideology on certain sections of the Party.

"The Party must take as the basis of its policy a resolute struggle both against those elements who represent the expression of bourgeois tendencies in our country and who try to evade the decision of the Fifteenth Congress 'to further develop the offensive against the kulak,' and also against those elements who strive to lend emergency and temporary measures the character of a lasting and prolonged policy, thereby endangering the cause of the alliance of the workers with the main mass of the peasantry."

By the summer of 1928, the Party was confronted even more clearly than at the time of the Fifteenth Congress with the need of decisive measures · in the domain of agriculture for the speediest solution of the grain problem. Petty, semi-self-sufficing peasant farming, the scale of which continued to decrease with every year, with the backward primitive technique in which even the use of a horse was not always profitable, could no longer continue as the principal grain base of the rapidly developing country.

"The creation of large-scale agricultural production, which constitutes the decisive method for overcoming the backwardness of agricultural labour, can be achieved either by creating large-scale kulak-capitalist farms or by creating large-scale socialist farms (Soviet farms, and amalgamations of small farms into collective farms, communes, artels, associations, etc.). Whether the peasant masses remain faithful to the alliance with the working class or permit the bourgeoisie to disunite them from the workers, depends upon which path the development of agriculture will take—the socialist path or the capitalist. And in accordance with this, who will direct *the development of the economy—the kulak or the socialist state*. The capitalist path of development of the countryside signifies, as is shown by the example of the capitalist countries, the creation of a powerful capitalist class (kulaks) in the countryside which, by mercilessly exploiting millions of small and very small farms, by ruining them and absorbing them, concentrates in its hands the bulk of the means of production and the bulk of the agricultural produce.

"To this capitalist path of creating *individual* large-scale farming, the Soviet power opposes the proletarian method of creating large-scale *socialised* farming, through co-operation in production, through collectivisation, which enable the small and very small farms, with the assistance and under the guidance of the Soviet power, to expand on the basis of collective labour and to rise to a higher level of technique and culture."

This passage from the resolution adopted a year later by the Sixteenth Conference of the Party on the methods of developing agriculture clearly outlines the perspectives for the further development of agriculture in the U.S.S.R. as they presented. themselves to the Party in the spring and summer of 1928.

To reject the idea of firmly carrying out the line laid down by the Fifteenth Conference for the socialist reconstruction of agriculture and the widespread development of Soviet and collective farms, meant in fact to rely upon the kulak, to take the capitalist path of agricultural development in the U.S.S.R. This was the essence of the Right opportunist deviation within the C.P.S.U., which began to crystallise in 1928 into a faction opposed to the Central Committee and to the whole Party.

At the Plenum of the Moscow Committee and the Moscow Control Commission in October 1928, Comrade Stalin characterised the tendencies of the Right deviation as follows:

"Under conditions of Soviet development, when capitalism has already been overthrown but has not yet been torn out by the roots, the Right deviation in communism represents an inclination, a tendency not yet formulated, it is true, and perhaps not even consciously realised, but nevertheless a tendency, on the part of a section of Communists, to depart from the general line of our Party toward the ideology of the bourgeoisie. When certain groups of our Communists strive to drag the Party back from the decisions of the Fifteenth Congress and deny the necessity for an offensive against the capitalist elements in the villages; or demand a contraction of our industry, in the belief that the present rate of development is ruinous for the country; or deny the expediency of subsidising the collective and Soviet farms, in the belief that it is throwing money to the winds; or deny the expediency of fighting against bureaucracy on the basis of self-criticism, in the belief that self-criticism shatters our organisation; or demand a slackening of the monopoly of foreign trade, etc., etc., it means that there are people in the ranks of our Party who are striving, perhaps without themselves realising it, to adapt our socialist development to the tastes and demands of the 'Soviet' bourgeoisie. The triumph of the Right deviation in our Party would mean that the capitalist elements in our country would be tremendously strengthened. And what would be the result of the strengthening of the capitalist elements in the country? The result would be that the proletarian dictatorship would be weakened and the chances of the restoration of capitalism would be increased. Hence, the triumph of the Right deviation in our Party would give rise to the conditions which are necessary for the *restoration* of capitalism in our country."*

The Comintern in the Struggle Against the Right Deviation As the Main Danger

During 1925-26, the principal sections of the Comintern had been carrying on a great struggle against the Trotskyist deviation, which was lapsing into the position of "Left" Menshevism. Its essence consisted in denying or obscuring the fact of the partial stabilisation of capitalism, in virtually refusing to work in the broad labour organisations controlled by the reformists, in refus-

* Stalin, *Leninism,* Vol. II.

ing to fight for winning over the Social-Democratic workers to Communism, in a tendency towards *Putschism*. Besides this, the Comintern did not cease to fight the Right opportunist tendencies in the Communist Parties—tendencies which were manifested in an overestimation of the stabilisation of capitalism, in conciliatory tendencies towards the bourgeoisie and Social-Democracy, particularly towards the trade union bureaucrats of the Amsterdam International. In May 1926, the leadership of the Communist Party of Poland committed a grave Right error by supporting Pilsudski at the moment when he was carrying through the fascist *coup*. Less crass but sufficiently serious Right errors were committed by the Communist Party of Great Britain during the general strike. And a number of gross opportunist errors were committed by the Chinese Communist Party in 1927.

As we have already noted in the preceding chapter, these errors were manifested in the fact that the Chinese Communist Party, in spite of the repeated directives of the E.C.C.I., did not take timely measures to develop the workers' and peasants' movement in the country, adapting itself in opportunist fashion to the moods of the Kuomintang bourgeoisie and shrinking from sharp clashes with it, and in the fact that the Party did not prepare itself for the desertion of this bourgeoisie to the side of counter-revolution and imperialism, that it was taken completely by surprise by this desertion of the bourgeoisie.

By the beginning of 1928, Trotskyism had been utterly smashed and exposed, not only in the C.P.S.U. but also in the principal sections of the Comintern. At the same time, certain new factors became apparent in the economic and political situation of the chief capitalist countries, which were pointed out by Comrade Stalin in the political report of the Central Committee to the Fifteenth Congress. The contradictions of capitalist stabilisation were growing more acute; Social-Democracy was revealed as playing an even more active role in supporting the capitalist regime, particularly was the role of the trade union apparatus revealed in sabotaging and disorganising the struggle of the workers for the most elementary economic demands; the war danger was increasing, particularly the danger of an attack on the Soviet Union.

This change in the general economic and political situation

of the capitalist countries urgently demanded of the Communist
Parties greater revolutionary activity both against the bourgeoisie
and against Social-Democracy. It was plainly necessary to intensify the struggle against Social-Democracy on account of the
active role the latter was playing in sabotaging the struggle of
the working class against the offensive of capital and in the
preparations for a war against the U.S.S.R.

Formerly the Amsterdam trade unions had opposed the
struggle for proletarian dictatorship by the counter-proposal of
some partial reforms or other, not rejecting strikes and other
methods of exerting pressure on the bourgeoisie for the realisation of these reforms. Now, however, the situation had radically
changed. The leaders of the Amsterdam trade unions systematically rejected each and every method of struggle against the
bourgeoisie even for reforms, and if the struggle broke out in
spite of them, they acted as strike-breakers. They argued as
follows. Capitalist rationalisation offers the employers great
opportunities to replace workers with machines, thus increasing
the army of unemployed. Under such conditions strike struggles
could not, in their opinion, have any chance of success.

There remained only the road of conciliation with the capitalists, the transformation of the trade unions into auxiliary organisations for the aid of the capitalists, which, in return for insignificant concessions to the upper stratum of the working class,
would enable the capitalists more easily to exploit without mercy
the masses of the workers. Hilferding, Naphtali and other theoreticians of Social-Democracy which had now become social-
fascism, christened this with the euphonious name of industrial
democracy. The Ninth Enlarged Plenum of the Comintern, which
met in February 1928, while summing up the results of the
struggle against Trotskyism on an international scale and declaring that Trotskyist ideology was incompatible with membership
of the Comintern, outlined a number of measures for the intensification of the struggle against Social-Democracy and declared
that for the ensuing period the Right opportunist danger was
the main danger in the Comintern. The intensification of the
struggle against Social-Democracy also denoted a blow against
those Right opportunist elements within the Communist Parties
who were lapsing into Social-Democracy.

It was natural that the Fourth Congress of the Profintern, which met in March 1929, should have adopted decisions on the tactics of the Communists in the trade union movement. The gist of these decisions was the rejection of the united front with the trade union leaders, the nomination of independent candidates in the elections to the factory committees (in opposition to the candidates of the Amsterdam trade union bureaucrats), the formation of independent strike committees to lead the economic struggles in spite of the Amsterdam trade union bureaucrats who sabotaged these struggles and the organisation, if need be, of independent trade unions, which did not at all mean abandoning activities in the reformist trade unions, but, on the contrary, implied an intensification of these activities.

The Sixth Congress of the Comintern

These same questions also confronted the Sixth Congress of the Comintern (in July and August 1928), which adopted a draft programme of the Comintern. The draft programme contained a detailed analysis of the situation in the capitalist and colonial countries, taking into account the new factors in this situation, and outlined the tactics of the Comintern accordingly. Comrade Stalin, in his report to the active members of the Leningrad organisation of the July Plenum of the Central Committee, characterised as follows the draft programme adopted by the Congress:

"1) The draft provides a programme not for any one or other of the national Communist Parties, but for all the Communist Parties together, embracing what is general and basic for all of them. Hence its character as a programme of principles and theory.

"2) Formerly it was the practice to provide a programme for the 'civilised' nations. Unlike this [Comrade Stalin is referring to the programmes of the Second International.—N.P.], the draft programme takes in all the nations of the world, white and black, the home countries and the colonial countries. Hence the all-embracing, profoundly international character of the draft programme.

"3) The draft takes as its starting point not the capitalism of one or another country, or part of the world, but the whole world system of capitalism, and contrasts it with a world system of communist economy. For this reason it differs from all previous programmes.

"4) The draft programme bases itself on the uneven development of world capitalism and deduces therefrom the possibility of the victory of socialism in separate countries, thence leading to the prospect of the creation of two parallel centres of gravity—a world centre of capitalism and a world centre of socialism—struggling between themselves for the conquest of the world.

"5) In place of the slogan of a United States of Europe the draft puts forward the slogan of a Federation of Soviet Republics of advanced countries and colonies which have broken away, or are breaking away, from the imperialist economic system, and which in its struggle for world socialism confronts the world capitalist system.

"6) The draft lays stress on the fact that Social-Democracy forms the main support of capitalism within the working class and the chief enemy of communism, considering that all other tendencies within the working class (anarchism, anarcho-syndicalism, guild social-ism, etc.) are, in actual fact, merely varieties of Social-Democracy.

"7) The draft attaches prime importance to the consolidation of the Communist Parties both in the West and in the East as a primary condition for securing the hegemony of the proletariat, and subsequently the dictatorship of the proletariat."*

The question of the programme had already been on the agenda of the two preceding Congresses of the Comintern but each time it was postponed.

"For the first time during the ten years of its existence," wrote Comrade Manuilsky, "after the victory of the proletarian dictatorship in the U.S.S.R., after a number of revolutionary movements in Central Europe, after the experience of the class battles which have occurred in the course of this decade, the Comintern has received a most important document, summing up and drawing the balance of the accumulated experience—a document which formulates scientifically the main problems of the Communist movement and the main ways of solving them. It is sufficient to read the programme to perceive the clarity and preciseness of the Stalinist formulations in the char-acterisation of the epoch of monopolist capitalism, on the question of the unevenness of development of world capitalism, on the question of the possibility of a victory of socialism in individual countries, on the question of the slogan of the federation of the Soviet Republics which have dropped out and are dropping out, as a result of revolution, from the imperialist system of economy, etc. As a result of the theoretical thoroughness with which Comrade Stalin has edited the programme of the Communist International, it is doubtful whether anyone of those who depart from the Marxist-Leninist position would succeed in seizing upon any 'vague' formula-tion in the programme in order to palm off his incorrect views in the sections of the Comintern. Thus, for instance, Bukharin's theory

*Stalin, *Leninism*, Vol. II.

of 'organised capitalism,' stands in clear contradiction to the thesis on the question of the role of monopolies and of competition given in the programme."

The resolution passed by the Congress on the tasks of the Comintern and its sections pointed out, first and foremost, the commencement of a third period in the development of post-war capitalism. The first period was characterised by an acute economic and political crisis, the second period by the partial stabilisation of capitalism. What was the distinguishing characteristic of the third period? Although capitalist stabilisation still continued, although production in the principal capitalist countries even exceeded the pre-war levels, nevertheless at the same time *all the external and internal contradictions of capitalist stabilisation were increasing, while the class struggle was growing more acute and the danger of war was maturing.*

"This third period renders inevitable a new phase of imperialist wars between the imperialist nations, of wars waged by them against the U.S.S.R., of wars of national liberation against imperialism and imperialist intervention, of gigantic class battles. Accentuating all international contradictions, accentuating the internal contradictions in the capitalist countries, unleashing colonial movements, this period inevitably leads, through the further development of the contradictions of capitalist stabilisation, to the further shattering of capitalist stabilisation."*

The masses were becoming revolutionised, were turning Leftward and beginning to take the offensive against capitalist stabilisation.

This atmosphere of the revolutionisation and Leftward trend of the masses made it necessary for the Communist Parties to launch a most determined offensive against Social-Democracy, in view of which the resolution pointed out the particular danger, for the Communist Parties, of the "Left" Social-Democrats and the need of taking all measures to expose them.

The function of the "Left" Social-Democrats may be summarised as that of "intercepting" the discontent of the masses, leading them astray by false "revolutionary" phrases and thereby restraining them from going over to Communism.

While endorsing the main political thesis of the Ninth Enlarged

---

* From the resolution of the Sixth Congress of the Comintern on the report of the E.C.C.I.

Plenum of the E.C.C.I. which spoke of the Right danger in the sections of the Comintern as the main danger, the resolution focused the attention of the Comintern sections not only on the Right danger but also on the danger of a conciliatory attitude towards it.*

The resolution, finally, emphasised that in view of the fact that Communist Parties were entering upon a phase of particularly sharp struggle against the bourgeoisie and Social-Democracy, it was essential to strengthen the ideological and organisational solidarity and discipline within these parties.

The analysis of the general situation of world capitalism given by the Sixth Congress of the Comintern had been brilliantly corroborated by the subsequent course of events. Its observations about the shattering of the partial stabilisation of capitalism were fully borne out. Later this was followed by the end of capitalist stabilisation.

The Sixth Congress of the Comintern confronted the principal sections of the Comintern with the question of a struggle not only against the Right danger as the main danger, but also against a conciliatory attitude towards it.

Comrade Stalin, in his speech at the October Plenum of the Moscow Committee and Moscow Control Commission of the C.P.S.U., gave the following comparative characterisation of the Right deviation from Communism under capitalist conditions, in the autumn of 1928:

"*Under capitalist conditions*, the Right deviation in Communism represents a tendency, an inclination, not yet formulated, it is true, and perhaps not even consciously realised, but nevertheless a tendency, on the part of a section of Communists to depart from the revolutionary line of Marxism in the direction of Social-Democracy. When certain groups of Communists deny the expediency of the slogan 'class against class' in election campaigns (France), or are opposed to the Communist Party putting up independent candidates (Great Britain), or are disinclined to make a sharp issue of the fight against 'Left' Social-Democracy (Germany), etc., etc., it means that there are individuals in the Communist Party who are striving to adapt Communism to Social-Democracy. The triumph of the Right deviation within the Communist Parties in capitalist countries would mean the ideological collapse of

---

* At the Fifteenth Congress of the C.P.S.U., Comrade Bukharin, in his concluding remarks on the report on the Comintern, tried to identify the Right danger with Trotskyism.

the Communist Parties, and a tremendous accession of strength to Social-Democracy. And what does an accession of strength to Social-Democracy mean? It means the consolidation and strengthening of capitalism, for Social-Democracy is the main bulwark of capitalism among the working class. Hence, the triumph of the Right deviation in the Communist Parties in capitalist countries favours the conditions necessary for the *preservation* of capitalism."*

The C.P.S.U. and the Comintern Expose the Anti-Leninist Platform of the Rights and Conciliators and Suppress their Factional Struggle

We must note that the key points in the resolution of the Sixth Congress on the tasks of the Comintern were not contained in the original draft of the resolution, but were inserted only after this draft had been discussed in the various delegations, particularly in the delegation of the C.P.S.U. In the original draft, which was drawn by Comrade Bukharin, the third period was characterised as a period of the further strengthening of capitalist stabilisation, as a period of the reconstruction of capitalism on a new technical base. In his report as well as in his closing remarks, Comrade Bukharin, moreover, expressed the opinion that a revolutionary situation was maturing, not as a result of the accentuation of the antagonism between capitalism and the working class, but as a result of the accentuation of the (external) contradictions between the capitalist countries, which would lead to revolution through war.

This tendency to obscure the internal contradictions of capitalism, not only the primary contradictions between capitalism and the working class but also the contradictions between capitalist groups (and individual capitalists) within the individual countries, flowed from the theory of "organised capitalism," elements of which were also contained in the previous writings of Bukharin.

It should be noted that Bukharin emphasised the possibility of an attack on the U.S.S.R. by the imperialists. However, this emphasis of Bukharin's was not so much a result of an analysis of the situation in the capitalist countries as, rather, of a desire to intimidate the Party and the Central Committee and to induce

* Stalin, *Leninism*, Vol. II.

them to make concessions to the kulaks, for otherwise, as he presumed, the peasantry would not support the Soviet government in time of war.

The German Rights and conciliators (the Ewart group) and the majority of the American delegation (the Lovestone-Pepper group), not to mention individual members of the Congress (Humbert-Droz, Serrat), were inclined to take Bukharin's standpoint at the Sixth Congress. Bukharin, however, did not absolutely insist upon the inclusion of his erroneous views in the programme of the Comintern and in the resolution on the report of the E.C.C.I. Thanks to this, both documents were adopted by the Congress unanimously.

Thus, the political essence of the Right deviation in the C.P.S.U. and in the Comintern consisted in collaboration with the bourgeoisie either through Social-Democracy (in the West) or directly (in the U.S.S.R.). The logical consequence in the West of such collaboration would have been the end of the independent existence of the Communist Parties, their dissolution in "Left" Social-Democracy, while in the U.S.S.R., it would have meant the realisation of bourgeois restoration.

The decision of the Sixth Congress of the Comintern regarding the necessity of focusing attention on the struggle against the Right danger, as the main danger, and against conciliating tendencies proved to have been most timely and opportune. Even before the delegates of the adjourned Congress could reach their respective countries, the Rights and conciliators launched an attack against the line of the Comintern. This attack assumed particularly widespread and bitter forms in Germany, where the temporary success of the partial stabilisation of capitalism had created a certain favourable environment for Right and conciliationist tendencies among certain sections of the Party. Following an unsuccessful attempt to remove the Party leadership, in particular Comrade Thälmann, by taking advantage of the so-called Wittorf * case—an attempt which utterly failed thanks to the resolute intervention of the Comintern, and despite the fact that Comrade Bukharin adopted a definitely tolerant position in this matter, tantamount to abetting the change of leadership and

---

* Wittorf: former secretary of the Hamburg Party organisation who embezzled Party funds.—*N.P.*

helping to place it in the hands of the Rights and conciliators—
the Rights commenced an open factional struggle against the
Central Committee. This struggle was headed by Brandler and
Thalheimer, who returned to Germany from the U.S.S.R. contrary
to the instructions of the Party. In defiance of the decision of the
Sixth Congress, the Rights contended that capitalist stabilisation
was further consolidating itself, thus following in the footsteps of
Bukharin on this question and lapsing into the theory of "organised capitalism." Instead of an intensified struggle against the
Left wing of Social-Democracy, they returned to the slogan of a
coalition with Left Social-Democracy (i.e., to the tactic of Brandler which had proved its bankruptcy at the end of 1923) and this
at a time when Social-Democracy had degenerated inot social-
fascism. Just as resolutely, the Rights rejected the trade union
tactic of an independent economic struggle, which they sought to
refute by trotting out the old hackneyed Social-Democratic arguments about a split in the trade union movement. The Rights
created their own factional press in order to defend their virtually
Social-Democratic views under the mask of Communism.*

* As was pointed out in the resolution adopted somewhat later by the
Central Committee of the Communist Party of Germany, the Right liquida-
tionists not only adopted a policy of organised factionalism, but broke completely with the ideological principles of Communism:
    "1) By rejecting the decisions of the Fifth and Sixth Congresses of the
Comintern and the decisions of the Fourth Congress of the Profintern and
opportunistically distorting the decisions of the Third Congress of the
Comintern;
    "2) By rejecting the strategic and tactical part of the programme of the
Comintern;
    "3) By rejecting the tactical turn decided upon by the Sixth Congress for
all sections of the Comintern;
    "4) By taking a stand against the democratic centralism and revolution-
ary internationalism of the world Party of Communism and demanding
autonomy for individual sections of the Comintern;
    "5) By rejecting the structure of the Party organisation on the factory
basis and proposing to return to Social-Democratic organisational methods;
    "6) By stubbornly insisting (in spite of the repeated decisions of the
Comintern) that a worker and peasant government as a transitional form
from the bourgeois to the proletarian state must be a coalition government
of Social-Democrats and Communists;
    "7) By demanding, under the bourgeois state, the universal arming of
the people in the form of a bourgeois militia;
    "8) By putting forward the demands of the transition period (workers'
control, etc.) in a non-revolutionary situation;
    "9) By taking a stand against revolutionary tactics in the trade unions and
against the Bolshevik strategy in the economic struggle."

The campaign of the Rights against the Comintern and the Central Committee of the Communist Party of Germany was supported by the conciliators. While formally declaring themselves in agreement with the decisions of the Sixth Congress of the Comintern, which they interpreted in an opportunist fashion (in the spirit of Bukharin's report and closing remarks, particularly on the question of capitalist stabilisation), the conciliators not only did not defend these decisions against the Rights but attacked the Central Committee with their full force, accusing the latter of violating inner-Party democracy (and this at a time when the Rights were conducting an open factional struggle against the Central Committee, establishing their own press, etc.).

However, the rank and file of the C.P.G. proved sufficiently mature politically to give a most decisive rebuff both to the Rights and to the conciliators as well. The leaders of the Right schismatics were expelled from the Party and found themselves in the position of generals without an army, while the conciliators were left in the same position of isolation within the Party. The Party rallied around the Central Committee on the basis of the Comintern line. The tactic of independent economic struggles was put into effect and produced positive results. After the Sixth Congress the Party made a considerable step forward towards winning over the majority of the working class of Germany, particularly in the large enterprises, which heretofore had been a bulwark of Social-Democracy.*

Even more insignificant in its results was the attempt of the Right and conciliationist elements to change the Party line and the Party leadership of the C.P.S.U. To be sure, they made use of all the experience gained by the Trotskyists in their struggle against the Party, including the patching together of *blocs* without any basis of principle. After the unanimous adoption of the resolution of the July Plenum, Comrade Bukharin approached Kamenev, who had just been re-admitted into the Party, and proposed to him (and through him to the other erstwhile, and

* Even after the expulsion of the Right elements from the German Party, the Right liquidationist elements of the Czecho-Slovakian Party, led by Hais, began an active struggle against the Comintern and attempted to get control of the leading organs of the Red trade unions. However, they found themselves isolated from the overwhelming majority of the Party and of the rank and file of the Red trade unions.

not merely "erstwhile," Trotskyists) to form a *bloc* against the Central Committee. These negotiations of Bukharin with Kamenev immediately became known to the Trotskyists, with whom Kamenev maintained contact. It was thus once again made clear to the Party that the Rights themselves were trying to form a *bloc* with the Trotskyists and semi-Trotskyist elements, that in their struggle against the Party they were ready to follow in the footsteps of the Trotskyists.

Instead of the slogan of a struggle on two fronts against the Right danger as the main danger and against the conciliationist tendencies—the slogan which had been put forward by the Sixth Congress of the Comintern—the Uglanov leadership of the Moscow Committee brought out the slogan of a struggle against an alleged recrudescence of Trotskyism (while maintaining complete silence regarding the Right danger). What they meant by this was not real Trotskyism—with which Bukharin, as his overtures to Kamenev proved, was ready to come to terms—but the line pursued by the Party since the Fifteenth Congress.

Following the example of the Trotskyists, the backstairs intriguers concentrated their main fire on the general secretary of the Central Committee, Comrade Stalin. Uglanov and others tried to prove that the leadership of the Central Committee was guilty of the commodity scarcity and the food difficulties, to overcome which the Central Committee had mobilised the whole Party. As against the line which was being carried out by the Party, they proposed concessions to the kulak and the private trader. Instead of "tying up" capital in heavy industry, they proposed to develop light industry alone, thus perpetuating the economic dependence of the U.S.S.R. on the surrounding capitalist countries.

In commencing the struggle against the line and leadership of the Central Committee in the Moscow organisation of the Party, the Uglanov leadership of the Moscow committee counted upon the support not only of the rank and file of the Moscow organisation but of other organisations as well. It was just at this time that Comrade Bukharin, in an article which he published in *Pravda* without consulting the Politburo, tried to provide an ideological basis for the campaign against the Central Committee which was being launched in Moscow. In this article, entitled *Notes of an Economist,* he raised the question of the alleged degra-

dation of agriculture which was going on in our country, at the
same time arguing strongly against the tempo of industrialisation
which the Party was pursuing, particularly against the figures
for the Five-Year Plan which were proposed by the State Planning Commission. However, all the hopes of those who had inspired the campaign against the Central Committee were completely dashed. The active Party workers and the rank and file
of the Moscow organisation simply removed the too presumptuous
associates of Uglanov. The whole story of the backstairs factional activity against the Central Committee came out at the
October Plenum of the Moscow Committee. And what came out
just as clearly was the pitiful impotence of its instigators to
lure away such an organisation as the Moscow organisation from
the Leninist path of the Party. As to the other organisations of
our Party, they extended unanimous and most determined support, not to the campaign against the Central Committee and the
line of the Fifteenth Congress which had been launched by the
Rights in Moscow, but to the Moscow organisation which had
repulsed this campaign.

The main political purport of the numerous Party resolutions
adopted in all corners of the country following the occurrences of
September and October in the Moscow organisation was not to
discontinue or to weaken the struggle against the remnants of
Trotskyist ideology within the Party, and, while waging a struggle both against the "Left" and Right deviations from the Leninist
line of the Party—thus waging a struggle on two fronts, at the
present stage of the struggle, in view of the general conditions of
the international situation and the situation within the country—
to pay especially strict attention to the Right deviation and to a
conciliationist attitude towards it.

The November Plenum of the Central Committee, in considering the control figures for the forthcoming economic year and the
question of regulating the growth of the Party, drew the balance
of all these decisions, giving a political characterisation of the
Right and "Left" deviations from the line laid down at the Fifteenth Party Congress:

"A Right (openly opportunist) deviation has come to light, which
finds its expression in efforts to slow down the tempo and to hold up
the further construction of large-scale industry, in a disparaging or

negative attitude towards the collective and Soviet farms, in a tendency to underestimate and obscure the class struggle, particularly the struggle against the kulak, in a bureaucratic disregard of the needs of the masses, in underrating the importance of the struggle against bureaucracy, underestimation of the war danger, etc. . . .

"At the same time there is a revival of the Social-Democratic, anti-middle peasant, super-industrialisation tendencies (Trotskyism), which employ "Left" phrases to conceal a semi-Menshevik Right attitude and which lead in reality to the same disastrous results as the open Right deviation."

Hence the task of a struggle on two fronts, against the Right deviation as the main danger and against conciliationnism.

"The plenum declares that at the present time the main danger in the C.P.S.U. is the danger of the Right, openly opportunist deviation. This is determined both by the present social-economic situation and by the fact that in the struggle against Trotskyist ideology the Party has already won a number of decisive successes."

The Mobilisation of the Masses for a Bolshevik Overcoming of Difficulties

The Plenum of November 1928 took note of the tremendous advance made by the industry of the Soviet Union during the past year (production increasing by 22 per cent, coupled with a large increase in the capital investments). In approving the control figures for the forthcoming year, the Plenum called for an acceleration of the tempo of industrialisation.

"The development of the iron and steel industry, the machine-building industry, electric power construction, and the chemical industry, the industrialisation and mechanisation of agriculture in every way, the systematic raising of the relative importance of the production of means of production—these constitute the essential conditions for the further development of the country, including agriculture, rendering particularly necessary the increasing rationalisation of the entire productive process, the increasing application of science, the fullest utilisation of the experience and knowledge of Western Europe and America. On the basis of the widespread enlistment of the masses in the process of socialist construction, the growth of their material welfare, the systematic adoption of the seven-hour working day, on the basis of the rising quality of the work of the technical cadres and the increasing unification of science, technique, economic management and economic practice in general, the Party must resolutely and firmly continue the policy aiming at the industrialisation of the country. The international situation, the mighty technical achievements of the capitalist nations, the war danger, etc., on their part render the realisation of these tasks a matter of absolute urgency. Bearing in mind the necessity of overtaking and outstripping the capitalist countries in technical and economic respects, the Plenum of the Central Committee declares that these tasks can only be carried out by attaining an intensive tempo in the development of industry and the industrialisation of the country in general, and by the maximum mobilisation of the Party and of the masses of workers and peasants."

However, one essential condition for the fulfilment of this plan was to make sure of an adequate supply of grain, and hence the successful carrying out of the grain collections, the further lowering of the cost of production and the raising of the productivity of labour. The grain problem, which was urgently raised after the Fifteenth Congress by the July Plenum, still occupied the centre of the Party's attention at the November Plenum. The Plenum decided to continue with unflagging energy the carrying out of the measures for the socialist reconstruction of agriculture (the organisation of Soviet farms, collective farms, machine and tractor stations, supplying of machinery, contractation, etc.), while giving a further stimulus to the individual farming of the poor and middle peasants. The session of the Central Executive Committee which was held after the Plenum passed a decree which called for a 35 per cent increase in the yield of peasant farms during the next five years by means of such simple measures as the cleaning and chemical treatment of seeds, fighting pests, etc. Besides this, a number of changes were outlined in the agricultural tax with a view to relieving the middle peasant and encouraging the expansion of the cultivated area of poor and middle peasant farms.

The carrying out of the grain collections was rendered extremely difficult by the serious crop failure, the destruction first of the winter crop and later also of the spring sowings in the principal grain districts of the Soviet Union—in the Ukraine and to some extent in the Northern Caucasus and the Central Black Soil Region. The Ukraine and, to a considerable extent, the Northern Caucasus and the Central Black Soil Region were thus incapacitated, and this explains why, despite the great increase in the grain collections in the eastern districts of the Union (Siberia, the Urals, Kazakstan), the country did not get a sufficient quantity of bread. The kulaks, as in the preceding year, organised a grain strike, boycotting the state organisations which had charge of the grain collections and preferring to sell their grain on the open market at exorbitant prices. The carrying out of the plans for lowering the cost of production and raising the productivity of labour also encountered great difficulties, on the one hand owing to unsatisfactory work on the part of the economic organisations and, on the other hand, owing to an insufficiently class conscious attitude towards labour in socialist industry on the part of a certain section of the workers, particularly of those who had but recently been recruited into industry from the countryside. Considerable success was achieved in carrying out the line laid down by the Fifteenth Congress, but this success was gained at the price of overcoming tremendous difficulties and further efforts were demanded.

While developing a widespread explanatory campaign among the poor and middle peasant masses regarding the decrees for raising the yield and modifying the agricultur tax, so that a considerable increase in the country's grain supplies might already be secured in the forthcoming year, and while continuing to carry out measures for the socialist reconstruction of agriculture at the most vigorous tempo, the Party found it necessary at the same time in order to ensure economy in the distribution of supplies, to establish norms for the regulation of consumption (food cards) and on the other hand, in a number of districts in which the kulaks retained considerable grain surpluses, to apply measures of social pressure to them. Village assemblies, under the leadership of the Party organisations, began to pass decisions for imposing a definite tax on the kulaks who concealed their grain surplus and refused to turn it over to the state. Thus the poor and middle peasant masses under the leadership of the Party were mobilised against the kulaks.

Confronted with the grain strike of the kulaks, the Party not only mercilessly exposed and rejected the capitulationist proposals of the Rights to slow down the tempo of industrialisation and to import grain from abroad, but, relying on the poor and middle peasant masses, broke the resistance of the kulaks, took the grain from them and secured the successful realisation of the tempo of industrialisation decided upon by the Fifteenth Congress.

The tasks outlined for raising the productivity of labour and lowering the cost of production could not be carried out without the most broad and active participation of the working masses and labour organisations. Particularly urgent was the question of intensifying the activity of the trade unions on the front of socialist construction. The Shakhty case had revealed elements of slothfulness, indolence and inertia in the work of the trade unions. The exposure and resolute criticism of these elements met with violent resistance on the part of a certain section of the trade union apparatus, which rose up in defence of these elements who were connected with tendencies of political indifference, of tolerance towards "tailist"* tendencies, of alienation from the Party and from the whole work of socialist construction—tendencies which during the previous few years had managed to find lodgment here and there in the apparatus of the trade unions. It was absolutely necessary mercilessly to repress these tendencies and moods in order that the trade unions might be able to fulfil their function of organising the working class and solving the tremendous problems which confronted it. The November Plenum of the Central Committee, in the resolution adopted in connection with Comrade Molotov's report on the recruiting of workers and on regulating the growth of the Party, pointed out that:

"Our mass organisations (trade unions and others) often do not manifest the necessary sensitiveness to the needs and requirements of the working men and women, in many cases lag behind the growing activity of the masses and for this reason make absolutely inadequate use of their very great opportunities for mobilising the forces of the working class in order to carry out the principal tasks which confront it and to overcome the difficulties of building socialism which are connected with these tasks. The trade unions are especially behindhand in their work with the new cadres of workers who have poured into the factories and mills during the last few years, in particular in their work with the immense and ever growing mass of seasonal workers as well as agricultural workers, the bulk of whom, without passing through the school of proletarian training in the trade unions, cannot enter the ranks of the real builders of socialism. A merciless struggle against bureaucratic isolation from the workers, a struggle both against official callousness in regard to their living conditions and also against an attitude of acquiescence towards the moods of their more backward sections, and in general against the still numerous elements of bureaucracy in mass work—such, under the present conditions, is the most

* Literally. Khvostist from the Russian word khvost which means "tail." A khvostist is one who drags at the tail of events.—Ed.

important task of the trade unions 'and of other mass organisations. In enforcing the slogan of self-criticism in practice and in the real development of trade union democracy, a decisive change for the better yet remains to be secured."

During the Eighth Congress of Trade Unions the Communist fraction of the Congress, as a result of a very obstinate struggle. against the Right opportunist leadership headed by Comrade Tomsky, succeeded in obtaining a formulation of the tasks of the trade unions which corresponded to the theses of the November Plenum and to the whole line of the Party, to the Bolshevik tempo of industrialisation which was being put into effect by the Party, and to those difficulties which had yet to be overcome in the struggle against the petty-bourgeois vacillations of certain sections of the working class.

The Eighth Congress of Trade Unions marked a turning point in the work of the trade unions, the beginning of a new period in this work. The very active participation of the trade unions in the campaign in connection with the new elections to the soviets, the organisation by them of workers' brigades for the countryside, and, finally, the active part played by the trade unions in the development of socialist competition among the workers of the various plants, districts and industries for the fulfilment of the industrial and financial plan, lowering the cost of production and raising the productivity of labour—all this was the result of the resolute way in which the decisions of the Eighth Congress were put into effect.

However, in order to overcome the difficulties and to solve the positive tasks of socialist construction, it was necessary to mobilise and to reconstruct not only the trade unions, but also the whole state and economic apparatus.

As a result of the intensification of the struggle of the hostile elements against the working class and the Soviet power, the bureaucratic distortions in the work of the state apparatus were ever more clearly becoming an expression of the pressure exerted on the working class by the kulaks, the urban bourgeoisie and the bourgeois intelligentsia.

Hence the task of a particularly tense struggle against bureaucracy, of putting fresh life into the Soviets and of further and more profoundly enlisting the participation of the masses in the whole work of the Soviet state. Hence the task of determinedly purging the state apparatus of all alien and careerist elements. But a similar task had also become necessary with regard to the Party. The existing situation most emphatically demanded the strengthening of the rock-like unity and fighting capacity of the Party ranks. For this reason the November 1928 Plenum put forward the tasks of a more intensive recruitment into the ranks of the Party of industrial and agricultural workers, simultaneously with a general purging of the Party of all elements of class degeneration and decay.

The Struggle Against the Revision of Leninism, the Anti-Party Slander and the Platform of the Rights

But at the very time when the Party was exerting all its efforts to solve the problems raised by the Fifteenth Congress, seeking support in the struggle against difficulties in developing the activity and self-criticism of the toiling masses, headed by the proletariat, in strengthening the leading role of the working class in relation to the poor and middle peasantry, in strengthening and putting fresh life into the work of the state apparatus and of all mass labour organisations, at the time when the overwhelming mass of the Party was rallying together on the basis of its general line, a small group of Central Committee members headed by Comrade Bukharin, having departed from the Party line, were lapsing ever further and further in the direction of open opportunism, of capitulation and lack of faith in the forces of the working class and were with ever greater insistence seeking a way out of the difficulties in concessions to the hostile elements, in a gradual withdrawal from the position of the proletarian dictatorship. On the eve of the November Plenum, Bukharin in his *Notes of an Economist* had already proposed slowing down the tempo of industrialisation on the pretext that there were no reserves and that it was necessary to adjust the tempo to the "tight places" (instead of directing the first and main blows at these "tight places").

It was also at this time that the Rights began very vigorously spreading abroad the idea of the degradation of agriculture. This idea, borrowed as it was from the bourgeois professors of the wrecker type, open ideologists of kulakdom and private capital, and adopted by the theoretcians of Right opportunism, this idea meant nothing more nor less than an assumption of the bankruptcy of the whole Soviet policy and an attempt to give grounds for a radical change of this policy in the interests of the kulak (of course, under the guise of conciliation of the middle peasant or something of that kind).

Finally, as we have already noted, the sharpening of the class struggle was interpreted as a direct outcome of our incorrect policy. The only possible conclusion to be drawn from this was that it was necessary to retract the slogan of an offensive against the kulak, in order to give him every chance of peacefully growing into socialism, without any accentuation of the struggle. It was quite in the spirit of this political line that Comrades Bukharin and Rykov proposed to abolish the individual taxation of the kulak elements in the countryside.

At the Eighth Congress of Trade Unions, the Right opportunists added another feature to their "ideological" arsenal by defending the elements of slothfulness, bureaucracy, political indifference and alienation from the Party in our trade union movement. Practically, it was a question of keeping the trade unions from actively supporting the line of the Party. From this it was only one step to the purely Menshevik attitude of placing the trade unions in antithesis to the Party. And when the question arose of securing by practical organisational methods that turn in the work of the trade unions which was envisaged in the decisions of the Eighth Congress, the Rights did not hesitate to attempt to set the fraction of the Congress at odds with the Central Committee. They tried to mobilise the Congress fraction against the election of Comrade Kaganovich, Secretary of the Central Committee, to the Presidium of the All-Union Central Council of Trade Unions. To be sure, these attempts ended in miserable failure. However. Comrade Tomsky, on finding himself in the minority in the Congress fraction, deemed it possible to withdraw from his work as chairman of the All-Union Central Council of the Trade Unions without permission from the Central Committee. Bukharin had already withdrawn from work on the *Pravda* and in the Comintern, also without waiting for leave.

The next stage in Bukharin's lapse into a Right opportunist

position was his speech on the political legacy of Lenin. In the late nineties of the last century, Eduard Bernstein, in his notorious book *The Problems of Socialism,* made a "daring" attempt to demolish Marxism through Marx and Engels. Bernstein contended that in the latter part of their lives Marx and Engels renounced the sins of their youth, repudiated the revolutionary illusions which had characterised their youthful views and became apostles of class collaboration. Now Bukharin attempted a similar manipulation with Lenin, claiming that Lenin in his last articles never said a word about the kulak but spoke of the peasantry as a whole, recommending to the Party an extremely circumspect attitude towards the peasantry, that in reality Lenin was opposed to the building of communism in the countryside and that he advised us to effect industrialisation only in quite infinitesimal doses.

It is scarcely necessary to spend our time in proving that this was a shameless calumny on Lenin.

Scores of quotations could be cited proving that Lenin attached exceptionally great importance to the socialist reconstruction of agriculture. The following is an excerpt from his speech delivered at the Eighth Congress of Soviets, at the end of 1920:

"As long as we live in a small-peasant country there will be a more solid economic base in Russia for capitalism than for communism. That must not be forgotten. Those who closely observe the life of the countryside, in comparison with that of the town, know that we have not eradicated the roots of capitalism and that we have not undermined the base and support of our internal enemy. The latter is supported by petty economy, and there is only one way of undermining him, to transform the economic life of the country, including agriculture, on a new technical basis, a technical basis of modern, large-scale production."*

And here is what Lenin wrote in his article *On the Tax in Kind* after the introduction of the N.E.P.:

"*If* we get electrification in ten or twenty years, the individualism of the petty agriculturist and the freedom of trade exercised *by him* locally are not dangerous in the least. *If we do not get* electrification, the return to capitalism is *in any case* inevitable."

In the same pamphlet Lenin also wrote:

"If peasant production is to develop further, we must definitely secure a further transition, and this transition must inevitably consist

* Lenin, *Collected Works,* Vol. XXVI.

in the extremely unprofitable and extremely backward petty, individual-
ised peasant production gradually combining and organising into
social large-scale agricultural production. This is how Socialists always
pictured it. And that is also the view of our Communist Party."*

Bukharin, who did not shrink from the crassest distortion of
Lenin's views, wanted 'to present to the Party a distorted Lenin,
a sleek and well-groomed Lenin. Moreover, Bukharin obscured
the fact that the question of the tempo of industrialisation and of
the struggle against the kulak was more acute in 1929 than at the
end of 1922 and beginning of 1923, when the restoration of industry was only commencing and when the international situation
did not as yet dictate with such imperative practical urgency the
slogan to overtake and outstrip the capitalist countries in economic respects.

After depicting Lenin as a kind of liberal professor, it was
not difficult to put forward against the Party the accusation, fab-
ricated by the wreckers, of military feudal exploitation of the
peasantry (which was gladly seized upon by Milyukov), to repeat
the Trotskyist calumnies about the bureaucratisation of the Party,
to repeat the Brandlerite slander about the decay of the Comintern and to complain that the "regime" which had been established in the Party was stifling the freedom of criticising the Party
line—that famous "freedom of criticism" which had been lauded
by all opportunists and which had already been castigated by
Lenin in *What Is To Be Done.* ¹The Rights descended to these
counter-revolutionary Trotskyist charges against the Party and
the Party regime during the discussion in the Central Committee
of the evidence regarding the attempts which Bukharin was already making in the summer of 1928 to conclude a *bloc* with
Kamenev and through him to establish contact with the Trotskyists for a struggle against the Party and its leadership.

At the April Plenum of the Central Committee the "trio" in
the Politburo** together with Uglanov came out in opposition to
the Central Committee with a complete Right opportunist programme.

The line which the Party was putting into effect was characterised by the trio through Comrade Bukharin as a lapse into

* *Ibid.*
** This "trio" consisted of Comrades Bukharin, Rykov and Tomsky.—*Ed.*

Trotskyism. Without formally expressing himself against the Five-Year Plan, Comrade Rykov, supported by his associates, proposed to reject it in fact, offering in its stead a so-called "two-year plan" containing a programme of measures aimed at raising the individual sector of agriculture, while the Soviet and collective farms were mentioned only for appearance's sake. Bukharin defended this on the ground that in any case we could not obtain grain from the socialised sector in large quantities for another five or ten years. The trio made a violent attack on the measures of social pressure that had been brought to bear against the kulak, characterising them as "the abolition of the N.E.P." They proposed that instead of taking from the kulak the grain which the country was in need of, it should be imported from abroad. This meant curtailing the import of industrial equipment. Bukharin also proposed to normalise market relations (*i.e.*, virtually to establish complete freedom of trade) and to introduce quarterly grain prices (*i.e.*, to raise them in the spring, when the grain was left principally in the hands of the kulaks, and to lower them in the autumn, when grain was being sold by the poor and middle peasants).

Essentially what Bukharin proposed was that the Soviet government sanction a complete orgy of kulak speculation and surrender to the mercy of the kulak.

Otherwise, according to Bukharin, the country had to expect an inevitable failure of the industrial plans and of the sowing campaign.

". . . There are, in fact, *two lines,*" said Comrade Stalin. "The first line is the general line of our Party, the revolutionary, Leninist line of our Party. The second line is the line of Comrade Bukharin. That second line is not yet clearly formulated, partly because incredible confusion of ideas exists in the ranks of Comrade Bukharin's group, and secondly, because, as they carry very little weight in the Party, efforts are made to mask this second line in one way or another. But, as you see, this line nevertheless exists, and it exists as a line *distinct* from the line of the Party, as a line which *puts itself in opposition* to the general line of the Party.... That second line is fundamentally a line of *Right* deviation. . . ."

"The fight against the Right deviation is not a secondary duty of our Party. The fight against the Right deviation is one of the most decisive duties of our Party. If we, in our own ranks, in our own Party, in the political General Staff of the proletariat, which leads the movement and leads the proletariat forward—if in this General Staff we tolerated the free existence and the free functioning of the Right deviators, who are trying to demobilise the Party, to demoralise the working class, to adapt our policy to the tastes of the "Soviet" bourgeoisie, and thus give way in face of the difficulties of our construction—if we tolerated all this, what would it mean? Would it not mean that we want to put the brake on the revolution, demoralise our socialist construction, flee from difficulties, surrender the position to the capitalist elements? Does Comrade Bukharin's group understand that to refuse to fight the Right deviation is to *betray* the working class, to *betray* the revolution?"*

The Sixteenth Party Conference

The keynote of the Sixteenth All-Union Party Conference which met immediately after the Plenum was the further unfolding of the tremendous tasks of the reconstruction epoch, outlined by the Fifteenth Congress, the surmounting of all the difficulties of growth connected with the carrying out of these tasks, the development of an unusually powerful mobilisation of the forces of the Party, the working class and the toiling masses around the concrete tasks of economic construction.

On the basis of the general directives adopted by the Fifteenth Congress for the drafting of the Five-Year Plan, the Sixteenth Conference, in its resolution "On the Five-Year Plan for the Development of National Economy," outlined a concrete plan for the five coming years.

The Five-Year Plan adopted by the Conference envisaged an increase of the total industrial output by 250 per cent (the draft plan considered at the Fifteenth Congress provided for an increase of less than 200 per cent) and of the output of heavy industry by 330 per cent. In accordance with Lenin's plan, the Five-Year Plan provided for a tremendous advance in the electrification of the country. The production of electric power was to increase more than fourfold.

Production of pig-iron, from 3,500,000 tons, was to be brought up to 10,000,000 tons. Production of coal, from 35,000,000 tons, to 75,000,000 tons. In the Donets Basin the plan called for the doubling of coal production. The gross output of the machine building industry was to increase 3.5 times according to the Five-Year Plan, and that of agricultural machine building—4.5 times.

* Stalin, "The Right Deviation in the C.P.S.U." *Leninism*, Vol. II.

In addition to a general increase in agricultural production of 150 per cent, the Five-Year Plan provided for a considerable revolution in the structure of agriculture. It envisaged the collectivisation of about 20 per cent of the total number of peasant farms.

It should be noted that in the autumn of 1928 Bukharin criticised the original draft of the State Planning Commission, which contained much more modest figures than the plan adopted by the Conference, saying that it was beyond the strength of our country.

The resolution adopted by the Sixteenth Conference on the methods of raising agriculture pointed out first and foremost the indisputable fact that agriculture was advancing, in spite of all the talk of degradation. In this resolution the measures for the socialist reconstruction of agriculture were indissolubly linked up with the task of raising the level of individual poor and middle peasant farming. The resolution once more emphasised that, for the entire mass of peasant farms, the path to socialism lay through the raising of the crop yield, supplying machinery, co-operation in production and collectivisation, and the squeezing out of the kulak capitalist elements. Meanwhile the Right opportunists, led by Bukharin, were propounding the theory that the kulak would "grow into" socialism—a theory which was connected with the idea of transforming the poor and middle peasant farms into kulak farms and of forming kulak co-operative nests.

It should be noted that certain comrades who spoke against the Right deviation in defence of the general line of the Party, nevertheless manifested a certain underestimation of the kulak danger and of the sharpening of the class struggle in the country. These comrades proposed that kulaks should not be prevented from joining collective farms if they were willing to turn over their land and stock to the collective farm.

Comrade Stalin somewhat later stated at the Conference of Marxist Agrarians that it was a ridiculous question

"whether we can admit the kulak into the collective farms. Of course not," answered Comrade Stalin, "as he is a sworn enemy of the collectivisation movement."*

---

* Stalin, *Leninism*, Vol. II.

However, individual comrades at the Sixteenth Party Conference answered this question in the affirmative, failing to perceive that, at a time when the collective farm movement was developing on a broad scale, the joining of collective farms by kulaks was a definite manoeuvre in the class struggle for the purpose of disrupting the collective farms from within.

The Struggle of the Party Against Bureaucracy. The General Purging of the Party Ranks and the Enrolment of Workers

The resolutions regarding the struggle against bureaucracy and the purging of the Party pointed out that the accentuation of the class struggle was reflected in the situation in the state apparatus, where the alien class elements were striving to sabotage the line of the Party and to transform individual links of the Soviet apparatus into walls separating the Party from the toiling masses.

"The bureaucratic distortions in the state apparatus are in some cases becoming an expression of the pressure of the kulak, urban bourgeoisie and bourgeois intelligentsia on the working class."

The determined socialist offensive against the kulak and the nepman sharply raised the question of a struggle against bureaucracy and distortions of the class line in the state apparatus as well as in the work of the broad labour organisations, above all of the trade unions.

"The struggle of the Party and of the soviets against bureaucratic distortions in the state apparatus, which often screen the real nature of the proletarian state from the broad toiling masses, is becoming one of the most important forms of the class struggle."*

In these questions, too, as it is well known, the Right deviators also departed from the line of the Party, fighting against the development of self-criticism and thereby virtually acting in defence of the bureaucratic and often downright degenerate elements in the Soviet economic organs and trade unions.

The November Plenum, in the resolution on Comrade Molotov's report regarding the enrolment of workers and the task of

* From the resolution of the Sixteenth Party Conference "On the Results and Immediate Tasks of the Struggle Against Bureaucracy."

regulating the growth of the Party, after noting the tremendous growth of the Party and the strengthening of its link with the working class, had already pointed out that the further

"extensive enrolment of workers must be combined with a strict verification of the present membership of the Party and with the most resolute *purging* of its ranks of the socially alien, careerist, bureaucratised and decayed elements."

The Sixteenth Conference emphasised that

"in the period of the reconstruction of the socialist economy of the country, connected as it is with the socialist offensive against the capitalist elements in town and countryside and with an intensification of the class struggle, the Party must review its ranks with especial care, in order to strengthen resistance to the influence of the petty-bourgois environment, to render the Party more homogeneous and to increase its fighting capacity for overcoming the difficulties of the socialist reconstruction of the national economy."

The Conference instructed the Central Control Commission to carry through a general purging of the ranks of the Party and to complete it before the Sixteenth Congress.

"The purging must mercilessly expel from the ranks of the Party all elements that are alien to it, that are harmful for its success, that are indifferent to its struggle—incorrigible bureaucrats, careerists, those who are connected with and aid the class enemy, who have become severed from the Party owing to the intrusion of economic, private property interests, anti-Semites, secret adherents of religious worship— exposing the concealed Trotskyists, Myasnikovists, Sapronovists* and adherents of other anti-Party groups, and cleaning them out of the Party. But the purging must at the same time strengthen the work of the organisation, check up the work of the nucleus, create more comradely relations between the members of the Party, raise the feeling of responsibility of each one for the policy, for the fate of the whole Party, provide an incentive for raising the level of political knowledge, strengthen the struggle against bureaucracy, increase the activity of all members of the organisation, strengthen their bond with the masses of workers and peasants, strengthen active participation in the socialist reconstruction of the countryside, in the rationalisation of production and management, in the raising of labour discipline, in eliminating all kinds of wastefulness, etc."**

The Sixteenth Conference addressed an appeal to the entire working class urging the development of socialist competition.

* Adherents of the counter-revolutionary Sapronovist group of "Democratic Centralism."—*N.P.*

Socialist competition, which had extended to an immense number 'of mills and factories, was an expression of the mighty enthusiasm of the masses, who rallied round the Party in the struggle to overcome difficulties and to fulfil the Five-Year Plan.

The Conference once more emphasised that the Right deviation in the Party as the main danger constituted a very serious obstacle to the overcoming of the difficulties of the. reconstruction period, inasmuch as it strove to disarm the Party in the struggle against these difficulties and to inculcate a defeatist and capitulationist psychology within the Party.

"The difficulties of the period of socialist reconstruction, particularly under conditions of an intensification of the class struggle," the Conference pointed out in its resolution on the Five-Year Plan, "inevitably call forth vacillations among the petty-bourgeois strata of the population, and this is reflected among some sections of the working class and even in the ranks of 'the Party. These vacillations, which reflect the influence of the petty-bourgeois environment, are manifested in a departure from the general line of the Party on fundamental questions, and above all on the question of the tempo of socialist industrialisation, on the question of the development of the socialist offensive against the kulak and against the capitalist elements in general, and on the question of strengthening in every way the socialist forms of economy in the countryside.

"In connection with this, the greatest danger within the Party, under the present conditions, is the Right danger, as the expression of a downright rejection of the Leninist policy of the Party, as an expression of the open opportunist surrender of the Leninist positions under the pressure of the class enemy. Only a merciless rebuff of all vacillations in the carry-. ing out of the general Bolshevik line, the realisation of which signifies the strengthening of the alliance of the working class with the peasantry while further strengthening the leading role of the working class, can secure the accomplishment of the tasks of socialist construction which have been set in the Five-Year Plan."

The Party in the Struggle on Two Fronts in the Period of the Extended Socialist Offensive

The resolution of the Conference regarding methods of raising the level of agriculture pointed out that:

"Despite the decision of the Fifteenth Congress, the Right deviators are striving to hold up and retard the development of Soviet farms and of the collective farm movement, which is important not only from the

** From the resolution of the Sixteenth Party Conference on the purging and verification of the members and candidates of the C.P.S.U.

standpoint of the future of the Soviet country, when these forms of farm-ing will take a predominant place in agriculture, but also from the stand-point of the present situation, when the development of large-scale agri-culture in state and collective forms is being placed by the proletarian state in antithesis to the kulak method of creating large-scale agriculture. The Party considers the policy of the Rights for abandoning the construction of large-scale socialist factories and discontinuing the ever increasing aid which is being given to the development of the collectives, for abandoning the systematic and persistent transfer of agriculture to a base of large-scale production, to be a direct desertion to the position of the kulaks, a direct rejection of the leading role of the working class in the development of agricultural production."

The Conference thus described the Right deviation as a direct desertion to the position of the kulaks. It was just because of this that all the forces favouring capitalist restoration within the U.S.S.R., starting with the bourgeois liberal professors, quite cor-rectly accounted the Right deviation their ally, their virtual agency in the ranks of the C.P.S.U. It was just because of this that the Mensheviks abroad, together with all other counter-revolutionaries, hailed with such delight the appearance of the Right opposition in the ranks of the C.P.S.U., promising it in advance the support of the "vital elements in the country."

Trotskyism, when it was still in the ranks of the C.P.S.U. tried to disseminate there a purely Social-Democratic view with regard to the peasantry. It was from the Second International that Trotskyism borrowed its basic idea that it was impossible to build socialism in the U.S.S.R. The "Left" phraseology of Trotskyism, with which it was constantly juggling, was and is the typical "Left" Social-Democratic phraseology by means of which Social-Democracy seeks to hoodwink the revolutionary workers. Out-ward lustre and inner vacuity, allowing it to be used as a cover for any kind of Right opportunist and even counter-revolutionary content—such is the principal characteristic of this phraseology. Finally, Trotskyism borrowed from the Mensheviks the idea of the Thermidorian degeneration of the Soviet government. But Trotskyism did not exhaust the entire stock of ideas of international and Russian Menshevism. There was still enough material left to supply "ideological" equipment for the Right deviation in the C.P.S.U. and its brethren in the other sections of the Comintern. This once more fully confirmed the Bolshevik truth, which was many times pointed out by Lenin, that both the

Right and the "Left" deviations from Communism lead into the swamp of Social-Democracy.

Prior to the October Revolution, the Mensheviks upheld the idea of an alliance of the working class with the bourgeoisie under the leadership of the latter.

After the October Revolution, after the expropriation of the bourgeoisie, when the peasantry remained the last capitalist class in our country, the Mensheviks linked up their main hopes for the restoration of capitalism with the kulak elements among the peasantry, particularly after they had become convinced that the urban bourgeoisie under the N.E.P. would not become a factor of any serious economic importance. And the lying demagogy of the Mensheviks on the subject of an alliance of the working class with the peasantry (combined, it goes without saying, with a denial of the leading role of the working class) was employed by them as a sort of figleaf with which to cover up the defence of their kulak policy which was directed to the restoration of capitalism and against the working class.

All the declarations of the Right opportunists within the C.P.S.U. in the years 1928-30 to the effect that the N.E.P. had been abolished, that the tempo of industrialisation which had been adopted was beyond the country's strength, that the Party line was lapsing into Trotskyism, that the building of Soviet and collective farms was a utopian and still-born venture—all this along with their practical proposals for the normalisation of market relations, for raising the prices on agricultural products and for concessions to the kulak, could have been read long before in the columns of the *Sotsialistichesky Vestnik*.

The theoreticians of the Right deviation got their ideological inspiration, in the main, from the bourgeois liberal professors of the type of Kondratyev.* It was the latter who provided the "scientific" foundation for the kulak viewpoint of the Rights. But a good share of this work must go to the credit of the Menshevism of the Groman type, which had specialised for a long time in the concoction of "Marxist" arguments about the necessity and inevitability of capitalist restoration in Russia—

*Kondratyev: professor of agronomy and former official in the People's Commissariat of Agriculture, involved in the plot to organize kulak counter revolution in 1930.

the Menshevism which was the lawful successor to Struve's apologetics of capitalism.**

The ideological connection between Bukharin's Right opposition and the Right opportunist tendencies of the past can be traced in a number of historical examples—on the eve of the 1905 Revolution, on the eve of the new upswing following the reaction of the Stolypin period and on the eve of the October Revolution.

By overcoming conciliationism towards Menshevism after the Second Congress (the essence of this deviation consisted in denying the need for an independent Bolshevik Party, in efforts to merge with Menshevism and thereby to subject the Bolsheviks to the ideological leadership of the bourgeoisie), Bolshevism was able to play a tremendous role in the Revolution of 1905-07, to take the position of an independent political party in this Revolution, to prevent the conversion of the working class into cannon fodder for the bourgeoisie, which is what the Mensheviks were trying to do, and to lay the first stones in the foundation for the victorious October Revolution.

The overcoming of conciliationism towards the liquidators of 1910-11 (the Bolshevik-conciliators) was mainly responsible for the fact that in the ensuing revolutionary upsurge the Party was able to rout the liquidators and to secure its own hegemony in the labour movement. This enabled the Party to display the maximum degree of political firmness after the outbreak of the war and the collapse of the Second International, once more to rout the Mensheviks in 1917 and thereby to pave the way for the victorious outcome of the October Revolution.

There is no need to emphasise how important it was for the Party that it overcame the Right opportunist line and strike-breaking action of Zinoviev and Kamenev in 1917. By exposing and overcoming it, the Party was able to win power and to

----

**As was revealed during the trial of the Union Bureau of the "Central Committee of the Russian Social-Democratic Labour Party" (Mensheviks) in the beginning of 1931, a number of prominent Mensheviks, professing to have broken with Menshevism, but in reality carrying out the Menshevik Party directives (Groman, Ginsburg, Sher Yakubovich and others) who held responsible positions in various leading Soviet organs, tried to put into effect the very same line for the restoration of capitalism which the Right opportunists defended in their struggle against the Central Committee.

maintain it after it had been won, instead of surrendering it
without a battle as was proposed by the then capitulators and
strike-breakers (Kamenev and Zinoviev), who were ready to
allow a majority in the government to the Mensheviks and Socialist-Revolutionaries and to remove Lenin from the position of
chairman of the government.

It was the same story now. Only by fighting against
opportunism on two fronts and against conciliationism, only by
relentlessly repressing the Right deviation as the main danger at
this stage, and inflicting on it a complete ideological defeat was
the Party able to secure the successful fulfilment of those tasks
of the reconstruction period from which the Rights were dragging the Party back in cowardly panic.

Beginning with the Sixth Congress of the Comintern, our Party,
in its most important political documents, pointed out that the
Right deviation (and the attitude of conciliation towards it) was
the main danger as compared with the "Left" (Trotskyist)
deviation. This, of course, did not mean that after the Fifteenth
Congress there was no basis left in the Party for the "Left"
deviation, for remnants of Trotskyist ideology.

In his speech at the November Plenum of the Central Committee, Comrade Stalin correctly said:

"... Is there really such a thing as a 'Left' deviation in the Party?
Is there in the Party an anti-middle peasant tendency—or a tendency
towards super-industrialisation, etc.? Yes, there is. What does it amount
to? It amounts to a deviation towards Trotskyism. That was said
by the July Plenum. I refer to the well-known resolution of the July
Plenum on the grain collection policy, where the fight on two fronts
is mentioned: the fight against those who want to retreat from the
Fifteenth Congress—the Rights, and the fight against those who want
to transform the emergency measures into the permanent policy of
the Party—the 'Lefts,' the tendency towards Trotskyism. It is clear
that elements of Trotskyism and a tendency towards Trotskyist
ideology exists in our Party. I believe about six thousand individuals
voted against our platform at the time of the discussion that took place
prior to the Fifteenth Party Congress (a voice: ten thousand). Well,
if ten thousand voted against, twice ten thousand Party members
sympathetic to Trotskyism did not vote at all, since they did not attend
the meetings. Those are the Trotskyist elements who have not left the
Party but who, it must be assumed, have not yet rid themselves of the
Trotskyist ideology. Moreover, I think that a number of Trotskyists who
later broke away from the Trotskyist organisations and returned to the

Party, have not yet abandoned the Trotskyist ideology and also, pre-
sumably, are not averse to spreading their views among the members
of the Party. Finally, there is the fact of (a recrudescence of the Trotskyist ideology in certain organisations of the Party. Combine all these
facts and you get all the necessary elements comprising a tendency
toward Trotskyism in our Party.

"And that is easily understood; it cannot be otherwise, in view
of the petty-bourgeois environment and the pressure of this environment on our Party, than that. Trotskyist tendencies should exist in
our Party. It is one thing to arrest and exile the Trotskyist cadres; it ·
is another thing to put an end to the Trotskyist ideology. That will
be more difficult. And we say that wherever there is a Right deviation,
there must be a 'Left' deviation. The 'Left' deviation is the shadow
of the. Right deviation. Lenin said with regard to the otzovists, that
the 'Lefts' are Mensheviks turned inside out. That is absolutely true.
The same thing can be said of the present day 'Lefts.' Those who
incline towards Trotskyism are in fact Rights turned inside out, they
are Rights concealing themselves behind 'Left' phrases.

"Hence the fight on two fronts—against the Right deviation and
against the 'Left' deviation.

"It may be asked: if the 'Left' deviation is in essence the same
as the Right opportunist deviation, then where is the difference between
them?

"...The difference consists in the fact that their platforms are
different, their demands are different and their approach and methods
are different. If, for instance, the Rights say: '*It is a mistake to build
Dnieprostroy,*' while the 'Lefts' on the contrary say: '*What is the
good of one Dnieprostroy? Give us a Dnieprostroy every year,*'
(*laughter*) it must be admitted that there is some difference between
them. If the Rights say: '*Do not interfere with the kulak, give him
freedom to develop,*' while the 'Lefts' on the contrary, say: '*Strike not
only at the kulak, but also at the middle peasant, since he is just as
much a private property owner as the kulak,*' it must be admitted that
there is some difference between them. If the Rights say: '*Difficulties
have set in, is it not time to quit?* while the 'Lefts,' on the contrary,
say: '*What are difficulties to us: a fig for difficulties, let us dash ahead*'
(*laughter*), it must be admitted that there is some difference between
them.

"And so you get a picture of the specific platform and the specific
methods of the 'Lefts.' And that explains why the 'Lefts' sometimes
succeed in winning over a part of the workers by their high-sounding
'Left' phrases and by depicting themselves as the most determined
opponents of the Rights, although all the world knows that the social
roots of the 'Lefts' are the same as those of the Rights, and that they
not infrequently arrive at an understanding and form a *bloc* with the
Rights in order to fight the Leninist line.

"That is why it is essential for us Leninists to conduct a fight on two fronts, against the Right deviations and against the 'Left' deviation."*

When Comrade Stalin spoke at the November Plenum, the Party did not as yet know that during the July Plenum, Bukharin, the leader of the Right opposition, had already gone to arrange a *bloc* with Kamenev, who only professed to repudiate Trotskyism, but in reality continued to maintain ideological and practical contacts with the Trotskyists.

After an interval of less than two years those same "Leftist" elements of the type of Shatskin and Sten, who in the autumn of 1928 had accused the Party of not fighting hard enough against the Rights, participated in the Right-"Leftist" *bloc*.

However, the semi-Trotskyist tendencies in the Party were on the wane after the Fifteenth Congress, apart from some insignificant zig-zags and waverings. The principal reason for this was the extremely intensive process of the collapse and putrefaction of Trotskyist ideology and of the Trotskyist organisation outside the ranks of the Party.

The Struggle Against Right Opportunism and Against the Conciliators in the Comintern

While continuing the struggle on two fronts, the Party, after the Sixteenth Conference just as prior to it, concentrated its main fire on Right opportunism, which in the U.S.S.R. was fostered chiefly by the growing resistance of the kulaks.

From the very first days of its crystallisation, the Right deviation within the C.P.S.U. became the centre of attraction for all opportunist and semi-Social-Democratic elements on an international scale. These elements were already trying to unite around Bukharin at the Sixth Congress of the Comintern. The attack launched by the Rights and the conciliators on the Central Committee of the German Communist Party after the Sixth Congress coincided with the sally of the Uglanov leadership of the Moscow Committee against the Central Committee of the C.P.S.U. and with the appearance of Bukharin's article "Notes of an Economist" in the *Pravda*.

*Stalin, *Leninism*, Vol. II.

The German Rights and conciliators based all their arguments on Bukharin's theses regarding the consolidation of capitalist stabilisation, the technical reconstruction of capitalism, etc. The Right group formed in the Communist Party of Czecho-Slovakia, led by Jilek, Bolen and Hais, also defended these theses, drawing from them the conclusion that it was necessary to pursue reformist tactics and to form a *bloc* with the "Left" Social-Democrats. A characteristic feature of the Czech Rights was a tendency to underrate Czecho-Slovakian imperialism and to consider Czecho-Slovakia as an oppressed colonial country. This led to a weakening of the struggle against the Czech bourgeoisie and Czech Social-Democracy. In thus taking a step towards Social-Democracy, the Czech Rights, following the Germans, produced a new charge against the Comintern—that of overestimating the danger of an attack on the U.S.S.R. As a result of their factional schismatic activities the Czech Rights also were expelled from the Comintern. A similar fate befell Bukharin's main bulwark at the Sixth Congress, *viz.*, the Lovestone group in the Central Committee of the Communist Party of the United States, which upheld the thesis of American exceptionalism, *i.e.*, that American imperialism was secure for a long time against crises and the shattering of stabilisation.

About the same time, a Right deviation clearly took shape in the Communist Party of Poland, characterised by a tendency to underestimate the role of Polish imperialism and its aggressiveness with respect to the U.S.S.R., to overestimate the contradictions within the fascist camp which ruled Poland and to regard these contradictions as a factor in the Polish revolution, and by patent illusions regarding the revolutionary role of Polish social-fascism. The basic political tendencies of the Rights in the Communist Party of Poland were along the same line as the errors committed by the Polish Party leadership in May 1926, when it regarded the fascist *coup* of Pilsudsky as the beginning of a bourgeois-democratic revolution in a colonial country. The ideological basis of these errors was the theory that post-war Poland was in the position of a colony—a theory which was foisted upon the Polish Communists by Bukharin in 1925.

Summing up the struggle against Right opportunism and conciliationism in various sections of the Comintern, above all in the German, Czecho-Slovakian and American sections, the Tenth Enlarged Plenum of the E.C.C.I. in July 1929 adopted a decision of extreme importance from the point of view of principle:

"The Plenum recognises as incompatible with membership of the Communist Party the defence by individual members of the views of the Right deviation which has been condemned by the Comintern as an anti-Party tendency, profoundly hostile to the interests of the proletarian revolutionary movement.

"The Plenum at the same time points out that the conciliationism, which has played the role of cowardly opportunism and served as a screen for open liquidationism, has of late lapsed into Right positions on all fundamental questions of the Communist movement and has taken upon itself the role of the Rights within the Communist International. After the expulsion of the Right liquidators, conciliationism has become the centre of attraction for all Right elements in the ranks of the Communist Parties, the mouthpiece of all defeatist tendencies and opportunist views. In view of this, the Plenum of the E.C.C.I. demands: a) that the conciliators openly and definitely dissociate themselves from the Right deviators; b) that they carry on an active struggle, not in words, but in deeds, against the Right deviation; c) that they submit unreservedly to all decisions of the Comintern and of its sections and actively carry them into effect. Anyone failing to carry out any one of these conditions will thereby place himself outside the ranks of the Comintern."

Bearing in mind the leading ideological role of Comrade Bukharin for the opportunist and conciliationist tendencies in the sections of the Comintern, and in view of the fact that Bukharin not only did not repudiate these opportunist views but continued to develop them further in his article on *Organised Capitalism* which he published even after the decisions of the Sixteenth Party Conference, the Tenth Plenum of the E.C.C.I decided to remove Bukharin from the Presidium of the E.C.C.I.

The article on *Organised Capitalism* was the crowning point as it were to the edifice of opportunist views which Bukharin had erected. To go further was impossible. In this article Bukharin contended that capitalism had succeeded in mitigating the internal crises, in eliminating competition, and in transforming itself into "organised" capitalism. Elements of this theory could be found in Bukharin's writings even earlier than this. But never before had he defended it in such a nakedly anti-Marxist and anti-Leninist form. Combined with Bukharin's views regarding the consolidation of capitalist stabilisation and the reconstruction of capitalism on a new technical base, the result was a complete, harmonious opportunist conception which would have done credit to any Social-Democratic theoretician.

But there was a "minor weakness" in this theory, namely, that it was utterly at war with the facts. In June 1929, Bukharin finally reconciled all the internal contradictions of capitalism. In October 1929, in the United States, the main citadel of capitalism, the main bulwark of the partial stabilisation of capitalism throughout the world, a violent crisis broke out which rapidly developed into a world crisis. This crisis accentuated to an extreme degree all the contradictions of the capitalist system—the contradictions between the bourgeoisie and the working class, between the imperialist countries and colonial countries, between the imperialist powers themselves, between the victorious and defeated countries of the World War. The crisis hastened on the process of capitalist rationalisation at the expense of the working class, intensified the struggle for markets, increased the war danger and created the necessary condition for the rapid growth of the elements of a revolutionary upsurge in the capitalist and colonial countries.

As Comrade Stalin pointed out in his Political Report to the Sixteenth Congress of the C.P.S.U.

"1) The crisis has most profoundly affected the *principal country of capitalism*, its citadel, the U.S.A., which concentrates in its hands not less than half of the whole production and consumption of the world. Obviously this circumstance cannot but lead to a colossal extension of the sphere of influence of the crisis, to the sharpening of the crisis and the accumulation of the 'unbudgeted' difficulties for world capitalism.

"2) In the course of development of the economic crisis, the industrial crisis in the chief capitalist countries has not simply coincided, but has become *interwoven* with the agricultural crisis in the agrarian countries, aggravating the difficulties and predetermining the inevitability of a general decline in economic activity. Needless to say, the industrial crisis will intensify the agricultural crisis and the agricultural crisis will protract the industrial crisis, and this cannot but lead to the deepening of the economic crisis as a whole.

"3) Present-day capitalism, as distinguished from older capitalism, is *monopolistic* capitalism, and this inevitably gives rise to the struggle between capitalist combines to maintain high monopolist prices of commodities in spite of over-production. Obviously, this circumstance, which makes the crisis particularly painful and ruinous for the mass of the people, who are the basic consumers of commodities, cannot but lead to the dragging out of the crisis, cannot but retard its dissipation.

"4) The present economic crisis is developing on the basis of the *general crisis* of capitalism, which began during the period of the imperialist war, undermined the foundations of capitalism and paved the way for the present economic crisis.

"What does this mean?

"It means first of all that the imperialist war and its aftermath have intensified the decay of capitalism and destroyed its equilibrium; that we are now living in the epoch of wars and revolutions; that capitalism no longer represents the *sole* and *all-embracing* system of world economy, that side by side with the *capitalist* system of economy there exists the *socialist* system, which is growing, which is flourishing, which is resisting the capitalist system, and which by the very fact of its existence is demonstrating the rottenness of capitalism and shaking its foundations.

"It means, furthermore, that the imperialist war and the victory of the revolution in the U.S.S.R. have shaken the foundations of imperialism in *the colonial and dependent* countries, that the prestige of imperialism in these countries has already been undermined, that it is no longer capable of governing in the old way in these countries.

"It means, further, that during the war and after it, a young, native capitalism appeared and grew up in the colonial and dependent countries, which competes successfully in the markets with the old capitalist countries, sharpening and complicating the struggle for markets.

"It means, finally, that the war has left to the majority of the capitalist countries a painful heritage in the shape of *chronic underemployment of factories* and *armies of unemployed running into millions,* which, moreover, have been transformed from reserve into *permanent* armies of unemployed. This created a mass of difficulties for capitalism even before the present economic crisis, and must still further complicate matters during the crisis.

"Such are the circumstances which aggravate and sharpen the world crisis.

"The present economic crisis is the most serious and profound world economic crisis that has ever occurred."*

The Plenum of the Central Committee in November 1929

In spite of the panic predictions of the Right opportunists at the April Plenum, the Party successfully completed the grain collections plan on the basis of the measures of social pressure brought to bear against the kulak, thus rendering entirely unnecessary the importation of grain from abroad which had been proposed by the Rights. The Party was just as successful in

*Stalin, *Leninism,* Vol. II.

carrying out the spring sowing campaign, achieving an extension of the area under cultivation. Careful elaboration of individual parts of the Five-Year Plan after the Sixteenth Party Conference showed that it was quite possible to alter it in the direction of greater expansion in a number of important industries. In the summer of 1929, the Central Committee of the C.P.S.U. adopted a number of decisions in favour of raising the original Five-Year Plan for the oil industry, for cotton, for the non-ferrous metal industry, etc. The transition to the five-day working week made it possible to raise the question of further accelerating the tempo of industrialisation.

The attempt of the imperialists in the summer and autumn of 1929 to force a war in the Far East upon the Soviet Union, and thus to disrupt our further work of industrialisation, met with complete discomfiture. The special Far-Eastern Army, commanded by Comrade Blücher, crushingly repulsed the Chinese militarists.

Instead of the failure of all the industrial plans as was predicted by Bukharin, the November Plenum of the Central Committee of the C.P.S.U. was able to record a considerable overfulfilment of the plans for the first year of the Five-Year Plan. Production of large-scale industry showed an increase of almost 24 per cent as compared with the 21.5 per cent increase called for by the plan. Production of heavy industry showed an increase of almost 30 per cent as against 26 per cent according to plan. But particularly marked was the overfulfilment of the plan in collectivisation, precisely in the field where the Rights considered the plan to be least practicable.

".... The unprecedented tempo of collectivisation, *exceeding the most optimistic projects,*" the November Plenum pointed out in its resolution on the control figures, "is evidence of the fact that, following the poor peasants, the movement has been joined by the real masses of *middle peasants,* who are becoming convinced through practical experience of the advantages of collective forms of agriculture."

The Plenum pointed out the bankruptcy and collapse of Right opportunism on the whole front of economic construction in the U.S.S.R.

"The *Rights* asserted the 'degradation' of agriculture. *In reality* we had a further growth of the poor and middle peasant farms, a general increase in the cultivated areas, an increase in the supply of machinery and a rise in the material, technical and agronomic level of development of agriculture.

"The *Rights* declared that there was a 'rupture' of the alliance between the poor and middle peasant masses and the working class. *In reality* we had a further strengthening of the alliance of the working class with the peasantry and a strengthening of the leading role of the proletariat in this alliance, which found its expression in the rapid development of collectivisation and in the building of Soviet farms.

"The *Rights* prophesied the inevitability of famine and of the importation of grain. *In reality* we had such an increase in the grain collection as secured the country grain of home production and assured the accumulation of a grain reserve fund of tens of millions of poods, coupled with a favourable trade balance and the accumulation of foreign currency.   .   '   \

"The *Rights* contended that the tempo of industrialisation which had been determined upon was beyond the country's strength. *In reality,* we have not only fulfilled but considerably exceeded the tasks set by the plan.

"The *Rights* declared that the tempo set for collectivisation and for the building of Soviet farms was impracticable, that the essential material and technical prerequisites were lacking and that the poor and middle peasantry was unwilling to pass over to collective forms of agriculture. *In reality* we have so rapid a development of collectivisation, so strong a tendency of the poor and middle peasants towards socialist forms of farming, that the collective farm movement, in actual fact, has already begun to grow into *all-round collectivisation of whole districts*. This signifies a new stage, a new phase in the period of transition from capitalism to socialism.   '

"The *Rights,* having no faith in the creative forces of the working class, demanded that the tempo be adjusted to the 'tight places,' that we passively adapt ourselves to difficulties. In *reality* the working class under the leadership of the Party, by actively overcoming these difficulties, has secured in excess of the plan a further growth of the productive forces in the direction of socialism.

"The *Rights* contended that a general economic crisis, *i.e.,* a disturbance of the normal course of production, and reproduction, was inevitable. *In reality* we have such a growth of production, such an acceleration of the tempo, as we could not even have dreamed of formerly, and which enables us actually to transform the optimum variant of the Five-Year Plan into a minimum variant.

"Only by resolutely overcoming the efforts of the Right opportunists, objectively the spokesmen of the economic and political interests of the petty-bourgeois elemental forces and of the kulak capitalist groups, to divert the Party from the general line of our development, have the working class and the Party been able to achieve a considerable step forward in the work of socialist construction."

The Plenum, in approving the control figures for 1929-30, outlined a further growth of planned industry, and on the basis of the report by Comrade Kaganovich adopted an important resolution for the training of technical and economic cadres for the rapidly growing industry. As Comrade Stalin had pointed out shortly before the Plenum in his historic article "A Year of Great Change," published in the *Pravda* of November 7, 1929, the problem of cadres had become the central problem of our socialist construction.

The Rights issued a declaration at the Plenum which, while recognising the achievements of the Party, stated that had the Party accepted their proposals in April, it could have achieved the same results with less exertion. The Rights attempted to prove that their differences with the Party did not go beyond disagreements regarding the extraordinary measures and drew the quite unexpected conclusion that these differences had ceased to exist.

While obliged to withdraw the platform which they had put forward in opposition to the Party and to declare that the differences had ceased to exist, the Rights nevertheless did not withdraw any of the accusations which they had previously hurled against the Party (the lapse into Trotskyism, military-feudal exploitation, the disintegration of the Comintern, the bureaucratisation of the Party).

For them it was only a question of discontinuing the struggle for the time being, avoiding a blow and—waiting for an accentuation of the difficulties.

"By refusing to admit their errors on questions of economic policy, on questions of the industrialisation of the country, the collectivisation of agriculture and the development of Soviet farms, by refusing to recognise their errors in appraising the class struggle, and their failure to grasp this struggle, finally by attempting to adopt methods of factional struggle against the Party, the Bukharin group has definitely exposed its anti-Leninist, anti-Bolshevik character. In connection with this, the plenum decided to recognise propaganda of the views of Right opportunism and of conciliationism with it as incompatible with membership of the C.P.S.U."

While adopting this decision, the Plenum at the same time decided to remove Comrade Bukharin, the ideologist of the Right deviation, from the Politburo and to warn the others that, in the event of the slightest effort on their part to continue the struggle against the line and decisions of the E.C.C.I. and of the Central Committee of the C.P.S.U., the Party would not hesitate to apply corresponding organisational measures in their case.

At the same time the November Plenum took note of the recrudescence of "Left" tendencies, of semi-Trotskyist incursions against the general line of the Party. Shortly before the Plenum, certain comrades (Shatskin, Sten, Lominadze), came forward with the slogan for the organisation of a union of the poor peasants —a slogan borrowed from the Trotskyist theses on the eve of the Fifteenth Congress—and with a number of semi-Trotskyist proposals with regard to the state apparatus and the Party. Against the Party leadership they put forward half-disguised accusations of centrism which were also borrowed from the stock-in-trade of Trotskyism.

A few days after the November Plenum the leaders of the Right opposition presented a statement admitting the correctness of the general line of the Party, recognising as erroneous the struggle which they had heretofore waged against this line, and expressing their readiness in the future to defend the Party line in actual fact and to fight against deviations from it.

The capitulation of the leaders of the Right deviation was clear evidence of the strength and unity shown by the Party in defending its general line, the more so since convincing evidence in favour of this line had been provided during an extremely brief period of time by the actual course of events.

But this capitulation was of a formal character and, as later development showed, was not sufficiently sincere.

The capitulation of the Right leaders did not at all relieve the Party of the necessity of further exposing the Right deviation and of fighting manifestations of the Right deviation both in theory and practice.

The Right opportunist Bukharinist school, along with its teacher at its head, left a considerable opportunist legacy in the domain of theory. Quite a prominent place in this legacy was and is taken by the theory of "equilibrium" between the sectors of our national economy. As Comrade Stalin stated, in his speech at the Conference of Marxist Agrarians at the end of December 1929:

"On the basis of this theory it is assumed that we have a socialist sector—in one compartment, as it were, and a *non-socialist* or if you like, a capitalist sector—in another compartment. These two compartments move on different rails and glide peacefully forward, without colliding with each other. Geometry has taught us that parallel lines do not meet. But the authors of this remarkable theory believe that their parallel lines will meet some day, and that the result will be socialism. . . .

"It is not difficult to comprehend that this theory has nothing in common with Leninism. It is not difficult to comprehend that this theory objectively pursues the aim of defending the position of individual peasant farming, of furnishing the kulak elements with a 'new' theoretical weapon in their struggle against the collective farms, and of discrediting the positions of the collective farms."*

Two roads face agriculture in the U.S.S.R.—either towards capitalism or towards socialism.

"There is no third way, and there cannot be one. The 'equilibrium' theory represents an attempt to find a third way, and for the very reason that it assumes that there is a third (non-existent) way, it is utopian and anti-Marxist."

In the same speech Comrade Stalin also exposed another Right opportunist theory, the theory of "automatic development":

"The authors of this theory assert approximately the following: Capitalism once existed in this country and industry developed on a capitalist basis, while the village followed the capitalist town spontaneously and automatically, and assumed the image of the capitalist town. Since *this* was the case under capitalism, why should the same not follow under Soviet economy. . . . Hence the question arises: Is it worth our while to bother about organising Soviet farms and collective farms . . . when the village can follow the socialist town without this?

"Here we have another theory, the aim of which, objectively, is to furnish fresh weapons to the capitalist elements in the rural districts in their struggle against the collective farms.

"Under capitalism the village followed the town spontaneously, for the reason that capitalist production in the town and small commodity production carried on by the peasant belong essentially to *one and the same type* of production. It goes without saying that small commodity production is not yet capitalist production. But fundamentally it belongs to the same type as capitalist production, for it is founded on the private ownership of the means of production.

* Stalin, *Leninism,* Vol. II.

"Otherwise Lenin would not have said that 'so long as we live in a small peasant country, capitalism has a firmer economic basis in Russia than communism.' Accordingly, the theory of 'automatic development' in the sphere of socialist construction is a rotten and anti-Leninist theory. Accordingly, in order that the small-peasant village may follow the socialist town, it is necessary, apart from everything else, to establish large-scale socialist economy in the rural districts in the form of Soviet and collective farms as the basis of socialism, which will be able to *lead* the main masses of the peasantry, under the guidance of the socialist town.

"The socialist town must *lead* the small-peasant village by introducing Soviet and collective farms in the rural districts and reorganising the village on a new socialist foundation."

Another theory, that of the "stability" of small peasant farming, was quite strongly embedded in the heads of the Right opportunists. It was this very theory which, even in the spring of 1928, inspired sceptical opinions with regard to the development of large Soviet farms on the ground that European and American practice allegedly had not confirmed the technical superiority of large-scale production in agriculture. In this the Right deviators were joined by the Narodnik and Cadet professors, by all the revisionists of Western Europe, by the whole synod of bourgeois scientists in the U.S.S.R. of the type of Kondratyev and Chayanov.* Under Soviet conditions, as Comrade Stalin said, "this anti-Marxist theory pursues one sole aim: to eulogise and strengthen the capitalist order."

Our Soviet farm construction, the organisation of large-scale Soviet farms, the cultivation by these farms of hundreds of thousands and millions of hectares of virgin soil are a blow at the Right opportunists who have forgotten the elementary truths of Marxism. The achievements of the Soviet farms have definitely settled the disputes of many decades in favour of large-scale socialist farming as the most powerful lever for raising the level of agriculture. On this important point they have inflicted a decisive blow on the bourgeois theoreticians of political economy and their Social-Democratic *claqueurs*.

The Party was confronted not only with the task of exposing the theories of Right opportunism which had joined hands with

* Chayanov: professor and official of the Commissariat of Agriculture, associated with Kondratyev in the plot to organise kulak counter-revolution.

bourgeois science, but also, in connection with this, with the task of waging a merciless struggle against manifestations of Right opportunism in practice, expressed in the efforts to undermine collectivisation and the grain 'collections, in collaboration with the kulak elements in the countryside, in the support given to these elements by individual links in the Soviet and co-operative apparatus and sometimes even by Party nuclei and individual members of the Party, in a tendency to do away with the Soviets in the districts of all-round collectivisation, and finally, in a tendency to admit kulaks into the collective farms.

The collective farm movement had already begun to develop rapidly after the Fifteenth Congress of the Party. But the rate of its growth became particularly rapid in the autumn of 1929. The growth of the collective farm movement was greatly facilitated by the organisation of machine and tractor stations (Comrade Stalin at the Fifteenth Congress told of the first experiment in the organisation of such stations which was made by the Shevchenko Soviet Farm).

Of great significance was the work of the large model Soviet farms (the Gigant Farm, the Scientific Experimental Farm, etc.) which were organized in the summer of 1928.

From Restricting and Squeezing Out the Kulak to the Liquidation of Kulakdom

In the autumn of 1929 a number of regions could already report districts where all-round collectivisation prevailed, and at the November Plenum the question arose of all-round collectivisation in whole regions (the Northern Caucasus, the Lower Volga, the steppe area of the Ukraine, the Trans-Volga part of the Middle Volga Territory) in the course of the next one and a half to two years. Following the November Plenum the tempo of the collectivisation increased even more throughout the whole Union, but particularly in the grain districts. Comrade Stalin was fully justified in stating, in his speech at the Conference of Marxist Agrarians (on December 27, 1929) that:

"... The collectivisation movement, which has assumed the character of a mighty and growing *anti-kulak avalanche*, is sweeping the resistance of the kulak from its path, breaking the kulak power and clearing the road for widespread socialist construction in the rural districts."*

The Party was confronted with a mighty turn of millions of the middle peasant masses towards the socialist path of development. What were the main causes of this turn?

On the one hand, the practical experience of socialist large-scale farming—of the Soviet farms and particularly of the machine and tractor stations which cultivated the collective farm fields. Soviet industry had already sufficiently developed to supply the countryside with scores of thousands of complex agricultural machines. But even the experiment of merely pooling the simplest agricultural implements in the collective farms was productive of positive results.

On the other hand, the middle peasant masses in the grain districts had witnessed three grain collection campaigns. During these campaigns the kulak had offered desperate resistance to the Soviet government. But the Soviet government came out victorious from these struggles, successfully overcoming the kulak resistance. The kulak, the representative of the capitalist path of agricultural development, had thus suffered a severe defeat. And the socialist path of development opened up broad and clear perspectives to the middle as well as to the poor peasant. And it was above all in the largest grain districts that the mass of the middle peasantry first made its choice.

The resolution adopted by the Sixteenth Congress on the report of the Central Committee states:

"*The decisive turn of the middle peasant masses towards socialism* as a result of the correct policy of the Party found its most vivid expression in the mighty collective farm movement, which at the end of 1929 embraced millions of peasant farms, thus creating *a new correlation of class forces in the country,* transforming the middle peasant who joined the collective farm into a bulwark of the Soviet power, creating the conditions for replacing kulak production of grain by the production of the Soviet and collective farms and enabling the Party to pass from the slogan of restricting and squeezing out the kulak to the slogan of liquidating the kulaks as a class on the basis of all-round collectivisation."

* Stalin, *Leninism,* Vol. II.

16*

This decisive and historic turn in the policy of the Party was explained in detail by Comrade Stalin in his speech at the Conference of Marxist Agrarians:

"In 1927, the kulak produced over 600,000,000 poods of grain, 130,000,000 of which he disposed of by exchange outside of the rural districts. That is a fairly serious force with which one must reckon. And how much did our Soviet and collective farms produce at that time? About 80,000,000 poods, of which they brought a little over 35,000,000 (marketable grain) to the market. Judge for yourselves whether at that time we were in a position to *replace* the production and the marketable grain of the kulaks by the production and the marketable grain of our Soviet and collective farms. It is clear that we could not have done so. . . .

"What is the position at present? We now have an adequate material basis from which to deliver a blow against the kulak, to break his resistance, to liquidate him as a class, and to *replace* his production by the production of the Soviet and collective farms. You are aware that the grain produced on the collective and Soviet farms in 1929 amounted to no less than about 400,000,000 poods. . . . You also know that the collective and Soviet farms delivered more than 130,000,000 poods of marketable grain (that is, more than the kulaks in 1927). And finally, you know that in 1930 the gross production of the collective and Soviet farms will amount to no less than 900,000,000 poods, (*i.e.,* more than the gross production of the kulaks in 1927) and they will supply not less than 400,000,000 poods of marketable grain (*i.e.,* incomparably more than the kulaks supplied in 1927). . . .

"That is the change that has taken place in the economics of the country. . . .

"As you see, the material basis exists today which enables us to *replace* kulak production by that of the collective and Soviet farms. That is why our attack on the kulaks has now met with undeniable success."*

This is the reason why we passed from the policy of restricting and squeezing out the kulak to the policy of liquidating kulakdom.

Both at the Fifteenth Congress and at the Sixteenth Conference the Party still adhered to the position of restricting and squeezing out the kulak.

"In the period of the Fifteenth Congress," Stalin wrote in his article *On the Policy of Liquidating the Kulaks as a Class,* "the policy of restricting the exploiting tendencies of the kulaks was merely tightened up by new and supplementary measures, as a consequence of which

* *Ibid.*

the squeezing out of individual sections of the kulaks could not but be intensified....

"On what assumption did the Fifteenth Congress proceed when it proclaimed the intensification of the policy of restricting (and *eliminating*) the capitalist elements of the countryside? On the assumption that, in spite of the restriction of the kulaks, the kulaks *as a class* for the time being *must remain*....

"Under the policy of restricting the exploiting tendencies of the kulak we can count only on squeezing out individual sections of the kulaks, which fact does not contradict, but, on the contrary, presumes the *retention*, for the time being, of the kulaks as a class. In order to squeeze the kulaks out as a class, a policy of restricting and squeezing out individual sections of the kulaks is not enough. In order to squeeze the kulaks out as a class we must *break down* the resistance of this class in open fight and *deprive* it of the productive sources of its existence and development (the free use of land, means of production, leases, the right to hire labour, etc.). This marks the *turn* toward the policy of liquidating the kulaks as a class. Without that, all talk of squeezing the kulaks out as a class is idle chatter, pleasing and profitable only to the Right deviators. Without that, serious, not to speak of mass collectivisation of the countryside is inconceivable. The poor and middle peasants in our village who are smashing up the kulaks and carrying out mass collectivisation have understood that quite well. Apparently, some of our comrades still fail to understand that.

"Hence, the present policy of our Party in the village is not a *continuation* of the old policy, but a *change* from the old policy of *restricting* (and squeezing out) the capitalist elements of the countryside to the new policy of liquidating the kulaks as a class."*

The Party in the Struggle Against Anti-Middle Peasant Excesses

On January 5, 1930, the Central Committee passed a decision regarding the tempo of collectivisation in various regions. According to the Five-Year Plan, we should have had 20 per cent of the peasant farms collectivised at the end of the five-year period. This figure had already been reached in many districts by the beginning of 1930. The Central Committee now decided that collectivisation in the chief grain districts should be completed in the main in the spring of 1931 (Northern Caucasus, Lower Volga and the trans-Volga part of the Middle Volga Region).

* *Ibid.*

postponing the completion of collectivisation in the other grain regions, and after these in the non-grain regions, to the following years.

Such a tempo of collectivisation, while far exceeding the pace set in the Five-Year Plan, was perfectly practicable. However, since the autumn of 1929, some comrades had already begun to yield to an unhealthy and reckless tendency to race after high tempoes without taking sufficient care to consolidate the results attained. And following this, in spite of the Central Committee's decision, a number of regional and local organisations, succumbing to "dizziness from success," began to figure on completing collectivisation in the spring of 1930.

This resulted in numerous and quite widespread distortions of the Party line with regard to the middle peasant.

These distortions were manifested in the violation of the principle of voluntary action, in ignoring the specific economic and national characteristics of the various districts and regions, in the creation of "giant collective farms," and finally in efforts to form collective farm communes at all costs by socialising all the peasant livestock and other possessions, including household goods.

Besides this, there were numerous cases in districts of all-round collectivisation where middle peasants were dispossessed along with the kulaks.

What was the nature of these anti-middle peasant excesses, which were in fundamental contradiction to the whole line and approach of the Party and to the repeated directives of the higher Party organs regarding the strictest observance of the principle of voluntary action on the part of the peasants in the carrying out of collectivisation? (Decision of the Sixteenth Party Conference, Comrade Stalin's article *A Year of Great Change*, the decision of the Central Committee of January 5, 1930.)

Inasmuch as the Party line was being replaced in such cases by violence against the middle peasant, which is hostile to Leninism, it was undoubtedly a manifestation of Trotskyist and semi-Trotskyist "Left" tendencies, of a recrudescence of these tendencies.

It also happened that in many places, practical workers of a Right tendency, finding themselves behindhand in the tempo of collectivisation and not having carried on any serious preliminary work among the poor peasants, tried to make up for these shortcomings by arbitrary administrative action. Finally, in many cases violence against the middle peasants on the part of local workers was inspired directly by kulak provocation. Most of the excesses and stupidities, however, must be attributed to "dizziness from success."

The result of these excesses was the formation of a large number of spurious collective farms, chiefly in the form of "giant communes." Everywhere the excesses aroused discontent among the middle peasants and in some places also among the poor peasant masses, thereby strengthening the position of the kulaks who were being liquidated.

On the basis of this discontent, combined with the desperate resistance of the kulaks to the carrying out of collectivisation and to the liquidation of kulakdom as a class, there occurred mass actions against collectivisation in various districts of the U.S.S.R.

The largest number of such actions occurred in districts where there had been least preparation for collectivisation, in the backward national minority districts.

The Central Committee opportunely issued a number of emphatic directives to correct the excesses which had been committed in various localities.

The spurious collective farms began to disintegrate. On the other hand, the discontent among the middle peasant masses resulting from the excesses of the "Leftists" caused a wave of withdrawals from the collective farms.

Here and there, there were local attempts to gloss over the "Leftist" excesses which had been exposed by the Central Committee of the Party and to resist their correction. Attempts were made to ascribe the withdrawals from the collective farms to "objective" causes, to the "inevitable" vacillations of the middle peasants.

The Central Committee insisted on the resolute correction of the excesses, not hesitating to resort to organisational measures. Of exceptional importance in getting rid of the excesses and in straightening out the line of those Party organisations which had permitted them were the articles of Comrade Stalin—"Dizzy With Success" and "A Reply to Comrades on the Collective Farms," published in the *Pravda*. The correction of the excesses had the effect of calming the middle peasant masses, arresting the wave of withdrawals from the collective farms, stabilising and consolidating in the collective farms a percentage of peasant farms which exceeded the original figures set for the entire period of the Five-Year Plan, and preparing for the successful carrying out of the spring sowing campaign, particularly in the collective farm sector.

The "Left" anti-middle peasant excesses strengthened not only the position of the kulak but also that of his Right opportunist agents within the Party. The Right opportunists attempted to interpret the wave of withdrawals from the collective farms caused by these excesses as the beginning of the collapse of the Party policy which they had long expected.

Together with the perpetrators of the "Left" excesses the Right opportunists interpreted the measures taken by the Central Committee to correct these excesses as the beginning of a new policy, as a retreat from the previous policy in the field of collective farm development. Many of yesterday's most violent perpetrators of excesses began to advocate a policy of "automatic development" in the collective farm movement. Here and there, the local organisations relaxed their energy in the struggle against the kulak and against Right opportunism. Cases were discovered where a liquidationist attitude had been shown to the main slogans of the Party at this stage—to the slogans of all-round collectivisation and the liquidation of the kulak as a class. Both the Right opportunists and the perpetrators of "Left" excesses tried to place the blame for the distortions committed locally on the general line of the Party, attempting to discredit the Central Committee.

The Party decisively repulsed all the opportunist attacks on its general line and on its leadership both on the part of the Rights and on the part of the "Lefts."

The Sixteenth Party Congress

The Sixteenth Party Congress was in session from June 26 to July 13, 1930. The Agenda of the Congress included the reports of the Central Committee, of the Central Control Commission and of the delegation of the C.P.S.U. to the E.C.C.I., questions regarding the results and future prospects of the fulfilment of the Five-Year Plan and of the Party's work in the socialist reconstruction of agriculture, and questions regarding the tasks of the trade unions in the reconstruction period.

The Congress coincided, as was noted by Comrade Stalin, with a turning point in the life of the capitalist countries and of the U.S.S.R.—a turning point which was characterised by a deep and acute economic crisis in the capitalist world and by an unprecedented, gigantic development of socialist construction in the U.S.S.R., by the entry of the Soviet Union into the period of socialism.

After hearing the reports of Comrades Stalin and Kaganovich, the Congress noted with satisfaction the tremendous part played by the C.P.S.U. and its Central Committee "in the work of Bolshevising the sections of the Communist International and purging them of opportunist elements."

The Congress was able to note a strengthening of the international position of the U.S.S.R. as a result of the correct policy pursued by the Central Committee of the C.P.S.U. This found its most striking expression in the settlement of the dispute on the Chinese Eastern Railway and in the resumption of diplomatic relations with Great Britain.

Proceeding on the assumption that the bourgeoisie would seek a way out of the ever-sharpening economic crisis in war, that the groups and cliques dominating the imperialist powers would strive to settle the contradictions between them at the expense of the U.S.S.R., and bearing in mind that this situation increased the war danger for the Soviet Union, the Congress instructed the Central Committee to take all measures towards strengthening the defensive capacity of the U.S.S.R., while continuing as formerly to pursue a policy of peace and persistently exposing the war preparations of the capitalist governments.

The Congress emphasised the great significance of a Bolshevik tempo in the industrialisation of the U.S.S.R. for securing its capacity for defence and for securing within the near future the economic independence of the U.S.S.R. from the surrounding bourgeois states.

The U.S.S.R. had achieved tremendous success in carrying

out Lenin's slogan to overtake and outstrip the advanced capitalist countries in technical and economic respects. No capitalist nation had ever dared even to dream of such a tempo of economic development as was achieved by the Soviet Union. While most of the capitalist countries, beginning with 1928, retrogressed in the level of their production, only France succeeding in raising its level of production by 13 per cent, in the U.S.S.R., production increased by 55 per cent. However, in spite of the great achievements of industrialisation in the U.S.S.R., we were still far behind the advanced capitalist countries in the most important economic indices. Electric power production in the U.S.S.R. amounted in 1929 to about 6,500,000 kw. hours, while in the U.S.A. it amounted to 126,000,000 kw. hours, in Canada to 18,000,000, in Germany to 33,000,000 and in Italy to about 11,000,000. In the production of pig iron we did not reach the pre-war level (5,500,000 tons) until 1929-30, while in 1929 the United States produced 42,000,000 tons, Germany about 13,500,000 tons, France about 10,500,000 tons and Great Britain about 8,000,000 tons.

Only by continuing to carry out a Bolshevik tempo of industrialisation could the U.S.S.R. secure its technical and economic independence from capitalist countries, and indeed its very existence.

And, as Comrade Stalin stated at the Sixteenth Congress:

"People who chatter about the necessity of *reducing* the rate of development of our industry are enemies of socialism, agents of our class enemies." *

On the basis of the report of the Central Committee, the Sixteenth Congress adopted some very important decisions on the carrying out of the Five-Year Plan in four years and on the completion of all-round collectivisation throughout the Soviet Union within the next few years, which meant also completing the liquidation of the kulaks as a class.

In how far was the slogan of fulfilling the Five-Year Plan in four years attainable—a slogan which issued from the very heart of the working masses who had entered into socialist competition?

As early as the summer of 1929, the Central Committee of

*Stalin. *Leninism*, Vol. II.

the C.P.S.U. re-examined the provisions of the Five-Year Plan for the non-ferrous metal industry and raised them 100 per cent.

The output of the oil industry, according to the Five-Year Plan, was to reach a value of 977,000,000 rubles in 1932-33. Actually, we had already reached 73 per cent of this figure in 1929-30.

In the peat industry, we had an output valued at 115,000,000 rubles in 1929-30, *i.e.,* 96 per cent of the figure set for the last year of the Five-Year Plan.

In general machine building the rate of development already attained assured the fulfilment of the Five-Year Plan in two and a half to three years. Similarly with agricultural machine building.

The powerful combine plants in Saratov, Rostov and Zaporozhie were not provided for at all in the Five-Year Plan, but represented additions to it.

Such was the situation with regard to the fulfilment of the Five-Year Plan in four years.

Of tremendous significance was the decision of the Central Committee, which was approved by the Congress, to create a new powerful coal and metallurgical base in the Urals-Kuznetsk area.

Heretofore, we had three main industrial districts—Moscow, Leningrad and the Ukraine (with the adjacent localities of the Northern Caucasus). Moscow and Leningrad (in addition to the powerful textile and food industry in Moscow and the Moscow Region) became the centres of Soviet machine building. The principal coal and metallurgical base in the U.S.S.R. was in the Ukraine, namely, the Donbas (coal) and Krivorozhe (iron ore). The southern plants produced about three-quarters of the total output of iron and steel.

The Five-Year Plan called for a doubling of the output of coal and iron ore in the Donbas and Krivorozhe.

Besides this, it called for tremendous reconstruction of a number of operating plants in the Ukraine (the Makeyevka plant, the Dzerzhinsky plant at Kamenskoye, the Voroshilov plant at Alchevskaya) and for the construction of a number of mighty new plants (the Azovstal plant at Mariupol and the plants at Zaporozhie and Krivorozhe).

But the gigantic rate of development of heavy metallurgy in the Ukraine did not cover the country's requirements. We could no longer rely in the future on one coal and metallurgical base. We had to create another base as rapidly as possible, utilising the colossal resources of iron ore in the Urals, of coal in the Kuzbas and of non-ferrous metals in Kazakstan.

". . . Can this alone in the future satisfy the requirements of the South, the Central Region of the U.S.S.R., the North, the Northeast, the Far East and Turkestan? Everything goes to show that this is impossible. One of the new features in our national economic development is, incidentally, the fact that this basis has already become inadequate for us. The new feature is that while continuing to develop this base in every possible way for the future, we must immediately begin to create a second coal and metallurgical base. This must be the Urals-Kuznetsk Combine, the combination of Kuznetsk coking coal with the ores of the Urals. The building of an automobile works at Nizhni, the tractor works at Chelyabinsk, the engineering works at Sverdlovsk, the combine building works at Saratov and Novosibirsk: the growing non-ferrous metal industry in Siberia and Kazakstan, which demands the creation of a network of repair shops and a number of basic metal works in the East: finally, the decision to build textile factories in Novosibirsk and Turkestan—all this imperatively demands an immediate commencement of the work of creating a second coal and metallurgical base in the Urals."*

The formation of a new coal and metallurgical base in the East will be of very great importance for the defence of the U.S.S.R.

The Sixteenth Congress squarely confronted the country with the question of developing and reconstructing the transport system. From the end of the war until 1930 the railway system of the U.S.S.R. increased by 12,800 kilometres (in 1930 we completed the construction of the first large railroad line built under the Soviet regime, the Turksib). However, the equipment of the transport system was left in the main unchanged. In this regard we were far behind the technique of the advanced capitalist countries (U.S.A., Japan). And meanwhile the freight turnover had doubled as compared with the pre-war period and tended to increase still more rapidly.

We were thus faced with the necessity of radically recon-

---

* Stalin, "Political Report of the Central Committee to the Sixteenth Congress of the C.P.S.U." *Leninism*, Vol. II.

structing our railway system. Without such reconstruction the transport could not cope with its task.

The congress devoted particular attention to the question of strengthening the communications between the central part of the country and the new industrial district which was being developed in the Urals and Siberia.

Comrade Stalin in his report laid stress on the disgraceful conditions of our water transport. In 1930 the Volga Steamship Company was carrying only 60 per cent of the pre-war freight traffic, while the Dnieper Steamship Company was carrying only 40 per cent. This situation had to be radically changed.

The Sixteenth Congress issued a new slogan of socialist construction in the U.S.S.R., the slogan of accelerating the development of the light industries producing articles of mass consumption. Having restored heavy industry, we were already in a position to provide more funds for light industries, which had heretofore been lagging behind the rate of development set by the Five-Year Plan. The principal cause of this backwardness was the shortage of raw materials. But in 1930 the Party succeeded in considerably enlarging the area under cotton, sugar beet and industrial crops in general. The achievements of industrialisation rendered it possible more rapidly to develop the light industries, particularly the textile and food industries, thus definitely overcoming the commodity shortage in the country and eliminating the difficulty of providing food supplies for the proletarian centres.

By persistent work for the socialist reconstruction of agriculture, by developing Soviet and collective farms, the Party succeeded in the main in solving the grain problem. This problem had occupied the centre of the Party's attention for two years. The basic argument of the Right opportunists in their struggle against the general line of the Party was to assert the degradation of agriculture, particularly in the grain regions. In a number of documents the Rights tried to prove that the area under grain crops had decreased. Even the drought in the Ukraine and Northern Caucasus in 1928 and the destruction of a part of the grain in these regions as a result of frosts was used by them as an argument against the policy of the Party. The solution of the grain problem, the overcoming of the grain crisis in the country and the creation of large grain reserves in the hands of the state constituted a supreme victory of the Party over the kulak and his Right opportunist agents in the ranks of the Party. But this victory had to be clinched by the further development of Soviet and collective farms, by the ploughing of millions of hectares of virgin soil in the Trans-Volga region, in the Urals, in Siberia and Kazakstan by the tractors of the Soviet and collective farms.*

But the solution of the grain problem confronted the Party with another very important problem—that of cattle breeding.

In this field a serious situation had arisen on the eve of the Congress as a result of the desperate resistance which the kulak offered to our work of socialist reconstruction.

The kulaks everywhere tried to persuade and to provoke the poor and middle peasants to kill off their cattle, particularly before they joined the collective farms, arguing either that "the collective farm would take them away anyhow" or that those who joined the collective farm without cattle would be given cattle by the state. Such cases of kulak provocation, designed to take advantage of the ignorance, backwardness and private property instincts of the peasant, became quite widespread. It was one of the forms of the class struggle of the kulak against the Soviet power. The kulak was considerably aided in this by the excesses which were committed with regard to socialising the cattle during the process of collectivisation.

As a result of this the country experienced a serious shortage of meat and dairy products.

The measures decided upon by the Sixteenth Congress of the Party for the solution of the cattle breeding problem were designed to effect a rapid development of cattle breeding, particularly of hog breeding Soviet farms, the importation of pedigree horned cattle suitable for early breeding, the development of the

---

* "The question of the cultivation of waste and virgin soil is of the utmost importance for our agriculture," said Comrade Stalin in his speech at the Conference of Marxist Agrarians. "We know that one of the aims of the agrarian movement was to do away with the lack of land. At that time there were many who believed that this shortage of land was absolute, that there was no more free cultivable land to be had. And what actually transpired? Now everyone sees plainly that there were and still are scores of millions of hectares of free soil in the Soviet Union. The peasant, however, was quite unable to till this soil with his wretched implements. Since

meat industry and the increased development of cattle breeding in the collective farms.

Large-scale cattle breeding Soviet farms, as a base for the meat and dairy industry, were being created primarily in the east of the U.S.S.R.

In addition to this the Party undertook the task of transforming the so-called consuming regions into producing regions, by developing industrial and fodder crops and also by the development of grain farming.

The further increase of food and raw material supplies of the country was possible only on the basis of the socialist reconstruction of agriculture, of its mechanisation and tractorisation and of the intensified development of the Soviet and collective farms.

The Sixteenth Congress outlined measures for the consolidation and further development of the collective farms.

"Of decisive significance for the work of the Party at this time," reads the resolution of the Sixteenth Congress on the report of the Central Committee, "is the task of further drawing the poor and middle peasant farms into collective farms on a voluntary basis, the problem of *organising* the work in the collective farms, the problem of *distributing* the crop within the collective farms, the problem of training collective farm cadres, of raising the cultural level of the collective farm masses, of overcoming petty-bourgeois vacillations within the collective farms, of *strengthening the collective farms* by all possible means as the foundations of socialist construction in the countryside.

"While carrying out the slogan of basing itself on the collective farmer, in all its practical work in the countryside, the Party must resolutely fight against all tendencies to ignore or to underestimate individual poor and middle peasant farming, extending aid to this farming, strengthening the independent organisations of the poor peasants in the Soviets, co-operatives and lower links of the collective farm movement, carrying on extensive work among the individual peasants and drawing them into the collective farms."

The Party paid particular attention to the organisation of collective farms in the districts raising beet, flax and other

he was unable to cultivate waste and virgin land, he inclined to 'soft soil,' the soil belonging to the landowners, the soil adapted to tillage with the aid of implements at the disposal of the peasants under the conditions of individual labour. This was the cause of the shortage of land'." (*Leninism.* Vol. II.)

industrial crops, thus ensuring the creation of a strong, raw material base for the light industries.

The Socialist Offensive Along the Whole Front

By what means was the Party fulfilling the tremendous tasks of building socialism which it had set itself, by what means was it overcoming the difficulties which were to be met with in the carrying out of these tasks and which were a result of our colossal economic and cultural backwardness and of the resistance offered by the hostile class elements?

It was doing it by determinedly launching a general socialist offensive on all fronts, an offensive which the Party commenced at the end of 1929—the year of great change.

"What is the essence of the Bolshevik offensive in present conditions?

"The essence of the Bolshevik offensive lies, first of all, in mobilising the class vigilance and revolutionary activity of the masses against the capitalist elements in our country; mobilising the creative initiative and independent activity of the masses against the bureaucracy in our institutions and organisations which keeps the colossal reserves concealed in the heart of our social system idle, and does not allow them to be utilised; organising competition and labour enthusiasm among the masses to increase the productivity of labour and develop socialist construction.

"Secondly, the essence of the Bolshevik offensive lies in organising the reconstruction of all the practical work of our trade union, cooperative, soviet and all other kinds of mass organisation in keeping with the demands of the reconstruction period; in organising in them a nucleus of the most active and revolutionary workers, pushing aside and isolating the opportunist, narrow craft unionist and bureaucratic elements; driving out of them the hostile and degenerate elements, promoting new workers from below.

"Furthermore, the essence of the Bolshevik offensive lies in mobilising the maximum resources for financing our industry, our Soviet farms and collective farms, and in putting the best members of our Party on the task of developing this work.

"Lastly, the essence of the Bolshevik offensive lies in mobilising the Party itself to organise the whole offensive; strengthening and pulling together the Party organisations, driving out the elements of bureaucracy and degeneration, isolating and pushing aside those who express Right and 'Left' deviations from the Leninist line, pushing real, steadfast Leninists into the front ranks."*

* Stalin, "Political Report of the Central Committee to the Sixteenth Congress of the C.P.S.U." *Leninism*, Vol. II.

The Congress focussed the attention of the Party and of the working masses on the problem of technical and economic cadres, which had become one of the central problems of socialist construction.

Clearly perceiving the close connection between the rate of industrialisation decided upon and the task of raising the cultural level of the toiling masses, the Congress resolved to accelerate the rate of cultural development and to establish universal elementary education in the U.S.S.R. beginning with 1930-31. The Congress summed up the prolonged phase of the Party's struggle for its Leninist general line against the Right and "Left" opportunists. Both the Right and "Left" opportunists were still continuing their struggle against the Central Committee in open and concealed forms. Comrade Kaganovich, in his organisational report on the work of the Central Committee, pointed out that, for instance:

"Uglanov to this day still works against the Central Committee, to this day still maintains his connections with the deviationist elements of the Moscow organisation, to this day still instigates people on the quiet, on the sly, against the Central Committee of the Party."

"Why is the Right deviation at present the principal danger in the Party?" said Comrade Stalin. "Because it reflects the kulak danger, while the kulak danger at the present time, at the time of our general offensive and our uprooting of capitalism, is the main danger in the country."*

The Congress emphatically repudiated all tendencies to minimise the Right danger and all conciliationism towards it— tendencies which demobilised the Party and undermined its fighting capacity at a time when we had not yet overcome the resistance of the kulak, when the kulak still continued by various methods to influence the anarchic petty-bourgeois forces and to direct them against the proletarian dictatorship, and when the desperate struggle of the kulak continued to be a steady source of inspiration for Right opportunism.

The Right deviation continued to be the main front opposing the general line of the Party, closely connected as it was with elements which were hostile to the proletarian dictatorship and which were fighting for the restoration of capitalism in the

* *Ibid.*

country. It is characteristic that on a great number of questions (the rate of socialist construction, collectivisation) Trotskyism should have adopted the viewpoint of the Right deviation and that of late there had been more frequent efforts of an ever more systematic character to create a united front of the Right and "Left" opportunists against the Party on the ideological basis of the Right deviation.*

Finally, a new and highly significant fact was the coalescence of Right opportunism, in the Party with anti-Soviet counter-revolutionary tendencies in the country. A large number of counter-revolutionary organisations in the country were found to have been connected by close ideological (and sometimes not only ideological) bonds with Right opportunism in the Party.

Bearing all this in mind, the Congress declared the views of the Right opposition to be incompatible with membership of the C.P.S.U.

The former leaders of the Right opposition, Rykov and Tomsky, found themselves once more forced to declare at the Congress that their former point of view was erroneous and that the general line of the Party was correct. The Congress, however, was not at all satisfied with the form of their statements which were characterised by an obvious desire to gloss over the errors they had committed. Moreover, the Congress had to take into account that the former leaders of the Right opposition had not fulfilled the pledge which they had already given the Party in November 1929 to wage an active struggle against the Right deviation and against conciliationism in regard to it. Nevertheless the Congress elected the former leaders of the Right opposition to the Central Committee, thus giving them the opportunity to show in actual fact that now at any rate, after the Congress, they were willing and able actively to defend the general line of the Party.

But the Congress included a special provision in the resolution on the report of the Central Committee, giving the Party a weapon against all hypocritical and double-faced manoeuvres, which it had reason to expect from the former leaders of the Right opposition.

---

* This was manifested particularly clearly after the Congress in the case of the unprincipled, double-faced Right-"Leftist" *bloc* of Syrtsov and Lominadze.

"The Congress draws the attention of the whole Party to the fact that opportunists of all shades, particularly the Rights, are resorting to a new manoeuvre, which finds its expression in a formal recognition of their errors and in a formal acceptance of the general line of the Party, but which does not corroborate this recognition by work and struggle for the general line. In reality, this signifies only a transition from an open struggle against the Party to a concealed struggle or to waiting for a more propitious moment for resuming the attack on the Party. The Party must declare a most merciless war against this sort of duplicity and deceit and must demand that all those who acknowledge their errors shall prove the sincerity of their admissions by actively defending the general line of the Party. Those who fail to live up to this demand should be dealt with by resolute organisational measures."

The social base of the "Left" deviation during the preceding years had been the decaying petty bourgeoisie and the declassed elements in town and countryside.

The rapid rate of the socialist industrialisation of the U.S.S.R. and of the collectivisation of agriculture had contracted and continued to contract this social base. But it still existed. And it continued to exert a certain influence on individual sections of the poor peasants and on individual groups of backward workers. It fostered the parasitic and equalitarian tendencies in the collective farms, which are usually covered up with "Left" phrases ("Leftist" equalitarianism). This petty-bourgeois social base still continues even now to be the source of "Left" excesses in collective farm construction.

The experience with the anti-middle peasant excesses of the spring of 1930 had already shown to what an extent the "Left" method of arbitrary administrative action, of running too far ahead, of the desire to exceed at all costs the pace determined upon by the Party, played into the hands of Right opportunism, the main danger within the Party, and of the kulak capitalist elements, whose agency it is.

For this reason the struggle against "Left" opportunism, against all kinds of "Left" excesses and against conciliationism in regard to them, against the "Leftist" dizziness from success, continued to be an immediate task of the Party, an essential condition for the overcoming of the main Right opportunist danger.

27*

During the years preceding the Sixteenth' Congress, the Party organisations underwent a considerable increase.

On January 1, 1928, the Party had 1,302,000 members and candidates.

On April 1, 1930 (at the conclusion of the purging), the Party had 1,852,000 members and candidates, including 1,210,000 members.

At the time of the Fourteenth Congress the working class core of the Party constituted 58 per cent of the total; by the time of the Sixteenth Congress it had risen to 68 per cent. At the time of the Fourteenth Congress, workers at the bench constituted about 36 per cent, and at the time of the Sixteenth Congress about 49 per cent.

The Plenum of the Central Committee of November 1928 had issued instructions to raise the number of workers at the bench in the Party to 50 per cent and these instructions had in the main been carried out.

The Congress fully approved:

"The work carried out by the Central Control Commission for purging the ranks of the Party of socially and ideologically alien elements, of careerists, degenerated and bureaucratised elements who hinder the extension of the socialist offensive."

The Sixteenth Party Conference, more than a year prior to the Congress, had expressed itself in favour of the periodic carrying out of such a purge.

The Congress fully endorsed the report of Comrade Molotov on the work of the C.P.S.U. delegation in the Executive Committee of the Communist International.

The Congress pointed out that the analysis of the international situation and the appraisal of the partial stabilisation of capitalism given by the previous Congresses, particularly by the Fifteenth Congress of the C.P.S.U. and by the Sixth Congress of the Comintern, had been completely confirmed and that the present time, with its acute world economic crisis, was the beginning of the end of capitalist stabilisation.

The Congress noted with satisfaction the active part played by the C.P.S.U. delegation in the solution of a number of very important questions of the Communist International—in outlining the tactics of independent leadership in the class battles, intensifying the struggle against Social-Democracy, which had become fascised, and against its agents in the ranks of the Communist movement, the Right opportunist deviators.

The Congress was able to record considerable achievement in the work of extending the influence of the Comintern sections among the broad masses of the working class and among the toilers in the colonies.

Following a report by Comrade Kuibyshev on the fulfilment of the Five-Year Plan, the Congress adopted a detailed resolution focussing attention particularly on the quality of the work of our industry and on the need to improve it.

The resolution pointed out that:

"It was only as a result of an irreconcilable struggle against the Right opportunists that the Party could have achieved, and did achieve its tremendous success in the fulfilment of the Five-Year Plan. Further achievements of socialist construction are possible only by continuing this struggle against the Right deviation as the main danger in the Party and against conciliationism in regard to it.

"At the same time it is necessary to carry on a most resolute struggle both against the remnants of Trotskyism and also against all excesses and "Leftist" exaggerations of a super-industrialisation type. The exposure and repression of "Left" opportunist exaggerations is an essential condition for a successful struggle against the Right opportunist deviation, which is the main danger in our Party."

The resolution of the Congress on the report of Comrade Yakovlev regarding the collective farm movement and the raising of agriculture summarised the results of the Party policy in the socialist reconstruction of agriculture and outlined the further prospects in this field.

The resolution sounded an emphatic warning against transferring the organisational system of Soviet farm management into the collective farms, since, unlike the Soviet farms, which are state enterprises created with the resources of the state, the collective farms are voluntary social unions of the peasants created with the resources of the peasants' themselves, with all the consequences arising therefrom.

The resolution emphasised that:

"The main form of the collective farm at this stage is the agricultural artel. To demand that the peasants, in joining the artel, should immediately renounce all individualistic habits and interests, and forego the possibility of engaging, in addition to socialist farming, in personal farming (a cow, sheep, poultry, vegetable garden), and the possibility of profiting by outside earnings, etc.—to demand this means to forget the A.B.C. of Marxism-Leninism....

"The artel *does not complete, but is only the beginning* of the creation of a new social discipline, of the task of teaching the peasants socialist construction. In the collective farms, the peasants will not finally outlive their petty-proprietor psychology, the desire for private accumulation, inherited from generations of small private owners, except as a result of years of persistent work directed towards placing the collective farms on a basis of large-scale mechanised farming, of persistent work for the creation of cadres from the ranks of the collective farmers and for raising the cultural level of the whole mass of collective farmers."

Finally, there was the resolution on the report of Comrade Shvernik regarding the tasks of the trade unions in the reconstruction period. This resolution gave a detailed appraisal of the old opportunist leadership of the trade unions which had endeavored to prevent the trade unions from taking part in socialist construction and which was dominated by backward petty-bourgeois tendencies. It called for a real turn in the work of the trade unions to face the tasks of industry, to face the basic questions of socialist construction, shock-brigade work and socialist competition. In this resolution the production tasks of the trade unions were organically linked up with the tasks of defending the material and cultural needs of the workers, with their cultural and political education. The resolution laid especial stress on the tasks of the trade unions as mass organisations of the proletariat in the work for the socialist reconstruction of agriculture, whereas the former Right opportunist leadership of the All-Union Central Council of Trade Unions headed by Tomsky had refused on principle to meddle with this task.

The most important political conclusion which the Sixteenth Congress of the Party drew from the enormous work which had been carried out by the Party in the period preceding the Congress was that we had now entered upon the period of socialism.

"Our period is usually called the period of transition from capitalism to socialism," said Comrade Stalin. "It was called the transition period in 1918, when Lenin, in his famous article, *On 'Left' Childishness,* first gave the description of this period with its five forms of economic life. It is called the transition period today in 1930, when some of these forms are obsolete and are already going to the bottom, while one of them, namely, the new order in the sphere of industry and agriculture, is growing and developing with unprecedented speed. Can it be said that these two transitional periods are identical, and are not radically different from each other? Clearly it cannot. What did we have in the economic sphere in 1918? Ruined industry and mechanical cigarette-lighters,* no collective or Soviet farms as a mass movement, the growth of the 'new' bourgeoisie in the towns and the kulaks in the country. What have we got today? Socialist industry which has been restored and is being reconstructed, a widespread system of Soviet and collective farms, embracing over 40 per cent of the total sown area of the U.S.S.R. in the spring sowing alone, a dying 'new' bourgeoisie in the town, a dying kulak class in the country. The first was a transitional period, the second is a transitional period. And yet they are as far apart from each other as heaven and earth. And no one can deny that we are on the eve of liquidating the last serious capitalist class, the kulak class. It is clear that we have already passed out of the transitional period in the old sense, and have entered the period of the direct and full-fledged building of socialism all along the line. It is clear that we have already entered the period of socialism, because the socialist sector now controls all the economic levers of the whole of national economy, although we are still a long way from the completion of socialist society and the abolition of class differences."**

The National Question at the Sixteenth Congress

Comrade Stalin devoted a great deal of attention in his political report to the national question at the present stage of socialist construction in the U.S.S.R. and to the struggle against nationalist deviations. Since the Twelfth Congress, this question had not been raised in full scope at the Party congresses and conferences. There was no need for this, since the decisions of the Twelfth Congress remained in full force and were unswervingly carried out in practice. The Twelfth Congress set the Party the tremendous task of eliminating the remnants of national inequality in the economic and cultural field and of the vestiges of Great Russian and local chauvinism connected with them and of overcoming the nationalist deviations within the Party, while concentrating its main fire on the Great Russian deviation.

---

* At the time, the metal industry was in a state of disorganisation and the factories were idle, and the workers were making cigarette lighters on their own account.

** Stalin, "Political Report of the Central Committee to the Sixteenth Congress of the C.P.S.U." *Leninism,* Vol. II.

Since 1923 there had been a mighty development of economic construction and of cultural work in the national minority republics and regions—in the Ukraine, White Russia, Transcaucasia, Central Asia, Kazakstan, etc.

In his speech "On the Political Tasks of the University of the Peoples of the East" delivered in 1925, Comrade Stalin emphasised the exceptional importance of work directed towards the development and raising of the national cultures of the various peoples of the Soviet Union, referring in this speech primarily to the Eastern peoples.

"But what is national culture? How are we to make national culture compatible with proletarian culture? Did not Lenin, in pre-war days, say that we had two cultures: bourgeois culture and proletarian culture, and that the slogan of 'national culture' was a reactionary slogan of the bourgeoisie, which is striving to infect the minds of the workers with the virus of nationalism? How are we to reconcile the development of national culture, the inauguration of schools and courses in the native languages, and the training of Communist cadres from among the local people, with the building of socialism, with the building of proletarian culture? Is this not an impenetrable contradiction? Of course not! We are now building proletarian culture. That is absolutely true. But it is also true that proletarian culture, which is socialist in content, is assuming different forms and different means of expression among the various peoples who have been drawn into the work of socialist construction, according to their language, their local customs and so forth. Proletarian in content and national in form—such is the human culture towards which socialism is marching. Proletarian culture does not cancel national culture, but gives it content. On the other hand, national culture does not cancel proletarian culture, but gives it form. The slogan of 'national culture' was a bourgeois slogan so long as the bourgeoisie was in power and the consolidation of nations proceeded under the aegis of the bourgeois system. The slogan of 'national culture' became a proletarian slogan when the proletariat came into power, and the consolidation of nations began to proceed under the aegis of the Soviet power. He who has not grasped the difference of principle between these two different situations will never understand Leninism, nor the substance of the national question from the Leninist point of view."*

But the enforcement of the national policy of the Party continued to encounter violent resistance on the part of bourgeois

* Stalin, *Leninism*, Vol. I.

chauvinist elements—a resistance which increased in some sections as the class struggle in the country became more acute.

Of late it had been Great Russian chauvinism which had shown the greatest activity, and this activity was undoubtedly in proportion to the relative importance of Russian kulakdom and of the Russian urban petty bourgeoisie and intelligentsia in the economic and cultural life of the Soviet Union and in individual national minority republics.

This activity was reflected within the Party in a tendency to revise the decisions of the Twelfth Congress and the very foundations of the national policy of the Party and of the Soviet government, in a tendency to interpret the increased measure of planning and centralisation in the guidance of the economy of the U.S.S.R. (the creation of an All-Union People's Commissariat of Agriculture, the concentration of control over the basic industries in the respective commissariats of the Soviet Union)—a process which was inevitable in the course of socialist construction—as a prelude to the abolition of the national minority republics, in efforts to utilise Lenin's struggle against the slogan of national culture under capitalist conditions as proof of the incorrectness of the Party line of creating and strengthening national Soviet Republics and of developing the cultures of the national minorities during the period of the proletarian dictatorship. On this basis a theory was developing of the fusion of all nationalities in the U.S.S.R. into one Russian nationality with one Russian language.

On the other hand, in the national minority republics, local chauvinism was also growing more active, supported as it was by the bourgeoisie and kulaks of the non-Russian peoples who were seeking salvation from the rapid growth of the socialist elements of the national economy, from the all-round collectivisation and the liquidation of the kulaks as a class in bourgeois counter-revolution under the banner of secession from the U.S.S.R. and in an orientation towards the capitalist neighbours of the Soviet Union (Poland, Rumania, Persia, Afghanistan).

The Congress resolved that:

"The main danger at the present stage is the Great Russian deviation, which endeavours to revise the foundations of the Leninist national policy and which, under the banner of internationalism, conceals the aspirations of the dying classes of the formerly dominant Great Russian nationality to regain their lost privileges. At the same time the deviation towards local nationalism, which weakens the unity of the peoples of the U.S.S.R. and plays into the hands of the interventionists, is also raising its head.

"The Party must intensify the struggle against both deviations on the national question and against conciliationism in regard to them, at the same time paying increased attention to the practical putting into effect of the Leninist national policy, to the elimination of the elements of national inequality and to the widespread development of the national cultures of the peoples of the Soviet Union."

The increased activity of the working class and of the poor and middle peasant masses in the national minority republics which constitute a considerable part of the U.S.S.R. and play a tremendous role in the economy of the Soviet Union,* is closely connected with the firm enforcement of the national policy, with the adoption of the native language of the local workers and peasants in the Party, trade union and Soviet apparatus, with the training of local cadres, with the task of developing in every way the cultures of all the peoples of the Soviet Union, national in form and socialist in content.

Without this it is impossible to secure the successful construction of socialism in the national minority republics; without this it is impossible finally to overcome the local nationalism which is seeking allies beyond the Soviet borders; without this it is impossible to transform the national minority republics into an unconquerable bulwark of the Soviet power against all external enemies.

In order fully to grasp the chauvinist stupidity of the "Communists" who favour the abolition of the national minority republics, it is sufficient to recall the intertwining of nationalities existing on both sides of the Soviet frontiers throughout their whole vast extent.

Beyond the western frontier of the Soviet Union, are entire districts populated by Karelians (in Finland), White Russians, Ukrainians and Moldavians (the Moldavians constitute a con-

---

* The Ukraine is the principal coal and metallurgical base of the U.S.S.R.: Azerbaijan is the principal base of the oil industry; Central Asia is the principal cotton base, and Kazakstan the principal base of non-ferrous metallurgy and of livestock breeding.—*N.P.*

siderable part of the population of the autonomous Moldavian Soviet Republic and also of Bessarabia which is under Rumanian bourgeois occupation). In all these districts the bourgeoisie is carrying on a rabid nationalist agitation. The "Communists" who favour the abolition of the national minority republics fail to understand what a powerful stimulus this agitation would get if the Soviet government decided to revise the Leninist national policy.

Now it is just the opposite. Polish fascism is forcibly "Polonising" the Ukrainian and White Russian population of western Ukraine and western White Russia, and this results in their being drawn towards the Soviet Union, not only on a social basis but on a national basis as well. A similar policy is being pursued by the Rumanian bourgeoisie in Bessarabia as regards the Moldavians, not to mention the other nationalities. And what is the situation along the Asiatic frontier of the U.S.S.R.?

The northern part of Persia bordering upon Transcaucasia is inhabited by Azerbaijan Tyurks, while Central Asia is inhabited by Turkomen. On the other side of our Afghanistan frontier there are again Turkomen as well as Uzbeks and Tajiks. Western China is inhabited by Kirghizians and Kazaks. Mongolia is inhabited by Mongols who speak the same language as our Buryat-Mongols.

Finally, the U.S.S.R. has been and remains a model laboratory for the solution of the national question for the whole world.

The interests of the international proletarian revolution, which are indissolubly bound up with the interests of internal socialist construction, demand of our Party that it resolutely extend the Leninist national policy, making its tempo conform to the general Bolshevik tempo of our socialist construction. This presupposes the waging of a most determined struggle against nationalist deviations within the Party, above all against the Great Russian deviation.

It was against this deviation that Comrade Stalin uttered the following trenchant words in his speech in reply to the debate at the Sixteenth Congress:

"The theory of the fusion of all the nations of, say, the U.S.S.R. into one common *Great Russian* nation with one common *Great-Russian* tongue is a national-jingoist, anti-Leninist theory, which is in contradiction to the basic principle of Leninism that national distinctions cannot disappear in the near future, and that they are bound to remain for a long time, even after the victory of the proletarian revolution *all over the world*. As for the development of national cultures and national tongues taken in more distant perspective, I have always maintained, and continue to maintain, the Leninist view that in the period of the victory of socialism *all over the world,* when socialism has been consolidated and become a matter of every-day life, the national languages. must inevitably fuse into one common language, which, of course, will be neither Great Russian nor German, but something new."

After the Sixteenth Congress**

The period after the Sixteenth Congress has been marked by new and mighty victories for the general line of the Party.

Having achieved the further growth and strengthening of heavy industry by carrying out the decisions of the Sixteenth Congress, the Party has secured the creation of our country's own base for the socialist reconstruction of the whole national economy, has secured the fulfilment of the main political tasks set us in the Five-Year Plan, has secured the fulfilment of the Five-Year Plan in four years in the largest branches of our industry and has done away with unemployment.

Of particularly great importance are the achievements of the Soviet Union in the development of high quality metal industries, formerly almost non-existent in our country; in the development of the construction of various types of machines which were not produced in tsarist Russia—automobile and tractor industry, heavy machinery construction (blooming mills, etc.); and in the development of the chemical industry. These are decisive achievements for securing the technical and economic independence of our country, for strengthening its defensive capacity and its international power.

On the basis of the powerful development of heavy industry, the Party, under the leadership of the Central Committee, is at the present time taking all measures for the maximum development of light industry and of the production of articles of mass consumption.

* Stalin, *Leninism,* Vol. II.
** This section brings down the history of the Party to the period before the Seventeenth Party Conference.—*Ed.*

The main form of agriculture in the Soviet Union during the period following the Sixteenth Congress has become the socialist agriculture of the Soviet and collective farms. The plan for collectivisation envisaged in the Five-Year Plan has been greatly exceeded. Agriculture in the Soviet Union has definitely taken the socialist path of development. The collective farmer has become the dominant figure in agriculture.

We have completed the construction of the foundation of socialist economy in our country. The question of "who will defeat whom" in the struggle of the socialist elements against the capitalist elements has been decided in favour of socialism.

The results of the historic contest between the two systems which have existed side by side for a period of fifteen years, the system of moribund capitalism and the system of rapidly growing socialism, are being revealed ever more clearly before the broad toiling masses of the whole world. Beyond the borders of the Soviet Union, in the capitalist countries, there is disintegration and crisis. Meanwhile the Soviet Union has drawn the balance of the victorious accomplishment of the first Five-Year Plan and is embarking on a practical programme for the building of a classless socialist society in the second Five-Year Plan.

But side by side with the tremendous achievements we still have a number of great defects in the work of socialist industry and agriculture—the backwardness of metallurgy and transport, the insufficient development of the production of articles of mass consumption, the low crop yield.

The Party is faced with the task of definitely eliminating these defects by further consistently enforcing the Six Conditions of Comrade Stalin—organised recruiting of workers and their retention in the given enterprise, eliminating the fluctuation of labour, improving the material and general living conditions of the workers, overcoming wage-levelling and lack of personal responsibility, solving the problem of cadres, training specialists from the ranks of the working class and correctly utilising the services of the old specialists, enforcing cost accounting, developing Soviet trade, in particular collective farm trade and commodity circulation on the basis of the further organisational and economic strengthening of the Soviet and collective farms; and further putting into effect Comrade Stalin's slogan to master technique.

We have in the main completed all-round collectivisation and the liquidation of the kulaks as a class in the principal agricultural districts of the country. But the remnants of kulakdom are still offering desperate resistance, influencing the individual farmers and the backward sections among the collective farmers, striving to disrupt the collective farms, to sabotage the sowing campaign, to undermine the carrying out of the state collections of grain and other agricultural products.

Insufficient Bolshevik vigilance and the fact that some of the village Party organisations are clogged with alien and degenerated elements aid the kulak in his counter-revolutionary activities which are aimed at disrupting the grain collections and sowing campaigns, as was the case in the Northern Caucasus (Kuban) in the latter part of 1932. By purging the Party organisations of alien and degenerated elements and by mobilising the masses of collective farmers to fight under the leadership of the Party against the remnants of kulak elements and for the fulfilment of the obligations to the state, the Party will secure the strengthening of the collective farms as a socialist form of economy and ensure the further development of agriculture.

"The new successes of socialism will be secured by the working class only in a struggle against the relics of capitalism, by pitilessly crushing the resistance of the perishing elements of capitalism, by overcoming the bourgeois and petty-bourgeois prejudices to be found among the toilers, and by persistent work in re-educating them along socialist lines.

"This means that an intensification in the class struggle will still be inevitable in future at certain periods and particularly in certain districts and certain sections of socialist construction, which at the same time emphasises the fact that bourgeois influences upon individual strata or groups of workers will inevitably remain and in some cases may even grow stronger, that for a long time to come class influences alien to the proletariat will inevitably penetrate the working class and even the Party. In view of this the Party faces the task of strengthening the proletarian dictatorship and of increasing its struggle against opportunism, especially the Right deviation which is the main danger at the given stage."*

Right opportunism, which is lapsing into the standpoint of counter-revolution, continues to be the agency of kulakdom within

---

* *Forward to the Second Five-Year Plan,* Resolutions of the Seventeenth Party Conference, p. 38.

the Party. "Leftist" excesses, "Leftist" tendencies to wild scheming and skipping over difficulties, play into the hands of Right opportunism and of the remnants of kulakdom which are at the back of it.

The task of fighting on two fronts continues to confront the Party in all its urgency. The Right danger remains as the main danger. Anyone who does not understand this is playing into the hands of the kulak elements.

The achievements of our Party in accomplishing the socialist industrialisation of the Soviet Union—a process which has already raised the economic and political power of our country to an unprecedented height—have helped the Soviet government to uphold the cause of peace in the struggle against international imperialism.

But the bourgeoisie is seeking a way out of the crisis in war. The rabid imperialist cliques in various countries of the East and West continue to prepare for intervention against the Soviet Union. The U.S.S.R. and the C.P.S.U. have to face, as a task of particular urgency, the problem of securing a continued Bolshevik tempo of industrialisation which, along with the revolutionary movement in the capitalist and colonial countries, constitutes a very real factor in the struggle against the war danger, as it is also a factor for the revolutionisation of the toiling masses beyond the borders of the Soviet Union.

"It is sometimes asked," said Comrade Stalin at the Conference of Managers of Soviet Industry on February 4, 1931, "whether it is not possible to slow down a bit in *tempo,* to retard the movement. No, comrades, this is impossible. It is impossible to reduce the *tempo!* On the contrary, it is necessary as far as possible to accelerate it. This necessity is dictated by our obligations to the workers and peasants of the U.S.S.R. This is dictated to us by our obligations to the working class of the whole world.

"To slacken the *tempo* means to fall behind. And the backward are always beaten. But we do not want to be beaten. No, we do not want this! Incidentally, the history of old Russia is the history of defeats due to backwardness. She was beaten by the Mongol Khans. She was beaten by the Turkish beys. She was beaten by the Swedish feudal barons. She was beaten by the Polish-Lithuanian "squires." She was beaten by the Anglo-French capitalists. She was beaten by the Japanese barons. All beat her for her backwardness, for military backwardness, for cultural backwardness, for governmental backwardness, for industrial backwardness, for agricultural backwardness. She was beaten because to beat her was profitable and could be done with impunity. Do you remember the words of the pre-revolutionary poet: 'You are both poor and abundant, you are both powerful and helpless, mother Russia.' These words of the old poet were well known to those gentlemen. They beat her saying: 'You are abundant,' so we can enrich ourselves at your expense. They beat her saying: 'You are poor and helpless,' so you can be beaten and plundered with impunity. Such is the law of capitalism—to beat the backward and the weak. The jungle law of capitalism. You are backward, you are weak, so you are wrong, hence you can be beaten and enslaved. You are mighty, so you are right, hence, we must be wary of you.

"That is why we must no longer be backward.

"In the past we did not and could not have any fatherland. But now that we have a working class government, we have a fatherland, and we will defend its independence. Do you want our socialist fatherland to be beaten and to lose its independence? If you do not want this you must put an end to this backwardness as speedily as possible and develop genuine Bolshevik speed in building up the socialist system of economy. There are no other ways. That is why Lenin said during the October Revolution: 'Either death, or we must overtake and surpass the advanced capitalist countries.'

"We are 50-100 years behind the advanced countries. We must cover this distance in ten years. Either we do this or they will crush us.

"This is what our obligation to the workers and peasants of the U.S.S.R. dictates to us. ·

"We have, however, still more serious and more important obligations. These are our obligations to the world proletariat. They coincide with our first obligations. But we regard them as being still higher. The working class of the U.S.S.R. is part of the world working class. We have triumphed not only as a result of the efforts of the working class of the U.S.S.R. but also as a result of the support of the working class of the world. Without this support we would long ago have been torn to pieces. It is said that our country is the shock-brigade of the proletariat of all countries. This is well said. This imposes very serious obligations upon us. Why does the international proletariat support us? How did we deserve this support? We merited it by the fact that we were the first to fling ourselves into the battle against capitalism, we were the first to establish a working class state, we were the first to begin building socialism. We merited it by the fact that we are working for a cause which, if successful, will change the whole world and free the entire working class. And what is wanted for success? The elimination of our backwardness, the development of a high Bolshevik *tempo* of construction. We must move forward so that the working class of the whole world, looking at us, might say: 'Here is my vanguard, here is my shock-brigade, here is my working class state, here is my fatherland; they are promoting their cause which is our cause, well, let us support them against the capitalists and spread the cause of the world revolution.' "*

The Party is advancing with the measured tread of its countless proletarian battalions to the consummation of socialism in our country, to the strengthening of the U.S.S.R. as the base of the international proletarian revolution, to the victory of the revolution on an international scale.

The Party in the course of decades has proved capable of creating a picked staff such as no army has ever had, a staff which is strong by virtue of its vast collective experience and its unshakable confidence in the forces of the working class, a staff which has never lost courage and has never wavered even at the most difficult moments.

During the years of the reconstruction period, during the years of the general socialist offensive on all fronts, the ranks of our Party have grown considerably stronger.

In exposing Trotskyism and Right opportunism, the Party has done a tremendous work to promote the ideological solidarity of its ranks, the ideological training of its cadres in Marxism-Leninism and the generalisation and assimilation of the great wealth of experience which we have gained in our socialist construction.

In the course of this work, the Party has exposed a number of hostile anti-Leninist ideological systems, which, hiding under the Soviet and sometimes even under the Communist flag, won over individual groups of Party members, but which in reality were directed against the Party and against the proletarian dictatorship (Rubinism, Menshevik idealism, etc.).

In the autumn of 1931 appeared Comrade Stalin's letter to the editors of *Proletarskaya Revolyutsia.* Comrade Stalin exposed the "rotten liberalism, which has spread, to a certain extent, among a section of the Bolsheviks," and drew the attention of the whole Party to the fact that with the aid of rotten liberalism, Trotskyist contraband, brazen slander against Lenin, against the Party and its policy in the interpretation of some very important questions regarding the history of Bolshevism was being smuggled into our historical literature.

Rotten liberalism is an attitude of conciliation, of toleration,

* Stalin, *Leninism,* Vol. II.

... towards directly hostile ... result of a relaxed or lost sense of ... the beginning of a direct departure from the position of ... of out-and-out degeneration. It thus becomes an outright ... a betrayal of the cause of the ...

Comrade Stalin's letter was of tremendous significance for the fraternal Communist ... mobilising them for a struggle against the remnants of Luxemburgism which hinder the resolute and correct carrying out ... Bolshevik policy.

Comrade Stalin focussed ... attention of the whole Party and above all of the Communist historians on Trotskyist contraband in literature dealing with the history of the Party—contraband which found its expression in the denial of the international role of Bolshevism, in efforts to depict Lenin as a centrist or semi-centrist, in slanderous misrepresentation of the Bolshevik strategy and tactics during the period of the 1905 Revolution.

"It seems to me that 'historians' and 'litterateurs' of the category of the Trotskyist smugglers are for the present trying to carry on their work of smuggling along two lines.

"First of all, they are trying to prove that Lenin in the period before the war underestimated the danger of centrism, while leaving the inexperienced reader to surmise that Lenin was not at that time a real revolutionary but became one only after the war, after he had been re-equipped with Trotsky's help. Slutsky may be regarded as a typical representative of such a type of smuggler. We have seen above that Slutsky and Co. are not worth our bothering about much.

"Secondly, they try to prove that Lenin in the pre-war period did not understand the necessity for the bourgeois-democratic revolution ... into the socialist revolution, while leaving the inexperienced ... surmise that Lenin was not at that time a real Bolshevik, that ... the necessity for such a development only after the war, after he had been re-equipped with Trotsky's help."

... Stalin's letter contributed enormously to the ideolog-... begin ... or a cau ... of the enti ... he entire ... o all sectors ... ion of our constructio ... he whole wor ... s my shock-bri ... and; they are p ...

to the work of raising the study c Party history to a real Bolshevik level.

In the struggle against opportuism and rotten liberalism, the Party is training its cadres in Bolsevik ideological intransigence, is rallying its ranks still more closy around its Leninist Central Committee, around its leader and eacher, Comrade Stalin. The forthcoming purging of the Party vill serve as a mighty weapon for the further strengthening of th Party's ideological solidarity.

The Party will demand of eac member a knowledge of the fundamental principles of its profamme and theory and of the main Party decisions, a readiness o fight for their enforcement in practice, to defend the general he of the Party in deeds, ruthlessly to expose the double-deale; and those who deceive the Party. The Party will purge its raks of decayed and degenerated elements, of hidden Trotskyists an Right opportunists.

By rallying the working class till more closely around itself, by strengthening the leading rol of the proletariat among the toiling masses, by purging its rans of opportunist and degenerated elements as well as of enenes who have sneaked into 'the Party, by enhancing in the dailystruggle its class homogeneity and fighting capacity and the Mrxist-Leninist consciousness of its members, by relying on the clossal experience of decades of heroic struggle, the Party will succed in overcoming all the difficulties which confront it in the vtorious construction of a classless socialist society.

not only towards opportunist, but also towards directly hostile ideas. Rotten liberalism is the result of a relaxed or lost sense of Party vigilance and sometimes the beginning of a direct departure from the position of the Party, of out-and-out degeneration. It thus becomes an outright crime, a betrayal of the cause of the working class.

Comrade Stalin's letter was of tremendous significance for the fraternal Communist Parties, mobilising them for a struggle against the remnants of Luxemburgism which hinder the resolute and correct carrying out of the Bolshevik policy.

Comrade Stalin focused the attention of the whole Party and above all of the Communist historians on Trotskyist contraband in literature dealing with the history of the Party—contraband which found its expression in the denial of the international role of Bolshevism, in efforts to depict Lenin as a centrist or semi-centrist, in slanderous misrepresentation of the Bolshevik strategy and tactics during the period of the 1905 Revolution.

"It seems to me that 'historians' and 'litterateurs' of the category of the Trotskyist smugglers are for the present trying to carry on their work of smuggling along two lines.

"First of all, they are trying to prove that Lenin in the period before the war underestimated the danger of centrism, while leaving the inexperienced reader to surmise that Lenin was not at that time a real revolutionary but became one only after the war, after he had been 're-equipped' with Trotsky's help. Slutsky may be regarded as a typical representative of such a type of smuggler. We have seen above that Slutsky and Co. are not worth our bothering about much.

"Secondly, they try to prove that Lenin in the pre-war period did not understand the necessity for the bourgeois-democratic revolution growing into the socialist revolution, while leaving the inexperienced reader to surmise that Lenin was not at that time a real Bolshevik, that he grasped the necessity for such a development only after the war, after he had been 're-equipped' with Trotsky's help." *

Comrade Stalin's letter contributed enormously to the ideological solidarity of the entire Party, to increasing the vigilance of the Party on all sectors of our struggle, both in the realm of theory and also in that of practice. It gave a powerful stimulus

* Stalin, "Questions Concerning the History of Bolshevism," *Leninism*, Vol. II.

to the work of raising the study of Party history to a real Bolshevik level.

In the struggle against opportunism and rotten liberalism, the Party is training its cadres in Bolshevik ideological intransigence, is rallying its ranks still more closely around its Leninist Central Committee, around its leader and teacher, Comrade Stalin. The forthcoming purging of the Party will serve as a mighty weapon for the further strengthening of the Party's ideological solidarity.

The Party will demand of each member a knowledge of the fundamental principles of its programme and theory and of the main Party decisions, a readiness to fight for their enforcement in practice, to defend the general line of the Party in deeds, ruthlessly to expose the double-dealers and those who deceive the Party. The Party will purge its ranks of decayed and degenerated elements, of hidden Trotskyists and Right opportunists.

By rallying the working class still more closely around itself, by strengthening the leading role of the proletariat among the toiling masses, by purging its ranks of opportunist and degenerated elements as well as of enemies who have sneaked into the Party, by enhancing in the daily struggle its class homogeneity and fighting capacity and the Marxist-Leninist consciousness of its members, by relying on the colossal experience of decades of heroic struggle, the Party will succeed in overcoming all the difficulties which confront it in the victorious construction of a classless socialist society.

BIOGRAPHICAL NOTES

BIOGRAPHICAL NOTES

(Of names appearing in both volumes of the *Outline History*)

ABRAMOVICH, R.—Prominent leader of the Bund and of the Menshevik Party. Participated in the Fourth and Fifth Congresses of the Party. At present a member of the Editorial Board of the Menshevik paper *Sotsialistichesky Vestnik*, published abroad. One of the most venomous enemies of the working class and of socialist construction in the U.S.S.R. Was exposed at the trial of the "Union Bureau" of the Mensheviks in the spring of 1931 as an active instigator of and participant in the preparations for armed intervention against the Soviet Union.

ADLER, F.—Leader of the Social-Democratic Party of Austria. One of the leaders of the social-fascist Second International, where he occupies a "Left" position, endeavouring to screen the present social-fascist policy of the Social-Democrats with "revolutionary" phrases.

ALEXEYEV, Peter—Textile worker; prominent revolutionary in the seventies of the last century; was an active member of the Moscow Narodnik circle of propagandists. In 1877 was tried together with other members of the circle ("The Trial of the Fifty"). Delivered a pronounced revolutionary speech at the trial which acquired widespread celebrity.

ALEXINSKY, G. A.—Participant in the Fourth and Fifth Congresses of the Party; was a member of the Second State Duma. In 1909, together with Bogdanov and others, broke with the Bolsheviks and joined the *Vperyod* group. On the outbreak of war, sided with the extreme social-patriots. In 1917 made foul and slanderous charges against Lenin and the Bolsheviks; was arrested in 1918 by the Cheka, was released on bail and escaped abroad. At present, a monarchist.

ARMAND, Ines—Party worker, participated in the Party Conference in 1913; represented the Bolshevik Central Committee at the Brussels Conference in the summer of 1914. Died in 1920.

ARTEM (SERGEYEV)—Old Party worker; delegate to the Fourth (Stockholm) Congress of the Party; one of the leaders of the October Revolution in the Ukraine, particularly at Kharkov and in the Donbas. Member of the Central Committee of the R.C.P. from 1917 to 1921. After the Tenth Congress of the Party, was elected chairman of the Central Committee of the Miners' Union. Was killed in a railway accident in July 1921.

AVKSENTYEV, N.—One of the leaders of the Socialist-Revolutionary Party. In 1917 joined the Kerensky government; was chairman of the so-called "pre-parliament" elected by the "democratic conference" in September 1917. In 1918 was president of the counter-revolutionary Ufa Directorate. Now a White émigré.

AXELROD, P. B.—An outstanding ideologist of Menshevism and an irreconcilable foe of Bolshevism. Played a prominent part in the Narodnik movement of the seventies of the last century; was one of the organisers of the "Cherny Peredel" and of the "Emancipation of Labour" group. Beginning with the Second Congress of the Russian Social-Democratic Labour Party, one of the most prominent leaders of Menshevism. After the October

Revolution, led the extreme Right wing of the Menshevik Party. One 'of the instigators and propagandists of foreign intervention against the U.S.S.R. Died in 1928.

BADAYEV, A.—Member of the Party since 1904; member of the Bolshevik fraction of the Fourth State Duma; participated in the Cracow and Poronin Conferences in 1912 and 1913. Member of the Central Committee of the C.P.S.U. and chairman of the Union of Consumers' Co-operatives of the Moscow Region.

BAKUNIN, M.—Well-known Russian revolutionary and anarchist. Left Russia in 1840; participated in the German revolution in 1848; was active in the First International, attempting to organise a secret alliance of the anarchists within its ranks. In 1872, on Marx's demand, was expelled from the First International for his disorganising activities. In the seventies of the last century, Bakunin's ideas were dominant among the Russian Narodnik intelligentsia. Died in 1876.

BAUER, Otto—Leader and theoretician of Austrian Social-Democracy; was Foreign Minister in the Austrian bourgeois government in 1918-19. In 1927, used all his influence for the suppression of the insurrection of the Vienna workers. Theoretician of the "Left" wing of the Second International; member of the Executive Committee of the Second International; enemy of the Soviet Union.

BAUMAN, N. E. (Grach)—Prominent Party worker in the early years of the present century; agent of the *Iskra;* delegate to the Second Congress of the R.S.D.L.P.; Bolshevik. Murdered by the Black Hundreds in Moscow during the October days of 1905.

BAZAROV, V.—Former Bolshevik. In 1917, was one of the editors of the conciliationist newspaper *Novaya Zhizn.* In 1929-30, played a leading role in the counter-revolutionary activities of the "Union Bureau" of the Mensheviks.

BEBEL, A.—One of the most outstanding leaders of German Social-Democracy and of the Second International; worker by origin. Adhered to the Centrist wing of German Social-Democracy. Died in 1913.

BERNSTEIN, Eduard—Prominent German Social-Democrat and revisionist. Author of the book *Problems of Socialism,* published in 1899, which criticised the foundations of Marxist doctrine on all fundamental questions of theory and policy. During the World War, Bernstein first occupied a social-chauvinist and later a Centrist position. At present, Bernstein's revisionist views have been officially recognised by the parties of the Second International. Died in 1932.

BLAGOYEV—Organised the first Social-Democratic group in Russia (in 1883); later belonged to the revolutionary wing of the Bulgarian labour movement and subsequently to the Communist Party of Bulgaria. Died in 1924.

BOGDANOV, A. A. (Maximov, Malinovsky, Ryadovoy)—Participated in the Social-Democratic circles of the 'nineties; one of the organisers of the Bureau of the Committees of the Majority in 1904; played an active part in the Third Congress of the Party; member of the Central Committee of the Party from 1905 to 1907; leader of the *Vperyod* group in 1909-10; author of a large number of works on economic and philosophical questions. In philosophy he upheld the idealist viewpoint of "empiro-monism," which was resolutely combated by Lenin who defended the viewpoint of dialectic materialism. After the October Revolution, Bogdanov held a Menshevik position, believing that our country was not ripe for a socialist revolution; was the ideological inspirer of the "Workers' Truth" group (in 1923), which put forward a Menshevik platform against the Party and its policy. Died in 1927.

BRANDLER, A.—Former German "Left" Social-Democrat and Luxemburgist, later a Communist. As leader of the Central Committee of the C.P.G. during the revolutionary events in Germany in 1923, pursued a Right opportunist policy; was removed from work in the C.P.G., in 1924. In 1928 was expelled from the Comintern for factional schismatic activities.

BUBNOV, A. S.—Old Bolshevik; began his revolutionary activity at Ivanovo. Voznesensk in 1903; participated in the Fourth, Fifth and all subsequent Congresses of the Party; in 1910 was a member of the Bolshevik Centre in Russia. On the eve of the October Revolution was a member of the committee of five entrusted with the task of organising the armed uprising. Member of the Central Committee of the C.P.S.U. At present, People's Commissar of Education of the R.S.F.S.R. Author of a number of books on the history of the Party.

BUDENNY, S. M.—Member of the Party since 1919; commander of the First Cavalry Army from 1919 to 1921, which won a number of brilliant victories over Generals Pokrovsky, Mamontov, Shkuro and Pavlov. The Cavalry Army played an important role in the defeat of Wrangel. At the Eighth Congress of Soviets, Budenny was elected to the All-Russian Central Executive Committee. At present, a member of the Revolutionary War Council of the U.S.S.R. and of the Central Executive Committee of the U.S.S.R.

BUKHARIN, N. I.—Member of the Party since 1906; in 1909 was a member of the Moscow Committee of the Party; after repeated arrests he went abroad where he took part in the work of the Bolshevik groups which aided the Party. After the February Revolution Bukharin became a member of the Central Committee; was editor of the *Pravda* from 1918 to 1928; was member of the Executive Committee of the Communist International. During the war was in opposition to the Leninist core of the Bolsheviks, upholding incorrect views on the nature of imperialism, on the state and the proletarian dictatorship. Bukharin disagreed with Lenin's slogan of the defeat of "one's own" government. During these years Bukharin developed semi-anarchist views on the state. After the February Revolution worked in Moscow, where he took part in the October Revolution. In 1918 was a "Left" Communist and was opposed to the conclusion of peace and to Lenin's economic plan. Took Trotsky's side during the discussion of the trade union question in 1921. In 1922 supported the proposal to abolish the monopoly of foreign trade. Is author of numerous works on economic, political and philosophical questions, containing many erroneous, anti-Marxist theses which were criticised by Lenin and Stalin. In 1928-29, Bukharin was the leader of the Right opposition in the C.P.S.U. and in the Comintern. In connection with this, was removed from the Presidium of the E.C.C.I. in July 1929, and in November 1929, from the Politburo of the Central Committee of the C.P.S.U. In November 1929, declared himself in agreement with the general line of the Party. At the present time a member of the Presidium of the Commissariat of Heavy Industry; member of the All-Union Academy of Science.

CHERNOV—Leader of the Socialist-Revolutionary Party. Was Minister of Agriculture in the Provisional Government of Kerensky; chairman of the Constituent Assembly; took an active part in the uprising of Czechs and Socialist-Revolutionaries on the Volga in 1918. An active enemy of the U.S.S.R.

CHICHERIN, G. V. (Ornatsky)—Menshevik up to 1917; joined the Communist Party after the October Revolution; member of the Central Committee of the C.P.S.U. from 1927 to 1930; People's Commissar of Foreign Affairs of the U.S.S.R. from 1918 to 1930.

CHUBAR, V. Y.—Member of the Party since 1907; member of the Central Committee and candidate for the Politburo of the Central Committee of the C.P.S.U.; chairman of the Council of People's Commissars of the Ukraine.

DAN, F. I. (Gurvich)—A leader of the Mensheviks; now a member of the Editorial Board of the Menshevik *Sotsialistichesky Vestnik*, published abroad. One of the most venomous enemies of the working class and of the U.S.S.R. An organiser of sabotage and of intervention.

DEUSCH, L. G.—Participated in the Narodnik movement in the seventies of the last century; one of the founders of the "Emancipation of Labour" group; later became a Menshevik. During the war a rabid defencist; at present non-Party.

DJAPARIDZE (Alyosha)—Prominent Party worker; Bolshevik; participated in the Third Congress. Took an active part in the October Revolution in Transcaucasia. One of the twenty-six Baku commissars shot in 1918.

DZERZHINSKY, F. E.—One of the most outstanding workers of the Bolshevik Party. For many years a member of the Central Committee of the Social-Democratic Party of Poland and Lithuania; delegate to the Fourth and subsequent Congresses of the Party; served a sentence of penal servitude from 1912 to 1917. After the Conference of April 1917, was a member of the Bolshevik Central Committee; one of the leaders of the October uprising. After the October Revolution, chairman of the Cheka and of the G.P.U. Later, People's Commissar of Home Affairs, People's Commissar of Transport and Chairman of the Supreme Council of National Economy of the U.S.S.R. Died in 1926.

DUBROVINSKY (Innokenty)—Prominent Party worker and organiser; took part in the work of the *Iskra* period and that of the first revolution. A member of the Central Committee from 1907 to 1910, during which time he was a Bolshevik conciliator. Returned to Russia for Party work and was arrested. Died in exile in Siberia in 1913.

EIDELMAN—Took part in and helped to organise the First Congress of the R.S.D.L.P. At present, a member of the C.P.S.U.

EREMEYEV—Member of the C.P.S.U. since 1906. Was an active collaborator in the *Pravda* from 1912 to 1914 and in the post-October period. Died in 1931.

ERMANSKY, A.—One of the leaders of the "Yuzhny Rabochy" (Southern Worker) group up to the Second Congress. An active Menshevik who carried on a constant struggle against the Bolshevik Party. In 1921, formally broke with the Menshevik Party. Author of works on economics and rationalisation of labour which upheld Menshevik views.

FRUNZE, M. V.—Member of the Party since 1905; delegate to the Fourth Congress; was sentenced to death in 1907, but the sentence was commuted to one of penal servitude. Took part in the armed uprising in Moscow in October 1917. Was commander of the armies on the Southern front which victoriously concluded the operations against Wrangel. After the demobilisation, was commander of the troops in the Ukraine and Crimea. From 1921, a member of the Central Committee of the C.P.S.U. From 1924 to 1925, Assistant People's Commissar, and later People's Commissar, of Military and Naval Affairs. He carried through the military reform in

1924, laying a firm foundation for the territorial militia system of the Red Army. Died in 1925.

GAY—Member of the C.P.S.U. since 1916. Secretary of the Central Committee of White Russia. At present, one of the secretaries of the Moscow Regional Committee of the C.P.S.U.

GORTER, H.—Leader of the Left wing of the Social-Democratic Party of Holland; author of a book *Historical Materialism;* opposed the Marxist viewpoint on a number of questions (the dictatorship of the proletariat, the national question, etc.). During the war fought against social-chauvinism. In 1919 joined the Comintern, but held an "ultra-Left" position and later withdrew from the Communist movement.

GROMAN, V. (Gorn)—An old member of the Menshevik Party. Worked for a number of years in the State Planning Commission. Participated in the counter-revolutionary Menshevik organisation ("Union Bureau") which engaged in organising wrecking activities and conspiring for intervention against the Soviet Union.

GUESDE, Jules—French Socialist; one of the most prominent leaders of the Second International. Prior to the war, adhered to the Left wing of the Second International; for many years waged a persistent struggle against opportunism in the French Party. In 1914, together with Plekhanov and other leaders of the Second International, he betrayed socialism. For a certain period, was minister in the French bourgeois government. Died in 1922.

GUSSEV, S. I.—Member of the Party since 1896. Delegate to the Second and Fourth Congresses of the Party. Was a member of the Bureau of the Committees of the Majority which prepared for the Third Congress of the Party. Took an active part in the Revolution of 1905. Participated in the October Revolution in Petrograd. During the Civil War played a leading role in military work. Later, a leading worker in the Comintern. Died in 1933.

HILFERDING, Rudolf—German Social-Democrat; author of the well-known book *Finance Capital,* published in 1909, containing an analysis of imperialism from the standpoint of Social-Democratic Centrism. Author of the theory of "organised capitalism" which serves as the platform of the social-fascists for the defence and justification of capitalist society. After the revolution of November 1918 in Germany, was on several occasions minister in the government of the German bourgeois republic. An enemy of the U.S.S.R. and of the revolutionary proletarian movement.

JORDANIA, Noah—Delegate to the Second, Fourth and Fifth Congresses; member of the Central Committee from 1907 to 1910; a Menshevik; one of the leaders of the "August *Bloc*" in 1913-14; member of the First State Duma. Chairman of the government of the Georgian Democratic Republic from 1918 to 1921 and instigator of the persecutions of Georgian Bolsheviks. At present an émigré. According to the latest data discovered in the archives, he was connected in the pre-revolutionary years with the tsarist secret police and gave evidence betraying his comrades.

JAURÉS, J.—Leader of the opportunist wing of the French Socialists; an outstanding parliamentary leader. Founder and editor of the paper *L'Humanité* (at present the organ of the French Communist Party); pursued a petty-bourgeois pacifist policy. Assassinated on July 31, 1914.

KAGANOVICH, L. M.—Leather-goods worker; member of the Party since 1911; prior to the revolution, carried on active Party work in the Ukraine; was arrested many times. After the February Revolution, worked in the military organisations of the Party. Following the October Revolution worked in the All-Russian Collegium for the organisation of the Red Army, and later at Voronezh, in the Party Committee and Executive Committee of Soviets of the Gorky (Nizhni-Novgorod) Gubernia. Member of the Central Committee of the C.P.S.U. since 1924. From 1925 to 1928 was General Secretary of the Central Committee of the Communist Party of the Ukraine. At present, Secretary of the Central Committee and of the Moscow Regional and Moscow City Committees of the C.P.S.U. Member of the Politburo of the Central Committee.

KALININ, M. I.—Metal worker; member of the Party since 1898; carried on Party work in St. Petersburg, Reval, Tiflis and Moscow; was delegate to the Fourth (Stockholm) Congress. An active worker during the years of underground activities. Since 1919, has been chairman of the All-Russian Central Executive Committee and since the formation of the U.S.S.R. chairman of the All-Union Central Executive Committee. Has been a member of the Central Committee of the C.P.S.U. since the Eighth Congress (1919). Is a member of the Politburo of the Central Committee of the C.P.S.U.

KAMENEV—Participated in the work of the Third (1905) and Fifth (1907) Congresses of the Party; was a member of the Editorial Board of the organ *Proletary;* in 1914 was sent to Russia as a representative of the Central Committee and, upon being arrested at the same time as the Bolshevik fraction of the State Duma, upheld an opportunist position at the trial. After the February Revolution came out against Lenin and the Party with a Right opportunist platform which repudiated the struggle for proletarian dictatorship. On the eve of the October uprising, he and Zinoviev took up a "strike-breaking" position, publishing a statement in the *Novaya Zhizn* in which they divulged the plans of the Party. After the October Revolution he favoured a return to bourgeois democracy and a rapprochement with the Mensheviks and Socialist-Revolutionaries. Kamenev's behaviour during this period was denounced by Lenin. In 1925 together with Zinoviev he headed the "New Opposition." In 1926-28 he was in the Trotskyist opposition *bloc.* At the Fifteenth Congress he was expelled from the Party; shortly after, upon submitting a statement declaring that he broke with Trotskyism, he was reinstated. In October 1932, was again expelled from the Party for duplicity, for deceiving the Party and maintaining contact with the counter-revolutionary kulak group of Ryutin. In 1933 Kamenev in a public statement thoroughly repudiated his errors and shortly before the Seventeenth Party Congress was re-admitted into the Party.

KARAKHAN, L. M.—Until 1917, a Menshevik, but opposed to liquidation; in 1917, worked in the organisation of the "Mezhrayontsi" in St. Petersburg and together with this organisation joined the Party at the Sixth Congress in 1917. Since the October Revolution has worked in the Commissariat of Foreign Affairs. At present, Assistant People's Commissar of Foreign Affairs of the U.S.S.R.

KARPOV, L.—Communist; member of the Central Committee of the Party in 1903-04. After the October Revolution worked in the economic organs of the Soviet government. One of the most prominent specialists in the chemical industry. Died in 1921.

KAUTSKY, Karl—Beginning with the early eighties of the last century published a fortnightly Social-Democratic magazine, *Die Neue Zeit,* in which he wrote on subjects of natural science, economics and politics. Author of the *Economic Principles of Karl Marx,* which is a popularisation of the first volume of *Capital;* author of the Erfurt Programme which was adopted by the German Social-Democratic Party in 1891. In his writings Kautsky calls himself a Marxist, but in reality he has diverged from Marx and on a number of fundamental questions (regarding the state, the proletarian dictatorship, etc.) he has given an opportunist distortion of Marx's doctrine. Kautsky defended the Centrist position in the German and international labour movement, screening the open opportunists. Kautsky supported the Russian opportunists, the Mensheviks, in their struggle against the Bolshevik Party and its policy. After the outbreak of the war he defended the conduct of the social-patriots in the various belligerent countries. When the German Social-Democratic Party split, he joined the Independent Socialist Party. Since the October Revolution he has acted as a bitter enemy of the Soviet power. At present he is in the right wing of the Second International, defending the idea of a prolonged coalition with the bourgeoisie and openly advocating intervention and the overthrow of the Soviet government by armed force (particularly in his pamphlet *Bolshevism in a Blind Alley*, published in 1930). In Kautsky's latest works, particularly in his two volumes on *The Materialist Interpretation of History*, published in 1927, the vulgarisation of Marxism has reached its extreme limit. Kautsky's position has been exposed in Lenin's *State and Revolution* and *The Proletarian Revolution and the Renegade Kautsky* (see Stalin, *Problems of Leninism*).

KHATAYEVICH—Member of the Party since 1913; member of the Central Committee of the C.P.S.U. From 1928 to 1932, secretary of the Party Committee of the Middle Volga territory. Was secretary of the Central Committee of the Communist Party of the Ukraine.

KIROV, S. N.—Old Bolshevik, member of the Party since 1904; prior to the revolution was engaged in illegal Party work; was a member of the Party Committee at Tomsk; worked in Irkutsk and Vladivostok. During the Civil War, played a leading role in military work. Beginning with 1922, a member of the Central Committee of the C.P.S.U. Since 1923 secretary of the Central Committee of the C.P. of Azerbaijan. Since the beginning of 1926, secretary of the Leningrad Regional Committee of the C.P.S.U. Member of the Politburo of the Central Committee since 1930.

KISELEV, A.—Metal worker. Has participated in the revolutionary movement since 1898; arrested many times in connection with his revolutionary Party activities; at the Sixth Congress of the Party (in 1917) was elected a candidate to the Central Committee. Since 1924 has been secretary of the All-Union Central Executive Committee.

KNIPOVICH ("Dyadenka")—Old Bolshevik. At the end of the seventies of the last century she joined the "People's Will" organisation, and at the beginning of the 'nineties she joined the Marxists; collaborated in the *Iskra*, participated in the Second and Fourth Congresses of the Party. After the split she joined the Bolsheviks; was a member of the St. Petersburg Party committee; beginning with 1908, owing to serious illness, was compelled temporarily to withdraw from Party activity. Resumed Party activity in 1917. Died in 1922.

KOLLONTAI, A. M.—Between 1904 and 1914 was a Menshevik; at the beginning of the war broke with the Mensheviks adopting an internationalist position. In 1917 was a member of the Central Committee of the R.C.P. After the October Revolution, became People's Commissar of Social Welfare. From 1920 to 1922 she was the ideological leader of the "Workers' Opposition," continuing factional activities for a certain period, after the decision of the Tenth Congress regarding the dissolution of factions. Signed the "statement of twenty-two" to the Comintern which was severely criticised and condemned by the Comintern. Later renounced her anti-Party views. At present, engaged in diplomatic work.

KOSSIOR, S. V.—Worker; member of the Party since 1907; was an active Party worker in the Ukraine. After the February Revolution was elected to the Petrograd committee of the Party. In 1920 became secretary of the Central Committee of the Communist Party of the Ukraine. From 1922 to 1925 was secretary of the Siberian Regional Committee of the Party. Has been a member of the Central Committee of the C.P.S.U. since the Twelfth Congress. At present, general secretary of the Central Committee of the Communist Party of the Ukraine and a member of the Politburo of the Central Committee of the C.P.S.U.

KRASSIKOV, P. A.—Member of the Party since 1892; member of the Organisational Committee which convened the Second Congress; after the Second Congress carried on active work for the organisation of the Third Congress. Under the Soviet government has been engaged in work in the Commissariat of Justice and in anti-religious propaganda. At present, a member of the Collegium of the People's Commissariat of Justice.

KRASSIN, L. B. (Nikitich, Zimin, Winter)—One of the outstanding Bolshevik workers of the period of the first revolution; was a member of the Central Committee; in 1904, took up a conciliationist position; participated in the Third and subsequent Congresses of the Party and in the Bolshevik Conference in 1909 (the enlarged conference of the Editorial Board of the Proletary). Showed exceptional organisational abilities in underground work; in 1909, at the time of the split among the Bolsheviks, lined up with the *Vperyod* group, later withdrawing for a prolonged period from the Party and from politics. Returned to active work in 1918, and from that time on occupied a number of important positions in economic and diplomatic fields. At the Thirteenth Congress of the Party was elected a member of the Central Committee of the C.P.S.U. Was People's Commissar of Foreign Trade and Soviet Ambassador to Great Britain. Died in November 1926.

KRZHIZHANOVSKY, G. M.—Took part in Social-Democratic activities in St. Petersburg in the nineties of the last century; member of the Central Committee of the R.S.D.L.P. in 1903; after the first revolution, withdrew from active Party work. Under the Soviet government has taken a leading part in the work of economic organisations. At the Eighth Congress of Soviets in December 1920 he reported on behalf of the "Goelro" on the electrification of the R.S.F.S.R. Was chairman of the State Planning Commission. Is a member of the Central Committee of the C.P.S.U. At present. a member of the Collegium of the People's Commissariat of Education.

KRUPSKAYA, N. K.—Old Bolshevik; participated in the St. Petersburg "League of Struggle for the Emancipation of the Working Class" in 1895-96; was secretary of the Editorial Board of the *Iskra* from 1900 to 1903; participated in the various Party Congresses. Since the October Revolution she has been a member of the Collegium of the People's Commissariat of Education.

KUBYAK—Member of the Party since 1898, participated in the Fourth and other Congresses of the Party. Is a member of the Central Committee of the C.P.S.U.

KUIBYSHEV, V. V.—Member of the Party since 1904. Was secretary of the Central Committee of the R.C.P. in 1922-23. Was chairman of the Central Control Commission from 1923 to 1926. At present is a member of the

Central Committee of the C.P.S.U.; member of the Politburo 'of the Central Committee since 1927; chairman of the State Planning Commission.

KUTUZOV. I. I.—Member of the C.P.S.U.; in 1921 he shared the views of the "Workers' Opposition." At the Tenth Congress was elected to the Central Committee. At present working in the All-Russian Central Executive Committee.

LAFARGUE, P.—Famous French Socialist; participated in the Paris Commune; in 1883, together with Guesde, he drafted the programme of the *Parti ouvrier français.* Fought for many years in the ranks of the Left wing of the French labour movement. Author of numerous brilliant pamphlets against capitalism and christianity.

LARIN, Y. (Lurie)—Prominent Menshevik up to 1917; in 1906 he defended the proposal for a Labour Congress and a "broad labour party"; during the period of reaction advocated liquidationism; during the war was a "Menshevik-internationalist." Joined the Bolshevik Party in 1917, after the Sixth Party Congress. After the October Revolution held a number of leading economic posts; was a member and candidate of the All-Russian Central Executive Committee and of the Central Executive Committee of the U.S.S.R. (of several Soviet Congresses). Died in 1932.

LASHEVICH, M.—Member of the Party since 1901. One of the active participants in the October Revolution in Petrograd. During the Civil War was engaged in military work. Later a member of the Central Committee of the C.P.S.U. In 1925, was one of the leaders of the "New Opposition." At the July Plenum of the Central Committee of the C.P.S.U. was removed from the list of candidates to the Central Committee for factional activities. Was expelled from the Party by the Fifteenth Party Congress for active participation in the Trotskyist opposition. After submitting a statement to the Central Control Commission condemning his errors in principle and repudiating the platform of the Trotskyists, was reinstated in the C.P.S.U. Died in the summer of 1928.

LASSALLE, F.—Famous German Socialist; participated in the Revolution of 1848. In the 'sixties, his brilliant agitation helped to revive the German labour movement. Won tremendous popularity with his speeches—"The Theory of the Constitution," "What Next?", "The Workers' Programme," etc. Lassalle's views diverged from the theory and practice of revolutionary Marxism. While fighting for universal suffrage, Lassalle carried on negotiations and tried to come to an understanding with the German chancellor Bismarck, which caused Marx and Engels to attack him severely. Lassalle's views were reflected in the work of the German Social-Democratic Party. (See Marx, *Critique of the Gotha Programme.*) At present Lassalle's anti-Marxist views are being utilised by the social-fascists to justify their policy of betrayal.

LEPESHINSKY, P.—Old Bolshevik, participated in the revolutionary movement since 1893; prominent *Iskra*-ist; began his revolutionary activities in a student circle of the "People's Will" group; was a member of the Organisational Committee which convened the Second Congress of the Party and participated in the preparations for the Third Congress. After the October Revolution worked in the People's Commissariat of Education. Author of works on the history of the revolutionary movement.

LIEBKNECHT, Karl—Son of Wilhelm Liebknecht, one of the founders of the German Social-Democratic Party. Prior to 1914 he was in the Left wing of the German Social-Democratic Party, advocating an active struggle against militarism and the church in spite of the official line of the Party which was opposed to work in the army and held that religion was the private affair of each member of the Party. Karl Liebknecht was the founder of the Youth International which was organised in 1907. After 1914, became world renowned by his heroic struggle against the war. In 1916, was sentenced to hard labour. Upon his release as a result of the Revolution of November 1918, he became one of the founders of the Communist Party of Germany. In his literary works, Liebknecht, together with Rosa Luxemburg, committed a number of opportunist, semi-Menshevik errors. He was assassinated in January 1919 by White Guards, who were armed, organised and inspired by the Scheidemann-Noske Social-Democratic government.

LITVINOV, M. M. (Vallakh, Maximovich)—Old Bolshevik; professional revolutionary; in the early years of the present century was an agent of the *Iskra;* in 1904-05 was a member of the Bureau of the Committee of the Majority; was a delegate to the Third Congress of the Party; in 1907 was a delegate and secretary of the Russian delegation to the International Socialist Congress at Stuttgart; participated in the Berne Conference (1912) and in the conference of the Entente Socialists (1915), where under the instructions of the Central Committee of the Party he protested against the Socialists supporting the war and withdrew from the conference. Was the first Soviet Ambassador to Great Britain, where he was arrested in 1918 as hostage and was exchanged for Lockhart. Was for several years Assistant People's Commissar of Foreign Affairs and since 1930, People's Commissar of Foreign Affairs. Member of the Central Executive Committee of the U.S.S.R. Elected to the Central Committee at the Seventeenth Party Congress.

LOBOV—Member of the Party since 1903. Member of the Central Committee of the C.P.S.U. At present, People's Commissar of the Timber Industries.

LOMOV (Oppokov)—Member of the C.P.S.U. At the Sixth Congress of the Party was elected to the Central Committee. Was Commissar of Justice in the First Council of People's Commissars. During the Brest-Litovsk period was a "Left" Communist. At present, a member of the Central Committee of the C.P.S.U. and vice-chairman of the State Planning Commission.

LOZOVSKY, A. (Dridzo)—Communist. In 1917, withdrew from our Party, returning in 1919 together with a group of so-called internationalists. After the October Revolution worked principally in the trade union movement. At present, general secretary of the Profintern and candidate to the Central Committee of the C.P.S.U.

LUNACHARSKY, A. V. (Voynov)—Took active part in the preparatory work for the Third Congress and in the Third Congress; member of the Editorial Board of the Bolshevik newspaper *Vperyod* in 1905; participated in the Fourth (Stockholm) Congress; during the period of reaction withdrew from the Bolshevik Party, joining the *Vperyod* group; in his philosophic writings Lunacharsky defended the Mach and Avenarius theory of cognition which conflicts with dialectic materialism, and attempted to reconcile socialism with religion. During the war he collaborated in Trotsky's paper *Nashe Slovo*. On returning to Russia in 1917, he worked in the organisation of the "Mezhrayontsi" and together with them joined the Bolshevik Party. After the October Revolution, was People's Commissar of Education of the R.S.F.S.R. until 1929. Later, chairman of the Scientific Committee attached to the Central Executive Committee and member of the Presidium of the Central Executive Committee of the U.S.S.R. Writer and playwright. In 1930, was elected a member of the Academy of Science of the U.S.S.R. In 1933 was appointed the first Soviet ambassador to Spain, but died before assuming his post.

LUXEMBURG, Rosa—Prominent Marxist, later a member of the Communist Party. In the early nineties of the last century, together with Marchlevski, Warski and Tyszko, founded the Social-Democratic Party of Poland which later assumed the name of the "Social-Democratic Party of Poland and Lithuania." Since the beginning of the century, while maintaining close contact with the Polish movement, she worked primarily in Germany, opposing opportunism and revisionism. After the first Russian revolution, was one of the leaders of the Left movement in the German Social-Democratic Party. Participated in the Fifth (London) Congress of the R.S.D.L.P. During the period of reaction she tried to take a middle course. At that time, as well as later, Rosa Luxemburg's views differed from Lenin's on the questions of the hegemony and dictatorship of the proletariat, on the role of the Party and of the Soviets, and on the peasant, national and organisational questions. Together with Parvus, Rosa Luxemburg developed "a utopian and semi-Menshevik scheme of permanent revolution" which was taken up by Trotsky and other Mensheviks and was "transformed into a weapon of struggle against Leninism." Rosa Luxemburg developed her own incorrect theory of imperialism which was strongly combated by Lenin. During the war, Rosa Luxemburg held an internationalist position, but was not sufficiently consistent in defending it, at times lapsing into a pacifist standpoint. She was subjected to frequent persecution. Upon her release from prison in November 1918, Rosa Luxemburg participated, together with Liebknecht, in the creation of the Communist Party of Germany and together with Liebknecht perished in the January days of 1919 at the hands of Social-Democratic assassins. Besides numerous pamphlets and articles on political questions, Rosa Luxemburg wrote several large theoretical works containing a number of semi-Menshevik errors.

LYADOV, M. N.—One of the founders of the Moscow "Workers' League" in the middle of the nineties of the last century. Participated in the Second, Third and Fifth Congresses of the Party; during the period of reaction adopted the standpoint of the "otzovists," joined the *Vperyod* group, and later withdrew from the Party for a long period. Returned to the Party and to active work after the October Revolution. Beginning with 1920 worked in Soviet economic organs. From 1923 to 1929 was head of the Sverdlov Communist University. In 1928 upheld Right deviationist views. Later worked in the People's Commissariat of Education of the R.S.F.S.R.

MANUILSKY, D. Z.—Member of the Party since 1904; after the split in the Bolshevik fraction in 1909, joined the *Vperyod* group. Participated in the October Revolution in Petrograd. From 1919 to 1923 worked in the Ukraine and later in the Comintern. Is a member of the Central Committee of the C.P.S.U. and of the E.C.C.I.

MARCHLEVSKI, Y.—One of the founders of the Social-Democratic Party of Poland. In 1920 was chairman of the Polish Revolutionary Committee. Died in 1925.

MARTOV (Zederbaum)—Participated in the St. Petersburg "League of Struggle for the Emancipation of the Working Class"; was a member of the Editorial Board of *Iskra*; a Menshevik after the split at the Second Congress and fought against the Bolshevik Party during all the ensuing years up to his death. Died in 1923.

MARTY, A.—French revolutionary; Communist. In 1918 led the insurrection of the sailors in the French Black Sea fleet, the French sailors refusing to carry out the orders of the imperialist interventionists to bombard Soviet Odessa. On May 27, 1919, Marty organised a rebellion on the battleship

"Waldeck-Rousseau." In July 1919, was sentenced by court martial to twenty years' hard labour, but under pressure of the proletariat was released in 1923. In 1924 was elected to parliament. Is a member of the Central Committee of the French Communist Party.

MARTYNOV, A. S.—Editor of the *Rabocheye Dyelo*; after the Second Congress and in the following years was a Menshevik and carried on an active struggle against the Bolsheviks; in 1904 was a member of the Editorial Board of the new (Menshevik) *Iskra;* participated in the Fourth and Fifth Congresses of the Party; during the war sided with the Menshevik-internationalists. Left the Mensheviks after the October Revolution and joined the C.P.S.U. in 1923. At present, working in the Comintern.

MASLOV, P.—Prominent Menshevik; liquidator; author of a number of works on the agrarian question in which he defends revisionist views. In 1903, in a pamphlet *On the Agrarian Programme,* written under the pen-name X., he opposed the agrarian part of the Party programme which was later adopted by the Second Congress; was a constant collaborator in Menshevik legal and illegal publications. During the period of the first revolution, made the proposal of "municipalising" the land—a proposal which he upheld at the Stockholm Congress in 1906 against Lenin's proposal for the nationalisation of the land. During the war sided with the defencists, later withdrawing from politics.

MEDVEDEV, S.—Participated in the Cracow Conference in 1912. From 1920 to 1922 participated in the "Workers' Opposition" group. In 1924 wrote a letter to his factional associates in Baku, expressing Menshevik views on a number of questions (Comintern, Profintern, policy towards the peasantry, concessions policy). In 1926 joined the so-called "opposition *bloc.*" In October 1926, together with Shlyapnikov, submitted a statement to the Central Committee of the C.P.S.U. in which he repudiated the views expressed in his letter and renounced factional activities within the Party. Expelled from the Party during the Party purging of 1933.

MEHRING, Franz—Famous German Social-Democrat, historian, philosopher and literary critic. Prior to the imperialist war, adhered to the Left wing of the German Social-Democratic Party. During the war, waged a determined struggle against the defencists; was imprisoned. Mehring was one of the founders of the Communist Party of Germany. Died in March 1919. Prior to his death, wrote a number of brilliant articles defending the Soviet government against the slanders of the bourgeoisie and Social-Democracy.

MENZHINSKY, V. R.—Old Party worker; during the period of reaction was a member of the *Vperyod* group. Took an active part in the October Revolution. At present chairman of the G.P.U. and a member of the Central Committee of the C.P.S.U.

MIKOYAN, A. I.—Member of the Party since 1915. Up to 1920 worked in Transcaucasia. From 1922 to 1926 was secretary of the Regional Party Committee of the Northern Caucasus. At present, People's Commissar of Supplies, a member of the Central Committee of the C.P.S.U. and candidate to the Politburo of the Central Committee.

MOLOTOV, V. M.—Member of the Party since 1906; on the staff of the *Pravda* from 1912 to 1914; was a member of the Russian Bureau of the Central Committee in 1917; took a leading part in the October Revolution. Secretary of the Central Committee of the C.P.S.U. in 1920-21. Secretary of the Central Committee since the Tenth Party Congress. One of the closest collaborators of Lenin. Since December 1930, chairman of the Council of

People's Commissars of the U.S.S.R. Is a member of the Politburo of the Central Committee of the C.P.S.U.

MURANOV, M.—Member of the C.P.S.U.; was a member of the Bolshevik fraction of the Fourth State Duma elected by the workers of the Kharkov Gubernia; was arrested in 1914 together with the whole Bolshevik fraction of the Duma on the charge of "feudalism" and was exiled to Siberia, whence he returned after the February Revolution. At present a member of the Central Control Commission of the C.P.S.U. and of the Presidium of the Supreme Court of the R.S.F.S.R.

MYASNIKOV, G.—Participated in the "Workers' Opposition" group in 1921-22. Was expelled from the Party in 1922. After his expulsion, attempted to create an illegal "workers' group," opposing the working class to the Soviet government in the spirit of Menshevism. Even before his expulsion Myasnikov propagated the idea that the Soviet government should extend full political freedom to all, from the monarchists to the anarchists.

NOGIN, V. P. ("Makar")—One of the oldest Bolshevik workers; participated in the *Rabocheye Znamya* group; later was an agent of the *Iskra;* member of the Central Committee in 1907 (after the Fifth Congress). During the period of reaction was one of the most active underground workers. In 1917, was the first Bolshevik chairman of the Moscow Soviet of Workers' and Soldiers' Deputies. At the Seventh Conference, April 1917, was elected to the Central Committee. Together with Kamenev and others, upheld Right opportunist views in opposition to Lenin. After the October Revolution was People's Commissar of Trade and Industry; resigned from the Council of People's Commissars, together with the other Rights, demanding a rapprochement with the Mensheviks and Socialist-Revolutionaries. Later was in charge of the textile industry. For a number of years was chairman of the Auditing Commission of the Central Committee of the C.P.S.U. Died in 1924.

OLMINSKY, M. S.—Was connected with the "People's Will" organisation at the end of the 'eighties; later became a Social-Democrat; after the Second Congress joined the Bolsheviks; in 1905 was on the staff of *Vperyod* and *Proletary* and from 1910 to 1914 of *Zvezda* and *Pravda.* During the February Revolution worked in the Moscow Committee of the Bolsheviks. Took an active part in the October Revolution. Until the end of 1924 was in charge of the Party History Committee attached to the Central Committee of the C.P.S.U. Was one of the directors of the Marx-Engels-Lenin Institute. Author of a number of valuable works on the history of the Party. Died in 1933.

ORJONIKIDZE, G. K.—Member of the Party since 1903; participated in the Prague Conference in 1912, where he was elected to the Central Committee of the Party; carried on leading Party work in Russia. During the Civil War played a leading role in military work. After 1921 directed the work of the Party and Soviets in Transcaucasia. From 1926 on, was chairman of the Central Control Commission of the C.P.S.U. and People's Commissar of the Workers' and Peasants' Inspection. Later, became chairman of the Supreme Council of National Economy and, after its reorganisation, People's Commissar of Heavy Industry. Is a member of the Politburo of the Central Committee of the C.P.S.U.

OSSINSKY, V.V. (Obolensky)—Member of the C.P.S.U.; took an active part in the October Revolution. In 1918, was chairman of the Supreme Council of National Economy. Was one of the leaders of the opposition groups of the "Left" Communists (in 1918) and of "Democratic Centralism" in 1920-21.

PETROVSKY, G. I.—Old Bolshevik, a worker; took an ctive part in the
labour movement in the Ukraine; participated in the Crcow Conference in
1912-13; was chairman of the Bolshevik fraction of the Furth State Duma;
was arrested in November 1914 together with the other olshevik deputies
and exiled in 1915 to Siberia. After the October Revoluon, was People's
Commissar of Home Affairs of the R.S.F.S.R. Since 191, has been chairman of the All-Ukrainian Central Executive Committee ad since 1922 has
held simultaneously the posts of chairman of the Centrl Executive Committee of the U.S.S.R. and of the All-Ukrainian Central Executive Committee.
Is a candidate for the Politburo of the Central Committee of the C.P.S.U.

PLEKHANOV, G. V. (N. Beltov, Volgin, Kamensky, Ushcov)—Participated
in the Narodnik movement in the seventies of the last citury; in 1883, together with Axelrod and others, he founded the Social-Lmocratic "Emancipation of Labour" group outside of Russia. In the suggle against the
Narodnik tendencies, Plekhanov obscured the revolutnary role of the
peasantry, which was pointed out by Lenin in his wors. From the end
of the 'nineties, he fought against revisionism in the Eurean labour movement but manifested a conciliationist attitude towards th Russian revisionists, the legal "Marxists." Was a member of the Editrial Board of the
Iskra from its foundation and author of a draft of theParty programme
which contained a number of incorrect theses (the charcterisation of capitalism in Russia, the proletarian dictatorship, the attude towards the
petty bourgeoisie) and which was severely criticised b Lenin. Together
with Lenin, he opposed the Mensheviks at the Second ongress. After the
Congress he joined the Mensheviks and fought against e Bolsheviks. He
was at the head of the Mensheviks at the Fourth anc Fifth Congresses
of the Party. At the end of 1908 he broke with theMenshevik leaders
and began to fight against liquidationism, but differedwith Lenin on a
number of political and organisational questions (thehegemony of the
proletariat, the attitude towards the bourgeoisie and owards the peasantry, etc.). In 1912-13, he published a paper *For theParty* in the name
of the Mensheviks opposed to liquidation. In 1914, he egan to publish a
paper *Yedinstvo*. After the outbreak of the World Ware associated himself with the social-patriots. On his return to Russia afr the outbreak of
the revolution in 1917, he waged a bitter struggle agast the Bolsheviks,
criticising even the defencist *bloc* of the Mensheviks ar Socialist Revolutionaries from a Right st   t. After the July days e adopted a completely counter-revolutio   on, upholding the id of a "strong gov-
ernm   However, aft   ober Revolution, he degorically refused
to   ame to any   ventures againsthe Soviet govern-
me   d in 1918.   ears of hisife Plekhanov was
c   heoreticians   tional, committing a number
o   t distortiol   tical wrks on philosophy
            questions   tarian ictatorship, etc.

POKROVSKY, M. :—An outstanding and world-famous Russian scholar and Marxist historiaı Began his literary activity in 1892. Definitely became a Marxist at the eɔ of the 'nineties. In 1905 joined the lecturers' group of the Moscow Comːittee of the Bolsheviks. In 1906-07 was a member of the Moscow Commiᴄe and a delegate to the Fifth Party Congress in London, where ⸱ was elected to the Bolshevik Centrè. From this time on lived illegall During the period of the inner Party struggle, he joined the *Vperɔd* group in Paris, remaining in its ranks until the spring of 1911. uring these years Pokrovsky wrote his principal work *History of Russ: From the Earliest Times* (in five volumes), the first work to give a [arxist interpretation to the whole course of Russian history. In Augu 1917, returned to Russia. After the October Revolution, was elected chainan of the Moscow Soviet of Workers' Deputies. Joined the group of "Lᴇ" Communists. From May 1918 until 1932 was Assistant People's Commisᴀr of Education. Died in 1932.

POSTYSHEV, P.—ⱱmber of the Party since 1904. During the years of reaction was in prison aᴤ in exile. After the October Revolution worked in the Far East and wᴤ one of the leaders of the Red partisan struggle against the White Guarᴄ and against the Japanese occupation troops. From 1924 to 1930 wᴤ engaged in leading Party work in the Ukraine. After the Sixteenth Corress became secretary of the Central Committee of the C P.S U. At presᴇ: secretary of the Communist Party of the Ukraine and of the Kharkov ⸱rty Committee.

POTRESOV, A. N. Starover)—Was active in the St. Petersburg "League of Struggle for tᴣ Emancipation of the Working Class"; was a member of the editorial ıard of the *Iskra;* after the Second Congress was one of the Menshevi leaders; in 1910, in the magazine *Nasha Zarya* (and prior to this in ıe collection of articles entitled *The Social Movement in Russia*) put tᴄward a glaringly liquidationist platform. During the war and later, aɟered to the extreme Right wing of the Mensheviks. At present an émigı carrying on counter-revolutionary work against the Soviet governmeı.

POZERN, B. P.—A olshevik; delegate to the Fourth Congress of the Party. At present, secretry of the Leningrad Regional and City Committee of the C.P.S.U.

PREOBRAZHENSKʾ E. A.—Member of the Party since 1903; worked in the Urals; was inexile until 1917. In 1918 adhered to the "Left" Communists. In 1920-ᴤ was one of the secretaries of the Central Committee of the R.C.P. Lied up with the Trotskyists at the time of the discussion on thᴄtrade union question. During the discussion in 1923 was one of the leders of the Trotskyist opposition. Author of a number of works in whichᴄe tried to provide a theoretical basis for the Trotskyist economic platforn of 1923-27. The characteristic tendency of his works was to ɸcounterpɯ the working clas⸱   e peasantry and to view the latter as a colonɟ to be exploited ᴣ   ıdustry. Was expelled from the Party in 1927for factional actiᴠ   ɔw broken with Trotskyism and been reinstatᴣ in th⸱

YATAKOV, L. L.—from ⸱   ik but opposed to liquidation. Joinᴇthe ⸱   War. During the war and at the ᴄnfereᴦ   ıxemburgist view- point on the natᴄal qu⸱   ⸱ne of the leaders of the Party in ᴣ Ukrᴣ   ⸱1918. In 1919-20

At present, is in charge of the Department of National Economic Accounting of the U.S.S.R. and candidate of the Central Committee of the C.P.S.U.

PARVUS L. (Helfand)—Took a prominent part in the German and Russian Social-Democratic Parties. At one time, adhered to the Left wing in the German Social-Democratic Party. In 1905, together with Rosa Luxemburg, advocated the semi-Menshevik theory of "permanent revolution." After the 1905 Revolution, became a large trader in grain and from the outbreak of the World War, became an upholder of German imperialism. Died in 1924.

PETROVSKY, G. I.—Old Bolshevik, a worker; took an active part in the labour movement in the Ukraine; participated in the Cracow Conference in 1912-13; was chairman of the Bolshevik fraction of the Fourth State Duma; was arrested in November 1914 together with the other Bolshevik deputies and exiled in 1915 to Siberia. After the October Revolution, was People's Commissar of Home Affairs of the R.S.F.S.R. Since 1919, has been chairman of the All-Ukrainian Central Executive Committee and since 1922 has held simultaneously the posts of chairman of the Central Executive Committee of the U.S.S.R. and of the All-Ukrainian Central Executive Committee. Is a candidate for the Politburo of the Central Committee of the C.P.S.U.

PLEKHANOV, G. V. (N. Beltov, Volgin, Kamensky, Ushakov)—Participated in the Narodnik movement in the seventies of the last century; in 1883, together with Axelrod and others, he founded the Social-Democratic "Emancipation of Labour" group outside of Russia. In the struggle against the Narodnik tendencies, Plekhanov obscured the revolutionary role of the peasantry, which was pointed out by Lenin in his works. From the end of the 'nineties, he fought against revisionism in the European labour movement but manifested a conciliationist attitude towards the Russian revisionists, the legal "Marxists." Was a member of the Editorial Board of the *Iskra* from its foundation and author of a draft of the Party programme which contained a number of incorrect theses (the characterisation of capitalism in Russia, the proletarian dictatorship, the attitude towards the petty bourgeoisie) and which was severely criticised by Lenin. Together with Lenin, he opposed the Mensheviks at the Second Congress. After the Congress he joined the Mensheviks and fought against the Bolsheviks. He was at the head of the Mensheviks at the Fourth and Fifth Congresses of the Party. At the end of 1908 he broke with the Menshevik leaders and began to fight against liquidationism, but differed with Lenin on a number of political and organisational questions (the hegemony of the proletariat, the attitude towards the bourgeoisie and towards the peasantry, etc.). In 1912-13, he published a paper *For the Party* in the name of the Mensheviks opposed to liquidation. In 1914, he began to publish a paper *Yedinstvo*. After the outbreak of the World War he associated himself with the social-patriots. On his return to Russia after the outbreak of the revolution in 1917, he waged a bitter struggle against the Bolsheviks, criticising even the defencist *bloc* of the Mensheviks and Socialist Revolutionaries from a Right standpoint. After the July days he adopted a completely counter-revolutionary position, upholding the idea of a "strong government." However, after the October Revolution, he categorically refused to lend his name to any White Guard adventures against the Soviet government. He died in 1918. For the last twenty years of his life Plekhanov was one of the theoreticians of the Second International, committing a number of opportunist distortions of Marxism in his theoretical works on philosophy regarding the questions of the state, of the proletarian dictatorship, etc.

POKROVSKY, M. N.—An outstanding and world-famous Russian scholar and Marxist historian. Began his literary activity in 1892. Definitely became a Marxist at the end of the 'nineties. In 1905 joined the lecturers' group of the Moscow Committee of the Bolsheviks. In 1906-07 was a member of the Moscow Committee and a delegate to the Fifth Party Congress in London, where he was elected to the Bolshevik Centre. From this time on lived illegally. During the period of the inner Party struggle, he joined the *Vperyod* group in Paris, remaining in its ranks until the spring of 1911. During these years Pokrovsky wrote his principal work *History of Russia From the Earliest Times* (in five volumes), the first work to give a Marxist interpretation to the whole course of Russian history. In August 1917, returned to Russia. After the October Revolution, was elected chairman of the Moscow Soviet of Workers' Deputies. Joined the group of "Left" Communists. From May 1918 until 1932 was Assistant People's Commissar of Education. Died in 1932.

POSTYSHEV, P.—Member of the Party since 1904. During the years of reaction was in prison and in exile. After the October Revolution worked in the Far East and was one of the leaders of the Red partisan struggle against the White Guards and against the Japanese occupation troops. From 1924 to 1930 was engaged in leading Party work in the Ukraine. After the Sixteenth Congress became secretary of the Central Committee of the C.P.S.U. At present secretary of the Communist Party of the Ukraine and of the Kharkov Party Committee.

POTRESOV, A. N. (Starover)—Was active in the St. Petersburg "League of Struggle for the Emancipation of the Working Class"; was a member of the editorial board of the *Iskra;* after the Second Congress was one of the Menshevik leaders; in 1910, in the magazine *Nasha Zarya* (and prior to this in the collection of articles entitled *The Social Movement in Russia*) put forward a glaringly liquidationist platform. During the war and later, adhered to the extreme Right wing of the Mensheviks. At present an émigré, carrying on counter-revolutionary work against the Soviet government.

POZERN, B. P.—A Bolshevik; delegate to the Fourth Congress of the Party. At present, secretary of the Leningrad Regional and City Committee of the C.P.S.U.

PREOBRAZHENSKY, E. A.—Member of the Party since 1903; worked in the Urals; was in exile until 1917. In 1918 adhered to the "Left" Communists. In 1920-21 was one of the secretaries of the Central Committee of the R.C.P. Lined up with the Trotskyists at the time of the discussion on the trade union question. During the discussion in 1923 was one of the leaders of the Trotskyist opposition. Author of a number of works in which he tried to provide a theoretical basis for the Trotskyist economic platform of 1923-27. The characteristic tendency of his works was to counterpose the working class to the peasantry and to view the latter as a colony, to be exploited by state industry. Was expelled from the Party in 1927 for factional activity. Has now broken with Trotskyism and been reinstated in the Party.

PYATAKOV, L. L.—From 1910 to 1914 was a Menshevik but opposed to liquidation. Joined the Bolsheviks during the World War. During the war and at the Conference of April 1917 upheld the Luxemburgist viewpoint on the national question. From 1917 to 1919 was one of the leaders of the Party in the Ukraine. Was a "Left" Communist in 1918. In 1919-20 was engaged in military work and later in economic work. Shared the views of Trotskyism in the discussions of 1920-21 and 1923-24; beginning with 1926 adhered to the opposition *bloc*. Was expelled from the Party by the Fifteenth Congress for active participation in the Trotskyist opposition. After the Fifteenth Congress, repudiated Trotskyist views and was reinstated in the Party. At present, Assistant People's Commissar of Heavy Industry and a member of the Central Committee of the C.P.S.U.

RADEK, Karl—Member of the Party since 1904. Played a prominent part in the German and Polish Social-Democratic Parties. Until 1914 adhered to the Left wing in both parties. During the World War took the standpoint of the Zimmerwald Left. Together with Rosa Luxemburg, held semi-Centrist views on a number of fundamental questions (the hegemony of the proletariat, the peasant and national-colonial questions). Since 1917 has worked in Russia. Was one of the leaders of the "Left" Communists in 1918. In 1923-24 adhered to the Trotskyist opposition within the C.P.S.U. and to the Right deviation in the Comintern which was condemned by the Fifth Congress of the Comintern. In 1926-27 participated in the opposition *bloc*. Was expelled from the Party by the Fifteenth Congress for active participation in the Trotskyist opposition. Broke with Trotskyism in 1929 and was reinstated in the Party. At present on the Editorial Staff of the *Izvestia*.

ROZHKOV, N. A.—Well-known historian. Was a Bolshevik during the period of the first revolution, and at the London Congress was elected to the Central Committee. During the years of reaction he became a liquidator. In October 1917 came out as an open enemy of the proletarian dictatorship. In later years engaged in scientific work. Died in 1927.

RUDZUTAK, Y. E.—Member of the Party since 1905. After the first revolution was in prison and in exile. After 1917 was engaged principally in trade union work. Defended Lenin's viewpoint during the discussion on the trade union question in 1920-21. Was elected to the Central Committee at the Tenth Congress. After the Twelfth Congress was secretary of the Central Committee and vice-chairman of the Council of People's Commissars of the U.S.S.R. Was a member of the Politburo of the Central Committee of the C.P.SU.

RUKHIMOVICH, M. L.—Member of the Party since 1913. In 1917, worked principally in the Ukraine. From 1923 to 1926 was chairman of the Donbas Coal Trust. From 1926 to 1930 was vice-chairman of the Supreme Council of National Economy and later People's Commissar of Ways and Communications. At present, chairman of the Kuzbas Coal Trust.

RUMYANTSEV, P. P.—Prominent Bolshevik worker during the period of the first revolution; was a member of the Central Committee in 1905-06; participated in the Fourth Congress. Later withdrew from the Party. Died in 1925.

RYAZANOV, D. B.—On the eve of the Second Congress was a member of the "Borba" group which was opposed to the *Iskra*. During the period of the first revolution, was active for a certain time in Odessa and St. Petersburg. Was a Centrist during the war and worked on the Trotskyist newspapers *Golos* and *Nashe Slovo*. Joined the Bolshevik Party in 1917. In October, advocated a compromise with the Mensheviks and Socialist-Revolutionaries. In 1918 withdrew from the Party owing to his opposition to the Brest Peace. Later was readmitted into the Party. In February 1931 was removed from his post of director of the Marx-Engels-Lenin Institute and expelled from the Party for betrayal of the Party and complicity with the Mensheviks and Interventionists.

RYKOV, A. I.—Member of the Party since 1902; member of the Central Committee in 1905-06; was a conciliator during the period of reaction. During the preparations for and at the time of the October Revolution took a Right opportunist stand and opposed the uprising together with Zinoviev and Kamenev. After the October Revolution was engaged primarily in directing economic work. Elected to the Central Committee of the C.P.S.U. at the Ninth Congress. From 1924 to 1930 was chairman of the Council of People's Commissars of the U.S.S.R. and R.S.F.S.R. In 1928-29 he was one of the leaders of the Right opposition in the C.P.S.U. In November 1929 publicly repudiated the Right opportunist views. In December 1930 was relieved of his duties as chairman of the Council of People's Commissars of the U.S.S.R. Since 1931 has been People's Commissar of Post and Telegraphs.

SAFAROV—Member of the Party since 1908. Was one of the leaders of the "New Opposition" in 1925. Was expelled from the Party at the Fifteenth Congress for active participation in the Trotskyist opposition. In 1928 repudiated the Trotskyist views and was reinstated in the Party. At present a worker in the Comintern.

SAMOYLOV, F. N.—Member of the C.P.S.U. In 1912 was on the staff of *Pravda;* was a member of the Fourth State Duma, elected by the workers of the Vladimir Gubernia. During the war was arrested together with the whole Bolshevik fraction of the Duma and exiled to Siberia. Returned from Siberia after the revolution, in 1917. Was in charge of the Party History Committee attached to the Moscow Committee of the C.P.S.U.

SAPRONOV, T.—Former member of the Party. Was a "Left" Communist in 1918; in 1920-21, was one of the leaders of the "Democratic Centralism" group. In 1923 signed the slanderous "statement of the forty-six" accusing the Central Committee of the Party of pursuing an incorrect policy. Took an active part in the 1923 discussion in which he supported the opposition. From 1925 to 1927 was one of the leaders of the opposition group "of fifteen." Was expelled from the Party by the Fifteenth Congress for factional and schismatic activities.

SCHWARTZ, Semyon—Member of the Party since 1904; was very active in the work for the re-establishment of the Party during the years of reaction, particularly in the convening of the Prague Conference. After the February Revolution worked in the Ukraine. Member of the Central Committee of the C.P.S.U. Was chairman of the Central Committee of the Miners' Union. At present engaged in economic work.

SEMASHKO, N. A. (Alexandrov)—Old Bolshevik; physician; has participated in the revolutionary movement since 1892. In 1905 went abroad, where he worked in the Bolshevik organisations in Paris and Geneva under the close guidance of Lenin. Was People's Commissar of Health from the formation of the Commissariat (in July 1918) up to 1930. At present a member of the Presidium of the All-Russian Central Executive Committee.

SHLYAPNIKOV, A.—After the October Revolution was appointed People's Commissar of Labour, but on November 17 resigned, together with the other Right wingers, from the Council of People's Commissars. Later was a trade union worker. In 1920-21 led the "Workers' Opposition." After the Tenth Congress, which prohibited the existence of factions, continued to participate in the opposition struggle against the Party. At present engaged in economic work. In his literary works on the 1917 Revolution he smuggled in Trotskyist contraband. After his writings had been exposed he repudiated the anti-Party views containedin them. In 1933 during the Party purging was expelled from the Party.

SHOTMAN, L.—Member of the Party since 18{; participated in the Second Congress and in the Party Conference of 913. At present engaged in economic work.

SKRYPNIK, L. A.—Member of the Party si:e 1897; a delegate to the Third Congress; took an active part in the olshevik Conference in 1909 (enlarged conference of the Editorial Board (the *Proletary);* was a Party worker during the years of reaction. After 917 worked continuously in the Ukraine except during its evacuation. Ws a member of the Central Committee of the C.P.S.U., member of the Cntral Committee of the C.P. of the Ukraine, member of the Presidium o the Central Executive Committee of the U.S.S.R. and People's Comissar of Education of the Ukrainian S.S.R. Was guilty of lack of gilance, succumbing to the machinations of counter-revolutionary natioil-chauvinist elements in the Ukraine. Committed suicide in 1933.

SOKOLNIKOV, G. Y.—Member of the Party sice 1905; in 1910-11 adhered to the group of the Bolshevik-conciliators; d:ing the World War worked on Trotsky's paper *Nashe Slovo.* Was a prornent military worker during the civil war. At the Sixth Congress, in 191, was elected to the Central Committee of the Party. From 1922 to 192(was People's Commissar of Finance. In 1925 adhered to the "New Oposition" and in 1926-27 to the united opposition *bloc.* Broke with th(opposition in 1927. At the Sixteenth Party Congress was elected candidte to the Central Committee of the C.P.S.U. Was Soviet Ambassador to ritain.

SOLTZ, A. A.—Member of the Party si 98; was a member of the *Rabocheye Znamya* group; became ꭐ fter the Second Congress; was arrested many times for his activities. Has been a member of the Presidium of the (l Commission ever since its organisation. Is Chairman of the

STEPANOV-SKVORTSOV, I. I.—Mer 1898; was a delegate to the Fourth Congress; one of the translators of Marx's *Capital* into ted in the attempt to establish a daily Bo w. At the Fourteenth Party Congress was tee of the C.P.S.U. From 1925 to 1928 wa m 1926 to 1928 director of the Lenin Ins

SUKHANOV, N.—Economist an ution and later, adhered to the Socialist- n to consider himself a Marxist. In 19 interna- tionalists. Author of the *M* whic contains a slanderous Mens' volutic Recently participated in the · ks. W found guilty at the trial of eas viks in 1931.

SULIMOV—Worker, member Urals Regional Committe Executive Committee of t Committee of the C.P.S.U missars of the R.S.F.S.R.

SUN YAT-SEN—Promine in exile. Was at the Chinese Revolution. On testament, advising hi of Soviet Russia and to cont.ue to fight for the regeneration of China. The Kuomintang Party founde by Sun Yat-sen is now a counter-revolutionary organisation, leading te struggle against the revolutionary movement of the Chinese workers id peasants.

SVERDLOV, J. M. ("Andrey")—ld member of the Party; one of the most active underground workers iring the period of reaction; one of the leaders of the October Revolion in Petrograd. Was a member of the Central Committee of the R.C. and chairman of the All-Russian Central Executive Committee from 19˙ to 1919, revealing brilliant organisational abilities in this work. Died in J19.

SYRTSOV—Member of the Par˙ since 1913. From 1927 to 1930 was a member of the Central Commiee of the C.P.S.U. and from 1929 to 1930 chairman of the Council of Piple's Commissars of the R.S.F.S.R. At the time of and after the Sixteent Congress of the Party, he, together with Lominadze, headed an unprincled double-dealing Right "Leftist" *bloc* with a Right opportunist platform. Vas expelled from the Central Committee of the C.P.S.U. At present engied in economic work.

TARATUTA (Victor)—Old memb of the Party; from 1907 to 1910 candidate to the Central Committee; piticipated in the Bolshevik Conference in 1909 (the enlarged conferenceof the Editorial Board of the *Proletary*). After the October Revolution vas engaged in economic work. Died in 1926.

TOMSKY, M. P.—Member of thiParty since 1904; participated in the Fifth Congress of the Party; attenid the Bolshevik Conference in 1909 (the enlarged conference of the Euipean Board of the *Proletary*) which consummated the split with the Veryod group. After serving a sentence of hard labour was exiled, retuiing after the February Revolution. Upon returning to Russia was assignt to trade union work. At the Eighth Conress of the Party (in 1919) ws elected to the Central Committee. From e end of 1917 until 1929 waschairman of the All-Union Central Council Trade Unions. In 1928-29 wi one of the leaders of the Right opposition the C.P.S.U. In November)29 submitted a statement renouncing the ight opportunist views.

)TSKY, L. D.—Headed the intrist tendency in the ranks of Russian ocial-Democracy (Trotskyism intil 1917 was a variety of Menshevism). oined our Party at the tim of the Sixth Congress, in August 1917, imporarily withdrawing his enshevik views. Trotskyism thus became a faction of communism, a Jition which wavered between Bolshevism nd Menshevism" and which ibsequently sank to the role of "advance uard of the counter-revolutioiry bourgeoisie." In September 1917, after he Bolsheviks had won a mairity in the Petrograd Soviet, was elected its chairman. After the Octob˙ Revolution was People's Commissar of Foreign Affairs and later Peopls Commissar of Military and Naval Affairs. Headed all opposition which iught against the Leninist Party (on the question of the Brest Peace, inhe trade union *bloc*, 1926-27). On the eve f the Fifteenth Congress of tl Party (at the end of 1927) was expelled rom the Party and later, for crying on illegal anti-Soviet activities, was xpelled from the USSR. An itive enemy of socialist construction in the U.S.S.R. and of the Communist iovement.

SERETELI, I. G.—Member of ie Second State Duma and leader of the Menshevik part of the Social-Diocratic fraction of the Duma; participated in the Fifth Congress of the .S.D.L.P. During the war adhered to the Menshevik-internationalists. Aft˙ the February Revolution became a rabid he repudiated the anti-Party views contained in them. In 1933 during the Party purging was expelled from the Party.

SHOTMAN, L.—Member of the Party since 1893; participated in the Second Congress and in the Party Conference of 1913. At present engaged in economic work.

SKRYPNIK, L. A.—Member of the Party since 1897; a delegate to the Third Congress; took an active part in the Bolshevik Conference in 1909 (enlarged conference of the Editorial Board of the *Proletary*); was a Party worker during the years of reaction. After 1917 worked continuously in the Ukraine except during its evacuation. Was a member of the Central Committee of the C.P.S.U., member of the Central Committee of the C.P. of the Ukraine, member of the Presidium of the Central Executive Committee of the U.S.S.R. and People's Commissar of Education of the Ukrainian S.S.R. Was guilty of lack of vigilance, succumbing to the machinations of counter-revolutionary national-chauvinist elements in the Ukraine. Committed suicide in 1933.

SOKOLNIKOV, G. Y.—Member of the Party since 1905; in 1910-11 adhered to the group of the Bolshevik-conciliators; during the World War worked on Trotsky's paper *Nashe Slovo*. Was a prominent military worker during the civil war. At the Sixth Congress, in 1917, was elected to the Central Committee of the Party. From 1922 to 1926 was People's Commissar of Finance. In 1925 adhered to the "New Opposition" and in 1926-27 to the united opposition *bloc*. Broke with the opposition in 1927. At the Sixteenth Party Congress was elected candidate to the Central Committee of the C.P.S.U. Was Soviet Ambassador to Britain.

SOLTZ, A. A.—Member of the Party since 1898; was a member of the *Rabocheye Znamya* group; became Bolshevik after the Second Congress; was arrested many times for his revolutionary activities. Has been a member of the Presidium of the Central Control Commission ever since its organisation. Is Chairman of the Supreme Court.

STEPANOV-SKVORTSOV, I. I.—Member of the Party since 1898; was a delegate to the Fourth Congress; a writer and economist; one of the translators of Marx's *Capital* into Russian. In 1913 participated in the attempt to establish a daily Bolshevik newspaper in Moscow. At the Fourteenth Party Congress was elected to the Central Committee of the C.P.S.U. From 1925 to 1928 was editor of the *Izvestia* and from 1926 to 1928 director of the Lenin Institute. Died in 1928.

SUKHANOV, N.—Economist and writer. During the first revolution and later, adhered to the Socialist-Revolutionaries; subsequently began to consider himself a Marxist. In 1917 officially joined the Menshevik internationalists. Author of the *Memoirs of the Revolution of 1917*, which contains a slanderous Menshevik appraisal of the October Revolution. Recently participated in the wrecking organisation of the Mensheviks. Was found guilty at the trial of the "Union Bureau" of the Russian Mensheviks in 1931.

SULIMOV—Worker, member of the Party since 1905. Was secretary of the Urals Regional Committee of the C.P.S.U. and chairman of the Urals Executive Committee of the Soviets. At present a member of the Central Committee of the C.P.S.U. and chairman of the Council of People's Commissars of the R.S.F.S.R.

SUN YAT-SEN—Prominent Chinese revolutionary. Lived for a long time in exile. Was at the head of the revolutionary government during the Chinese Revolution. On the eve of his death, Sun Yat-sen wrote a political testament, advising his followers to maintain contact with the government of Soviet Russia and to continue to fight for the regeneration of China. The Kuomintang Party founded by Sun Yat-sen is now a counter-revolutionary organisation, leading the struggle against the revolutionary movement of the Chinese workers and peasants.

SVERDLOV, J. M. ("Andrey")—Old member of the Party; one of the most active underground workers during the period of reaction; one of the leaders of the October Revolution in Petrograd. Was a member of the Central Committee of the R.C.P. and chairman of the All-Russian Central Executive Committee from 1917 to 1919, revealing brilliant organisational abilities in this work. Died in 1919.

SYRTSOV—Member of the Party since 1913. From 1927 to 1930 was a member of the Central Committee of the C.P.S.U. and from 1929 to 1930 chairman of the Council of People's Commissars of the R.S.F.S.R. At the time of and after the Sixteenth Congress of the Party, he, together with Lominadze, headed an unprincipled double-dealing Right "Leftist" bloc with a Right opportunist platform. Was expelled from the Central Committee of the C.P.S.U. At present engaged in economic work.

TARATUTA (Victor)—Old member of the Party; from 1907 to 1910 candidate to the Central Committee; participated in the Bolshevik Conference in 1909 (the enlarged conference of the Editorial Board of the *Proletary*). After the October Revolution was engaged in economic work. Died in 1926.

TOMSKY, M. P.—Member of the Party since 1904; participated in the Fifth Congress of the Party; attended the Bolshevik Conference in 1909 (the enlarged conference of the European Board of the *Proletary*) which consummated the split with the *Vperyod* group. After serving a sentence of hard labour was exiled, returning after the February Revolution. Upon returning to Russia was assigned to trade union work. At the Eighth Congress of the Party (in 1919) was elected to the Central Committee. From the end of 1917 until 1929 was chairman of the All-Union Central Council of Trade Unions. In 1928-29 was one of the leaders of the Right opposition in the C.P.S.U. In November 1929 submitted a statement renouncing the Right opportunist views.

TROTSKY, L. D.—Headed the Centrist tendency in the ranks of Russian Social-Democracy (Trotskyism until 1917 was a variety of Menshevism). Joined our Party at the time of the Sixth Congress, in August 1917, temporarily withdrawing his Menshevik views. Trotskyism thus became "a faction of communism, a faction which wavered between Bolshevism and Menshevism" and which subsequently sank to the role of "advance guard of the counter-revolutionary bourgeoisie." In September 1917, after the Bolsheviks had won a majority in the Petrograd Soviet, was elected its chairman. After the October Revolution was People's Commissar of Foreign Affairs and later People's Commissar of Military and Naval Affairs. Headed all opposition which fought against the Leninist Party (on the question of the Brest Peace, in the trade union *bloc*, 1926-27). On the eve of the Fifteenth Congress of the Party (at the end of 1927) was expelled from the Party and later, for carrying on illegal anti-Soviet activities, was expelled from the U.S.S.R. An active enemy of socialist construction in the U.S.S.R. and of the Communist movement.

TSERETELI, I. G.—Member of the Second State Duma and leader of the Menshevik part of the Social-Democratic fraction of the Duma; participated in the Fifth Congress of the R.S.D.L.P. During the war adhered to the Menshevik-internationalists. After the February Revolution became a rabid defencist, was a minister in the Kerensky coalition-government. Tse-reteli is a violent enemy of the U.S.S.R.

TSKHAKAYA, M. (Barsov)—One of the oldest Georgian Bolsheviks; was a delegate to the Third, Fifth and several subsequent Congresses of the Party. After the February Revolution carried on a severe struggle against the Mensheviks in Georgia. After the soviets were established in Georgia, became chairman of the Transcaucasian Central Executive Committee. At present working in the International Control Commission.

TYSZKO (Leo Yogiches)—One of the founders of the Social-Democratic Party of Poland. At the Fifth (London) Congress of our Party was elected a candidate to the Central Committee. During the World War was active in Germany. One of the organisers of the Spartakus Bund and of the German Communist Party. Was assassinated by the German White Guards in 1919.

UGLANOV, N. A.—Joined the Party in 1905. From 1924 to 1928 was secretary of the Moscow Committee of the Party, being relieved of this post at the end of 1928. During his last months as secretary of the Moscow Committee, attempted to carry on factional activities against the Central Committee and against the line of the Fifteenth Congress but encountered a unanimous rebuff by the Moscow organisation. Was one of the leaders of the Right opposition in the ranks of the C.P.S.U. in 1928-29. Aided the counter-revolutionary work of the Ryutin group in 1932 and was expelled from the Party.

UNSHLICHT—Prominent member of the Polish Social-Democratic Party. In 1912 was the leader of the Warsaw organisation which opposed the central leadership of the Polish Party and formed a *bloc* with the Bolsheviks. After the October Revolution was a prominent military worker and Assistant People's Commissar of Military and Naval Affairs. At present is engaged in economic work.

URITSKY, M. (Boretsky)—Participated in the Social-Democratic movement since the 'nineties; was a member of the Trotskyist group which published the Vienna *Pravda* from 1909 to 1911. After the February Revolution was one of the leaders of the "Mezhrayontsi" in Petrograd, joining the Bolshevik Party together with this group. Was elected to the Central Committee at the Sixth Congress of the Party. After the October Revolution was chairman of the Petrograd Cheka. Was assassinated in 1918 by the Right-Socialist-Revolutionary Kanegiser.

VANDERVELDE, E.—One of the leaders of the Second International and one of the outstanding representatives of European reformism, which has now become social-fascism. Chairman of the International Socialist Bureau before the World War. From the beginning of the war until recently was a minister in the Belgian bourgeois government. Is an enemy of the Soviet Union and of the revolutionary labour movement.

VAREYKIS—Member of the C.P.S.U. since 1913; member of the Central Committee of the C.P.S.U. and Secretary of the Regional Committee of the Central Black Soil Region.

VLADIMIROV, M. K. (Lyova)—Participated in the Third Congress of the Party. In 1910-11 belonged to the group of Bolshevik-conciliators. From 1914 to 1916, worked on Trotsky's paper *Nashe Slovo*. After the February Revolution belonged to the organisation of the "Mezhrayontsi," joining the Bolshevik Party together with them at the Sixth Congress in August 1917. After the October Revolution held a number of leading administrative and economic positions. Died in 1925.

VLADIMIRSKY, M. F.—Member of the Party since 1894. Participated in the armed uprising in Moscow in 1905. At present a member of the Auditing Commission of the Central Committee of the C.P.S.U.

VOLODARSKY, V.—A Party worker. Emigrated abroad after the 1905 Revolution. Fought against social-chauvinism during the war. Upon returning to Russia in 1917 joined the Bolsheviks and became prominent as an outstanding speaker and organiser. Played an important role in the October Revolution in Petrograd. Was assassinated by a Socialist-Revolutionary terrorist in June 1918.

VOROSHILOV, K. E.—Member of the Party since 1903; a worker. Was a delegate to the Fourth and Fifth Congresses. Began his Party activity in the Donbas (Lugansk and Alchevskaya). From 1906 to 1917 Voroshilov carried on active underground work in Baku, St. Petersburg and other cities, being arrested and exiled. Took part in the organisation of the October Revolution; was one of the organisers of the Cheka and of Red Guard detachments. One of the outstanding military workers during the Civil War. From 1918 to 1921 took part in the fighting before Tsaritsin (the present Stalingrad), in the Ukraine, Kronstadt, etc. Since the Tenth Congress has been a member of the Central Committee of the C.P.S.U. At present, a member of the Politburo of the Central Committee and People's Commissar of Military and Naval Affairs of the U.S.S.R.

VOROVSKY, V. V. (Orlovsky)—Was a member of the Editorial Board of the Bolshevik Vperyod in 1905; participated in the Third and Fourth Congresses of the Party; prominent Party worker and writer. After the October Revolution was Soviet Ambassador in several capitalist countries. In 1923 was assassinated at Lausanne by the Russian monarchist, Conradi.

VOYKOV, P. L.—Member of the Party since 1905; worked in the Crimea. After the October Revolution worked in the Urals. From 1924 to 1927 was Soviet Ambassador to Poland. In 1927 was assassinated in Warsaw by the White Guard, Koverda.

YAKOVLEV, Y. A.—Member of the Party since 1913. After the February Revolution was secretary of the Dniepropetrovsk Committee of the Red Army. In 1923 was in charge of the Press department of the Central Committee of the R.C.P. In 1926 was appointed Assistant People's Commissar of the Workers' and Peasants' Inspection. Since 1929 has been People's Commissar of Agriculture of the U.S.S.R. Is a member of the Central Committee of the C.P.S.U.

YAROSLAVSKY, E.—Member of the Party since 1898; participated in the Fourth, Fifth and subsequent Congresses of the Party. Between 1907 and 1917 was in prison and exile. In 1918 was a "Left" Communist. From 1921 to 1923 was a member of the Central Committee of the R.C.P. At present, a member of the Presidium and Secretary of the Central Control Commission of the C.P.S.U.

YURENEV, K. K.—Was one of the leaders of the "Mezhrayontsi" organisation in Petrograd in 1917, joining the Bolshevik Party at the Sixth Congress. Was one of the organisers of the Red Guards. In recent years has been engaged in diplomatic work.

ZALUTSKY—Member of the Party since 1907; was a delegate to the Sixth (Prague) Conference of the Party in 1912. At the time of the February Revolution was a member of the Bureau of the Bolshevik Central Committee. In 1925 was secretary of the Leningrad Committee of the Party and one of the leaders of the "New Opposition." Was expelled from the Party by the Fifteenth Congress for active participation in the Trotskyist opposition. Upon submitting a statement repudiating the Trotskyist views, was reinstated in the Party.

ZASULICH, V. I.—Took part in the revolutionary movement of the 'seventies; member of the "Emancipation of Labour" group; member of the Editorial Board of the *Iskra*; after the Second Congress became a Menshevik. Took a liquidationist standpoint during the years of reaction. During the war, together with Plekhanov, adhered to the extreme social-chauvinists. Died in 1919.

ZELENSKY, I.—Member of the Party since 1906; a member of the Central Committee of the C.P.S.U. From 1922 to 1924 was secretary of the Moscow Committee of the Party; from 1924 to 1931 was secretary of the Party Bureau of Central Asia. At present is chairman of the Centrosoyuz.*

ZEMLYACHKA (Samoylova)—Member of the Party since 1896; professional revolutionary. Participated in the Second Congress of the Party; was a member of the Central Committee and of the Bureau of the Committees of the Majority for the preparation of the Third Congress; took part in the subsequent Congresses of the Party. Was an active participant in the Civil War. Was a member of the Central Control Commission of the C.P.S.U. and Assistant People's Commissar of Ways of Communication.

ZETKIN, Klara—Oldest revolutionary; active for many years in the organisation of the working class women's movement; fought against opportunism in the Second International. During the World War took an internationalist standpoint. Fought in the ranks of the Communist Party of Germany since its formation; was a member of the E.C.C.I. Died in 1933.

ZEVIN—One of the twenty-six Baku commissars who were shot; participated in the labour movement since 1904. Became a Bolshevik after 1914; was arrested many times. After the February Revolution worked for a time in the Moscow Soviet. Beginning with August 1917 was a leading Party worker in Baku.

ZINOVIEV—Joined the Bolsheviks after the Second Congress and the split (1903). During the years of reaction was on the editorial staff of the *Proletary*. During the war participated in the Zimmerwald and Kienthal Conferences. After the October Revolution was chairman of the Leningrad Soviet, and later, from 1919 to 1926, Chairman of the E.C.C.I.

During the period of the preparations for the October Revolution Zinoviev, together with Kamenev, adopted a "strike-breaking" position. After the victory of the October Revolution he advocated the formation of a government together with the Mensheviks and Socialist-Revolutionaries. Zinoviev's (and Kamenev's) position was denounced by Lenin.

In 1925, Zinoviev led the "New Opposition." In 1926 he formed a *bloc* with Trotsky. On the eve of the Fifteenth Congress was expelled, together with Trotsky, from the C.P.S.U. In May 1928 Zinoviev submitted a statement declaring that he broke with Trotskyism and was reinstated in the Party. In October 1932, for duplicity and deceiving the Party and for having had contact with the counter-revolutionary kulak group of Ryutin, was expelled from the Party. In 1933 he again publicly renounced his errors. Before the Seventeenth Congress was reinstated in the Party.

---

* Centrosoyuz—the Central Union of Consumers' Cooperatives—*Ed.*

CPSIA information can be obtained
at www.ICGtesting.com
Printed in the USA
BVHW071525140119
537775BV00005B/179/P